GW00792180

 Interrogating Orientalism

INTERROGATING ORIENTALISM

Contextual Approaches and Pedagogical Practices

Edited by
Diane Long Hoeveler and Jeffrey Cass

THE OHIO STATE UNIVERSITY PRESS
Columbus

Library of Congress Cataloging-in-Publication Data

Interrogating orientalism : contextual approaches and pedagogical practices / edited by Diane Long Hoeveler and Jeffrey Cass.
        p. cm.
    Includes bibliographical references and index.
    ISBN-13: 978-0-8142-1032-1 (alk. paper)
    ISBN-10: 0-8142-1032-5 (alk. paper)
    ISBN-13: 978-0-8142-9109-2 (cd-rom)
    ISBN-10: 0-8142-9109-0 (cd-rom)
    1. English literature—19th century—History and criticism. 2. Orientalism in literature. 3. Orient—In literature. 4. Orientalism—Study and teaching. 5. English literature—18th century—History and criticism. 6. Travelers' writings, English—Orient—History and criticism. I. Hoeveler, Diane Long. II. Cass, Jeffrey, 1949.
    PR468.O74I58 2006
    820.9'325—dc22
                            2006009989

Cover design by Janna Thompson-Chordas.
Text design and typesetting by Jennifer Shoffey Forsythe.
Printed by Thomson-Shore, Inc.

The paper used in this publication meets the minimum requirements of the American National Standard for Information Sciences—Permanence of Paper for Printed Library Materials. ANSI Z39.48–1992.

9 8 7 6 5 4 3 2 1

CONTENTS

List of Illustrations   vii

INTRODUCTION: Mapping Orientalism: Representations and Pedagogies
Diane Long Hoeveler and Jeffrey Cass   1

PART ONE. Contextual Approaches

1. Interrogating Orientalism: Theories and Practices
   Jeffrey Cass   25

2. The Female Captivity Narrative: Blood, Water, and Orientalism
   Diane Long Hoeveler   46

3. "Better than the Reality": The Egyptian Market in Nineteenth-Century British Travel Writing
   Emily A. Haddad   72

4. Colonial Counterflow: From Orientalism to Buddhism
   Mark Lussier   90

5. Homoerotics and Orientalism in William Beckford's *Vathek*: Liberalism and the Problem of Pederasty
   Jeffrey Cass   107

6. Orientalism in Disraeli's *Alroy*
   Sheila A. Spector   121

PART TWO. Pedagogic Practices

7. Teaching the Quintessential Turkish Tale: Montagu's *Turkish Embassy Letters*
   Jeanne Dubino   139

8. Representing India in Drawing-Room and Classroom; or, Miss Owenson and "Those Gay Gentlemen, Brahma, Vishnu, and Co."
   Michael J. Franklin   159

9. "Unlettered Tartars" and "Torpid Barbarians": Teaching the Figure of the Turk in Shelley and De Quincey
   Filiz Turhan   182

10. "Boundless Thoughts and Free Souls": Teaching Byron's *Sardanapalus,*
    Lara, and *The Corsair*
    G. Todd Davis   198

11. Byron's *The Giaour:* Teaching Orientalism in the Wake of September 11
    Alan Richardson   213

12. Teaching Nineteenth-Century Orientalist Entertainments
    Edward Ziter   224

Works Cited   245
Notes on Contributors   265
Index   269

LIST OF ILLUSTRATIONS

Figure 1: Portrait of Lady Mary Wortley Montagu by Jonathan Richardson, ca. 1726   4

Figure 2: Map of travels by Lady Mary Wortley Montagu   5

Figure 3: Portrait of Lord Byron in Oriental costume by Thomas Phillips, ca. 1835   6

Figure 4: Map of travels by Byron   7

Figure 5: Photograph of Sir Richard Burton as pilgrim   9

Figure 6: Map of travels by Burton   10

Figure 7: French postcard of Algerian woman   53

Figure 8: Flyleaf from *The Female Captive*   60

Figure 9: William Musgrave's annotations to *The Female Captive*   61

Figure 10: Snake charmers at Regent's Park Zoo, from the *Illustrated London News,* June 15, 1850   230

Figure 11: Visitors to the Crystal Palace, from Henry Mayhew–George Cruikshank's *1851, or, The Adventures of Mr. and Mrs. Sandboys and Family*   232

Figure 12: Tunisian court, from the *Illustrated London News,* May 21, 1851   233

Figure 13: Algerian family at Vauxhall Gardens, from the *Illustrated London News,* July 12, 1851   235

Mapping Orientalism

Representations and Pedagogies

DIANE LONG HOEVELER AND JEFFREY CASS

I. Mapping Orientalism: Three Case Histories

In order to understand Orientalism it is necessary to realize, as Vincent T. Harlow has noted, that there were "two British empires." The first empire consisted of the colonies in America and the West Indies and was established in the seventeenth century, with the explorations in the Pacific, and the trading networks that developed with Asia and Africa. The "second British empire" dates from 1783 and resulted from the loss of America, which in turn forced Britain to formulate new ideas about and approaches to its empire. The Colonial Office was set up in 1801, and, as Harlow observed, Britain experienced a "Swing to the East," to India and the Asian colonies (Harlow, 2:1–11). The conquests of India (1798–1804) expanded Britain's empire to such an extent that the losses of America and the old West Indian colonies were not felt economically (Johnson, 13–14), and given the success of the British Raj after 1813 and especially 1857, it seems clear that the imperial desire was to keep the profits of the East while maintaining as strict a social and intellectual distance as possible from its cultures and peoples. Although the nature and continuously changing shape of the British Empire has been subject to a fair amount of debate and is still a controversial topic, we begin this volume with an attempt to map the rough contours of the shifting British Empire in order to historically situate this collection of essays. We also begin with a premise: literature written about or out of an awareness of this empire participated in an ongoing, complex attempt to understand what it meant for the British to come into contact with other alien (both attractive and repellent) societies, languages, cultures, and religions. Or, as the bishop of Avila so succinctly observed to Queen Isabella in 1492, "Language is the perfect instrument of empire" (quoted in Hulme, 1).

We begin this volume, therefore, by mapping three exemplars of Oriental pleasure travel as tropes for the readers of this book. By situating three particular individuals in three Orientalist costumes and then positioning those costumed bodies against the journeys that they undertook throughout what they understood as the "Oriental" world, we intend to suggest the topics that will be addressed in this volume. We also intend by selecting these three case studies to map the Oriental social body and body politic, with three different gendered states represented (female, bisexual, and male), and three different realms (the private, the spectacularly public, and the private within the public space). Finally, our three case studies represent the most acceptable types of travelers to the Orient (the elite lady, the potentate, and the religious devotee). We might also add that the travels of these three individuals cover most of the recognized areas of the "Oriental" world during the time period that we are addressing (from Spain, to the Levant, Turkey, Albania and the Ottoman Empire, and finally India).

As James Clifford has noted in *Routes,* "travels and contacts are crucial sites for an unfinished modernity," while it is more accurate to understand the "human location as constituted by displacement rather than stasis" (1). Europe, as he observes, has been "constantly remade, and traversed, by influences beyond its borders" (3). The travels undertaken during the eighteenth and nineteenth centuries by a number of Europeans can be seen as manifestations of Clifford's observation. British citizens traveling throughout the Oriental world did so not simply because they were motivated by adventure, economic exploitation, or cultural objectification, but actually for much more complex and reciprocal reasons. They were not seeking some "Oriental Other" to appropriate or control (as Edward Said has claimed in *Orientalism*). They were doing something much more interesting and complex: they were hybridizing (as Homi Bhabha has defined the concept) and modernizing. In fact, to understand where critical approaches to Orientalism are now, one needs to consider the valuable observation made by Timothy Powell:

> It has become clear in recent years . . . that a binary form of analysis that collapses a myriad of distinct culture voices into the overly simplistic category of "Other" defined in relationship to a European "Self" is theoretically problematic. The time has come, therefore, to initiate a new critical epoch, a period of cultural *reconstruction* in which "identity" is reconfigured in the midst of a multiplicity of cultural influences that more closely resembles what Homi Bhabha has called the "lived perplexity" of people's lives. (1; original emphasis)

The donning of indigenous garb by Lady Mary Wortley Montagu, Lord

Byron, and Sir Richard Burton suggests for us one of the ways that the "lived perplexity" of Orientalism can be approached. The stories that recount their adoption of native dress—as well as the maps of their journeys—become what we will identify as fitting sites for analyzing the emerging representational strategies that are to be found in British Orientalist literature of the eighteenth and nineteenth centuries. Hence, their examples concretely illustrate the ongoing importance of and critical interest in British Orientalism as a more complex, nondualistic paradigm. As Daniel Carey has demonstrated about early modern cultural exchange, English writers consistently stressed "the potential interchangeability of self and other rather than the radical opposition between the two" (34). For Carey, English writers "worried about the impact of travel precisely because they accepted the commensurability of human beings, and therefore the capacity of the English to become like those they observed and with whom they lived" (40). It is this hybridity or what Bhabha calls the "liminal space, in-between the [binary] designations of identity" that we attempt to capture with these three representations: "this interstitial passage between fixed identifications [that] opens up the possibility of a cultural hybridity that entertains difference without an assumed or imposed hierarchy" (Bhabha, *Location of Culture*, 4).

The first figure, Lady Mary Wortley Montagu, imitates the elite Oriental female dress of the private realm and, as such, she represents the world of the harem, the social elite, and the domestic realm. In 1716, Alexander Pope hinted that Montagu's decision to travel with her husband, the newly appointed ambassador to the Ottoman Empire, was effectively a decision to travel "to another world" (Grundy, 114). As Isobel Grundy affirms, Pope "appl[ies] the metaphor of death" to discourage Montagu from leaving (114), but Pope also underscores the enormous cultural differences a woman writer will have to confront in addressing the Oriental subject. After traveling in Europe for six months, she and her husband arrive in Adrianopolis (present-day Edirne) in February of 1717. By April, Montagu has already assimilated herself into Turkish culture and entertained her sister, Lady Mar, with a letter describing her resolve to dress in native attire, to publicly display herself as an appropriately dressed Muslim woman. She writes of her "Turkish habit":

The first piece of my dresse is a pair of drawers, very full, that reach to my shoes and conceal the legs more modestly than your Petticoats. They are of a thin rose colour damask brocaded with silver flowers, my shoes of white kid Leather embroider'd with Gold. Over this hangs my Smock of a fine white silk Gause edg'd with Embroidiery. This smock has wide sleeves hanging halfe way down the Arm and is clos'd at the Neck with a diamond button,

Figure 1. Portrait of Lady Mary Wortley Montagu by Jonathan Richardson, ca. 1726. Reproduced with the kind permission of The Earl of Harrowby.

but the shape and colour of the bosom very well to be distinguish'd through it. . . . My caftan of the same stuff with my Drawers is a robe exactly fited to my shape and reaching to my feet with very long strait falling sleeves. . . . (*Letters* 1:326)

Montagu's description of herself in this Orientalist dress confirms several artistic representations of her in Turkish "habit," including those by Jean-Baptiste Vanmour, Charles Jervas, Godfrey Kneller, and Jonathan Richardson (fig. 1). Her travels (fig. 2) reveal one version of the "Grand Tour" as it would have been made by an elite lady, an inhabitant of a definitively private sphere who undertook this chaperoned journey to "another world" in the company of an aristocratic and powerful male.

The passage quoted above is similar to another in which Montagu describes to Lady Mar the dress of her acquaintance Fatima: "She was dress'd

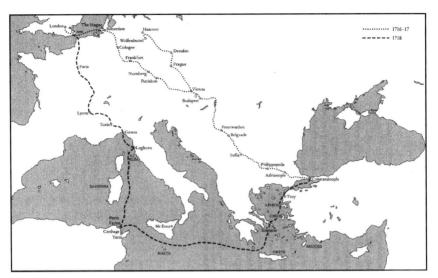

Figure 2. Map of travels by Lady Mary Wortley Montagu, 1716–1718, from *Lady Mary Wortley Montagu,* by Isobel Grundy. Reprinted with permission of Oxford University Press.

in a Caftan of Gold brocade flowered with Silver, very well fited to her Shape and shewing to advantage the beauty of her Bosom, only shaded by the thin Gause of her shift" (*Letters* 1:350). These passages demonstrate what Laura Brown has observed about the use of female clothing to mystify colonial ideology, particularly important for Montagu because she maps for her readers the attendant ambiguities of female dress in the Oriental world, at once confining and liberating, "fiting to shape" yet surprisingly roomy and free. Properly attired, Montagu's female traveler uses "privilege and power" to enter zones forbidden to men, such as harems, and interrogate the ways in which women occupy, manage, and control contested spaces. Her letters to her sister form what is now understood to be "domestic ethnography as a female genre, initially aristocratic then from the early nineteenth century distinctly middle class" (Melman 2002, 111). The female traveler in the Oriental world focused her "imperial eye" (Pratt) almost exclusively on detailed accounts of domestic and feminine spaces (harems and houses of the Turkish-Circassian elite in Istanbul) in an attempt to understand the differences (both positive and negative) in women's lives under a system of polygamy.

The second example of what we might call the attendant ambiguities of costuming occurs in the case of Lord Byron. In 1809, Byron and his friend John Cam Hobhouse visited Albania. Invited to Tepeleni by Ali Pasha in October of that year, Byron and Hobhouse rode several days and observed the military uniforms of the Albanian soldiers. Byron described "the Albanians in their dresses" in a letter to his mother: "[They] consist of a long

Figure 3. Portrait of Lord Byron in Oriental costume by Thomas Phillips, ca. 1835. Reproduced with permission of the National Portrait Gallery, London.

white kilt, gold worked cloak, crimson velvet gold laced jacket & waistcoat, silver mounted pistols & daggers" (Byron's italics, *BLJ,* 227). Enthralled by the spectacle of their clothes, Byron purchased several expensive "Albanian suits" which he wore to meetings with Ali Pasha. Several years later, soon after the publication of *The Corsair* in February 1814, Byron commissioned Thomas Phillips to paint the now-famous portrait of an Orientalized Byron (fig. 3), "for which Byron wore one of the 'magnifique' Albanian dresses he had purchased on his travels" (MacCarthy, 216). Benita Eisler speculates that "Byron took special delight in this costume" because while he was wearing it he fancied that he had become "an Oriental potentate, powerful and free, to whom nothing was forbidden" (223).

Clearly the costume represents Byron's allegiance to an elite political and military corps while the map of his journeys suggests an interest in the historical and military contours of the Ottoman Empire (fig. 4). To Western eyes, however, the outfit was sexually ambiguous, marking Byron as embodying an intermediary gender, although still very firmly placed in the

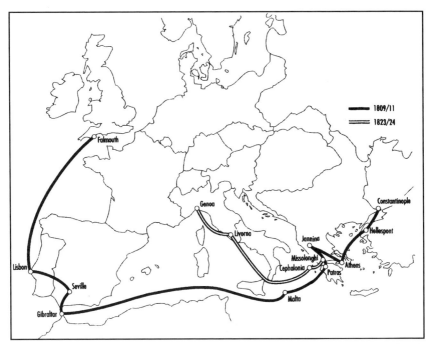

Figure 4. "Byron's Eastern Journeys," from *Byron: The Flawed Angel*, by Phyllis Grosskurth. Reprinted by permission of Houghton Mifflin Company. All rights reserved.

public realm. We might also note that Byron's Orientalist pose appears to be part of a sales strategy that Byron had enunciated a few years before to his friend Thomas Moore. In 1813, Byron had advised Moore to read Antoine Laurent Castellan's *Moeurs, usages, costumes des Othomans* (1812) for poetic materials:

> Stick to the East; the oracle, Staël, told me it was the only poetic policy. The North, South, and West, have all been exhausted; but from the East, we have nothing but Southey's unsaleables. . . . The little I have done in that way is merely a "voice in the wilderness" for you; and, if it has had any success, that also will prove that the public are orientalizing, and pave the path for you. (*Letters and Journals* 3:101)

Moore took Byron's advice and published his successful Oriental romance *Lalla Rookh* in 1817, a poem that described an India that the traveler Victor Jacquemont did not recognize: "Thomas Moore is not only a perfumer, but a liar to boot. I am now pursuing the same route that Lalla Rookh formerly did; and I have scarcely seen a tree since I left Delhi" (*BLJ* 1:360). The poetic Orient constructed for public consumption within Europe was clearly not the geographical reality that an experienced traveler into India would recognize.

Our third representation, Sir Richard Burton, initially went to India as a member of the British army and almost immediately decided to appropriate Oriental costuming as a means of interacting more fully with his new surroundings: "The first difficulty was to pass for an Oriental, and this was as necessary as it was difficult. The European official in India seldom, if ever, sees anything in its real light, so dense is the veil which the fearfulness, the duplicity, the prejudice, and the superstitions of the natives hang before his eyes" (Burton, *Selected Papers,* 22). Burton went so far as to stain his skin with walnut juice in an attempt to move as a native in an alien culture that he wanted to master by understanding and experiencing it from within, so to speak. Such an experience recalls the situation of James Kirkpatrick, another British imperialist who between 1797 and 1805 adopted Hyderbadi (Indian) clothing and ways of life, so much so that he married an Indian woman according to Muslim law (Dalrymple, xxxviii). As Dalrymple notes, such a case reveals a much more hybrid colonial world than the one that Edward Said has charted: "with far less clearly defined ethnic, national and religious borders. . . . It was as if this early promiscuous mingling of races and ideas, modes of dress and ways of living, was something that was on no one's agenda and suited nobody's version of events. All sides seemed, for different reasons, to be slightly embarrassed by this moment of crossover, which they preferred to pretend had never happened. It is, after all, easier to see things in black and white" (xlv).

Years later, in 1853, Burton made a "pilgrimage to Mecca," the *Hajj,* a feat accomplished by other Europeans, but not in indigenous dress, and not with the intent of convincing his fellow travelers that he was a practicing Muslim. Non-Muslims are, of course, prohibited from entering the Holy City of Mecca upon pain of death, and so the decision on Burton's part was daring to say the least. Burton decided to resurrect a character he had once developed for British Intelligence in the 1840s, namely, Mirza Abdullah the Bushiri, "a half-Iranian, half-Arab traveler in fine linens and jewellery" (quoted in Lovell, 53). As the painting made of Burton as "Mirza Abdullah the Bushiri" illustrates, his "dress" was disarmingly familiar to Middle Eastern inhabitants. As Burton indicates in his letters, he would wear:

> A muslin pirhan, or shirt with handing arms, and skirts like a blouse buttoned around your neck . . . a pair of blue silk shalwars or drawers . . . tight around the ankles and gathered in with plaits around the waist. . . . [The] coat is a long, white cotton garment . . . then a pair of yellow leather papooshes [slippers], worked with silk flowers, a shawl by way of a girdle

Figure 5. Photograph of Sir Richard Burton as pilgrim. Reproduced with permission of Corbis Corporation.

and in it a small Persian knife, with ivory handle and a watered blade. . . .
(quoted in Lovell, 51)

Feeling that this character might be too conspicuous for his deceptive purposes, Burton transformed Abdullah into a "wandering dervish with a knowledge of magic and horoscopes" (Lovell, 122). He wore a plainer robe and did not display quite the linguistic mastery of Arabic that his first Abdullah manifested. Burton's meticulous attention to the details of his Muslim impersonation did not merely reflect a desire to comprehend the life and experiences of the Oriental Other; rather, he transcended his ethnological interests in "passing as an Oriental" (Rice, 181) by engaging in unethical sociological practice (for which he was criticized in some quarters), as well as for indulging in the sheer pleasure of his wanderlust, what his biographer Lovell calls "the pure romance of the *Hajj*" (132), as the famous photograph of his *Hajj* persona suggests (fig. 5).

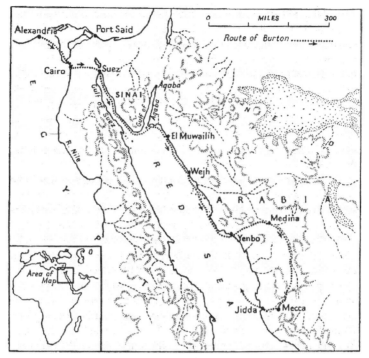

Figure 6. Map: "Pilgrimage to Mecca," from *Burton: A Biography of Sir Richard Francis Burton,* by Byron Farwell. Reprinted by permission of Penguin Books Ltd.

Burton's impersonation is an exhibition of his intellectual superiority and physical stamina, overcoming massive logistical problems simply to pursue his subject, the composition of his *Personal Narrative of a Pilgrimage to Al-Madinah and Meccah* in 1856, while it also acknowledges his complicity with British imperialism. Burton's persistent appropriation of Oriental costume, this time the private dress of a pilgrim, suggests the ability of a male to enter a public space with a private intent. Further, in assuming a garb that is alien to his class he becomes in a sense a member of an ambiguous caste. And his compulsive documentation of the sexual practices of Chinese, Indian, African, and "other" peoples places him firmly in the ultramasculine realm. We can also note by examining the map of Burton's travels (fig. 6) that his career trajectory coincided with the imperializing mission of the British Empire.

These three historical cases of famous writer/travelers confirm certain basic theoretical assumptions about Orientalism, notably their connections to British imperialism and what we now understand to be cultural hybridity. Though ensconced in widely different literary periods, stretching from the early eighteenth century to the middle of the nineteenth century, the portraits of Montagu and Byron and the photograph of Burton construct and reinforce Orientalized and continuously commodified versions of the British traveler in the East. This "traveler" consistently inhabits the popular imagination (at all class levels) because Mary Wortley Montagu's Turkish lady, Byron's Albanian potentate, and Burton's devout Muslim pilgrim mirror the process of colonization through stylized representation. These strangers in strange lands do not merely exoticize the Oriental Other, entertaining readers with the oddities of cultural difference. Indeed, Montagu, Byron, and Burton impersonate in order to instruct their readers as well as to titillate their senses. But they were always interacting with cultures that had their own long and rich history, and that is what is often overlooked in Western attempts to decode Orientalism. Nicholas Thomas has recently discussed some of the challenges of wrestling with colonial history, and he has observed that it is crucial to "avoid reproducing one of the central assumptions of Orientalism: that prospectively or already colonized places are a *tabula rasa* for the projection of European power and European representations" (36).

II: The Essays in the Collection

Not coincidentally, then, the essays in this collection frequently confront the problematics of Orientalist definition and representation. Moving chronologically, the first section of the volume explores a variety of the theoretical approaches to British Orientalism. In an essay titled "Interrogating Orientalism: Theories and Practices," Jeffrey Cass defines the many Orientalisms that have populated the theoretical field. Cass interrogates the concept and surveys the ways that Orientalism has been approached in literary and cultural studies. Also, he historically outlines various iterations of Orientalism although it is Edward Said's famous exploration of the term in *Orientalism* that has dominated theoretical discussions for over twenty-five years. Cass indicates how and why postcolonial critics challenge Saidian Orientalism. Writers such as Homi Bhabha, Ali Behdad, Ania Loomba, Dennis Porter, James Clifford, and Sara Mills construct a critique that attempts to render the field of Orientalism and its representations more dynamic, more capable of producing a critical model that explains the complex interchanges between Orient and Occident. While Said's critics to some extent acknowledge the explanatory power of his interpretive model and its lingering presence in the field of literary and cultural studies, they nonetheless ascertain that Said's central impulse—to tease out imperialist presumptions from Orientalist tropes—should itself be subject to a kind of ideological scrutiny. This scrutiny focuses not only on Saidian Orientalism but on Said's relationship with humanism and its promises of liberation through individual self-consciousness. Though *Orientalism* protests the ideological collusion between humanism and colonialism, Said still flirts with the humanist's hope of the transcendence of self through an aesthetic appreciation of literature and the arts, an unexamined pleasure of the text. For Bhabha and others, this hope actually constitutes a kind of subjection, a subsumption of the other into the valorized confines of humanism's big tent and a betrayal of the postcolonial desire to interrogate social, cultural, and political difference. Cass provides several perspectives on this important issue within Said's work, including critiques by Emily Apter, Mustapha Marrouchi, Kojin Karatani, Aamir Mufti, and Harry Harootunian. Cass concludes by describing the ways in which Orientalism has migrated into literary studies, iterated into new formats and texts, periods and genres. In particular, the period between 1750 and 1850 becomes a convenient snapshot for an analysis of Orientalist discourse(s) before, during, and following the historical date that Said supplies as the genesis of the professional study of Orientalism—the 1797 invasion of Egypt by Napoleon.

Diane Long Hoeveler's essay, "The Female Captivity Narrative: Blood, Water, and Orientalism," suggests that another trope besides self and other may be "even more germane to an understanding of British and French cultural productions: blood and water." Using the trope of blood and water, Hoeveler examines the female captivity narrative, which generally castigates Islam for its treatment of women, permitting, for example, the practice of polygamy. For Hoeveler, "blood and water" become essential figures in texts such as Elizabeth Marsh's *The Female Captive* and Robert Bage's *The Fair Syrian* because of the fear long associated with the captivity of Christian women within Muslim harems that stems from "the threatened circulation of female blood and control of bloodlines." Female captivity narratives thus impel imperialist logics because they reify the threat to British middle-class domesticity, the life's blood of the "home" and, by extension, the empire. Hoeveler thus makes use of the trope of blood and water in order to stress the internal contradiction between the British fascination with the Orient and its concomitant moral condemnations of "Oriental" behavior from within a framework of "muscular" Christianity. Furthermore, while Said ignores the works of British women writers in *Orientalism*, Hoeveler demonstrates their complicity in constructing "a female imperialist gaze toward the Oriental sphere." For Hoeveler, while British middle-class women writers like Aubin, Wollstonecraft, and Marsh are "critical of Islam's perceived denigration of women," they also represent women's bodies that appeal "to an aggressive Islamic male gaze."

In "'Better than the Reality': The Egyptian Market in Nineteenth-Century Travel Writing," Emily Haddad develops the "implications" of another master trope within Orientalist texts—the market. From Haddad's perspective, this trope epitomizes the relationship between the British traveler and the Egyptian market, but it does so in a way that collapses the conventional hierarchies between colonizer and colonized. By entering the Egyptian bazaar and becoming a consumer, the traveler is thrown off balance, occupying "a subject position not fully congruent with colonial hegemonic practice." The standard Egyptian practice of asking for a gratuity—*baksheesh*—even when no services have been performed gives the Egyptian "a measure of control over the British customer," for the British traveler can only be successful in acquiring goods and services with the active cooperation of the locals. The gratuity thus becomes the bribe; the gratified traveler is transformed into the fleeced consumer. In the end, *baksheesh* destabilizes the conventionally static and comfortable representations of Egypt—its ancient monuments, its desert landscapes, and its "picturesque bazaars"—and instead represents the compromised and vulnerable status of the British traveler.

In "Colonial Counterflow: From Orientalism to Buddhism," Mark Lussier considers the possibility that the "Orient" may have had an important effect on its own representation within Western thought. Using the term "colonial counterflow," Lussier contends that Buddhism emerges into European consciousness within the nineteenth century as a philosophical and spiritual counterweight to Enlightenment rationalism and that, somewhat ironically, European imperial interests make possible this "engagement with and representation of indigenous materials." Consequently, while Lussier views *Orientalism* as a text that reifies the West's power over the Orient, he also believes that Buddhism becomes a "counter-influence" over and against the colonialist project that interestingly coincides with the appearance of Romanticism. In particular, Tibetan Buddhism "cast[s] long shadows across the West" and even "take[s] up residence within it." Beginning with Alexander the Great, Lussier outlines the historical interactions between Buddhism and the West, stressing the British influence on the Himalayan region at the end of the eighteenth century, which begins a new phase of spiritual colonialism, and which the Jesuits had attempted to initiate in Japan and China. For Lussier, the most important test case for counterflow is that of Alexander Csoma, the Hungarian father of Tibetan studies, whose sojourn to Tibet produces the first systematic investigations of Tibetan grammar and the origins of the Tibetan language. Although under the aegis of Sir William Jones's Asiatick Society of Bengal and the patronage of British colonial agents like

William Moorcroft, Csoma nonetheless makes available for the first time to readers in English the entire Buddhist canon, as well as the *Tibetan-English Dictionary* and *Tibetan Grammar in English*. Csoma's work vigorously circulates Buddhist thought in the West, the reception of which undermines the "European commitment to its own epistemic form of enlightenment" since the Buddhist "dharma" deconstructs its positivistic worldview. The incorporation of Buddhism within Western philosophy culminates in the work of Arthur Schopenhauer and Friedrich Nietzsche, who embody the effects of the counterflow that Lussier outlines throughout his essay.

The fifth essay in the collection is Jeffrey Cass's "Homoerotics and Orientalism in William Beckford's *Vathek:* Liberalism and the Problem of Pederasty." Cass explores the whole conflicted representation of the Orient as a site of dangerous sexual hygiene, in which "liberal" thinking seeks to erase queer difference, uncomfortable with Beckford's horrifying conflation of homosexuality and pederasty, in fact, utterly discomfited by any real examination of queer desire or practice. Citing remarks Homi Bhabha makes about the intersections of postcolonial theory and sexuality, Cass argues for a recontextualization of Beckford's work within the framework of queer theory. In particular, Cass makes use of the work of Cindy Paton and Benigno Sánchez-Eppler to question whether or not the ending of *Vathek,* in which Beckford condemns his principal characters (Vathek, Carathis, and Nouronihar) to the Orientalized hell of Eblis, represents Beckford's own guilt at having an affair with thirteen-year-old William Courtenay. Cass examines this critical commonplace within the work of several of Beckford's critics who assume that Vathek's fate is a psychosexual projection of Beckford's and which, Cass finds, is a more comfortable critical solution than the one that also offers itself at the end of the novel—that Beckford feels no guilt whatsoever and that he fully expects to live a full life with his shameless appetites intact. Cass argues that the more conventional moralistic solution signals a kind of panic on the part of Beckford's critics (both heterosexual and homosexual) who refuse to confront the "problem of pederasty" in *Vathek*. Horrified that Beckford does not feel real guilt over his pederasty, perhaps even enjoying it, and concerned that he uses Orientalist representations to mask his perverse sexual desire and sexual politics, many of Beckford's critics attempt to separate the pederastic from the homosexual by erasing the former and reconstructing the latter. Ironically, the last word in the novel is given to the "good old genius" who presides over Gulchenrouz and the heaven of boys, which Cass interprets as the Orientalized paradise that Beckford not only covets but refuses to acknowledge as being perverse or licentious. Beckford's sexual politics threaten far more than a simple interpretation of the novel's conclusion by occasionally prudish but mainstream critics. Indeed, his Orientalist homoerotics not only challenge "the legitimacy of such readers to pass these judgments," they constitute a field of queer, pederastic play that "liberal" critics would prefer to remain buried with Beckford's presumed psychosexual guilt that the text only apparently affirms.

In the next essay, "Orientalism in Disraeli's *Alroy*," Sheila Spector explores the representation of the Orientalized Jew in Disraeli's *Alroy*, rightly viewing Disraeli's work through the prism of his politics. Spector argues that the central conflict of the novel between Jew and Muslim has implications for our understanding of Disraeli's decision to become a Tory, as well as his foreign policy during his years as prime minister. Just as Disraeli works out his politics of the 1840s in his "Young England" trilogy (*Coningsby, Sybil,* and *Tancred*), so in the 1830s, he acts out his emerging social and political views. In *Alroy*, Spector argues, Disraeli "uses the Middle East as a kind of negative laboratory," for he urges a government that balances its state obligations with its religious affiliations; he desires a golden mean that avoids the dangers of religious extremism. Drawing on an obscure episode from twelfth-century Jewish history, Disraeli advocates a constitutional relationship between church and state that is productive as it is receptive to the needs of the nation. The novel thus becomes a political and religious allegory, complicated by its numerous allusions and appropriations of Spenser's *Faerie Queene* and by the fact that Alroy, unlike the Red Cross Knight, makes choices he cannot undo or for which he cannot atone. Most interestingly, Alroy may be as Orientalized as his evil Turkish foe, for despite his good intentions, he is "othered" by his lack of Christian virtue. Hence, although the novel "conflates several versions of a common trope of Middle Eastern culture, the slaying of an unjust overseer," Alroy's heroism against that Orientalized evil is pointless precisely because his religion cannot adequately address the danger, thus dooming his empire to infidel invaders. As an Orientalist allegory, *Alroy* anticipates British imperial policies in the Middle East, for drawing on cultural stereotypes of Jews as helpless pawns in the face of infidel aggression, the British view themselves as virtuous protectors whose stability depends on balancing religious and secular interests throughout their empire. In the end, Spector darkly implies, Disraeli denies the efficacy of his Jewish heritage because it cannot win (or help him win).

This volume, however, does more than present textual analyses of Orientalist representations, which, to be sure, are interesting and important pieces of scholarship in their own right. The volume also intends to promote the teaching of Orientalism in the classroom by focusing on student engagement with the pragmatics of Orientalist representation. "Interrogating Orientalism" means, therefore, introducing students—at all levels—to the ways in which Orientalism exists in their everyday lives, and not only in the complex and nuanced close readings of distant and strange texts. University professors, college instructors, and other professional practitioners will be able to read not only about the interpretive practices that underwrite scholarship in Orientalism, but about the pedagogical strategies that shape the processes of individual student learning, as well as assist the transformation of groups of students into genuine learning communities. In a very real and practical sense, the study of Orientalism means more than investigating the ways in which the cultural landscapes of the "Other" penetrate and formulate the political minds of students. It means creating a space of self-reflexive interrogation in which students cannot and should not remain separate or insulated from one another, powerlessly inhabiting the social and cultural peripheries, or at least believing they do. Instead, deciphering the Oriental "Other" becomes an expansive enterprise. Without some regard for the ideological contexts of Orientalism, discussions about the nature of representation appear moot, for they fail to stimulate a transformative praxis that ties such discussions to the everyday lives and actions of their participants. The essays in the second section of this volume focus, therefore, on "performing" Orientalism in the classroom, and not only in demonstrating its intellectual properties.

For example, in the first essay of this section, "Teaching the Quintessential Turkish Tale: Montagu's *Turkish Embassy Letters,*" Jeanne Dubino examines teaching the Turkish tale by using Lady Mary Wortley Montagu's highly accessible *Turkish Embassy Letters,* the first secular text by a woman about the Middle East. Dubino finds the book an effective way of introducing Orientalism to students and, taking her theoretical cues from Meyda Yegenoglu, Lisa Lowe, Mary Louise Pratt, and Anna Secor, complicating the concept so that students learn that Orientalism is not a "unified" concept. Following Secor, Dubino suggests that the "Turkish tale" is a play on the term "traveler's tale"—a space of negotiated intercultural contact in which students investigate the effects of a new and feminized genre on Western readership. More importantly, Dubino exposes students to the multiplicity of discourses affected by the feminization of the Turkish (or traveler's) tale. Indeed, disciplines such as literature, history, sociology, anthropology/ethnography, politics, and cultural studies comprise what Barbara Korte refers to as an "*omnium-gatherum,*" that is to say, the "multifarious" travel book that gathers into itself multiple methodologies, discourses, disciplinary data, and perspectives with the intent of analyzing representations of travel. Despite Montagu's ethnographic intention of accurately depicting Turkish lives, however, her efforts principally succeed in "capturing the 'otherness of the other.'" Or, perhaps more succinctly, Montagu "cannot altogether avoid the tropes of Orientalism." To a large extent, then, Montagu inscribes these tropes within *The Turkish Embassy Letters,* presenting students with the opportunity of exploring Montagu's text as unconventional epistolary novel, travel tale, social and cultural history, feminist manifesto, and site of Oriental Othering. At the end of the essay, Dubino suggests a course format that includes possible required and reserve readings, as well as course objectives and assignments.

In the second essay in this section, "Representing India in Drawing Room and Classroom; or, Miss Owenson and 'Those Gay Gentlemen, Brahma, Vishnu, and Co.,'" Michael Franklin is concerned with a wide range of theoretical issues, including the social and political alignments in Romantic era literature and history, the conception of female genius and the function of the female artist within constricting gender ideologies, the pressing need for a discrimination among Orientalisms, and the contemporary relevance of pluralism and similitude (rather than difference and otherness). In his essay Franklin uses Sidney Owenson's *The Missionary* as a text that mediates these issues for the classroom. Like G. Todd Davis (below), Franklin is also concerned with reception theory, or the ways in which "earlier generations of critics and readers have shaped our conception" of texts and authors. Franklin wishes to teach students how to read "against the grain of [*The Missionary's*] particular agenda" in order to engage in "dialogue between past and present postcolonialisms" and have the students confront and respond to the textual dialectic between the anxieties of their own readerly expectations and personal experiences and the anxieties of empire, both of which control and contain those expectations and experiences. In the case of *The Missionary,* Franklin views Owenson's domestic trope of the drawing room as a supreme figure for the politics of empire, inasmuch as "the novel was composed in the library to provide luxurious listening" for a readership "for whom Orientalism might prove congenial amusement" but who are also in agreement with British imperial ambitions. Franklin thus connects the "performative expectations of [Owenson's] audience" with classroom performance, finally disrupting students from the comfort of their own Orientalist perches. Bringing "those gay gentlemen, Brahma, Vishnu, and Co" (a reference to a reviewer from the *Critical Review*) into the classroom at first confirms and then subtly subverts the students' Orientalist expectations because Owenson's "sentimental" text deliberately manipulates Orientalist stereotypes to "dispel prejudice." She uses the overheated language of sentimental fiction, which, following Ina Ferris, Franklin believes is a discourse of romantic theatricality that functions as a cover story for her political and ideological interventions. At the heart of this story are the Hindu priestess Luxima and the Catholic priest Hilarion, whose excessive (and appropriately forbidden) ardor for one another serves to highlight the "common ground" between

"Vedantic and Christian concepts of mystic love." In short, Owenson master-fully employs Orientalism to assert a cultural pluralism that undermines the inherent cultural differences (typified by religion) between East and West, finally harmonizing and reconciling the two. For students, the interpretive challenge lies in deconstructing the binaries that Owenson deliberately sets up—climate, culture, gender, and religion—and by recognizing that they are still configured in the students' expectations of these categories.

In "'Unlettered Tartars' and 'Torpid Barbarians': Teaching the Figure of the Turk in Shelley and De Quincey," Filiz Turhan speaks of the figural nature of the Turk in both writers who rely "on a presentation of the Turks as a trope for racial difference." Though contextualizing the historical relations between the British and the Turks, Turhan rightly points out that complex events like the Greek uprising of 1821 do not necessarily alter the Orientalist representations of the Turk and, in the cases of Shelley and De Quincey, "are given to descriptions that shock and titillate through the narrative of explicit horror and violence." In Shelley's poem *Hellas,* the Turks are wild animals, wholly incapable (unlike the Greeks) of establishing modern political or social institutions. In De Quincey's *Confessions of an English Opium Eater,* opium eating not only serves to reinforce Orientalist stereotypes, it actually confirms the superiority of the British. The Turks remain torpid after opium use; the British persevere in their habits of mind even after opium consumption. In other words, the British are better opium eaters than the Turks; they can control themselves, which makes them worthy of their imperial ambitions, while the Ottoman Turks cannot succeed in maintaining theirs.

In "'Boundless Thoughts and Free Souls': Teaching Byron's *Sardanapalus, Lara,* and *The Corsair,*" G. Todd Davis notes that his students often find Byron "irresistible," particularly *Don Juan,* but that they are more guarded and suspicious of his Oriental tales, "finding the language and context too difficult and foreign to fathom." Students are also resistant to critical theory, and Davis reveals how he uses reception theory to break down the barriers of the Oriental text. Teasing out students' expectations about the Oriental tale becomes paramount for Davis. By employing Jauss's "horizons-of-experience" for the Orientalist contexts Said defines, Davis feels that students will employ their own familiarity with and experience of the Oriental Other in unpacking the strange and unfamiliar textual representations of works such as *Sardanapalus, Lara,* and *The Corsair.* Contemporary constructions of the Orient in film—*Crouching Tiger, Hidden Dragon; The Matrix Trilogy;* and *Kill Bill, Volume I* and *Kill Bill, Volume II*—rivet the students' attention to Orientalism in popular culture. Their experience of these "texts" mediates their reading of other Orientalist texts, providing a language and a vocabulary with which to interpret them and decipher their strangeness. Furthermore, Davis guides his students to the notion that reception itself is an Orientalist trope in Byron's work, for Byron worries about how his readers will receive him and his work. In the case of *The Giaour,* for example, Byron makes use of the vampire (a Gothic villain frequently Orientalized in literature and film) to trope the idea of prey and predator. Just as the audience would devour him/his work, so Byron manufactures an Oriental Other who would assault and prey upon his audience. Thus, the meaning of the text lies in the reader's expectation and fear of being consumed, even as he or she performs "consumption" through the act of reading.

Byron's sexuality, too, becomes a transactional flashpoint between reader, writer, and text, and Davis promotes different horizons-of-experience for Byron before and after his Grand Tour, thus shaping a variety of interesting comparison/contrast topics. The Orientalized landscape of the East alters the nature of possible representations, and students will expect a more detect-able homoeroticism, which they will uncover in Byron's relevant journals and letters, as well as in works such as *Sardanapalus.* Finally, Davis wishes students to share and examine their own and each other's expectations of the Orientalist text, and he uses electronic communications to facilitate these interactions. Requiring students to write to one another guides them to more critical, less passive interpretive roles. Asking his students "to recreate Byron in their own constructed image and to situate him within a historical and cultural milieu" is possible because Davis exploits the students' internal-ized stereotypes of the Oriental Other and then explodes them by examining their expectations. Davis ultimately uses their horizons-of-experience to probe their fear of the Oriental Other and thereby transform their personal interpretive landscapes.

In his essay "Byron's *The Giaour:* Teaching Orientalism in the Wake of September 11," Alan Richardson highlights the process of bringing more living contexts to Orientalist texts such as William Beckford's *Vathek,* a task that Richardson successfully addresses in his edited volume *Three Oriental Tales.* The terrorist attacks of September 11, 2001, irrevocably alter, however, the "conditions for teaching Orientalism," and Richardson recalls that in the first days following the attacks, the media initially recirculate the "old binaries"—East and West, fanatic and secular, Islam and Christendom—that speak to the "stereotypical Oriental Other" that typically feeds media, filmic, and literary representations of Asian and African cultures. As Richardson argues, however, because anti-Muslim hate crimes did not rise as precipi-tously as might have been expected and because the media finally conveyed a less monolithic, more complex version of Islam, the public began to under-stand that Osama bin Laden did not "typify" Islam any more than Jerry

Falwell embodies Christianity. Richardson's purpose is to connect this historical outcome to a textual reading of Byron's *The Giaour*. It, too, "begins much as did the immediate public reaction to the horrors of September 11 by seeming to confirm a simplistically and remorselessly dichotomous view of East and West, Europe and its Oriental Other." Like the narrator of *The Giaour*, students will at first view the Oriental tale as a standard division of a democratic Greece and a despotic Asia, a free Europe and an imprisoned East. And yet, for Richardson, properly contextualizing *The Giaour*—both with current events and with the facts of Byron's life—ensures that students will recognize that the Orient is no more unified or hegemonic a concept than is the "West." Even so, Richardson urges the teaching of Orientalism (and its representations) with texts like Byron's not merely because of his desire for better, more sophisticated readers, but because he wishes students to break Orientalist habits of thought, in particular those that inhabit clever disinformation campaigns aimed at elevating the passions and circumventing the intellect.

In the final essay in the collection, "Teaching Nineteenth-Century Orientalist Entertainments," Edward Ziter begins with the premise that "the tropes of the Orientalist entertainment industry . . . have long informed public opinion in the West," and he goes on to examine the "Orientalist imagery" of the Great Exhibition in 1851. With an eye toward a teaching of Orientalism that focuses on broadly consumed visual forms, Ziter inveigles students into a study of the literal production of a commercial and consumable Orientalism that extends to contemporary practices, visual and performance forms, and state policy. The circulation of Orientalism within British popular culture, and reified by the Great Exhibition at the Crystal Palace, not only "unpacks" its history, but unearths as well the unexamined ideology that connects the Great Exhibition to the construction of academic fields such as ethnography. These fields construct "a new vocabulary of exoticism," even as they also "perpetuate older tropes of Orientalism." Ziter feels that while students will recognize the nearly inevitable continuation of Orientalist tropes, they will discover how these tropes can also be "manipulated and resisted." Ziter acknowledges the deictic nature of "entertainment" and popular diversion. As a result, he employs many nontraditional texts that contextualize specific events like the Great Exhibition. To be sure, nineteenth-century magazines and newspapers assist in this process, but "marginal iconography" in the forms of newspaper illustrations, tinsel prints, caricatures, and even academic painting are the most successful "texts" that enable students to interrogate the proliferation of cultural metaphors and metonymies. These figures explain the manufacture of British identity in relation to the Oriental Other, even as the British seek to contain and control the marginalized

Other through entertainments, museums, and a profusion of ethnographic displays. Students discern that as a Victorian theme park, the Great Exhibition is as much about the exercise of imperial power and colonial politics as it is a scientific, historic testament to Victorian progress.

While the essays in this volume certainly enter the arena of raucous academic debate surrounding Orientalism and postcolonialism, they are intended for both specialists and students. Focusing on the numerous and problematic representations of the Orient in eighteenth- and nineteenth-century British literature, they cover both hermeneutical and pedagogical practices. As such, they seek to expand our understanding of how Orientalism has functioned and, indeed, continues to function in our world.

Part One

CONTEXTUAL APPROACHES

CHAPTER 1

Interrogating Orientalism

Theories and Practices

JEFFREY CASS

I. Definitions, Revisions, and Critiques of Orientalism

Defining Orientalism is a difficult task because its historical origins do not always coincide with its contemporary parlance or the very wide range of its past and current theoretical uses. Michael Payne's *A Dictionary of Critical and Cultural Theory* offers the following definition of Orientalism: "A term for the European invention or the idea of the Orient, associated with the thought of Edward Said" (392). Payne goes on to say that Said's theories bear traces of Foucault's work on discourse and epistemological power and Derrida's theory of "European hallucination" in which Europe fantasized its completeness in the idealized other that was absent to it. More concretely, in his book *Orientalism*, A. L. Macfie borrows from the *Oxford English Dictionary* and outlines three traditional definitions of Orientalism: the historical field of an Orientalist, "a scholar versed in the language and literatures of the East" (3); the denotation or connotation in the arts of "a character, style or quality commonly associated with the Eastern nations" (3); and, finally, the identification of a "'conservative or romantic' approach to the problems of government" (3), which in the context of the nineteenth century signified a reliance on the East India Company to enact and enforce an "Anglicist" approach to nation-building. Macfie then describes the conceptual evolution of Orientalism following the Second World War, the historical contours of which include the work of Annouar Abdel-Malek, A. L. Tibawi, Bryan S. Turner, and, of course, Edward Said (4). For Macfie, these critics transform Orientalism into "an effective challenge to European hegemony, not only in the military and political, but also in the intellectual sphere" (5). But it is Said's work that remains the most influential and the most controversial. Macfie makes much the same case about the problems of defining

Orientalism and Said's relationship to the concept in his book of readings on and about Orientalism. In his introduction to the volume, Macfie concisely summarizes the problem as an intellectual debate between a theorist who "tends to view his subject through the prism of modern and postmodern philosophy" and his critics who "remain, for the most part, firmly wedded to a traditional (realist) approach to the writing of history" (5).

For many critics, Said's work fragments the steadiness of the *OED* definitions into differing, even opposing, versions of "intellectual" Orientalism. As compilers Barbara Harlow and Mia Carter acknowledge in their book *Imperialism and Orientalism: A Documentary Sourcebook*, Edward Said's definition of Orientalism as a Western restructuring of and assertion of authority over the Orient has generally prevailed since the publication of *Orientalism*, although both also cite the long history of Orientalism "with its own disciplinary in the course of the last two centuries in the Euro-American Academy" (49). Dismissing even this semblance of professional consensus, Ziauddin Sardar is even more blunt, stating that "There is nothing about Orientalism that is neutral or objective. By definition it is a partial and partisan subject" (vii). This movement away from generally accepted definitions has ignited controversy precisely because a critic's partisanship, his or her ideological commitments and loyalties, inflects his or her use of Orientalism.

For example, in a special issue of *Southern Review* titled *Alterity and Orientalism* (1993), Cathy Greenfield remains vague about narrow definitions of Orientalism in order to be as inclusive as possible, even bracketing the critical term as "Orientalism" and suggesting that it "has become an available and easy term for scholars in cultural literary studies to use." "Something like 'postcolonialism,' she continues, "it can signal (though not guarantee) a knowledge of the range of contemporary theoretical arguments which accompany Orientalism, as well as a particular well-intentioned (though not always well-practiced) ethical position towards or as part of subject populations" (311). Such circumlocutions serve the interests of diversity and inclusion, but such intentional lack of clarity makes possible the critical use of literature as a vehicle for ideological expression, which is at a far remove from a humanistic perspective that views literature as having a vital role in the production of cultural truth, but does not also consider that role an ideological one.

Not surprisingly, therefore, a sampling of the postcolonial critique of Saidian Orientalism principally focuses on what Michael Dutton and Peter Williams call Said's "valorization" of literature. This privileging "entails a lingering, in some ways ambivalent but resilient valuing of literature from different national canons" (331). As we shall see, this suspicion of literature as Western hegemonic discourse is closely tied to Said's humanism. And although Said revisits Orientalism throughout his career, even condemning the "sovereignty" of literature in *Culture and Imperialism* and asserting that his cultural criticism and political ideologies are truly relevant and germane to discussions of U.S. foreign policy, Said remains firmly planted in the field of comparative literature and the Eurocentric texts that occupy its domain. In other words, Dutton and Williams make an important point: Said never permits literature to utterly relinquish the humanistic role that it has occupied in the academy and in the outside world. By "fudging" the definitional boundaries of Orientalism (and, in his later work, on culture and imperialism), Said has loosed "incompatible periodisations" and "overlapping and/or mutually exclusive definitions of 'Orientalism' that, in turn, have given license to extremely loose and totalizing notions of 'Orientalism'" (328). In the end, however, Dutton and Williams do not define Orientalism with precision, nor do they take "Orientalism" outside the apostrophes for fear of the very theoretical totalizing they eschew.

The pithiest description of Said's *Orientalism* is Ania Loomba's. "This is a book," Loomba writes, "not about non-Western cultures, but about the Western representation of these cultures" (43). It is a simple but signal distinction that we should not forget, for it is relatively easy to focus on the theoretical problems of *Orientalism*—the seemingly static, unchanging nature of the Orient, the paradox between Said's sympathy for humanism and his reliance on antihumanist discourse theory, his reverence for canonical European texts—but it is equally important to comprehend the continuing appeal of Said's theories for literary critics. Indeed, one might well wonder how and why, in the face of enormous and serious postcolonial critique, some of this revisionism from Said himself, Orientalism continues to remain one of the hottest fields of literary study. As we shall see, that appeal principally lies in the complexities of Orientalist representation. Of course, that appeal has also given birth to a number of acute criticisms of Saidian Orientalism.

One of the most cogent critiques, particularly of Said's unquestioned use of Eurocentric models and literature, comes from Ali Behdad, who uncovers Said's "essentialist distinctions" that harden the Orient and the Occident as theoretical (and textual) terms, even if they do "create a useful paradigm to justify the appropriation of the Oriental Other" (10). "[Said's] insistence on the monolithic character of Orientalism," Behdad continues a bit later, "seems paradoxically consistent with the logic of Orientalism/colonialism" (11). The "formalization" of Orientalism thus "cannot account for the complexities of its *micro*practices . . . its dispersed network of representations that include strategic irregularities, historical discontinuities, and discursive heterogeneity" (12; original emphasis). Behdad wishes to push for a more flexible model, one that comports with the "dynamic exchange" between Orient and Occident, between the Oriental and European power, or, as Mark Lussier suggests later in this volume, between flow and counterflow.

Likewise, Homi Bhabha believes that Saidian Orientalism "could be extended to engage with the alterity and ambivalence of Orientalist discourse" ("The Other Question," 102), but Said forecloses this possibility by introducing a unified Western "intention" to "advance securely and *unmetaphorically* upon the Orient" (102; original emphasis). Although Bhabha acknowledges that Said appropriates "Foucault's concepts of power and discourse" (103), this appropriation, in Bhabha's view, is a misuse of Foucauldian theory, inasmuch as Said's binarism of West and Orient places both in a symmetrical power relation that can be "subverted by being inverted" (103), a result that seems to contravene the very resistances to such symmetries that Foucault's theories promises.

Furthermore, Said's acceptance of a coherent textuality within Orientalism "unif[ies] the subject of colonial enunciation" and sustains the very colonial fantasies that Said disdains. Bhabha writes: "This results in Said's inadequate attention to representation as a concept that articulates the historical and fantasy (as the scene of desire) in the production of the 'political' effects of discourse" (72). Following Fanon, Bhabha feels literary representation is the humanistic "fetish" that perpetuates colonialist stereotypes and imperial power—to be sure, a strong indictment, to which even the "emancipatory" humanism that Apter outlines in her essay on Saidian humanism can only uneasily answer.

While critiques of Saidian Orientalism by James Clifford, Dennis Porter, and Sara Mills will be discussed in section III of this chapter, other relevant revisions of Orientalism include those of Payne, Harlow and Carter, Macfie, Dutton and Williams, and Sardar. Moore-Gilbert (and his colleagues Gareth Stanton and Willy Maley) produce another historical riff on how Orientalist discourse "mediates" the relationship between East and West, saying that "the most immediate concern of Orientalism is analysis of the degree to which the West's system of scholarship, and its canon of aesthetic representation, have been implicated in the long history of the West's material and political domination of the non-Western world" (22). Brian Niro takes issue with Moore-Gilbert's criticism of Said's attempt to separate "the European fabrication of the Orient" from the "material dominance of that same thing" (137). Instead, Niro prefers the "strange magic" that differentiates the historical Orientalism prior to Said and Said's version of Orientalism: "To a certain extent, discussing the theoretical framework of Orientalism before the publication of Said's text is a bit like discussing gravity before Newton. Yes, the phenomenon existed, but the articulation of the precise phenomenon does not call the exact thing into existence until the point of its utterance" (135).

More to the point, Niro believes that Orientalism opens a space for a new form of "critical attention" (136). Instead of the "leering West" deriving pleasure from its fixation on the Orient as "source of wonder and fascination," Niro writes, "Orientalism stares back" (136). Niro's statement suggests that Orientalist representations, despite Moore-Gilbert's dim view of the "radical contradiction" between "discursive Orientalism and the material practices and politics of imperialism" (136–37), are positive spaces for critical self-reflection and textual interaction. Hence, Orientalism neither traps the reader nor imprisons the culture within an unalterable paradigm; rather, Orientalism urges "an adversarial critique" of the "sociocultural situation" that at once makes possible and sustains the repertory of Orientalism. Said's intention with *Orientalism* is to outline "a structure erected in the thick of an imperial contest whose dominant wing it represented and elaborated not only as scholarship but as a partisan ideology. Yet Orientalism hid the contest beneath scholarly and aesthetic idioms" ("Representing the Colonized," 299). For Said, literary representation becomes the critical medium through which this hidden "contest" can be unearthed and scrutinized. Though postcolonial critics bridle (with good reason) at the politics of Orientalism and the role they play in the construction of academic practices and literary interpretations, Niro nonetheless concludes that these critics ought to resist the theoretical straightjackets they attempt to wrestle onto Orientalist representations, which ultimately cannot be so easily marshaled or corralled. Reminiscent of Paul Ricoeur's linkage of suspicion and metaphor, some postcolonial critics subscribe to a hermeneutics of textual suspicion. Precisely because they doubt that the "Oriental" referents of the literary text do point to uncontainable, undifferentiated meaning(s), they become (one might argue), much like Orientalism itself, far too "inclusive" (Niro, 138). In this way, postcolonial critics come to resemble the universalizing colonizers they abhor because they unintentionally use the same critical devices and to the same ends. As Niro pointedly asks: "How can one claim status as an exoticized individual and maintain that distinction while employing, or even in the employment of, the discursive tools of the Orientalist?" (138).

But even if postcolonial critics cannot dismantle the "oppressor's house with the tools of his making" (Niro, 139), they are clearly right, as Timothy Brennan argues in "The Illusion of a Future: *Orientalism* as Traveling Theory," to be suspicious of *Orientalism* as a foundational text because Saidian Orientalism ironically stands as a "proleptic" critique of postcoloniality and not merely its historical precursor (576). For Brennan, *Orientalism*'s historicity implicitly glosses (and opposes) postcolonial studies, which "has understandably worn the clothing of identity in the often obtuse and willful psychoanalytic register of the 'subject position'"(576). Oddly, postcolonial critics may fit a Bloomian model, unwittingly and effectively suffering from the anxiety of influence: Said stands in for the "strong" literary father, away from whom postcolonial critics must swerve to formulate their own critique of exile, their own image of diaspora. In the end, postcolonial studies, Brennan feels, have not only misunderstood their relationship to Orientalism, they have unfortunately not been "altogether accurate in assessing *Orientalism*'s worth, in spite of having many bones to pick with Said and in spite of the fact that many of their critiques of postcolonial studies are desperately needed and long overdue" (579).

Finally, Malini Johar Schueller recapitulates Said's notions of Orientalism for American contexts, in which the United States constructs the Orient in "proto-imperial" fashion, setting up "the dichotomies of USAmerican righteousness, morality, energy, and vibrancy versus Oriental corruption, deviance, lassitude, and passivity" (ix). Schueller describes Said's version of Orientalism as "a male domain" and desire as "exclusively male" (x). Taking a feminist perspective, Schueller's work underscores a strand of Orientalist scholarship that is vital to Romantic studies—the conflicted work of women writers, in particular British women writers who occupy a subaltern social and sexual position in their own culture yet who also embody, often unwillingly, the very imperialist logics and Orientalist practices with which they express unease and philosophical concern. As Said notes in *Culture and Imperialism*, the cultural "readiness to assume and enjoy the experience of Empire" underwrites narratives such as Jane Austen's, "which their formal inclusiveness, historical honesty, and prophetic suggestiveness cannot completely hide" (96).

II. Theorizing Orientalism and the Role of Humanism[1]

[H]umanism is the only, and I would go so far as to say, the final resistance we have against the inhuman practices and injustices that disfigure human history. . . . The human, and humanistic, desire or enlightenment and emancipation is not easily deferred, despite the incredible strength of the opposition to it that comes from the Rumsfelds, bin Ladens, Sharons, and Bushes of the world. I would like to believe that *Orientalism* has had a place in the long and often interrupted road to human freedom. (xxix–xxx)
—Edward Said, "The Horizon of R. P. Blackmur"

What is this ethical pressure to "account for ourselves"—but only partially—with a political theater of agonism, bureaucratic obfuscation, violence and violation? Is this political desire for partial identification a beautifully human, even pathetic attempt to disavow the realization . . . that the techniques and technologies of politics need not be *humanizing* at all, in no way endorsing of what we need to understand to be the human—humanist?—predicament. (93)

—Homi Bhabha, "Interrogating Identity"

In one of the epigraphs cited above, Homi Bhabha asks two searching questions, and both of them contradict Said's statement that humanism is the "final resistance" against the disfigurement of "human history." As one of those "discontented" with humanism, Bhabha expresses what he sees as our "pathetic" efforts to "humanize" the world of politics, to render it ethically productive and morally pure. In so doing, Bhabha calls into question the basic universalizing and liberating elements of humanism. He finds that the humanistic promise of individual freedom and autonomy for all ("accounting for ourselves") is illusory, a call to a false ideological consciousness that unthinkingly remains complicit with "textual or narrative subjections—be they governmental, judicial or artistic" (92). Bhabha deliberately leaves unanswered the "open question" of "how we are to rethink ourselves once we have undermined the immediacy and autonomy of self-consciousness" (92). And clearly that is the task Bhabha wishes to take on, "to constitute a postcolonial, critical discourse," which, in his words, "contests modernity through the establishment of other historical sites and other forms of enunciation" (*Location of Culture*, 366).

Bhabha's desire to open up criticism to "other historical sites and other forms of enunciation" leave little doubt why Said's career-long desire to dive into the wreck of humanism and salvage some of its ideological and theoretical power forces Said's critics to point to the relationship between humanism and Orientalism. The "question" of Said's humanism is notably problematic when connected to Orientalism because Said appears to vigorously contest the very types of discourse that feed into humanistic ideology and theoretical inquiry. Such is the argument that James Clifford makes in his essay "On *Orientalism*." In this piece, Clifford presents Said as someone who "qualifies himself positively," despite his oppositional stance, "as a humanist" (263). As a result, Said's position "presuppose[s] a particularist, even individualist attitude combined with cosmopolitanism and a general valorization of creative process" (263). Clifford repeatedly reiterates Said's commitment to "cosmopolitan values" and to the "cultural hermeneutics of Erich Auerbach, Ernst Robert Curtius, and Clifford Geertz" (263). Clifford also argues that Said's theoretical methods, which Clifford believes Said borrows from Foucault, actually contradict his humanistic values that privilege literary discourse. The problem with this approach, as Clifford sees it, is that in deriving a "discourse" from a "tradition," Said "relapses into traditional intellectual history" that flatly contravenes the kind of cultural criticism that

Foucault envisions (268). Moreover, by employing only "nineteenth-century modes of thought," Clifford concludes that Said "gives himself too easy a target." What else could overdetermined Orientalist representations do but reveal Orientalist "modes of thought"?[2]

Emily Apter describes Said as "tenaciously" clinging to "humanist precepts and exegetical practices," even though he amply shows in *Orientalism* that "humanism and empire are revealed in mutual compact" ("Saidian Humanism," 35). Yet Said does so, according to Apter, because he envisions "other humanisms that survive the compromise with imperialism: emancipatory humanism, the ethics of coexistence, figural paradigms of ontogenesis in world-historical forms of culture, and the ideal of *translatio* as portal to a universal or sacred language" (35). It is possible to argue that Apter's "ideal of *translatio*" saves humanism because *translatio* implies the possibility of a universal aesthetics that can free interpreters from the prison house of linguistic and cultural barriers. Despite the "material unevenness" (Harootunian's phrase, 442) of an unchanging West and a permanently constructed "Orient," Saidian Orientalism imagines a "world system," which Apter believes, "takes account of the vast traffic in inter-national learnedness informing Greek-Arab-Judeo-Christian practices of cultural translation from the early Middle Ages to the present" (45). Connected to "sacred narratives of divine ontogenesis" (53), such as Dante's *Commedia* (and, more pointedly, Auerbach's version of it), this *translatio* highlights the "effects" of an intellectual will to power.

Similar to Harootunian's conclusion about the Saidian "'infinity of traces' to which we have yet to attend" (442) and Apter's suggestion that Saidian humanism aims to recuperate "a utopian politics of paradise" ("Saidian," 53), Aamir R. Mufti alludes to the global reach of Orientalism and its continuing and future significance, for despite the postcolonial efforts "to reclaim traditions whose social basis is seen to have been destroyed by the processes of capitalist-colonial modernization" ("Global," 482), these efforts cannot simply "bypass" Orientalism, which Mufti defines as "the organizing, refractive, globally ambitious, and, in the sense that Said has made us to understand, inventive culture of the modern West" (482). Mufti cites Apter's global *translatio* as Orientalism's "inventive" radicalism, hinting yet again at a brand of future humanism. Mufti writes: "The very point of humanistic culture is to make it adequate to the imagining of a postimperial world" (483). In her essay on the global *translatio,* Apter employs the term "transnational humanism" in her efforts to analyze Said's relationship to Auerbach (82). She concludes that Auerbach's "legacy of philological humanism is not and never was a Western versus non-Western problematic; it was, and remains, a history of intellectual import and export in which the provenance labels have been torn off" (82). Both Mufti and Apter, therefore, put positive and productive spin on the theoretical connections between Orientalism and humanism, though they do not entirely address the problems of humanism that postcolonial theorists such as Bhabha identify.

Regardless, the "postimperial world" Mufti envisions and the "global *translatio*" Apter highlights will force critics of Saidian Orientalism to confront, yet once more, the theoretical issues that arise when embracing the aesthetic experiences which humanism promises. Though no agent of "Old Comparative Literature," the demise of which Spivak takes some relish in proclaiming in her recent book *Death of a Discipline*, Said paradoxically enjoys immersing himself in the pleasures of European literature at the same time that he decries Eurocentrism. Even when he appears determined to move beyond the social and political limitations of humanism, urging scholars to connect their work to "commitment," to make their scholarship "serviceable" as he does in a presidential column for the Modern Language Association ("Humanism?" 3), he never quite relinquishes the pleasure principle that underlies the interpretive delights of humanism. As John M. Mackenzie acerbically asserts: "[Said] seeks to expose the humanistic tradition, while essentially writing within it himself" (6). When Said tells the story of the racist publisher who would not put Nobel laureate Maguib Mahfouz into print because "Arabic is a controversial language" (4), Said does not really convince the reader that he has definitively exposed the sociopolitical inadequacies of humanism; indeed, what seems at stake are the imaginative limitations of its practitioners who are not sufficiently universalist to recognize the merits of a Mahfouz or to incorporate his work readily into the proscenium of canonical world literature.

Said's "contrapuntal" readings of the nineteenth century not only betray a stubborn humanist strain, they reveal as well a thinly disguised aestheticism that seems jarringly at odds with his chosen identity politics. Mustapha Marrouchi does not, however, necessarily see this as an insurmountable problem, and in his *Edward Said at the Limits*, he confirms and explains this paradox:

> Like his outer- and intermappings of the globe, Said's mythic *bricolage* is based in Palestine but expands beyond it. Reading *contrapuntally* may be his lasting contribution to the study of literature whereby he amalgamates many narratives to a vision—namely, humanism. . . . A *contrapuntal* reading is therefore uniquely carried by literature in which the ideology of a period is transformed into a new historicist way by the imagination, forming new and surprising wholes such as emancipation, enlightenment. (58; original emphasis)

Marrouchi retrieves Said's humanism from the "mythic *bricolage*" that Said has constructed out of both his "intermappings of the globe" and his personal exile from a Palestinian neighborhood that no longer exists. But if this is humanism, it is one that never reaches a destination or affirms an unchanging value system. Even Said's "surprising wholes" are always unstable, ever in flux, like the currents he speaks of in *Out of Place*. Being in ethnic diaspora and theoretical counterpoint has forced critics to describe Said in terms of instability. As Abdirahman Hussein has recently suggested, "Most critics have found it necessary to use the notion of boundary or in-betweenness as an almost self-evident point of purchase from which to draw various implications" (2). In reading Said's work, he adds: "It is not uncommon to come across words like 'ambivalence,' 'vacillation,' 'neutrality,' 'contradiction,' 'paradox'" (2). Hussein builds upon this "in-betweenness" by detailing Said's "critical consciousness" as "de-defining, derailing, and dismantling" conventional methodologies—a view, it seems to me, very close to Marrouchi's "contrapuntal" reading. The difficulties that critics of Said face, and Marrouchi and Hussein are typical examples, derive from Said's deliberate and perhaps obdurate hindering of such an overarching characterization, for he ranges effortlessly over a variety of genres. For instance, his stance is theoretical in such writings as *The World, the Text, and the Critic* and *Intention and Method;* overtly political diatribe and apology in *After the Last Sky;* to playful but powerful exegetical historicism in *Culture and Imperialism*. Yet the breadth of Said's work depends principally on literary representations of reality in Western literature. In fact, exploring the nature of representation forms the mainspring of Said's comparatist practices, which in his most important work on representation—*Orientalism*—finally reveals not only the depth of Said's literary interests, but also the formulation of a theoretical system that pits humanistic desire against ideological commitment, aesthetic pleasure in imperial texts against the ever-renewing production and dissemination of imperial knowledge and colonialist propaganda.

In his essay "Uses of Aesthetics: After Orientalism," Kojin Karatani identifies one of the central problems of Orientalist representation—the self-deluding belief that admiration of the Oriental "Other" betokens respect for non-Western traditions:

One of the points Said made clear in [*Orientalism*] is "Orientalism" sees people of the non-West as convenient objects of analysis for the social sciences but ignores their intellectual and ethical existence. This undoubtedly designates non-Westerners as intellectually and ethically inferior. But what is more gnarled about this stance is that it goes hand in hand with an aesthetic worship of the very inferior other. This worship, in turn, produces an ineradicable self-deceit: Those with an Orientalist attitude come to believe that they, unlike others, treat non-Westerners more than equally—they treat them with respect. (147)

Of the "aesthetic worship" inherent in Orientalism, Karatani's criticism harshly exposes the contradiction between the aesthetic pleasure that one might take in Western versions of "oriental" culture and the prejudice and bigotry that these versions may evoke. Indeed, Orientalist productions of the last two centuries disguise this "ineradicable" self-deceit very well by enjoying the Oriental "Other" even as they reinforce both positive and negative racial stereotypes (i.e., a period staging of *Aida*, a trip to Luxor Las Vegas, a visit to a Delacroix or Gerome exhibition, a screening of Disney's *Aladdin*, a performance of Rimsky-Korsakoff's *Scheherazade*). Said recognizes that the comparatist work of Auerbach and Curtius, though intended as "an enlargement of the scholar's awareness of his sense of the brotherhood of man, of the universality of certain principles of human behavior" (261), nonetheless disintegrates in the face of Orientalist representation. Comparatism devolves into a retrograde affirmation of geographic and national otherness, in which present-day Islam can never lay equal claim with the West to social, cultural, or scientific achievement. There will not be a transcendence of difference; instead, there will actually be "a sharpened sense of difference between Orient and Occident" (261).

As Mitchell contends in "Secular Divination: Edward Said's Humanism," "continuing the conversation" (402) with Said guarantees additional inquiry into the ideological shortcomings of Orientalism, particularly as it becomes fused with humanism(s). In his book *Orientalism, Postmodernism, & Globalism*, Bryan Turner, noted Marxist critic in the social sciences, observes that the rise of subaltern studies in the 1990s derives from ways in which Said's work on Orientalism sparked critical debates surrounding decolonization and the "writing of history" (3). But these debates also draw sharp criticism from postcolonial theorists whose anti-Orientalism is of a piece with the antihumanist arguments of postmodernism. Despite Said's "very profound critique of liberalism by showing how power and knowledge are inevitably combined and how power relations [are] produced through discourse" (4), Turner outlines his principal historical criticism of Said by underscoring Said's questionable "concentration on textuality and textualism" (7). Such "textualism" for Turner has "resulted in a vicious solipsism in which there can be no distinction between fictional writing and social reality" (7). He then cites Baudrillard's claim that the [first] Gulf War "was merely a television event" as an example of the danger in decoupling text from history (7). Turner's comment also reveals a firmly entrenched ideological commitment against the idea that depictions of a powerless, victimized, and dehistoricized Oriental "Other" can ever really be innocent.

James Clifford's summary of *Orientalism* as a work that "frequently relapses into the essentializing modes it attacks and is ambivalently enmeshed in the totalizing habits of Western humanism" (271) comports with Turner's analysis and anticipates others' evaluations of Saidian Orientalism. For example, Dennis Porter directly confronts the problems inherent in Said's lingering humanism by arguing that Said "ignores" the warning issued by Raymond Williams about those who live on the periphery, "who are in one way or another outside or at the edge of specific hegemony" (152). Porter continues: "The failure to take account of such efforts and contributions not only opens Said to the charge of promoting Occidentalism, it also contributes to the perpetuation of that Orientalist thought he set out to demystify" (152). This is especially true because in *Orientalism* Said "discovers hegemonic unity" from a "heterogeneous" selection of texts. Even a text such as T. E. Lawrence's *The Seven Pillars of Wisdom*, written from a "position of privilege and authority" (155), still "allows counter-hegemonic voices to be heard within it," thus demonstrating that arch-Orientalist texts may be "re-read" as "fissured with doubt and contradiction" (155). In the case of *The Seven Pillars of Wisdom*, Lawrence—"no political ingenú, no Beau Geste"—creates an overdetermined literary work that exhibits an amazing "generic heterogeneity" (156). This heterogeneity culminates in a breakdown of categories and a "potential" for change that would not be countenanced by the "dominant hegemonic discourse" (160). In other words, a Saidian reading of Lawrence's book would produce a far less inflected, more totalizing result because such an assessment would only confirm the text's "arch-Orientalist" status. "Said is unable to suggest alternatives to the hegemonic discourse of Orientalism," Porter concludes, because "Said fails to historicize adequately the texts he cites and summarizes" and because "he does not acknowledge the semi-autonomous and overdetermined character of aesthetic artifacts" (160).

Though not directly confronting the connections between humanism and Orientalism, Sara Mills mirrors Clifford and Porter in her work on women's travel writing. While admitting that "Said's basic contention is correct—that texts do attempt to place, or have been read as placing, the other nation into a position of inferiority" (50–51), Mills also believes that "the texts themselves are much more complex than that, particularly women's texts" (51). For Mills, Said fails to distinguish between the "dominant reading" ("self-evident" meaning) of texts and those "elements" within the texts that can be construed as complicating or subversive to the dominant (52). Because the colonial texts produced by women never achieved "official status," as did those written by men, women's writings remained "at the level of the personal" and thus do not fit the theoretical model that Said proposes, in which the reception and the production of the text assist in the construction of its Orientalized representations. The reception and the production of women's texts differ markedly from those Said has identified as emblematic of Orientalist discourse. Further, she agrees with Porter that by unifying Western discourse in the manner Said describes in *Orientalism,* the "irreducible otherness" of the Orient (which Porter identifies) "runs the risk of confirming Orientalist knowledge in its powerful position rather than challenging it, since it seems to suggest that Orientalism has always and will always exist" (52). If, however, Orientalism is not the unified discourse that Said asserts, then the "diverse elements" of a text may "contest and affirm the dominant discourse" (55).[3]

Said's reliance on literary texts becomes, therefore, the *bête noire* for some postcolonial theorists who wish to problematize these kinds of representations and their meanings by favoring social and political criticism that views literature as itself complicit with imperial order and that demands that cultural critics, literary or otherwise, tease out and make explicit their ideological loyalties. As a result, Benita Parry decries a postcolonial cosmopolitanism, to which Said subscribes, that "proclaims its multiple detachments and occupancy of a hybrid discursive space" (19). The antihumanist strain contained by this assertion suggests that for these critics, one cannot simultaneously occupy aesthetic and literary spaces, and sociocultural or sociopolitical spaces. For Parry, Said contradicts himself because he affirms a definite "political alignment" at the same time that he acknowledges moving from one identity to another, essentially confirming a "hybrid" identity that somehow subsumes and homogenizes the inevitable dislocations and ambivalences that, being both European and Palestinian, both colonizer and colonized, ought to entail. "Said's remarks" (on his identity), Parry continues, "signal the dilemma for intellectuals in a climate where the militancy of anti-essentialist critiques inhibits their conceding the power of imaginary organic collectivities constructed under conditions of subjugation and conserved in the process of liberation struggles" (20). In the end, Parry seems to say, one must not only choose, but choose rightly and utterly. There can be no critical middle ground or vacillating ideological compromises.

That humanism for Said is the "final resistance" to abject dehumanization and squalid injustices confirms Timothy Brennan's description of the virtues of *Orientalism* as a text: "My own view is that *Orientalism* mattered in part because of how much it preserved a culinary humanism. It allowed people uncomfortably aware of contemporary empire to talk about imperialism in an acceptably humanist language" ("The Illusion of a Future," 579). Whatever one's political loyalties, Said's powerful statement about the real-world effects of a "culinary" humanism stakes a claim for *Orientalism* with regard to the as yet unsettled critical zone between Orientalism and humanism, a relationship that for scholars and teachers alike is deeply rooted in engaging with literary representations and the liberating force that representation seemingly offers. For many writers, Said's book is not another fading milestone marker within the graveyard of critical theory; indeed, it retains, even after more than a quarter century, its intellectual freshness and textual acuity.

III. Orientalism and Literature, 1750–1850

Though effectively challenged by postcolonial theorists, many of Said's ideas in *Orientalism* have managed to migrate—sometimes wholesale, sometimes with varying degrees of modification and success—into a variety of literary studies; in fact, there has been an explosion of criticism on Orientalism in the past fifteen years, stretching, expanding, and contorting Said's original concept almost beyond recognition, but into new and fascinating shapes. Todd Kontje expounds on German Orientalism. Madeline Dobie and Michele Longino explore French Orientalism. Joseph Dennon identifies the literary and intellectual history of Irish Orientalism, and Julia A. Kushigian mines the unlikely field of Orientalism in the Hispanic literary tradition. Jane Schneider explores Orientalism in Italy while Kalpana Sahni roots out the problems of Russian Orientalism and the colonization of Central Asia. K. E. Fleming offers an insightful portrait of Ali Pasha and Orientalism in Greece. Richmond Barbour discusses Orientalism on the London stage in the late sixteenth and early seventeenth centuries (before there was Orientalism, at least as Said conceives it), while Zhaoming Qian and Cynthia Stamy aim at engaging Orientalism in the modern poetry of Ezra Pound, William Carlos Williams, and Marianne Moore. Inge E. Boer's recently edited collection of essays on Orientalism covers an enormous swath of European history, culture, and literature, with essays on Barthes's exploration of Japanese artifacts, Palestinian popular culture, Venetian representations of "Turks," modern Arab travel narratives, and postcolonial cinema. Richard King and M. Faruk Zein conduct discourse analysis of Orientalism and religion; Fred Dallmayr summarizes the interconnections between Western philosophy and Eastern thought in order to move beyond the literary limits of Orientalism, or, as one of his contributors suggests, to "exit" Orientalism. Most recently, Bill V. Mullen has opened the door to a new field of Orientalist inquiry—Afro-Orientalism—and, in Lasansky and McLaren's collection of essays on architecture and tourism, Jeffrey Cass has coined the term "postmodern orientalism" to discuss the steroidal Egyptomania at the Luxor Las Vegas and the role consumerism plays in the newest iterations in popular culture of Orientalism-for-profit.

Yet even for critics who question the essentialism of Said's version of Orientalism—particularly the essentialist contrasts between East and West, a common criticism of Said's work—the explanatory power of Orientalism nonetheless lies in interrogating representation and the "realities" they evoke. Lisa Lowe destabilizes Orientalism in an attempt to gauge the heterogeneity of Orientalist representations in Lady Mary Montagu, Montesquieu, and E. M. Forster, yet she outlines the "postcolonial orientalism" of Barthes and Kristeva (and in the journal *Tel quel*) by identifying their figural narratives as "representations [that] constituted China as a utopian antithesis to French society and culture" (140). Reina Lewis also desires to underscore the ambiguities of Orientalist representation in the works by women who "produce imperialist images" but who also comprehend "the interdependence of ideologies of race and gender in the colonial discourse of the period" (*Gendering*, 3). Thus, for Lewis, women writers and artists both challenge and affirm their culture's political beliefs and cultural assumptions through their Orientalist representations. And in Meyda Yegenoglu's feminist reading of Orientalism, she boldly contends that her book "is about the cultural representation of the West to *itself* by way of a detour through the other" (1; original emphasis). Indeed, Yegenoglu defends Said's theoretical position on Orientalism and, following Clifford, argues that "the theoretical status of representation in his work can best be described as fraught with dilemmas and ambivalences" (17). To be sure, Lowe, Lewis, and Yegenoglu may perceive theoretical shortcomings in Said's work, but they finally agree that the critical relevance (and not merely the historical importance) of Said's work lies in interrogating the multidisciplinary representations of the Oriental Other, and not in describing "extratextual referents" from which one might construct a politics of postcolonial interpretation.

In *Rethinking Orientalism: Women, Travel, and the Ottoman Harem*, Reina Lewis extends her interdisciplinary arguments further. Providing evidence from Ottoman sources, Lewis challenges Orientalist notions of female passivity, arguing instead for a more developed notion of female agency, which subscribes to "practices of resistance that are charged by differences of both ethnicity and gender" (3). Though demonstrating "the other side of the classic Orientalist paradigm" (3), Lewis does not intend a singular Orientalized status for these voices, nor does she wish to construct yet another "homogeneous or stable category" (4). Rather, she asserts that women's voices point to "hybrid reformulations of Western cultural forms that emerge from the specific social, cultural, and political historical situations from which these individuals speak" (4). Not only do these voices undermine conventional representations of Orientalized women, they also hint at various reading publics; that is to say, these women writers speak to one another, and not merely because their works are transformed into commodified artifacts, produced for the consumption of colonial readers. Though enclosed, the harem becomes a site of cultural production and resistance. Lewis contends that the restoration of these voices through Ottoman sources "contributes to the recasting of critical thinking about the institutional and symbolic significance of the harem—that most fertile space of the Orientalist imagination" (4).

Lewis's exemplary work is an important indicator of the huge increase in, and popularity of, interdisciplinary scholarship in Orientalism within the last fifteen years. In fact, the fastest growth has been in the area of the visual arts. As Linda Nochlin suggests at the conclusion of her provocative essay "The Imaginary Orient": "As a fresh visual territory to be investigated by scholars armed with historical and political awareness and analytical sophistication, Orientalism—or rather its deconstruction—offers a challenge to art historians, as do many other similarly obfuscated areas of our discipline" (57). Written in 1989, Nochlin's essay accurately forecasts the avalanche of important studies in Orientalism and the visual arts, including Mark Crinson's work on Orientalism and Victorian architecture; Jill Beaulieu and Mary Roberts's edited collection on Orientalism in painting, architecture, and photography; John M. MacKenzie's investigations into the theory and history of Orientalism in the arts; Christine Peltre's exquisitely crafted book on Orientalism and art; Holly Edwards and her collaborators' foray into American Orientalism in art, film, and popular culture; Frederick Bohrer's book on Orientalism and visual culture in nineteenth-century Europe; Anthony Lee's study of art and Orientalism in San Francisco's Chinatown; and Bernstein and Studlar's collection of essays on Orientalism and film.

Furthermore, this outpouring of interest in Orientalism and artistic representation has spawned other industries—Occidentalism, or the ways in which Asian literature and media represent the West, and Ornamentalism, or the ways in which the British Empire represents itself in terms of class, as a "transoceanic construct of substance and sentiment" (122). Ian Buruma and Avishai Margalit define Occidentalism as "the dehumanizing picture of the West painted by its enemies," and their intention is "to examine this cluster of prejudices and trace their historical roots" (5). James Carrier's collection of essays on Occidentalism explicitly issues from a reflection on Said's *Orientalism*, the title of which "encouraged an easy inversion" (viii). Though anthropological in its disciplinary content, Carrier's collection also raises an important theoretical issue on representation, namely, "the ways that Westerners represent the West to themselves" (ix). Judith Snodgrass's book on presenting Japanese Buddhism to the West defines Occidentalism as "Asian recourse to the West as a resource for various domestic strategies" (11). It is not an inversion of Orientalism, but rather a discourse strategy that restores agency to Asian nationalist imperatives over and against the designs of Western-educated Asian elites who wish to maintain the status quo. Like Orientalism, Occidentalism constructs a "stylized image" that conforms to stereotypes, in this case an idealized version of the West as soulless, mechanistic, heartless, and bullying. Operating from the perspective of class rather than race, Ornamentalism, as conceived by David Cannadine, binds British imperial society together by virtue of domestic metonymies, the images of home and family, as well as the "presumption" that representing the periphery of empire, far from being a recovery of the exotic and of otherness, as Said conceives it, is actually a reaffirmation of the homely and the familiar, "the comprehending and the reordering of the foreign in parallel, analogous, equivalent, resemblant terms" (xix).

Of the plethora of Orientalisms that shape current scholarship, however, none has thrived more than British Orientalism, especially that of the eighteenth and nineteenth centuries, and frequently within the comparatist contexts that shaped Said's worldview, the same contexts that impel and shape the narrative of *Orientalism*. Of striking note is his brief discussion of M. H. Abrams and *Natural Supernaturalism*, a classic of traditional comparative literature, in which Abrams depends inordinately on the works of the British Romantic poets, in particular Wordsworth and Coleridge. In his book, Abrams attempts to explain, in Said's words, how a "reconstituted theology" in the late eighteenth century transforms the nineteenth century's passionate relationship between man's love of (and desire to be renewed by) the God-in-Nature and the equally compulsive desire to control, manage, and contain that same God-in-Nature within poetic discourse (*Orientalism*, 114). Analogously, Said seems to suggest, the project of Orientalism also begins in the late eighteenth century and represents the West's simultaneous yearning for and love of Eastern exoticism at the same time that it conquers and subdues Eastern lands in order to control, manage, and contain them. Indeed, the West's desire to colonize Asia reflects, rather paradoxically, its equally compelling desire to be regenerated by it, which as Said says, "was a very influential Romantic idea" (335).

In 1989, Gary Kelly was one of the first to use the term "Romantic Orientalism" in his essay "Social Conflict, Nation and Empire: From Gothicism to Romantic Orientalism." In this piece, Kelly outlines the literary and historical connections between the Gothic and the Oriental, analyzing what are now important areas of discussion for Romantic Orientalism—Robert Southey's *Thalaba* (1801) and *The Curse of Kehama* (1810), Charlotte Dacre's *Zofloya; or, the Moor* (1807), and Morier's *The Adventures of Hajji Baba, of Ispahan* (1824). By 2002, Shyamal Bagchee lists Romantic Orientalism as "a distinct sub-discipline of Orientalism" but which is "emerging as a field in its own right" (1). As evidence of this assertion, Bagchee cites the conference on Romantic Orientalism at the University of Wales, Aberystwyth (http://www.aber.ac.uk/english/conferences/romorprog.html). Less concerned about the thorny elements of postcolonial theory and more attentive to the Oriental details of novels, opera, history, travel literature, religion, and poetry, this illustrious group of international scholars (some of whose work is included in this collection) legitimated the interrogation of Orientalisms (in particular, British Orientalism) and the manifold ways in which Orientalist representation may take shape. Indeed, a partial list of important scholars of Romantic Orientalism includes some of the most important names of Romantic scholarship as a whole—Tim Fulford, Saree Makdisi, Peter Kitson, Joseph Lew, Michael Franklin, Gary Kelley, Nigel Leask, Billie Melman, Alan Richardson, Timothy Morton, Caroline Franklin, Malcolm Kelsall, Debbie Lee, Anne Mellor, Eric Meyer, Mohammed Sharafuddin, and Diego Saglia.

An integral part of the future of Romantic Orientalism lies in the postcolonial critique of Orientalism. Specifically, this form of critical analysis resists the "unidirectionality of colonial power" (Bhabha's phrase, *The Location of Culture*, 103) exemplified in Codell and Macleod's recent book, *Orientalism Transposed: The Impact of the Colonies on British Culture*. In that book, they contend, "native informants intervened in the discourse of Orientalism, applying Orientalist stereotypes to subalterns or even to the British themselves, to serve their own fluctuating political ends" (14). As applicable to Romantic studies, one need look no further than Fulford, Lee, and Kitson's book *Literature, Science, and Exploration in the Romantic Era: Bodies of Knowledge*. Arguing that "the complexity and variety of representations of indigenous people cannot be accounted for by a binary model" (26), Fulford, Lee, and Kitson contest the "binary oppositions" that *Orientalism* launches and urge instead "a post-Saidian approach" (26). Following Homi Bhabha, Fulford, Lee, and Kitson suggest this approach acknowledges "a disturbing hybridity" that "haunts the colonial encounter" (26). This hybridity "prevent[s] it from ever ossifying into a settled binary and ensur[es] that the coloniser's assumption of centrality and superiority is continually under threat" (26). Rather than follow Foucault's lead in showing how these encounters lead to the development of disciplines and the creation of a bureaucratized state, which then "surveyed and controlled its subjects" (27), the authors "build" upon the critical model provided by Bruno Latour. Unlike Foucault, Latour proposes that these disciplines consist of "linked individuals and centres across national boundaries" (27). The flexibility provided by Latour's model allows the authors to demonstrate how colonial encounters "were cycled and recycled through different, but interconnected, information systems" (27). Their method has implications for future Romantic scholarship because this analysis of "information systems" reiterates and reinforces the notion that encounters between colonizers and colonized are not binary, static, or one-way. In a chapter titled "Indian Flowers and Romantic Orientalism," the authors use the discipline of botany as an example to illustrate that the outputs and effects of colonial encounters are multivalent. They explore the case of Sir Joseph Banks, who directed the East India Company, but who also influenced the "spread of botanical gardens into the subcontinent" (71). Though Banks's botany "was imperial and commercial" (71), his stimulation of Indian botany unintentionally affected the production of Romantic poetry. The "networks" that Banks initiated, the authors assert, "helped precipitate new kinds of Orientalist scholarship and the new forms of verse that have come to be called Romantic" (71).

The "Romantic idea" that Said identifies, however, not only has its origins in the eighteenth century, it apparently extends well into the Victorian period. Its proliferation prompts Erin O'Connor to dub the phenomenon "Victorientalism." Not coincidentally, Said analyzes the Orientalist representations in the Victorian period, with discussions of Darwin, Carlyle, Disraeli, and Conrad. Like Romantic Orientalism, examples of Victorian Orientalism abound. Edward Ziter engages Orientalism on the Victorian stage. Emily Haddad identifies Orientalist poetics in English and French poetry throughout the nineteenth century. Jeffrey Cass writes about Orientalism in Charlotte Brontë's *Jane Eyre* and Elizabeth Gaskell's *Cranford*. Javed Majeed analyzes the role of the utilitarian philosophy of James Mill and Jeremy Bentham in the construction of an Orientalized India. Bart Moore-Gilbert outlines Orientalism in the work of Rudyard Kipling. Norman J. Girardot's study of missionary work and the comparative science of religions has recently been published in the emerging field of Sinological Orientalism. Many other critics have contributed enormously to the field of colonialism and Orientalism in the Victorian era: Jenny Sharpe (*Allegories of Empire*), Ann McClintock (*Imperial Leather*), Simon Gikandi (*Maps of Englishness*), Moira Ferguson (*Colonialism and Gender Relations from Mary Wollstonecraft to Jamacia Kincaid*), Deirdre David (*Rule Britannia*),

Christopher Lane (*The Ruling Passion*), and Patrick Brantlinger (*Dark Vanishings*), to name a few.

Although Timothy Brennan wistfully writes, "The history of *Orientalism* is already slipping away" ("The Illusion of a Future," 558), *Orientalism* has not seen its own demise. Even Said vacillated in his own appraisal of his most famous work. For his "Afterword" in 1994, Said speaks of the book nostalgically, regarding it as an opening salvo in the ongoing struggle against imperialism. He recalls: "Looking back at it from the distance afforded by fifteen eventful years and availability of a massive new interpretive and scholarly enterprise to reduce the effects of imperialist shackles on thought and human relations, *Orientalism* at least had the merit of enlisting itself openly in the struggle, which continues of course in 'West' and 'East' together" (352). In 2003, however, for a new introduction to *Orientalism*, he appears to have retreated from his retreat, suggesting boldly that George W. Bush and his "Arab hawk" advisers conceive the post-9/11 struggle in Orientalist terms and invaded Iraq with Orientalist stereotypes still very active in the formation of American political repertory (xx). Said angrily states: "Without a well-organized sense that these people over there were not like 'us' and didn't appreciate 'our' values—the very core of traditional Orientalist dogma as I describe its creation and circulation in this book—there would have been no [Second Gulf] war" (xx).

However debatable this last statement may be to critics on both the Left and the Right, in Said's mind, *Orientalism* still supported a potent explanatory and interpretive model. Even with the flood of news from the Arab world, even with the glut of information available on the Internet about Islam and the history of its adherents, even with the president urging an inflamed American public to discriminate between terrorists who were Muslim extremists and average Muslims who were peaceful and law-abiding, for Said, Orientalist representations nonetheless continued to circulate and recirculate, instigating not only cultural misunderstanding, but causing war for a crucial commodity—oil. Alarmingly, disarmingly, Said's book still commands our attention, not merely because of its historical importance to the development of postcolonial studies or its appropriation across disciplines, but because it remains a richly provocative text that challenges our theoretical and ideological assumptions, our interpretive and professional practices, and our spoken and unspoken politics.

NOTES

1. In a recent issue of *Critical Inquiry* (2005), Homi Bhabha and W. J. T. Mitchell edit a special section of essays that engage the death of Edward Said by addressing the ongoing importance of his work. Appropriately titled "Edward Said: Continuing the Conversation," this special section moves beyond empty hagiographic testimony and instead reveals the conflicted emotions that his most loyal friends (and ardent critics) still feel about the nature and scope of Said's influence. They reminisce about many versions of Said—Said the man; Said the theorist; Said the letter correspondent and media interviewee; Said the teacher. As Mitchell suggests in the opening essay: "We have sought rather to trace the living filaments of Said's thought as they were woven into the presence of his voice in his writing and speaking, his public persona and his private self" (366). Perhaps the most interesting elegies to Said in *CI* come from Gayatri Spivak and Homi Bhabha.

2. Interestingly, the fault line for critics on either side of Said's complex relationship to humanism derives from Said's equally complex relationship with fellow comparatist Erich Auerbach. In his essay "Auerbach in Istanbul: Edward Said, Secular Criticism, and the Question of Minority Culture," Aamir Mufti takes issue with Aijaz Ahmad (as well as with other critics who write about Auerbach and Said), suggesting that Said's rendering of Auerbach reveals a collision of fragmentary voices; *Mimesis* is not, for Mufti, a unified account of European realism from antiquity to modernity. Rather, Auerbach's magnum opus embodies a web of voices, which, recalling Said's work in *The World, The Text, and the Critic*, are affiliative and marginal. Their very decenteredness becomes the necessary precondition for launching a critique against the social and political forces that cause exile and displacement in the first place. Consequently, Mufti argues that "Said's turn to Auerbach" is not indicative of a Said who embraces "traditional and affirmative notions of culture and authority" (239). Rather, this "turn" embodies the possibility of rupturing the very seamlessness that underlies Western "liberal culture" (239). This interpretive rupture occurs because Said's "secularism" does not oppose religion but nationalism. Secularism, as Said conceives it, "contains the charge that the organicism of national belonging, its mobilization of the filiative metaphors of kinship and regeneration, obscures its exclusionary nature. . . . Secular criticism seeks continually to make it perceptible that the experience of being at home can only be produced by rendering some other homeless" (239). Opposing an affiliative network of many voices with the filiative nation of one voice is not only at the heart of Mufti's criticism, it is central to his description of Said's career-long interest in Auerbach's philological methods.

3. In similar fashion, Carol A. Breckenridge and Peter van der Veer engage Said's views by suggesting that Said's use of discourse is "already highly problematic" because he "points to a singular, transhistorical orientalist discourse" that has "complicated extra-textual and nondiscursive implications and consequences" (5). Pathak, Sengupta, and Purkayastha concur in their analysis of Orientalism, contentiously labeling Said's concept a "prisonhouse" because the "white texts" written by colonial writers about indigenous inhabitants (e.g., Forester's *A Passage to India*, Conrad's *Lord Jim*, Greene's *The Quiet American*) create a self-perpetuating and privileged discourse in which the nationalist identity of the Oriental Other remains within the "interpretive grid" of the Orientalist (196). Not surprisingly, the authors do not endorse an aesthetic promulgated by these "white texts" because aestheticism merely contributes to the pleasures of the prison house. Rather, they intend "a political reading . . . that is multiply determined by interests of race, class, caste, religion and gender; never finished, always in process" (198).

CHAPTER 2

The Female Captivity Narrative

Blood, Water, and Orientalism

DIANE LONG HOEVELER

It is in the Orient that we must search for the highest Romanticism.
—Friedrich Schlegel

I. History

The story of how Europeans institutionalized, commodified, and controlled their anxious projections about Muslim "Others" is a long, complex, and ultimately tragic saga that the term "Orientalism" only partially conveys. Historians as well as literary, religious, political, and cultural critics have attempted for close to four hundred years to come to terms with the meaning of Islam and more broadly with the challenges that the Eastern world presents to the West. More importantly for the purposes of this essay, it is necessary to recognize that the binary model (Self/Other) adopted by Edward Said to define Orientalism has been challenged and modified by recent feminist literary critics as both gender and class-blind. Famously, Said has defined his understanding of the cultural practice of Orientalism as a "Western style for dominating, restructuring, and having authority over the Orient" (3), while he has asserted that Orientalism is a discourse system that cannot be understood apart from recognizing it as "the enormously systematic discipline by which European culture was able to manage—and even produce—the Orient politically, sociologically, militarily, ideologically, scientifically, and imaginatively during the post-Enlightenment period" (3). For Said, there has never been an innocent use of the *topos* of the European in contact with Indians, Arabs, Turks, or Moors, for such a representation automatically places the spectator/reader in a binary system of difference and Otherness intended to "safeguard the legitimate interests" (100) of the West and contain, denigrate, or demonize the Oriental or, for my purposes in this essay, the Muslim. But Said certainly has had his critics and a number

46

of them have taken him to task for his blindness in regard to issues of gender, class, and methodology. For more recent critics like Lisa Lowe or Sara Suleri, Orientalism is not simply a rigid discourse system that remains static over long periods of time and space, or that privileges Self over Other, but instead Orientalism is a complex, multivalent, indeterminate, and heterogeneous narrative that needs to be situated in specific historical moments and national traditions in order to be understood.[1]

There is no question that Orientalism as a discourse system—whether viewed as binary or multivalent—is so vast and complex as to be intellectually unwieldy. But by narrowing one's focus to British (and to some extent French) Orientalism from approximately 1750 to 1800 one can examine at least one nexus of texts. This essay will address some of the texts written during this period by women or about women as captives of Muslims, and doing so, I think, will reveal a strong element of Christian anxiety and superiority as well as clear if not virulent anti-Islamic sentiments. Obviously an essay of this length cannot address all aspects of the non-Western world, nor do I have the space to consider Hinduism or the impact of Hinduism on Europe post–William Jones.

As Daniel J. Vitkus has recently noted, the early modern period (from the late sixteenth century through the seventeenth century) was characterized by a "violent contradiction: the old forces of ethnocentric, sectarian and nationalist feeling produced a repulsion for the alien, while at the same time the attractive forces of colonial land, valuable commodities and the general appeal of the exotic drew English culture out to mix with other cultures beyond their shores." For Vitkus, English culture during this period "produced representations of exotic, cross-cultural encounters and conversions that sought desperately to define English identity in an increasingly unstable context. For the early modern English, one of the most anxious and conflicted cross-cultural exchanges was the encounter with Islamic culture, in both the Ottoman dominions and in the Barbary States of North Africa" (1999, 23). Viewed as a false system of belief founded by a false prophet, Islam was demonized as the dark and yet seductive and attractive "Other" to Christianity, reflected in a variety of literary texts as if in a distorting funhouse mirror. If Christianity was the true religion of the blood, then Islam was presented as a cult built on water: ephemeral, fleeting, and ultimately deceptive.

This essay will take up what I will call the story of blood and water in 1479, when the coregents Ferdinand and Isabella, in their intense desire to unify the warring factions and contentious states of Spain, attempted to impose religious conformity throughout their territories. In short, they revived the Spanish Inquisition in Seville, a city that the Orientalizing Byron would celebrate in 1818 as the birthplace of Don Juan, his last poetic alter ego. The first targets of the Spanish Inquisition were Jews, and specifically the issue that concerned the Inquisition was the suspect sincerity of Jews as recently converted Christians (called alternately *Marranos* or *Conversos*), whose only chance of remaining in Spain required a sudden change of heart about their hereditary religious and cultural allegiances. In 1481, Muslims living in Spain became the next target, and by 1492, when Granada, the last Moorish stronghold on the peninsula, fell to the Catholic monarchs, the Muslims found themselves outcasts in the country they had ruled since 711 CE. Like the Jews, Muslims initially had the option to convert to Christianity and become what was known as *Moriscos*, but again their original religious identity was believed to be inscribed in their blood, and as such, they, like the Jews, were viewed as possessing "tainted blood" (the word *marrano* originally meant "swine," but in the Arabic root the meaning is actually "prohibited thing" or "outsider," or one who refused to eat the prohibited thing, pork; Crow, 142–44). Although there was a widespread practice of intermarriage between "old" Christians and *Moriscos* or *Marranos*, the possession of *sangre pura* (or untainted blood) became the new standard by which class status and national loyalty were defined in Spain (Crow, 144). From this point on, "blood" becomes shorthand for not simply family heredity and lineage, but for nationality and full political and religious membership in the newly modern nation-state and, as such, it assumes privileged status in not just Spanish consciousness, but throughout Christian Europe as well.

All Jewish-*Marranos* (at least 150,000) were expelled from Spain in 1492, and the ax fell on Muslim-*Moriscos* in 1609, when they were herded onto ships, transported to Morocco, and unceremoniously dumped there (Crow, 224). This horrific scene actually was a reversed mirror image of the events of 1126, when the Muslims, then rulers of Spain, deported thousands of Christians to Morocco as slaves (Carr, 84). The Muslim presence in Spain had been strong for over seven hundred years, so strong in fact that the forces of the Islamic Umayyad dynasty pushed to within two hundred miles of Paris and were finally defeated in their bid to control France by Charles Martel in 732 at the Battle of Poitiers. In short, Spain—and by extension Europe—lived with a powerful Islamic presence within its midst until the sixteenth century. Sometimes referred to as the "Asiatic tidal wave," Islam was more technologically advanced than Rome and its mathematical and technological discoveries threatened to leave early modern Christian Europe a backwater (Said, 74). As Albert Hourani has noted, Westerners considered the Muslim East threatening because it embodied an alternative culture that was frighteningly close to home (10–11). The persistent presence of Oriental despots, corrupt prophets, religious fanatics, noble Arab nomads, and lascivious Oriental houris could be seen on the London stage throughout the Renaissance, as all of them were featured endlessly in a number of dramatic productions (cf. Chew; Barbour). But in addition to these flat and stereotypical characters there were also portrayals of the renegade, the convert, or the shepherd turned emperor, "all figures that embody cultural flexibility, mobility, and adaptability. In the early modern period, the cross-cultural exchanges that took place in the Mediterranean were particularly paradoxical in their fusion of oppositionality and mutuality, autonomy and dependency. . . . [V]arious binarisms (English-foreign, friend-enemy, black-white, Christian-infidel) are broken down and deconstructed as often as they are upheld" (Vitkus 2003, 22–23).

In 1571 the Ottoman Empire was finally dealt a serious blow by the Spanish navy at the Battle of Lepanto, a siege also famous for the presence of Cervantes as a foot soldier (Carr, 161). Although not yet exactly the "sick man of Europe," the Ottoman Empire never fully recovered from this defeat, at least as a power in the West, and from this point on it existed uneasily on the fringes of European borders as well as its consciousness. Certainly its continued presence as a threatening, hyperbolic construction in a variety of literary texts suggests the persistent historical power of this once-powerful and feared anti-Christian force. As Alain Grosrichard has observed, by the seventeenth century and well into the eighteenth century, Christian critics

> [v]ied to discredit it [Islam] as a religion and set it in opposition to the "true religion." But anathema and insult were replaced by arguments and explanatory accounts of a historical, geographical, climactic, sociological or political nature. If Mahomet was able to install this power wherein an entire people were enslaved to the letter of his Law, it was because he was able to turn skillfully to his own advantage a situation of division, and exploit the character and natural inclinations of those who heard him: a burning-hot climate, making them tend towards a laziness of mind and a lasciviousness of body, had ever prepared them to accept the doctrine of predestination, and to propel them fiercely towards a belief in a purely carnal paradise, to the point where they wished to die for their religion in order to reach it all the more quickly. (Grosrichard, 106)

Faced with a religion that would encourage political martyrdom for the sake of sexually possessing virgins in the afterlife, Christians viewed Muslims as irrational fanatics, as antithetical to membership in a system of rationalistic, secularized nation-states. Further, Grosrichard reveals how Montesquieu, Voltaire, and Rousseau presented Islam as not simply an authoritarian religion, but also as a politically despotic system. For the Western Enlightenment political theorist, it was necessary to construct an elaborately seductive and phantasmagoric Orient (the sultan's court, the seraglio, oriental rugs, perfumes, spices, etc.) to serve as an analogy to the corruption that could also be found in Western despotic monarchies (specifically the courts of Louis XIV and Louis XVI). But by doing so, they created in their writings a new Enlightenment ideal, a constitutional government that could be set against and above both the Western absolutist monarchies and Eastern corrupt feudal states.

There is a certain amount of persistent bad faith, however, in both the British and French attempts to position themselves as crusaders against the dark and basely primitive forces of Islam. Both countries had long been practitioners of slavery themselves, while Napoleon had restored slavery and the slave trade in the French colonies in 1802 and the British did not abolish the slave trade until January 1, 1808. My contention is that in many ways Orientalist texts written in the late eighteenth century were specifically written to function as distracting mechanisms. By demonizing Islam and highlighting its sinister crimes and by employing the rhetorics of suppression and displacement, these texts became an effective means of allowing their readers the luxury of avoiding an honest and critical examination of their own society's flaws. In other words, female captivity narratives or narratives about white women living as captives in Islamic harems constituted a way of refusing to address forms of racial, social, and sexual discriminations that were actually endemic within the body of Europe itself.

Not all Orientalist texts, of course, avoided the ugly and unpleasant subject of slavery. Hannah Cowley's *A Day in Turkey; or Russian Slaves: A Comedy* (1791) ostensibly explores the complicated political maneuvering conducted by Russia, France, Turkey, and Britain during the earlier part of 1791 when Russia seized the Crimea and the Ottoman Empire sunk further into its status as "the sick man of Europe." Using conventional Orientalist tropes borrowed from Isaac Bickerstaff's *The Sultan* (performed 1775; published 1787), Cowley's play differs from that earlier work by addressing the subject of slavery straightforwardly. At one point in the play one of the Turkish characters notes that Christians themselves own slaves "in one of the northern islands" and that such a fact proves "by act of parliament that freedom is no blessing at all" (10; quoted in Cirakman, 163). Another Turk sarcastically observes that Christians have proven that slavery has a sexual as well as an economic motivation and that it suits only those with dark complexions, not whites: "Pretty creatures as this [a Circassian, a white Russian slave] they'd think it a blessing to give every freedom and take every freedom" (10; quoted in Cirakman, 163). Although the play uses some of the same devices that Lady Mary Wortley Montagu had employed earlier in her *Letters*, pointing out the analogies between East and West, *A Day in Turkey* goes further in confronting London audiences with their own political, social, racial, and sexual hypocrisies. As such, it caused a critical furor and never gained a royal audience (O'Quinn, 19).

II. Vignettes

Villain, I fear you not, I'll sacrifice you to preserve my Vertue; die Infidel, and tell your blasphemous Prophet, when you come to Hell, a Christian spilt your Blood.

—Penelope Aubin, *The Noble Slaves* (1722)

In the autumn of 1678 the French playwright Jean-François Regnard (1655–1709) was enjoying a pleasant sea voyage aboard a British Royal Navy frigate sailing along the Italian coast. Regnard thought he was making his way to Marseilles from Rome, but off the coast of Corsica, his ship was attacked by Saracen pirates, and Regnard and a French noblewoman on board the ship, Madame de Prade, were taken to Algeria and sold as slaves to the sultan, Achmet-Talem. In addition to being the successful author of *Le Légataire universel* (*The Sole Heir*), Regnard luckily possessed culinary skills, and he was immediately employed in the sultan's kitchen; in addition, he had a resourceful family that within ten months was able to raise the twelve-thousand-pound ransom necessary for his release and return to France. The fate of Madame de Prade, however, was not so fortunate. Consigned to the sultan's harem and never heard from again, her figure haunted the margins of French and British culture, so potent that more than one hundred years later the British hypochondriac Tobias Smollett refused to travel by sea to Nice, preferring to take a donkey overland instead (Ted Jones, xii–xiii, 212).

The horrific example of women like Madame de Prade could not have survived in British cultural consciousness, however, without the literary assistance of Penelope Aubin (1679–1731), one of the most potent exponents of the plight of the besieged and sexually ravished noblewoman. Aubin was the author of *The Noble Slaves: Being an Entertaining History of the Surprising Adventures, and Remarkable Deliverances, from Algerine Slavery, of Several Spanish Noblemen and Ladies of Quality* (1722; six printings), so popular that it was reprinted in both England and America over the next two hundred years. Almost as successful and sensational were her *The Strange Adventures of the Count de Vinevil and His Family; Being an account of what happened to them whilst they resided at Constantinople* (1721; three printings), as well as *The Life and Amorous Adventures of Lucinda* (1722) and *The Life of Charlotta*

Du Pont (1723), all of which employed a few choice scenarios of disaster on the high seas: kidnappings, as well as extended stints in Algerian harems or slave markets as part and parcel of these women in jeopardy narratives (cf. Baer). As Snader notes, Aubin "focuses on continental captives, especially passive noblemen, proselytizing priests, and women, character types that are essentially absent from factual accounts of Barbary captivity" (2000, 149). In doing so, she created a new genre of female-authored captivity narratives that sought to present female mastery over Oriental culture by heroines who adapt their clothing, alter their skin color, and skillfully outwit and outmaneuver their Muslim captors.

But Aubin's novels are not simply innocent escapist fare. Like the Barbary captivity narratives that had been published in England since the 1580s, Aubin's later novels attempted to represent Islam as a threat to British shipping and trading interests in the Mediterranean, and they developed a highly insular, self-assertive, self-controlled, and individualistic heroine who was complicit with the British colonialist agenda (Snader 2000, 149). According to Snader, Aubin's *The Noble Slaves* was the first female-authored work to advance the nationalistic and individualistic ideologies of the British as opposed to an Orient that was a zone of "polymorphous, uncontrollable, and predacious sexuality" (2000, 150). In her preface to the novel Aubin makes this explicit when she observes:

> In our nation, where the Subjects are born free, where Liberty and Property is so preserv'd to us by laws, that no Prince can enslave us, the Notion of Slavery is a perfect Stranger. We cannot think without Horror, of the Miseries that attend those, who, in countries where the Monarchs are absolute, and standing armies awe the People, are made slaves to others. The Turks and Moors have been ever famous for these Cruelties. . . . There the Monarch gives a loose to his Passions, and thinks it no Crime to keep as many Women for his Use, as his lustful Appetite excites him to like. (x; quoted in Snader 2000, 150)

Eliza Haywood quickly followed Aubin into the field, producing a series of novels that presented still more variations on the captivity plot, and sometimes showed Oriental captors to be more humane than Europeans. In such works as *Idalia* (1723), *The Fruitless Enquiry* (1727), and *Philidore and Placentia* (1727), Haywood highlights the skills of an aggressive female heroine who finds herself sometimes at the mercy of Oriental despots or who sometimes welcomes their kindness after brushes with European brutes. The variety in her works, however, belies a consistent theme: "[T]he European woman in the seraglio appears not as a suffering protagonist, not

Figure 7. French postcard of Algerian woman.
Reproduced with kind permission of the University
of Minnesota Press.

as a determined captive fighting for her chastity and national integrity, but
as a figure of illicit carnality and despotism, corrupted and empowered by a
dangerous sexual system" (Snader 2000, 160).

Other critics, notably Michelle Burnham and G. A. Starr, have tried to
trace the origins of captivity narratives to either the rise of the sentimental
genre, the secularized spiritual autobiographical tradition, or to the capitalist, progressive ideologies emerging at this time. Given the wealth of cultural,
religious, social, and economic influences that were converging, I would
argue that the female captivity narrative (fact or fiction) participated in a
larger ideological and cultural project: making the world safe for British
Christians who happened to find themselves traveling to foreign ports, that
is, engaged in imperialistic enterprises that were by definition risky business.
In short, British women writers—so pointedly ignored by Said—were com-
plicitous in advancing what I would label a female imperialist *gaze* toward
the Oriental sphere. This female *gaze* is complicated, however, in its assumption of two contradictory positions. On one hand, it is imperialistic, not simply in its support for British naval outposts throughout the Mediterranean,

but also in its sarcastic and derogatory contempt for the social, religious, and political organization of the Muslim world. More specifically, British middle-class women writers like Aubin, Haywood, Mary Wollstonecraft, and Elizabeth Marsh were particularly critical of Islam's perceived denigration of women. On the other hand, the Western female *gaze* is exotic, erotic, and deeply masochistic in its presentation of women's bodies as dehumanized, fetishized, part-objects designed to appeal to an aggressive Islamic male *gaze*. Perhaps no better visual depiction captures this second, abjected position better than figure 7, a late-nineteenth-century picture postcard produced in Algeria and intended for French male tourists.[2]

There certainly can be no doubt that Europeans experienced a very real fear of the Muslim world, but fear is less than half the story. In addition, there was throughout Europe an intense vogue for all things with an Orientalist flavor and this can be seen by considering yet another telling historical vignette. In 1781, Emperor Joseph II began to prepare for a state visit from Grand Duke Paul Petrovich of Russia, with whom he was to negotiate a secret agreement that would enable Russia and Austria to claim parts of the Ottoman Empire for themselves. In order to entertain the visiting Russian, Joseph requested that Mozart write an opera with a Turkish theme, and the result was Mozart's *Die Entführung aus dem Serail* (*The Abduction from the Seraglio*). Adapting Christoph Friedrich Bretzner's earlier story *Belmont und Constanze,* Mozart and his librettist Gottlieb Stephanie the Younger created a light-hearted romp through a harem, complete with an endangered and kidnapped heroine, Konstanze, sexually threatened by the pasha and rescued by her lover, Belmonte, only to become captive once again when she falls into the clutches of the evil and scheming overseer of the harem, Osmin. As Nicholas Till has observed, the opera was commissioned with the express intention of inflaming the Russian diplomat, and "would serve the emperor's propagandist campaign against the Turks." The locus of the most intense popular interest in the opera was precisely in its campy presentation of the Turkish harem, fascinating and terrifying in its configuration as a highly charged, polygamist site of the polymorphously perverse. Mozart's opera was tremendously popular upon its premiere, and its tropes of capture and escape were, of course, repeated in such gothic rescue operas as Cherubini's *Lodoiska*, Beethoven's *Fidelio*, Rossini's *Italian in Algiers*, and Weber's *Oberon*.[3]

If Orientalist opera was one potent site of ideological struggle between the European and the Muslim worlds, literature was another, earlier venue for the spread of Orientalist sexual stereotypes. For instance, Frances Sheridan's *History of Nourjahad* (1767) is one of many examples of the literary Orientalist fantasy so popular in England throughout the eighteenth and nineteenth centuries. Nourjahad, Prince Schemzeddin's favorite courtier, finds himself under what he thinks is the enchantment of immortality. He cannot die, but only periodically sleep and awake after many years, suddenly finding his young harem women have become old crones while he himself is perpetually young and hence continually forced to be on the market for new flesh. This particular Orientalist fantasy indulges in gross Eastern stereotypes and some very heavy-handed Western morality, but finally it is less about the Orient than it is about a Western woman's fear of aging and finding herself replaced by the next season's new and improved model of female flesh. In short, by the time Sheridan was writing, the Oriental tale had become so conventional that it essentially functioned as a blank screen onto which British authors could project their own particular political, social, religious, or sexual anxieties. Like Beckford's *Vathek* or Byron's *Giaour*, the Oriental tale constructed an abjected territory, an alien Eden that was fallen, sinful, and perverse.[4]

The situation was not much different in France, as witnessed by the fact that Voltaire's most popular drama, *The Tragedy of Zara* (1733), is an Orientalist saga concerned with a family of kidnapped Christian slaves living uneasily in a Turkish compound. The protagonists, Zara and her brother Nerestan, were captured as children and forced to convert to Islam, although Zara continued to wear an ornamental cross around her neck as a talismanic reminder of her true identity. Nerestan was never willing to forfeit his Christian identity, however, and as a young man requested permission to return to France in order to raise the funds necessary to ransom ten of the Christian slaves being held, including his sister and an elderly man he knew only as Lusignan, descended from the ancient kings of Jerusalem. In her brother's absence, Zara has fallen in love with Osman, the sultan's son, and agrees to marry him when he promises that Zara will be his only wife and empress. The plot takes both gothic and melodramatic turns, however, when Lusignan recognizes the cross around Zara's neck as the one worn by his long-lost daughter, while the scars on Nerestan allow the old man next to identify his son as well. With the family circle now complete, both father and son are appalled at the idea of Zara marrying a Muslim, and they insist that she be baptized (again?) in secret before her marriage takes place. Suspicious about her request to delay their nuptials, Osman follows Zara to her clandestine baptism, thinks she is meeting another lover, and stabs her, declaring: "This to thy heart—'Tis not the traitor, meet thee, / 'Tis the betray'd—who write it, in thy blood" (V.i.60). Blood is foregrounded again shortly later when Osman needs to see and touch Zara's blood in order to believe that she is truly dead. At Nerestan's reappearance, he also focuses on the primacy of his blood in understanding the monstrosity of his sister's murder by the Muslim: "She was my sister—All, that, now, is left thee, / Dispatch—From my distracted heart, drain, next, / The remnant of the royal, christian, blood" (V.i.61). Lusignan dies immediately from grief upon hearing the news of his daughter's murder and, unable to forgive himself, Osman commits suicide, declaring: "Tell 'em—with this, I murder'd her, her, I lov'd; / The noblest, and most virtuous, among women! / The soul of innocence, and pride of truth!/ Tell 'em I laid my empire at her feet; / Tell 'em, I plung'd my dagger in her blood; / Tell 'em, I so ador'd—and, thus, reveng'd her" (V.i.62). Loosely translated into English by Aaron Hill three years after its French premiere, *Zara* was performed well into the mid-nineteenth century throughout England.

Another one of Voltaire's Orientalist dramas, *Mahomet: ou le Fanatisme*, also bears scrutiny as a point of contrast to *Zara*. *Mahomet* was not as popular, and, indeed, it was censored not simply in 1742 but again in 1994 when a revival was attempted in Geneva. Many literary critics have claimed that Voltaire was not attacking Mohammed in this play, rather that his main targets, thinly disguised, were religious fanatics in general, and Christian fanatics in particular. When the play was first performed in Paris on August 9, 1742, Catholic Jansenists suspected that they were actually the intended objects of Voltaire's barbs, and they complained to the authorities who quietly pressured Voltaire to close the production. But there is also no denying the fact that Mahomet is presented in the play as a fraud, a lecherous adulterer, and a manipulator of people weak enough to be duped, and it was—significantly—Muslims who censored the 1994 performance, not Christians. As Voltaire observed about his creation of the antihero Mahomet:

> I have made *Mahomet* in this tragedy guilty of a crime which in reality he was not capable of committing. The count de *Boulainvilliers*, some time since, wrote the life of this prophet, whom he endeavored to represent as a great man, appointed by Providence to punish the Christian world, and change the face of at least one-half of the globe. Mr. Sale likewise . . . has given us an excellent translation of the Koran into English. . . . [But] for a driver of camels to stir up a faction in his village; to associate himself with a set of wretched Koreish . . . to boast that he was carried up to heaven, and there received part of that unintelligible book which contradicts common sense in every page; that in order to procure respect for this ridiculous performance he should carry fire and sword into his country, murder fathers and ravish their daughters—this is surely what no man will pretend to vindicate, unless he was born a Turk, and superstition had totally extinguished in him the light of nature. (*Mahomet*, 10)

For Voltaire, all manner of "superstition" is heinous, but clearly Islam is demonized for both its military ("murdering fathers") and its sexual practices (the "ravishing of daughters"), two emphases that recur throughout British fictions published in this period. Seeing the play as a successor to Montesquieu's *Lettres Persanes* (*Persian Letters*, 1721), Angela Pao recognizes that *Mahomet* "criticize[s] aspects of contemporary French society [and also] participat[es] in a pre-colonial Orientalist discourse that would eventually be used to support the French invasion and colonization of the Middle East and North Africa" (59). And certainly it is no surprise that British Orientalist works of the same period were used to shore up Britain's claims to Gibraltar, Mallorca, and Minorca, and eventually led to an empire that stretched around the globe.

III. Theories

> The Islamic claim to supercede a flawed and incomplete Christianity was an unthinkable phenomenon, and so it was denied in various ways, including a definition of Islam as a "pagan" misbelief akin to other forms of idolatrous paganism that Western Europeans associated with the Middle East.
> —Vitkus 1999, 208

Religion clearly stands as one of the central issues in much Orientalist literature, but I intend now to focus on the representations of women within this displaced religious discourse, women as objects of the Islamic male *gaze*, as well as Western women as gazers on the harem, the site of privileged male activity. Emily Apter has argued that the harem genre itself functioned as a "cultural supplement" for the West, a site of voyeuristic and scopophilic fulfillment of desires that were repressed in Europe ("Female Trouble," 219). For Reina Lewis, the harem genre "mirrors the ambivalence of colonial discourse itself—simultaneously shoring up and challenging a vision of absolute phallic power" (2002, 112), while Sarah Mills claims that women who produced Orientalist travel accounts were already influenced by the "always-mediated nature of representation," so that they could only depict women travelers as empathetic, personal, and emotional rather than objective, scientific, and rational (99). These various attempts to understand the complex representation of the harem are certainly provocative and useful, but none of them addresses the class or religious—the *sangre pura*—issues in the way that I think they need to be recognized.

I would claim instead that this fabulously constructed Eastern harem was also the literary site of a highly charged ideological struggle between

upper- and middle-class British writers, all of whom attempted to appropriate this contested sexual and religious terrain for their own purposes. For an
aristocratic writer like Lady Mary Wortley Montagu arriving in Turkey in
1717, women in Eastern harems were "free," powerful, and independent (see
Dubino's essay in this volume), while for a distinctly middle-class woman
writer like Elizabeth Marsh, author of the little-known *The Female Captive*,
women in the Eastern harem were either pawns or abused sex slaves. Writing
to her sister Lady Mar, Montagu waves the banner of religious tolerance by
proclaiming, "As to their Morality or good Conduct, I can say like Arlequin
'tis just as 'tis with you, and the Turkish Ladys don't commit one sin the less
for not being Christians." She went on in the same letter to observe:

> 'Tis very easy to see they have more Liberty than we have, no Woman of what
> rank so ever being permitted to go in the streets without 2 muslins, one that
> covers her face all but her Eyes and another that hides the whole dress of her
> head. . . . This perpetual Masquerade gives them entire Liberty of following
> their Inclinations without danger of Discovery. . . . Neither have they much
> to apprehend from the resentment of their Husbands, those Ladys that
> are rich having all their money in their own hands, which they take with
> 'em upon a divorce with an addition which he is oblig'd to give 'em. Upon
> the Whole, I look upon the Turkish Women as the only free people in the
> Empire. (*CL*, 327–29)

Montagu actually went further, claiming that the slave market was no
different from the marriage market in England: "In my opinion [women] are
bought and sold as publickly and more infamously in all our Christian great
Citys" (*CL*, 406). Ironically, the class privileges—not to mention the anti-
Catholicism and Latitudinarianism that buttressed Montagu's life—extended even to her view of women in Istanbul. As Dobie has recently noted,
Montagu is part of a "feminocentric" tradition that challenges received
beliefs about the Orient, including the (still widely held) view that "Islam is
uniformly oppressive to women" (127). In fact, there is a certain contrariness
in Montagu's *Letters,* as the epistolary descriptions of visits that Montagu
made to a variety of harems are eroticized and romanticized to a degree
that the modern reader (at least this reader) finds more than slightly suspicious. Characterized as a series of highly displaced sexual scenes and almost
perverse attempts to deny the oppression staring her in the face, Montagu's
Letters exemplify what Mary Louise Pratt has called the narrative of the
anticonquest in which imperial relations are depicted as a harmless and in
fact a benign process of reciprocity and mutual exchange (5–7). Montagu's
logic of anticonquest seems to be based on this unstated assumption: if I am

free to write as I please and to live a comfortable and safe life in the Turkish embassy as the wife of the ambassador to Turkey, then all women living in Eastern patriarchal societies must also enjoy the same freedoms I do.

Montagu's position, informed by her early-eighteenth-century aristocratic attitudes, seems to have truly offended later and decidedly middle-class writers like Robert Bage and Elizabeth Marsh. The literary commodification and codification of the white British female captive, sold into sexual slavery to live in a harem or seraglio presided over by a tyrannical and polygamous Muslim, became an effective tool in the hands of a variety of disparate writers with an even wider set of political, social, and religious agendas.[5] Both Bage and Marsh would appear to be composing what I would label Christian Orientalist texts in order to counter Montagu's smug assessment of the free and independent situation of women in Eastern harems (Montagu's *Turkish Embassy Letters* was published posthumously in 1763 and Marsh's novel in 1769). This move actually replicates Montagu's own earlier motivation, for she had written her *Turkish Letters* as a counter and opposing view to those put forward by Aaron Hill in his vehement denunciation of Islam in *The Present State of the Ottoman Empire* (1709).

IV. *The Female Captive*

> For the life of the flesh is in the blood; and I have given it to you upon the altar to make an atonement for your souls; for it is the blood that maketh an atonement for the soul.
> —Leviticus 17:11

Only recently have we been able to locate information about the life and travels of Elizabeth Marsh, author of *The Female Captive* (1769), the only Barbary captivity narrative written and published by a British woman in the eighteenth century (Colley 2003, 139). Prior to Linda Colley's research, all we knew about Marsh were the very scanty pieces of information recorded by Sir William Musgrave on the flyleaf of one of the three surviving copies of her two-volume novel (fig. 8 provides a sample of his handwriting). This copy of the novel, now in the British Museum, was once the property of Musgrave (1735–1800), a onetime neighbor of the Marsh family and compiler of the very useful *England, Scotland, Ireland: Musgrave's Obituaries Prior to 1800, with reference to the books where the persons are mentioned, and where some account of their character is to be found*. According to Musgrave, the novel is an accurate transcription of events that took place when Marsh actually was a captive off the coast of Barbary (North Africa) in 1756, where

Figure 8. Flyleaf from *The Female Captive*

she was living with her father, Milborn Marsh, a naval dockyard adminis-
trator stationed at the British outpost of Gibraltar. After 1748, Britain was
engaged with Spain in a series of skirmishes in which Spain attempted to
regain control of both Gibraltar and Minorca. Although Spain's Charles III
kept Gibraltar under siege for more than a year, the British managed to hold
onto Gibraltar; after the 1779–83 campaign, Spain regained Minorca from
the British (Carr, 175).

Musgrave's handwritten annotations throughout this copy of the novel
inform us that Marsh later married a Mr. James Crisp, a London merchant
who appears in the narrative as a "friend" who travels with and assists the
heroine. He also informs us that Mrs. Crisp eventually moved to India with
her husband where she died, leaving behind this novel as a record of her
earlier adventures (fig. 9). What is most interesting about the novel—apart
from Musgrave's compulsive need to fill in every dash in Marsh's text with
the missing name or place—is its very direct, first-person, eyewitness
appeal to its readers. Marsh insists continually throughout the text that her
story is true and based on events that she personally experienced, and not
"embellished by any Ornaments of Language, or Flights of Fancy" (3). Class-

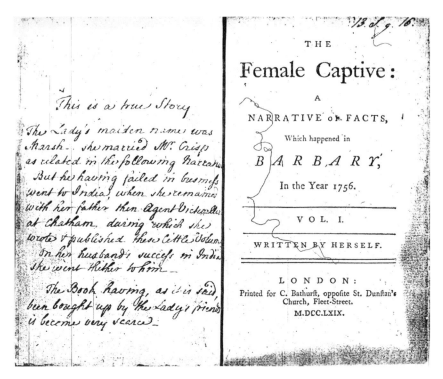

Figure 9. William Musgrave's annotations to *The Female Captive*

consciousness as well as self-consciousness about class is evident through-out the text, but Marsh also seems almost to be bragging that her narrative is the more reliable and truthful for her lack of poetic or linguistic skills. Forced to flee after the port of Minorca falls to the French in 1756, Marsh very quickly finds herself a captive of the Moors, by whom she is held for four months, and they are originally interested in using her as an object of barter with the British garrison stationed in Gibraltar. Once she returned to England, married Crisp, and had two children, Marsh found herself strapped for cash when her husband went bankrupt in the mid-1760s. She appears then to have decided to turn her hand to writing and she traded on the one extraordinary experience of her life: her brief captivity (Colley 2002, 43). Deciding that she had a credible eyewitness vantage point, Marsh writes first an early draft of her experiences (now in the Young Research Library, UCLA) in which she gives free rein to her double-barreled agenda. It becomes clear throughout the earlier as well as the later published text that Marsh is anti-Muslim for two reasons: because of the religion's beliefs as well as its treat-ment of women. But in the final analysis, these issues actually appear to be one and the same.

The presentation of Islam in Marsh's published female captivity narrative centers on one continual fixation: Islam is a religion that permits the legal practice of polygamy and hence it sanctions the buying and selling of women. As much as Montagu and later Wollstonecraft would make the same point about the corrupt marriage market in Europe, there was also a need on the part of bourgeois British writers to establish Christianity as the only force strong enough to counter the evils inherent in Islam. In addition to justifying polygamy, Islam also fostered the belief that women had no souls and hence did not deserve humane, let alone equal, treatment. For both positions, Islam was viewed as a dangerous form of cultural regression; a primitive, atavistic, and hypermasculine force that needed to be suppressed, if not destroyed, for social progress and the very survival of women and the bourgeois family to occur. I have to differ from Colley, however, who has argued that Marsh's published version of *The Female Captive* differs from the manuscript draft version in "omit[ting] virtually all references to religious conflict between Christianity and Islam" (2002, 127). Colley, who has studied the earlier version of the text, notes, for instance, that Marsh actually quoted in her draft version from John Hughes's popular drama *The Siege of Damascus* (1715) the following lines:

> Now in the name of Heav'n, what faith is this
> That stalks gigantick forth thus arm'd with terrors
> As if it meant to ruin, not to save?
> That leads embattel'd legions to the Field,
> And marks its progress out with blood and slaughter. (Quoted in Colley 2002, 127)

Marsh may not have included this passage in the final published version of *The Female Captive*, but she certainly retained in the central trajectory of her narrative the emphasis on Islam's tendency to "blood and slaughter." In fact, I would argue that religious conflict is central to *The Female Captive*, and that blood is at the very forefront of the dispute.

After one full volume of camel rides and abortive boat trips, Marsh finds herself in the Moorish prince's seraglio. At this particular and very crucial juncture, she is befriended by a Frenchman who is inexplicably living in the harem, and his interference is just the beginning of her very serious problems. This Frenchman (and anti-French, anti-Semitic, and antiblack statements suffuse the text) encourages Marsh to try to repeat some of the words that are being spoken in the harem by the women. Without intending anything more than simply trying to mimic the accents of the harem women, the heroine-author suddenly discovers that she has just verbally declared her belief that

Islam is the only religion and Allah is the only god (2:27). This statement is known as the Shahadah, or the Tawhid, a declaration of faith in the oneness of Allah and all that is necessary to make one a Muslim. From this point on, Marsh's ability to leave Morocco is compromised because witnesses declare that she has renounced her Christian faith and become a Muslim. Very shortly she is informed that she must immediately attend Sidi Muhammad, the Moorish prince, and with only an interpreter in his private quarters.

This is, of course, the moment we have been expecting since the title page. The well-rehearsed signs of the Orient, the heavy use of ideological codes of representation in this passage, suggest that even by the mid-eighteenth century the Oriental harem had become a cliché. Descriptions of Persian carpets and mosaic columns come thick and fast as Marsh makes her way to Muhammad's den and he makes his offer: "[H]is Imperial Highness wished to know if I would become a *Moor*, and remain in his Palace; desiring me to be convinced of his Esteem, hoping that I would properly consider the Advantages resulting from doing as he desired, and promising me every Indulgence that he could possibly favour me with" (2:36–37). What is most interesting about this scene is that it is less a sexual threat than it is a religious temptation; in fact, this scenario is strongly reminiscent of Satan's temptation of Jesus after Jesus' forty days in the wilderness. After refusing the prince's offer to convert, Marsh informs us that he "was disgusted with my Answer, from his remaining silent for some Minutes, throwing off the Mask he had hitherto worn, he cruelly informed me, that I had that very Morning, renounced the *Christian* Faith, and turned *Mahoteman;* and that a capital Punishment, namely, *Burning*, was, by their Laws, inflicted on all who recanted from, or disclaimed *their* Religion" (2:38–39; original emphasis).

Forced to flee for her life and after many scenes of flight and rescue, and mob cries for her capture, as well as escaping in the nick of time, the heroine finally finds her way back to Mr. Crisp and the British contingent. Only after she becomes so ill that she is bled by a British doctor does the prince relent: "Bleeding in that Country, being looked on as very extraordinary, and never practiced but in Cases of Extremity" (2:46). Shortly thereafter a dark-skinned man, an intermediary named Muly Dris, appears to reassure Marsh that all is going well in the negotiations to rid herself of the prince. Marsh describes Muly Dris somewhat curiously as "a Prince of the Blood" (2:51). The fact that he speaks Spanish in all of his exchanges with Marsh and her friends suggests that he is, in fact, a *Marisco*, an Islamic Spaniard (a Moor) living in Morocco and attempting to mediate between Christians and Muslims in the country. The term "Prince of the Blood," however, also suggests that Muslims define themselves by their heritage, their blood, their religion as thoroughly as do Christians. But in fact, it is the shedding of Marsh's blood that liberates her from Muslim clutches. The prince is finally willing to forego his dangerous sexual and religious designs on her and accepts in lieu of either the knowledge that her blood has been shed.

Islam, like other desert and tribal religions, privileges water, but in a manner that is distinctly different from Christianity. Water fountains are at the center of Islamic buildings, towns, and the Moorish baths that were notorious throughout Christianized Spain as identificatory tags associated with Muslim-*Moriscos*. Water is not sacred to Muslims, however, the way it is to Christians. Whereas Christians use water to ritually purify and baptize, Muslims have placed their baths in public areas, desacralizing them, and using water in strictly secular ways. But blood sacrifice continues to be practiced by Muslims even today, although only in relation to ritual animal sacrifice, an annual ceremony called the sacrifice of the sheep, one of the four great Muslim rites. Witnessed by Edith Wharton when she visited Rabat, the blood-sacrifice is not based on Koranic injunctions, but on the "Souna" or record of the Prophet's "customs." As Wharton notes, "the Moslem blood-sacrifice comes, by way of the Semitic ritual, from far beyond and behind it; and the belief that the Sultan's prosperity for the coming year depends on the animal's protracted agony seems to relate the ceremony to the dark magic so deeply rooted in the mysterious tribes peopling North Africa long ages before the first Phoenician prows had rounded its coast" (190).

Although this is not the venue to discuss the anthropological and sociological similarities and differences between Islam and Christianity (and by extension Judaism and Hinduism), it is important to note that Muslims still perform a ritual animal sacrifice on the day of the Great Feast, *Id al-Kabir*, to commemorate Abraham's sacrifice of the ram instead of his son (Benthall, 260). In fact, Islam and Hinduism are the only major religions to continue to practice ritual animal sacrifice and to shed literal blood in their ceremonies. The crucifixion of Jesus, demanded by His father, can be understood as a regression to that earlier form of ritualized human sacrifice, and since that time the sacrament of communion within the Christian community has been designated as a symbolic, metaphoric reenactment of the earlier ritualistic blood sacrifice of a human being.[6] Although all four majors religions (Hinduism, Judaism, Christianity, and Islam) privilege blood and water in contradictory fashions, as alternately both unclean and as sources of purification (see Leviticus 15:19; 17:11), I would suggest that there are certain perceived differences between the religions that became pronounced in the Orientalist texts of the eighteenth century. Christianity became for the Western mind a religion that privileges blood in its metaphorical and purely human (rational, symbolic, and decidedly not animal) associations, and it represented that blood primarily through familial descent, patrilineal claims, and more complex kingship systems. *Sangre pura,* a concept actually based in the earliest kinship-based societies, was revived in this period and became implicated in modern nation-building, in the attempt to produce pure racial stock that was understood as untainted Christian descent (i.e., as we have seen in the example of Spain). What appears finally to be at issue in the Western bourgeois female captivity narrative is the threatened circulation of female blood and control of bloodlines. Ergo, the valorization of monogamy within Christianity.

Billie Melman has argued in her work on nineteenth-century British women's writings on the Orient that collectively these works actually desexualized the harem, domesticating it in order to create the *haremlik* (the segregated quarters of women and children) as an "image of the middle-class 'home': domestic, feminine and autonomous" (1992, 101). According to Melman, women writers edited out evidence of the oppression of Muslim women in order to preserve the "domesticated" image of the harem as a locus for Western women to condemn (1992, 308–9). But such would not appear to be the case with Marsh's narrative. She obsessively focuses on the subjugated female bodies within the harem and the imminent sexual threat posed to a young British virgin by the demands of an irrational Muslim. Such a focus actually works to stabilize the position of the Western woman as a victim of the Orient's rapacious and perverse demands. The fact that Marsh escapes only because her blood is shed suggests that in Muslim eyes she has assumed the position of a sacrificial animal (the sheep), and therefore is an unclean object for an Islamic male. As Snader has argued, all of the Barbary captivity narratives were always imperialistic, Orientalist, and "enforcing [of] an expansionist ideology" (1997, 268), and certainly Marsh's text is no exception. The female imperialist *gaze* at work here, however, is a distinctly and muscularly Christian one, not a purely masochistic female gaze (Mulvey, 12–13). Although Marsh comes dangerously close to enslavement in the harem, she escapes through the timely intercession of good British soldiers and her own spilled blood, which paradoxically establishes her in the status of a victim and thereby seems to soil her in the eyes of the prince.

V. *The Fair Syrian*

Sacrificially constituted descent, incorporating women's mortal children into an "eternal" (enduring through generations) kin group, in which membership is recognized by sacrificial ritual, not merely by birth, enables a patrilineal descent group to transcend mortality by the same process in which it transcends birth. In this sense, sacrifice is doubly a remedy for having been born of woman.

—Nancy Jay (297)

Robert Bage's *The Fair Syrian* (1787) is another one of many little-remembered Orientalist titles published in Britain around the middle of the eighteenth century. Ironically, Eliza Haywood had composed a seraglio tragedy entitled *The Fair Captive* in 1721, with an epilogue written by Aaron Hill warning women that they will lose their power in England if their husbands ever learn of the Islamic model of polygamous marriage. The title of Bage's novel plays then on Haywood's earlier drama as well as Marsh's novel, recalling them both and situating itself within a century-long dialogue of Orientalist discourse. Bage himself (1720–1801) was originally a Quaker who eventually became a sympathizer with the French Revolution and a freethinker deeply influenced by the theories of Rousseau, Diderot, and Voltaire. But unlike his *Hermsprong, or Man as He Is Not* (1796), his *Fair Syrian* became so obscure that at one point it was easier to find French translations of the work in England than to find it in its original English version.

Like Marsh's *The Female Captive*, *The Fair Syrian* employs the rhetoric of the slow tease, the first volume building ponderously to the young British virgin's kidnapping and descent into the clutches of the Moroccan prince or, in Bage's case, the Syrian Saif Ebn Abu. Also like *The Female Captive*, the heroine of Bage's novel, appropriately named Honoria Warren, is rescued in the nick of time before she is subjected to the sexual and religious indignities that the text has been teasing us with for the first two hundred pages. It is necessary, however, to recognize that damsels in distress in Damascus are nonetheless still damsels in distress, and that a large portion of the general reading public in Britain would have recognized certain sentimental genre conventions operating in the bourgeois female captivity narrative. The differences, I think, occur when the issue of an alien religion is factored in, and these texts do make much of the peculiarities of the Muslim religion, particularly polygamy and the ability of Muslim men to buy and sell female sexual slaves because women are believed to be soulless. The disparate use of these themes, however, played into the agendas of both conservative and liberal writers of the day. It seems clear that Marsh's text is decidedly conservative and ideologically intent on enforcing British expansionism as a religious right and duty. The subscribers who paid to have Marsh's book published and whose names are listed at the front of the volume provide us with an interesting perspective on how keen the middle and professional classes were to keep Britain as a world power because that was where money and trade could be found. A liberal like Bage, however, had a different agenda. If Montagu pointed out the similarities between the aristocratic marriage market and the harem system, Bage was intent on attacking and reforming both the aristocratic and the bourgeois marriage markets.

In *The Fair Syrian*, Honoria is aggressively pursued by the aging and lecherous aristocrat, Lord Bembridge, at the very time she is living under the protection of his wife, Lady Bembridge, sister of the man who intends to marry Honoria, Lord John Amington. Lord Bembridge is later killed in a duel caused by one of his many infidelities; Lady Bembridge is pleased to be free of her British harem master; Honoria and Lord John marry and live in monogamous, mixed-class harmony with her long-lost father, who turns up in Constantinople and finally is able to return home to England. Bage's novel may be liberal on the question of marriage but it is decidedly conservative when it approaches the issue of religion. Like Marsh's novel, Bage's text also presents what I would identify as the conservative or religiously imperialist ideological appropriation of the Orientalist agenda. Bage's work repeats the charge that the existence and the spread of Islam stand as direct and dangerous threats to Christianity and what is seen as the civilizing process of Christian values and beliefs on all societies.

In *The Fair Syrian,* at one point the Saif visits Honoria's home and proposes to make the beautiful Christian his first and most important wife if she will "make outward profession of Islam." Mr. Warren explodes, "Assuming coxcomb! Change her religion, to be thy wife! . . . Wretch! leave my house—I will kill my daughter with my own hands, rather than she should have any connection with a base, unprincipled, abandoned man such as you." To which the Saif replies, "Yes, Christian dog, I will go to thy destruction" (2:47–48), and very quickly financial ruin, kidnapping, and slavery ensue for the Warren family. The notion that one's daughter would be better off dead than Muslim is a variation on the theme of the need for honor killings that occurs throughout these texts. The stakes are so high for both sides, not simply because virginity and the shedding of female blood are at risk, but because two warring religious worldviews have been put in competition with one another for imperial domination and control of both property (lands and goods) and women.

It is also important to note that Bage's novel employs rhetoric that is adapted virtually verbatim some ten years later by Mary Wollstonecraft in her *Vindication of the Rights of Woman* (1791) as well as in her *The Wrongs of Woman, or Maria* (1798). Bage's heroine, Honoria, is traded from Damascus to Basra and finally finds herself sold into a harem in Aleppo. Here she becomes the property of what she describes as a typical Turk: "To smoke tobacco with aromatics, to drink coffee, to chew opium, and repose upon a sofa were the regular occupations of the day. Add to these, luxurious suppers, wine, and women, and you have every thing a Turk thinks of value upon earth. I have been told, the love of wine increases with the use; the love of woman, not. Our master, at least, was no instance to the contrary. His sickly appetite called for a perpetual variety of women, whilst his passions were never sufficiently alive to make him give himself the trouble of selection. This was the business of the eunuchs" (2:86–87). In short, the Syrian harem in Bage's novel is consistently compared to the sorry state of Western bourgeois marriages as later depicted in the novels of Mary Robinson, Thomas Holcroft, Charlotte Smith, Wollstonecraft, and William Godwin. In fact, what has been termed Wollstonecraft's "feminist Orientalism" derives from this very practice of exploiting Eastern stereotypes in order to argue the feminist case in the West (Yeazell, 78).

The liberal appropriation of Bage's Orientalist agenda leads directly to Wollstonecraft's statements in *Vindication of the Rights of Woman* in which she alludes to "the husband who lords it in his little haram" (73) or to those women, "weak beings" whose educations have caused them to be "only fit for a seraglio!" (10). Mimicking Bage almost to the word, Wollstonecraft states that "the epicure must have his palate tickled, or he will sink into apathy; but have women so little ambition as to be satisfied with such a condition?" Wollstonecraft very interestingly reverses the critique, however, and goes on to compare bourgeois women to Oriental harem sex slaves, noting: "Can they supinely dream life away in the lap of pleasure, or the languour of weariness, rather than assert their claim to pursue reasonable pleasures and render themselves conspicuous by practicing the virtues which dignify mankind? Surely she has not an immortal soul who can loiter life away merely employed to adorn her person, that she may amuse the languid hours, and soften the care of a fellow-creature who is willing to be enlivened by her smiles and tricks, when the serious business of life is over" (29).

As numerous critics have noted, Wollstonecraft uses the term "Mahometanism" as a veiled charge against the British patriarchy itself, a system that she sees as denying women their equal status as political, intellectual, and spiritual beings.[7] For Wollstonecraft, Rousseau's writings are composed "in the true style of Mahometanism, [for women] are treated as a kind of subordinate being, and not as a part of the human species, when improvable reason is allowed to be the dignified distinction which raises men above the brute creation, and puts a natural scepter in a feeble hand." So if men hold illegitimate power it is because they have subjugated women, turning them into beasts of burden that have been effectively "Othered" out of their fully human and spiritual identities. And for Wollstonecraft, Christian men living in the great cities of high European culture are as guilty of this offense as are the Muslim harem-masters.

But finally there is a flaw in the Orientalist agenda of Wollstonecraft and other liberal supporters of the rights of women. If one opposes Islam because it is one of the representatives of the tyranny of religion, then isn't one also forced to see Christianity as yet another tyrannical religion? And if one does condemn Christianity, as surely Voltaire, Godwin, and Holcroft did, what does one place against Islam as a counterweight? Montagu would have endorsed Protestant hegemony and the efficacy of the 1699 Act of Toleration, which excluded Catholics from political positions. But by the time Wollstonecraft is writing, the situation is considerably more complicated. Unable to embrace one politically stable form of Christianity, the liberal Orientalists found themselves impotent, railing against a system for which they had no effective antidote.

The middle-class political and religious Orientalist agenda reached a dead end in the writings of Wollstonecraft, and from this point on the abjection of the Orientalized Western woman took on a distinctly different appearance. With the military containment of the Ottoman Empire, and no longer able to effectively condemn Muslims as an aggressive religious and political threat, women writers turned increasingly to a purely sexual focus on the East. Mary Shelley's portrait of the Turkish Safie in *Frankenstein* (1818) is a picture drawn straight out of her mother's Orientalist feminist agenda. Escaping a tyrannical and morally and financially corrupt father, Safie seeks rescue in the arms of the De Laceys, a substitute and idealized Christian family whose son Felix ("happiness") promises monogamy. In contrast, Charlotte Brontë's portrait of a fleshy and voluptuous Cleopatra in *Villette* (1854) bears strong witness to how thoroughly the Orientalized woman had become a figure of sexual nausea and dread for the female British imagination by mid-nineteenth century (cf. Zonana). And by the time that Edith Wharton visited harems in Fez (1919), the attitude had become one of barely concealed hostility and condescension. Taken into their innermost sanctuaries, Wharton views these women as "cellar-grown flowers, pale, heavy, fuller but frailer than the garden sort. . . . But what struck me was the apathy of the younger women." Later, after trying in vain to talk to them, Wharton notes, "[T]here are few points of contact between the open-air occidental mind and beings imprisoned in a conception of sexual and domestic life based on slave-service and incessant espionage" (204). So we return yet again to the leitmotif of slavery, and the easy and comfortable posture of condemning in Others what we have ourselves just recently practiced.

Clearly, by the early to mid-nineteenth century the works of the female Orientalists had become a heterogeneous, polyglot language, no longer fixed firmly in either religious condemnation or imperialistic fantasies of superiority and conquest. British middle-class authors were working out a number of class and religious anxieties within their own culture when they gazed on the "Other" that they had made of the Orient. As Lewis has noted, the accounts we have of Oriental harems and female captives can only be understood as a series of "heterogeneous and contradictory" texts: "They offered clashing commentaries based on differing amounts of access and expertise, and, though marketed on the 'truth factor' of their having actually been in a harem, must not be read as simply realistic, unmediated or unembellished. Their writings were historically contingent, so that whilst they all contributed to a shift towards a comparative social evaluation of the harem, the terms of their interest changed according to their own domestic concerns" (2004, 13). Clearly, the concerns of Marsh were different from those of Montagu, even though both had spent time in actual harems and both were in a position to claim that they were speaking from a position of "truth." I would like to conclude with a particularly apt observation made by Eric Meyer who has noted, "[W]hat we see when we look at the other, then, is our own disfigured image as it is revealed in the blind spots of our cultural field of vision, its incoherences, its contradictions, and its two-facedness in (mis)perceiving its veiled imperial desire" (693). An intricate dance of domination and demonization characterized the West's literary commodification and appropriation of the Muslim, as well as the Western woman. In short, one does not simply project onto the Other without at some point becoming the Other, and that is the point at which the binary breaks.

NOTES

1. In addition to the critiques of Dobie, Lowe, Melman, and Suleri, see, for instance, the cultural critique by MacKenzie and the religious and nationalist critiques by Vitkus, Cirakman, and Sardar. Porter claims that the "fundamental contradiction" at the heart of Said's study, that all representation is misrepresentation, is due to the inherently contradictory positions of the two dominant theorists that Said uses, Foucault and Gramsci (151).

2. See the final visual plate in Alloulah's collection (fig. 7) for an extended discussion of this provocative image. Alloulah observes: "To track through the colonial representations of Algerian women—the figures of a phantasm—is to attempt a double operation: first, to uncover the nature and meaning of the colonialist gaze; then, to subvert the stereotype that is so tenaciously attached to the bodies of women" (5).

3. Nicholas Till, quoted in www.mozartproject.org/compositions/k_383_.html (accessed March 1, 2004). According to Wilson, there were at least fourteen harem-abduction operas produced during the last half of the eighteenth century. Also see Hoeveler and Cordova for a more extensive discussion of gothic "rescue" operas as a genre.

4. Richardson's new Riverside edition contains the three specifically named titles. Barrell has argued that the erasure of Asian cultures within Orientalist texts created the very "blank screens" on which Westerners could project their own wishful fantasies (8).

5. Marsh's novel has recently (and rather inexplicably) been reprinted in an English paperback edition by an Islamic publishing house in Rabat, Morocco. All quotations from the novel will be from the original two-volume book. My sense of the complexity of Orientalist tropes builds on the work of Marilyn Butler, who identifies the British literary construction of Orientalism in the 1790s as "intellectually ambitious." Disagreeing with Said's argument that the West created the East as "effeminate" and "weak," and therefore easily controllable, Butler claims instead that the literature of the romantic period constructed a complicated discourse around the question of the East that was "powerfully imaginative" and constituted "an intellectually ambitious strain of Romanticism" (397–98).

6. The subject of blood ritual and sacrifice in religious worship is tremendously complicated and beyond the scope of this essay. According to Jay, cultic blood-shedding appears to have a gender-related organization and to be found most frequently in precapitalistic societies with some degree of technological development so that rights to durable ("real") property are highly valued and kinship is determined through patrilineal descent groups (289). For a useful summary of other theorists on the subject, see Gilders. For a discussion of the communion service as a "narcissistic sacrifice," see Beers.

7. Wollstonecraft was most likely familiar with the writings of M. Aikin, L.L.D., who identifies Mahomet as an "Imposter" in his *Memoirs of Religious Imposters, from the Seventh to the Nineteenth Century* (London: 1822), but originally published as essays by a variety of authors between the 1790s to 1814.

CHAPTER 3

"Better than the Reality"

The Egyptian Market in Nineteenth-Century British Travel Writing

EMILY A. HADDAD

The attention of the Egyptian authorities has been frequently drawn . . . to the evils resulting from the indiscriminate bestowal of "baḳshîsh" to the inhabitants of the Nile villages. . . . [W]e venture to express a hope that our fellow-countrymen, when travelling in Egypt, will lend their aid to . . . reform by abstaining from the distribution of money in response to mere demands for "baḳshîsh." . . . Tourists should especially abstain from throwing money from the decks of steamers on to the landing stages or on to the banks of the Nile for the purpose of witnessing the scramble for the coins; such exhibitions are mischievous as well as degrading.

—from "Baḳshîsh: Important Notice," ascribed to Evelyn Baring, Lord Cromer, British Agent and Consul General in Egypt from 1883 to 1907, and his German and American counterparts, and printed as a preface to the twelfth edition of *Thomas Cook's Handbook for Travelers in Egypt* (1912)

When William Thackeray announces his visit to the Pyramids in *Notes of a Journey from Cornhill to Grand Cairo* (1846), he does not at first mention them by name. His reader will know what he means when he says "those famous edifices" (90). The accompanying sketch, Thackeray's own, shows a dark-skinned boy seated on some rocks that could as easily be a cliff outcropping as the top of a pyramid. The description that follows depicts the boy and the landscape, but not the Pyramids themselves. Finally Thackeray pauses to impersonate the reader: "—And this is all you have to tell about the Pyramids? Oh! for shame! Not a compliment to their size and age? Not a big phrase,—not a rapture? Do you mean to say that you had no feeling of respect and awe? Try, man, and build up a monument of words as lofty as they are" (91–92). But Thackeray has already explained his narrative's evasion of the scene:

> It is poor work this landscape-painting in print. Shelley's two sonnets are the best views that I know of the Pyramids—better than the reality; for a man may lay down the book, and in quiet fancy conjure up a picture out of these magnificent words, which shan't be disturbed by any pettiness or mean realities,—such as the swarms of howling beggars, who jostle you about the actual place, and scream in your ears incessantly, and hang on your skirts, and bawl for money. (90)

Shelley did not go to Egypt, and neither of his Egyptian sonnets—"To the Nile" and of course "Ozymandias"—mentions the Pyramids. Thackeray might have had in mind the evocative descriptions in "Queen Mab" (2.126–40, 9.26–37) or "The Witch of Atlas" (496–504).[1] However, the importance of his explanation lies not in the precise reference, but rather in how it evinces the struggles of a midcentury British traveler to write about Egypt.

In nineteenth-century British discourse on Egypt, the Pyramids themselves are significant not only as a destination for sightseers, but also as what Judith Johnston calls "a site of desire," "the subject of an intense Victorian imperialist gaze" (71, 73). That Thackeray is willing to look at them only obliquely is, at bottom, a consequence of their having been so much gazed upon already. His attempts to record his impressions of the Pyramids, then, are both informed and restricted by what Edward Said calls Orientalism's "textual attitude," the idea "that people, places, and experiences can always be described by a book, so much so that the book (or text) acquires a greater authority, and use, even than the actuality it describes" (93). Concomitantly, Thackeray evinces a strong sense of "belatedness," as defined by Ali Behdad: the "anxiety of coming after what had come before" (13).[2] Caught between the attraction of earlier texts and the anxiety they engender, Thackeray appears to lay claim instead to realities other than those which his predecessors depict. These are the "mean realities" of the "actual place," with its swarming, bawling beggars. Any reader of nineteenth-century British writing about Egypt will recognize that the beggars are just as cliché as the Pyramids, yet Thackeray and most of his contemporaries express no anxiety about depicting them and no doubt about their reality.[3]

Several critics have given careful attention to the challenge that Thackeray and other midcentury Britons face in writing anew about an Egypt already so well recorded. Timothy Mitchell, in *Colonising Egypt* (1988), and Derek Gregory, in "Scripting Egypt: Orientalism and the Cultures of Travel" (1999), offer complementary Saidian analyses that provide a sound basis for my study here. Quoting Edward Lane, one of the nineteenth century's most important Orientalists, Mitchell explains that like visitors "to an exhibition, travellers wanted to immerse themselves in the Orient and 'touch with their fingers a strange civilization'" (26). On arriving in Egypt with that aim, "[t]hey thought of themselves . . . as actually moving from the exhibit to the real thing" (28). However, the Egypt they perceived was so fully constrained both by their understanding of reality as "that which can be represented" and by the image of the Orient already produced by representations in exhibits, illustrations, and texts that "[i]n the end the European tried to grasp the Orient as though it were an exhibition of itself" (29). Mitchell concludes:

> The Orient was something one only ever rediscovered. To be grasped representationally, as the picture of something, it was inevitably to be grasped as the reoccurrence of a picture one had seen before, as a map one already carried in one's head, as the reiteration of an earlier description. . . . To describe the Orient . . . became more and more a process of redescribing these representations. (30)

Building on Mitchell's argument as well as Said's, Derek Gregory develops the master-trope of the theater rather than the exhibition to reach a similar conclusion about Egypt's apparent intangibility. Travelers protect their sense of "the authenticity of their own experience" by "scripting" it to "provide and police the sights of a (still) exotic Egypt" (119). The results are, first, "the fabrication of [Egypt as] a space of constructed visibility," and second, the "constitution of the modern tourist as spectator-voyeur, as consumer-collector and, above all, as sovereign-subject"—such that tourists could "experience and command Egypt as a series of scenes set up for their own edification and entertainment" (145–46).[4]

The present essay will develop the implications of a different master-trope, that of the market. Like the exhibition and the theater, this trope functions to define and enforce distance between the traveler and Egypt, yet paradoxically the figuring of Egypt as a market also establishes a basis for apparently "real" and immediate encounters between travelers and their locale. Within the trope of the market, then, an aspect of the Egyptian experience emerges that is not encompassed by either of the other two master-tropes already analyzed. Whereas Gregory indicates that the constitution of the traveler as "consumer-collector" affirms his or her participation in "the powers and practices of colonialism" (146), I would suggest that by becoming a consumer (or at least a shopper) the traveler leaves, if reluctantly and temporarily, the theater and the exhibit hall and begins to occupy a subject position not fully congruent with colonial hegemonic practice.

My investigation of the trope of the market will be grounded in reference to nearly a dozen writers traveling in the middle half of the nineteenth century. Some are figures of indubitable status—Thackeray, of course, but also Richard Burton and Edward Lane, two of the century's most influential Arabists. Others—Amelia Edwards, Harriet Martineau, Eliot Warburton—are less prominent but were widely read in their time and have drawn renewed attention as emerging theoretical approaches (feminism, postcolonial studies) have helped to reveal the significance of their work.[5] The remainder—Samuel Bevan, Frederick Fairholt, William Hamley, William Loftie, Samuel Manning, Isabella Romer—are more obscure. Most of the writers I discuss stayed in Egypt for months rather than years and most traveled mainly as tourists. All wrote book-length accounts based on their experiences. Not only do these texts form a heterogeneous group, but also few, if any, of the individual accounts are ideologically or imagistically consistent throughout. Like any scholar of travel writing, therefore, I offer my argument with the knowledge that a careful reading of any of the texts I cite will inevitably produce evidence that appears to contradict my view.

This chapter follows three threads, one having to do with subject position and agency, another with interpretation and representation (in Mitchell's sense), and the third with value and price. All can be traced through the three motifs prominent in writers' deployment of the market as a trope: Egypt's bazaars themselves, the process of bargaining, and the Egyptian custom of begging for *bakshish,* or tips. Travelers who, like Thackeray, might have been stymied in their efforts to describe the Pyramids and other monuments rarely seem troubled in their descriptions of the bazaars. Although this sense of freedom and comfort implies an unmediated experience of the bazaars, the heavily textual nature of the descriptions themselves disturbs such an implication. Rather, the bazaar depictions approximate the paradigm supplied by Mitchell and Gregory.[6] The distancing which that paradigm stipulates between the scene and the experiencing subject is confirmed in several texts by the visitor's reluctance to purchase, to engage in the material exchange that is the basis of a bazaar's reality—for as Mitchell puts it in a different context, "what commercialism offers is always the real thing" (10). When the visitor abandons disengagement by starting to bargain, whether at a bazaar or elsewhere, he or she is thereby also repositioned ontologically. No longer the "sovereign-subject" of Gregory's analysis, the traveler instead must accept compromised agency, for while bargaining the shopper behaves responsively more than proactively. Further complicating the traveler's experience here is the instability of value implied by the very possibility of bargaining. Coming from what Mitchell diagnoses as a "world of signs" (14), British visitors are confronted in Egypt by a different world, one in which representation appears absent or insecure. This problem is acutely manifested in travelers' inability to attach prices to objects. Finally, the erosion of agency constituted by bargaining is exacerbated in the case of *bakshish,* whereas travelers can both initiate and terminate a bargaining process, they can only rarely prevent Egyptians from pestering them for tips. More importantly, persistent demands for *bakshish* confirm what travel narratives construe as Egypt's semiotic weakness, for *bakshish,* is a price without an object—in effect, the sign without the referent.

While bargaining and begging are, like the bazaar, common motifs in travelers' narratives, they are not as amenable as the bazaar to being "made picture-like and legible" (Mitchell, 33) within Orientalist convention.[7] Begging and bargaining cannot be encompassed hermeneutically—mainly, I would argue, because the incorporation of the European observer into the scene prevents him or her from occupying the disengaged position on which the accustomed hermeneutic strategies rely. Moreover, if Mitchell is right that in European exhibitions at midcentury, "[w]hat was on exhibit was the conversion of the world to modern capitalist production and exchange" (16), it is especially important that the hermeneutic structure of the exhibition be able to encompass the market system of nineteenth-century Egypt, precisely because that market exemplifies the converse of the modernity supposedly on display. By eluding the exhibition, the market would inevitably undermine the universalizing effect of the exhibition, and diminish its validity as a confirmation of the progress of modern capitalism. My analysis suggests that the market is particularly resistant to the exhibition's framework of meaning first because of its particular features, but also more importantly because of the situation in which it places the foreign traveler, whose agency and subject positions are not fully elaborated in Mitchell's discussion.[8] The failure of the exhibition to capture and contain the Egyptian market within its hermeneutic framework implies a weakness in the master-narrative of historical progress that underlies that framework. What the examination of the market as a trope reveals, finally, is both the urgency and the limits of nineteenth-century British writers' rhetorical appropriation of Egypt.

Bazaars—Just Looking

One midcentury visitor observes that "the Bazaars . . . form the stranger's chief object of attraction in an oriental town" (Bevan, 30).[9] Concomitantly, the marketplace becomes a nearly obligatory ingredient in nineteenth-century British narratives' establishment not only of local color, but also, more importantly, of the cultural authenticity of the East and thereby of the traveler's Eastern experience.[10] In the inevitable replication of descriptions from one text to the next, the marketplace also becomes a characteristic venue for the interpenetration of the seen and the previously envisioned. As Thackeray says of his first day in Smyrna (now Izmir, in western Turkey),

> Walk into the bazaar, and the East is unveiled to you; how often and often have you tried to fancy this, lying out on a summer holiday at school! It is wonderful, too, how *like* it is; you may imagine that you have been in the place before, you seem to know it so well! (29; original emphasis)

For Thackeray the bazaar harbors the essence of the East's difference, one that in the usual paradoxical way he "know[s] so well" because texts and illustrations have enabled him to preconceive it.[11] He can also experience it repeatedly; Cairo's indigenous shops, "the interminable vast bazaars with their barbaric splendor," fulfill the same desire as their Turkish counterparts, as he observes with pleasure that "[t]here is a picture in every street, and at every bazaar stall" (85). As Mitchell's argument would predict, he becomes enthusiastic about the scenes before him to the degree that they both recall what he knows and are amenable to being represented yet again.

Amelia Edwards's narrative of her 1873 trip, *A Thousand Miles up the Nile* (1877), is equally precise in its reproduction of the Egyptian market setting as a display, extraordinary yet expected:[12]

> in order thoroughly to enjoy an overwhelming, ineffaceable first impression of oriental out-of-door life one should begin in Cairo with a day in the native bazaars; neither buying, nor sketching, nor seeking information, but just taking in scene after scene, with its manifold combinations of light and shade, color, costume, and architectural detail. Every shop front, every street corner, every turbaned group is a ready-made picture . . .—they all look as if they had been put there expressly to be painted. (3)

Edwards's description of the markets consumes five pages of smallish print, more than a third of the opening chapter of her account. Fully aligned with the conventional Orientalist picturesque and entirely consistent with the paradigm outlined by Mitchell and Gregory, Edwards's description of Cairo's markets provides a primarily visual definition of Egypt's otherness. In placing Egypt on display, Edwards remains apart from it—and indeed she confirms this position by, as she says, "[not] buying." Moreover, throughout her extended verbal exploration of the bazaars, purchase itself is neither sought nor accomplished. She comes no closer in Cairo than a role-play in Khan al-Khalili, the most famous of the bazaars, where she repeatedly visits the precious metal merchants, "practicing Arabic" and "try[ing] on all their bracelets . . . again and again without buying" (8). Even though the goods in

Khan el-Khalili are "real" and the venue is authentically Oriental, the nature of the visitor's (non)engagement with it constructs it as an exhibit, as a space of representation. Later, during her journey up the Nile, Edwards does finally purchase some baskets, but there she reconstructs the bazaar as exhibit by pointing out that a certain design "of which specimens are preserved in the British Museum, seems still to be the pattern most in demand at Assûan" (166). Her own position as customer is effaced not only in her pose as a museum-goer but also in her use of "we" rather than "I" to document the transactions.

Edwards's deflection of the market as a venue for exchange is mirrored in Eliot Warburton's account of visiting Cairo's bazaars.[13] Like Edwards, he uses multiple rhetorical tactics to distance himself from the setting. Calling on both the exhibit and the theater, Warburton remarks that "the turbaned merchants . . . look as if they were for ever sitting for their portraits, and seldom move a muscle" (31). He declines to specify whether he bought anything. Instead, as he describes the aftermath of a hypothetical purchase, he conceals himself behind a generic "you" even more effectively than Edwards hid as "we." This "you" quickly becomes a part of the setting, seated on the counter in a shop and smoking, so as to "add to the almost imperceptible yet fragrant cloud that fills the bazaar" (32). However, this apparent participation in the scene turns out to be merely a cover by which the experiencing subject attains "full leisure for observation" (32). In short, the bazaar is just as much an exhibition and the visitor a looker-on as in Edwards's narrative or Thackeray's. The market remains authentic only as a display and the visitor as an observer; in none of these instances is the visitor willing to confess his or her status as shopper directly, or to admit that the bazaar is a site of transaction as well as of representation.

Bargaining—How Much?

When the bazaar functions as an exhibition rather than a marketplace, the items for sale have neither use value nor exchange value, but only visual value, and their price is of no great concern. If the visitor wishes to buy, on the other hand, he or she must both ascertain the price of the item and determine whether the price is fair. These are deeply difficult endeavors for most travelers. Sometimes the goods in question are unfamiliar and their value unknown. However, the greater obstacle is typically what travelers perceive as the instability of price. As Frederick Fairholt explains in his 1862 book *Up the Nile and Home Again*, "There is no fixed price for anything; hence you cannot, as in Europe, ask for an article, pay its value, and leave a shop with it in the course of five minutes" (19).[14] Consequently, many travelers do what they can to avoid "run[ning] the risk of a lengthy bargain in a shop" (Bevan, 32).

The few Britons who know Arabic well and/or are resident in Egypt for an extended period seem less troubled by this frustration. Richard Burton, for instance, gives a detailed list of "the necessary expenses of a bachelor residing in Cairo" in 1853 (64).[15] He presents the prices of various items, from rent to servants' wages to tobacco to rice, as clear and unambiguous (64–65). Edward Lane offers an equally detailed list of basic Egyptian commodities, with prices indicated in both piastres and pounds sterling (312).[16] Burton and Lane are exceptional both in their knowledge of expected prices and in their confidence that price and value might coincide. Evidently aware that most British visitors do not share his perspective, Lane also describes the more usual reaction:

> Buying and selling are here very tiresome processes to persons unaccustomed to such modes of bargaining. When a shopkeeper is asked the price of any of his goods, he generally demands more than he expects to receive; the customer declares the price exorbitant, and offers about half or two-thirds of the sum first-named; the price thus bidden is, of course, rejected: but the shopkeeper lowers his demand; and then the customer, in his turn, bids somewhat higher than before: thus they usually go on until they meet about half-way between the sum first demanded and that first offered, and so the bargain is concluded. But I believe that most of the tradesmen are, by European travellers, unjustly blamed for thus acting, since I have ascertained that many an Egyptian shopkeeper will sell an article for a profit of one *per cent.*, and even less. (315, 317)

No doubt Lane is correct that the instability of price is largely illusory, a matter of style more than of substance.[17] Nonetheless, British travelers persist in worrying that they do not get quite what they pay for in their transactions with Egyptian merchants and service providers. Even when they cite prices, they doubt that costs reflect real value. Fairholt, for example, is amazed that the price of donkeys can "run from £3 or £4 up to £150" (35). Bevan pays ten piastres to use the bath, but notes that "[t]he price of the Arab bath varies considerably," with Egyptians expecting to pay only three or four piastres for the same service (74). Martineau says that her party paid £40 per month for the dahabiya they hired, but that other travelers two years earlier had paid only £12 for a similar arrangement (*Eastern Life*, 17).[18] In none of these instances is price presented either as stable or as well correlated with value. Moreover, where detailed price lists exist, as in handbooks for travelers, they may manifest anxiety about cost and value better than they remedy it. The 1847 edition of John Gardner Wilkinson's widely used *Handbook for Travellers in Egypt*, for example, includes not only tables showing the change in prices between 1827 and 1841–42, but also five pages of "corrections and additions" consisting mostly of updated lists of prices. Baedeker's *Egypt* of 1878 has abandoned the effort to update, admitting that "it is hardly possible to give the traveller any idea of the prices of the various commodities" and warning against "the Oriental merchants themselves, with whom bargaining is difficult and troublesome" (250).

Although travelers might be amused to observe the process of reaching agreement on price under such exotic circumstances, they are—as both Lane and Baedeker suggest—typically discomfited when required to participate themselves. Amelia Edwards's reaction to shopping for a houseboat to rent will serve as an example. By the time of her stay in Egypt, the sailing trip up the Nile by dahabiya had been, as Gregory explains, "constructed as the defining experience of tourism in Egypt" for several decades already (120). Edwards goes to the Cairo suburb of "Boulak . . . where some two or three hundred Nile boats lay moored for hire" (9). Her struggle to select a boat is compounded by her inability to tell one "black or copper-colored" captain from another, by the captains' penchant for shifting the positions of their boats along the riverbank, by the boats' varied sizes and outfits, and so forth. Chief among her complaints, though, is the uncertainty of price. There are "boats that are only twice as dear as they ought to be, and boats with that defect five or six times multiplied." Worse yet, "prices . . . vary from day to day" (9). Edwards and her party fail to rent a boat at all in their ten days of effort; some twenty pages later she finally reveals, without detail, that they have joined with another party and hired a bigger vessel.[19] When Edwards is trying on bracelets while posing as a customer in Khan al-Khalili, she gets something (amusement, language practice) for nothing every time. There she is acting the customer, not being the customer; the bazaar need never become real and she need never feel subordinate to the Egyptian shopkeepers. When, on the other hand, she attempts to become, and not just act as, a shopper in the boat rental market, she becomes subject to the intentions of the captains, and she leads "a miserable life," "deliberating, haggling, comparing, hesitating" (10).

During his 1869 visit to Egypt, William Hamley succeeds much more easily at hiring a boat in Cairo, but the ideological content of his account is strikingly similar to Edwards's.[20] His initial description recalls the situation Edwards encounters: "There were plenty of passengers wanting boats," he observes, "and there were plenty of boats wanting passengers; but the difficulty was to get a passenger into a boat. . . . How such proceedings could ever end in embarkations I cannot imagine" (Hamley, 362–63). After some delay, Hamley and his companions simply "boarded and took possession of a craft" whose owners are not on board. The owners return shortly, and "with their appetite for jabber painfully excited, . . . wanted to draw us into foolish disputation, which we, with stern forbearance, declined" (363). Rather than engage in the lengthy process of selection and negotiation that stymies Edwards's party, Hamley and his fellow travelers strike their satisfying bargain precisely by not bargaining. At no point do they make any meaningful accommodation to local market practices; instead, their actions reproduce colonial tactics of occupation.

The significance of this episode becomes even clearer when it is compared with Hamley's description of his visit to Cairo's bazaars. Replete with stylized references to the *Thousand and One Nights* ("Arabian Nights"), his portrayal of the markets themselves is conventionally Orientalist. Unlike Edwards, however, Hamley is there to buy, at least at the outset, and a long report on bargaining is included, narrated, like its counterpart in Warburton's book, mainly in the second person. Several decorative items are purchased with some difficulty. Toward the end of the visit to the bazaar, however, "your education has advanced, . . . [and] you treat [the dealers] without ceremony, depreciating their wares, and offering for them a tenth of what they ask" (360). This traveler/customer's return to dominance is ultimately exemplified by his refusal to buy a circlet he admires from a salesman whom he considers too assertive (360). In short, when a practicing customer, the traveler cannot maintain the authoritative position necessary to his comfort; authority can once again be assumed only as the attempt to purchase is abandoned.

Hamley expresses this compulsion toward dominance in explicitly nationalist and racialist terms that are fully compatible with his subsequent colonization of the rental boat. On first entering the jewelry bazaar Hamley ("you") is distracted by a press of dealers and onlookers, but "you recover your Anglo-Saxon self-possession" and proceed (359). After making his first purchase, he finds himself newly disoriented, but again recalls his origins to steady himself: "You . . . show symptoms of hesitation, but, recollecting that this will never do for a free-born Briton among a gang of ignorant savages, you resolve to show the villains that you know what you are about" (359). Once the traveler has learned what he is about, he no longer purchases, and—not coincidentally—the market reverts to the realm of the imagined. In the paragraph after the one in which Hamley describes refusing to buy the circlet, he writes:

The parade of so much gorgeous stuff in so poor a place produces an effect of barbarous grandeur which is rather impressive. Most likely the same goods exhibited in a commodious, well-fitted European shop, would make a very paltry show. But undoubtedly imagination is busily at work here, and it is much wiser to believe that things are as you see them, than to seek to remove the glamour. Everything in Egypt is more or less enchanted. If the "Nights" were written, as some of the learned have supposed, by an Egyptian or Egyptians, their magic is accounted for. The difficulty in that land is not to believe in marvels. (360)

The market appears real in Hamley's narrative only while he is a customer. As soon as he returns to observation, the reality of the bazaar dissipates and he reverts to a fanciful vision allied with the most familiar of Oriental representations, the *Thousand and One Nights*. This episode in Hamley's narrative reveals with especial precision how the market imperils the detached, discrete subjectivity delineated by Mitchell and Gregory. Contrary to Gregory's argument, however, it is in becoming a "consumer-collector," and in contending with the uncertainty of price and value that accompanies that position in Egypt, that Hamley is temporarily displaced from the status of "sovereign-subject" (Gregory, 145–46), the same status that enables him elsewhere to experience Egypt as representation rather than reality. Hamley's eagerness to resume that status confirms Thackeray's contention that representation is "better than the reality"—and indeed once Hamley is again comfortable in his (Anglo-Saxon) sovereignty he reproduces the conventional representation of the market to the detriment of the reality that he has apparently just experienced.

The market is of course a place of exchange. As the object of a tourist's gaze, however, the market and its commodities have value mainly as what James Buzard would call a "token of authenticity" (6). Travelers can derive full benefit from a bazaar simply by observing and documenting it. When, on the other hand, they seek to buy an item, two changes occur. First, they must consider the value of the item, and determine, usually through bargaining, the price to be paid. Second, as part of the bargaining process, they cede the inherently superior position of observers for that of participants—and moreover participants who have less knowledge of both price and value than their partner/opponent in the bargaining. Thus it is principally the necessity for bargaining that sets the market apart from the master-tropes of theater and exhibition. While shopping, travelers can no longer remain confidently detached from what they observe, as they might in the theater or exhibit hall. If only temporarily, they occupy a subject position constrained by, rather than empowered by, the Egyptian setting. Further, because the traveler can purchase only with the dealer's active cooperation, the Egyptian tradesperson or boat captain acquires a measure of control over the British customer. Whereas the bazaar when observed produces a sense of reality that is in fact "fantasy . . . confirmed" (Gregory, 139), the bazaar when shopped in attains a more genuine (if less appealing) reality.

Beggars—Go Away!

The irritation and confusion travelers express about bargaining is, however, moderate in comparison with their reactions to the Egyptian tradition of tipping, or "bakshish." *Bakshish* is, according to Isabella Romer's 1846 account, "the first Arab word an [*sic*] European learns here *to his cost*, as it is addressed to him from all quarters, and means a present in money" (1:88; original emphasis).[21] By the time of W. J. Loftie's sojourn in Egypt in the late 1870s, *bakshish* was such a well-known phenomenon that he identifies it as the inauguration of his Egyptian experience; "When I heard that magic word," he gushes, "I realised for the first time that I was at length in the East, the land of romance, the scenery of the *Arabian Nights*, the glorious country of the rising sun, which poets have sung and artists have painted; . . . I had made the pilgrimage at last and set foot in Egypt: 'Backsheesh!'" (63). Few travelers were so enthusiastic. Edwards's account of her arrival at Luxor expresses more characteristic sentiments:

> And now there is a rush of donkeys and donkey boys, beggars, guides and antiquity-dealers, to the shore—the children screaming for backshîsh; the dealers exhibiting strings of imitation scarabs; the donkey boys vociferating the names and praises of their beasts; all alike regarding us as their lawful prey. (122–23)

Many visitors reacted to such scenes "with stout sticks" (Martineau, *Eastern Life*, 4), "the cold muzzle of a pistol" (Warburton, 168), or "a huge whip" (Bevan, 25). Richard Burton fends off the pleas for bakshish by dressing in Eastern costume and by speaking fluent Arabic, options available to few British travelers:

> The infant population spared me the compliments usually addressed to hatted heads; and when a little boy, presuming that the occasion might possibly open the hand of generosity, looked in my face and exclaimed "Bakhshîsh," he obtained in reply a "Mafîsh;" which convinced the bystanders that the sheep-skin covered a real sheep. (*Pilgrimage*, 8)[22]

That immunity to the demand for *bakshish* symbolizes for Burton the success of his disguise suggests the extent to which vulnerability to begging defines the European experience of Egypt.[23]

Harriet Martineau and her party are so troubled by this harassment that they include freedom from begging in their bargain with guides at the Pyramids:

> We had bargained before starting that we should not be asked for baksheesh "while going up the Pyramid." Our guides took this literally, and began begging the moment we put our feet upon the summit. And all the way down my guides never let me alone, although they knew I had no money about me. (198)[24]

At the time of her trip to Egypt in 1847, Harriet Martineau had already produced three books in the field of economics, including *Illustrations of Political Economy*, a major work published in multiple volumes between 1832 and 1834. She was also the writer of a book entitled *How to Observe: Morals and Manners* (1838), which one editor has called "the first substantive treatise on sociological methodology" (Hill, xi). Yet despite this extraordinary expertise and her considerable reading about Egypt, she remains perplexed by Egyptians' begging. For example, she is amazed that even after discovering that she is deaf and can hear well only with an ear trumpet, the inhabitants of the upper Egyptian city of Aswan

> pressed forwards to shout into my ears "baksheesh! baksheesh," till Alee [her dragoman] pushed and flogged them away. I wonder at their perseverance in thus incessantly begging of strangers; for we could not learn that they ever got anything by it. If, as it appeared to me, travellers give only in return for service, or in consideration of some infirmity, the perseverance in begging seems wonderful. (*Eastern Life*, 48)

Her personal irritation with beggars aside, Martineau seems to be bothered by *bakshish* mainly because it appears to her economically irrational. In *How to Observe*, she makes a clear case that both morality and conduct operate according to universal rather than culturally specific principles, and she applies those principles confidently to economic problems, including beggary in Spain (38–39). Yet in Egypt she is at a loss. Why, she wonders, does begging persist when no reward is ever given? Why do the guides ask incessantly for tips from a deaf woman who has no money on her? Why do chained prisoners on death row "cr[y] 'baksheesh' as vigorously as any idler in the place" (*Eastern Life*, 137)? These questions suggest that Egyptian economic assumptions differ fundamentally from British ones—or as she puts it more specifically elsewhere, "taxes in Egypt are not the same thing as taxes in Europe" (*Eastern Life*, 64).[25] So, too, the interdependence of labor, production, and compensation cannot as easily be assumed in Egypt as in Europe. For example, at a "sugar-refinery" near Cairo, the workers are compensated, legitimately enough, in molasses, but "they have to bribe the measurer of the molasses to give them due measure" (*Eastern Life*, 250). When *bakshish* is asked of tourists, as when a bribe is paid to the man measuring molasses, no labor has been expended and no commodity or service has been produced, yet compensation is expected anyway.

Like bargaining, then, *bakshish* is a troubling phenomenon to British travelers in several ways. Most practically, as Samuel Manning says of his visit to the Pyramids in the early 1870s, the pestering makes it "difficult . . . to abandon oneself to the full enjoyment of the scene" (61).[26] In the terms of Mitchell's and Gregory's arguments, the persistent and even "threatening" (Fairholt, 241) demands for *bakshish* prevent travelers from remaining the disengaged, superior observers at the exhibit hall or theater. Beggars rupture the integrity of the exhibit and the drama, requiring the spectator to act as well as gaze. The spectator's implied disempowerment is exacerbated by the fact that the entreaties for *bakshish* come unbidden and can be escaped only with difficulty, since "*bachshish* forms the pith and marrow of every transaction, be it social or commercial" (Romer, 2:113). Whereas bargains can be entered by choice and ended at will, beggars have the traveler at their mercy. Even though European travelers are targets for *bakshish* because of their hegemonic position (as manifested in their wealth), clearly most feel victimized rather than empowered by the Egyptians' pleas.

In addition, the dissonance of price and value entailed in bargaining is experienced even more intensely in begging. It is bad enough that at the end of a bargain travelers feel that they have paid more than the goods or services are worth, but in the *bakshish* market, they are expected to pay without receiving any goods or services at all. Thus, the demand for *bakshish* (with the need to pay it on occasion as well) furthers the destabilization of value already entailed in bargaining. If bargaining implies variability in commodity values, *bakshish* suggests the absence of value altogether.[27]

By midcentury most travelers have probably read accounts of new arrivals being assaulted by donkey boys (a submotif in themselves), or of would-be Pyramid climbers being hassled by aggressive guides—yet whereas prior descriptions of the Nile, the Pyramids, or other commonly visited Egyptian monuments often provoke authorial anxiety, comparable descriptions of bazaars, bargaining, and beggars do not. Even when such descriptions bear clear traces of the textual attitude identified by Said, the narratives themselves

rarely express concern at their belatedness. In short, the existence of antecedent texts does not appear to impinge upon travelers' sense that they are
perceiving their experience of beggars or shopkeepers as a reality unmediated by prior texts.

Most British travelers claim to prefer the attenuated, citationary reality of
the monuments, the landscape, and even the picturesque bazaars (when just
looking) to the unpredictable and intimate reality of bargains and *bakshish*.
Yet their participation in that reality suggests that the master-tropes of the
exhibit hall and the theater, with their emphasis on distance and disengagement, do not fully encompass the typical range of experiences depicted in
travelers' narratives. When constituted as customers (willing or not), travelers do set aside the artifice of the exhibition and the drama, and along with
it the inherent superiority of the spectator's position. Few are comfortable
with this compromised status; their accounts often implicitly define success
in a market interaction as the resumption of supremacy, whether by driving
a hard bargain or by resisting the cries for *bakshish*. But unlike the exhibit or
the drama, the market resists secure signification; instead it stands for uncertainty of value. A bargain is typically hard only in relation to the originally
quoted price, not in relation to the absolute value of the item. Moreover, the
marketplace in Egypt is pervasive; as Edwards complains in Luxor, "every
man, woman and child about the place is bent on selling a bargain" (371).
Thus whereas the exhibit hall and the theater are sites within which well-
defined meanings are produced, the market is a site of both unstable signification and indeterminate boundaries. The insecurity of the market explains
the desirability of the exhibit hall and the theater. The theater-goer and the
visitor to the exhibition can make sense of what they see in ways that travelers faced with the demands of bargaining and *bakshish* often cannot.

Analyzing *From Cornhill to Grand Cairo*, Patrick Brantlinger notes that
"[p]rogress through commerce is the axiom of Thackeray's free trade imperialism" (138). Harriet Martineau offers a more fraternalistic approach to a
similar conclusion:

> Seeing in commerce the instrument by which all the inhabitants of the earth
> are in time to be brought into common possession of all true ideas, and
> sympathy in all good feelings, [the observer] will mark the progress made by
> the society he visits towards this end. (*How to Observe*, 165)

For Martineau and Thackeray, commerce is the indicator both of cultural
progress and of participation in the world community. Travelers to Egypt,
however, struggle to interpret and to function within Egypt's particular version of commerce, the market. Derek Gregory is right to call British travel

to Egypt "an intrinsically hermeneutic project" (115). By their engagement in the market of Egypt—whether shopping for baskets, bargaining for boat rental, or fending off beggars—travelers signal the disintegration of that project.

NOTES

1. "To the Nile" was written in 1818 but not published until 1876; Thackeray is very unlikely to have known it in 1846. For a complementary discussion of Thackeray's perspective on Egypt, see Johnston, 74–78.

2. James Duncan and Derek Gregory provide a concise summary of scholarship on such traveler-writer's anxiety; see Duncan and Gregory, 7–8, as well as Gregory, 119.

3. Further examples could be drawn from most of the writers discussed in this essay; few Britons wrote about visiting Egypt without some nervous comment on the Pyramids. Of especial interest is Samuel Manning, who narrates his interactions with the local Bedouins in some detail before observing: "All this may seem quite out of keeping with the feelings proper to a visit to the Pyramids—as no doubt it is—but I have been so much annoyed by the unreality and sentimentalism of many books of travel, that I prefer to state facts exactly as they happened" (61).

4. These two tropes—the exhibition and the theater—are not, of course, the only ones critics have identified. Mary Louis Pratt's influential 1992 book seeks "to use the study of tropes as much to disunify as to unify what one might call a rhetoric of travel writing"; her book's "theme is how travel books by Europeans about non-European parts of the world went (and go) about creating the 'domestic subject' of Euroimperialism" (Pratt, 11, 4). James Buzard grounds his 1993 analysis of nineteenth-century travel writing in the "master-trope . . . of the *beaten track*" (4; original emphasis). Neither of these valuable works addresses nineteenth-century travel writers' representations of Egypt, however. Nor does Barbara Korte's 1996 overview of British travel writing, although her focus on the panorama as a trope could usefully be adapted for analysis of writing about Egypt, as Mitchell's brief discussion of panoramas suggests (Korte, 85; Mitchell, 23–24). Laura E. Franey's trope of choice is violence; her 2003 book discusses Egypt, but does not substantively differentiate Egypt's place in nineteenth-century discourse from the places occupied by other parts of Africa. The well-defined tradition of writing about Egypt, as well as the cultural and political specificity of Egypt in the nineteenth-century popular imagination, seems to me to render such a differentiation necessary. Nigel Leask identifies "curiosity" as the preeminent trope of Romantic-period travel writing (4); his 2002 book includes a lengthy chapter on "Romantic Egyptomania." Also of interest is Paula Sanders's discussion, in a 2003 article, of the medieval as a trope in Victorian depictions of Cairo.

5. A number of critics have analyzed women's travel writing to show that women's attitudes and experiences as travelers are characteristically distinct from men's. I did not find a significant gender-based difference in the deployment of the market as trope. While my essay treats both male and female writers, it will not take up the larger question of gendered travel.

6. Gregory also comments on the interaction of textuality and reality in portrayals of the bazaar; see 139–40.

7. Amelia Edwards's account renders this metaphor of legibility directly: "the land of Egypt is . . . a great book—not very easy reading, perhaps, under any circumstances" (66; see also 127).

8. Mitchell notes that many travelers desired "direct and physical contact with the exotic" (27), but most of his discussion focuses on the viewer's position as detached rather than embedded; he speaks, for instance, of "the figure on the viewing platform" (9) and "[t]he person . . . as something set apart from a physical world, like the visitor to an exhibition or the worker attending a machine, as the one who observes and controls it" (19). When a traveler does achieve cultural immersion, it is through disguise (Lane is Mitchell's example), a tactic which enables the visitor to "carr[y] out the characteristic cognitive manoeuvre of the modern subject, who separates himself from an object-world and observes it from a position that is invisible and set apart" (28). However, I would point out that the effect of such direct contact is heavily mediated by the disguise, and therefore does not adequately model the engagement undertaken by those (the great majority) who remain easily identifiable as European. In a significant sense, my essay is about what happens when detachment yields to interaction without the shield provided by disguise.

9. Samuel Bevan went to Egypt as an employee of a transit company. He seems to have had few accomplishments apart from his *Sand and Canvas; a Narrative of Adventures in Egypt* (1849), a book which was not reprinted.

10. As several critics have pointed out, tourist travel to Egypt, especially in the Victorian period, followed a predictable itinerary, which in turn engendered a certain narrative uniformity, at least superficially. For further discussion, see Barrell; Gregory, 134–37; and Johnston, 73–74. Given the modernization of Egypt during the nineteenth century (especially by Muhammad Ali, who ruled Egypt from 1806 to 1847, and more erratically by his successors), authenticity was an urgent matter. Few travelers appreciated the Europeanization of Egypt's cities, as much as they enjoyed the improvements in security and transportation that also resulted from Egyptian leaders' attraction to things European; see Gregory, 122, 127 and Sanders, 188–89 for related discussions. For a useful general analysis of authenticity in the context of travel, see Buzard, 6–11.

11. It should be noted that some writers distinguish between "markets" and "bazaars"; see, for example, Edwards, 78; Fairholt, 174, 340; and Warburton, 144. Strictly speaking, a bazaar consisted of permanently established shops, often clustered by commodity, with jewelers in one area, arms dealers in another, and so on. A market usually sold more perishable goods, including food, and (especially in smaller towns) might be an open-air affair with an intermittent schedule. The tourist trade was a more prominent feature of bazaars, and Europeans were more likely to visit bazaars than markets, especially if they were staying in hotels or had employed dragomans or other servants who would arrange the purchase of food and other necessities. For the purposes of my argument, however, the two terms can be used interchangeably, as British travelers' experiences of the two venues appear consistently similar.

12. At the time of her trip to Egypt, Edwards (1831–1892) had already published several novels, a history, and two travel accounts. She later undertook an American lecture tour on Egyptian subjects, and became an active contributor to the field of Egyptology. *A Thousand Miles* was reprinted many times.

13. Warburton (1810–1852) published his popular book, *The Crescent and the Cross; or Romance and Realities of Eastern Travel*, in 1844.

14. Fairholt (1814–1866) was an artist and historian. His book on Egypt was not reprinted, although he met greater success with other publications.

15. Burton (1821–1890) was a capable and active Arabist and Orientalist. He spent time in Egypt at the start of the journey that he records in *Personal Narrative of a Pilgrimage to al-Madinah and Mecca* (1855).

16. Lane (1801–1876) is best known for his Arabic-English dictionary and for his *An Account of the Manners and Customs of the Modern Egyptians*, a book considered definitive for many decades after its publication in 1836.

17. Lane also describes the system by which Cairene markets are inspected to ensure that weights and measures are accurate and that no shopkeeper sells "above the regular market price" (122).

18. Martineau (1802–1876) was a novelist and economist who went to Egypt in 1847. Her account of her sojourn, *Eastern Life, Present and Past* (1848), will be discussed in greater detail below.

19. In an appendix entitled "Hints to Travellers in the East," Warburton includes advice on bargaining for a boat as well as other arrangements for travel on the Nile (353–54); see for comparison Fairholt's discussion of costs (82–85).

20. In Egypt to attend the opening of the Suez Canal, Hamley (1815–1893) was a colonel in the Corps of Royal Engineers and a longtime contributor to one of the premier Victorian periodicals, *Blackwood's Edinburgh Magazine,* in which his travel account was first published serially under the pseudonym "Scamper." The four lengthy articles were collected and published as a book entitled *A New Sea and an Old Land* (1871).

21. Her two-volume *A Pilgrimage to the Temples and Tombs of Egypt, Nubia, and Palestine, in 1845–6* is the second travel book Romer (d. 1852) published. It was reprinted at least once.

22. Burton glosses "mafish" as "there is none" (8). Hats were widely recognized in Egypt as exclusively European attire—hence the reference to "hatted heads" drawing demands for *bakshish*. Burton was at this early point in his travels acting the part of a Persian dervish.

23. This is not to say that Egyptians never paid *bakshish*. In fact, Egyptians of even limited means would typically have expected to tip (or bribe) in order to grease the wheels of government bureaucracy, to be exempted from some obligation, to receive a service, and the like, as well as in charity to the poor or disabled. However, they would not usually have been approached on sight, as Europeans often were, with demands for tips, except in the case of charitable giving (see, for example, Burton, 82–83, 189).

24. Manning makes a similar, but more satisfying bargain, paying a shilling to a Bedouin shaykh "on condition that he allowed no one to speak to me for a quarter of an hour" (61).

25. Martineau's next topic is an extended critique of the Egyptian government's handling of agricultural policy. The subtext of this critique is the same as that of her comments on *bakshish*—that the Pasha neglects basic principles of political economy (specifically, in this case, the "security of property or other rights" [*Eastern Life*, 247]), and is thereby acting against the interests of his country.

26. Manning (1822–1881) was an editor, writer, and artist who published numerous illustrated travel books in addition to *The Land of the Pharaohs: Egypt and Sinai*, a book which seems to have appeared in at least three versions between 1870 and 1890. I am using an undated copy, probably from 1875.

27. Gregory offers a variant but useful perspective on Egyptians' manipulations of value and price for the tourist market (124).

CHAPTER 4

Colonial Counterflow

From Orientalism to Buddhism

MARK LUSSIER

I. Colonial Counterflow

This essay explores the emergence of Buddhism into European consciousness across the nineteenth century and establishes an intensified focus on
British activities relative to Tibet, for reasons that will become apparent.
Eventually I intend to analyze cultural encounters across what I only half-
jokingly term the "long" Romantic period (ca. 1270–present), and I offer
here a short summation of these concerns in order to contextualize the
counterflow that Orientalism establishes. In the later phase of encounter (the
period that overlaps with the periodic range of Romanticism), I will examine
how various texts function as the temporal and historical backdrop for complex dialogic negotiations between seemingly polarized epistemologies of
the Enlightenment. Basically, while the initial phase of encounter was driven
by spiritual colonialism (hence by spiritual materialism), the second phase
of encounter was driven by Enlightenment materialism, which established a
turbulent semiotic stream that rippled from colony to country (margin to
center) and which structures this discussion.

This summation, therefore, serves to introduce the primary concerns of
this essay: (1) the first British delegation, headed by Scotsman George Bogle,
to establish contact with Tibet; (2) the arrival of Sir William Jones to India
a decade later, which clearly signaled a shift in colonial thinking and which
stimulated a textual torrent returning to the European sphere; (3) the singular effort undertaken by Alexander Csoma to translate Tibetan into English
(thereby providing a crucial supplement to European understanding of
Buddhism), an endeavor underwritten by institutions established by Jones

himself, and (4) the accelerated accumulation of linguistic knowledge within European centers of Orientalism across the nineteenth century, a semiotic stream through which scholars distinguished Buddhism from other Eastern religious systems and therein ignited it, in Sir William Arnold's immortal phrase, as *The Light of Asia.*

The focus on contact between British colonial administration and Tibet clearly brings several layers of colonial counterflow into sharper view, yet this type of counterflow from circumference to center has already figured prominently in numerous discussions of Orientalism, colonialism, and imperialism post-Said. However, within contemporary critical discussions of Orientalism, Buddhism has remained absent, perhaps reflecting its status as spiritual wanderer from its initial home in northern India and Nepal, and knowledge of it as a distinct theology and philosophy flowed somewhat late down the information highway of British colonialism now well established critically. Nigel Leask maps one current of this inflow by exploring "the manner in which British Romantic writers consciously and unconsciously articulated their anxieties about the Other" (Leask, *Romantic Writers*, 2). The influx of Orientalist cultural information into works by major Romantic writers (from Byron to De Quincey), the source for an "anxiety of empire" rippling across the period, attests to the impact Romantic Orientalism exerted on literary forms and artistic imagination. Travel literature certainly defined one linguistic layer feeding this anxiety of counterinfluence, and in the work selected for exploration, Samuel Turner's *Account of an Embassy to the Court of the Teshoo Lama in Tibet*, such anxieties emerge in the "contradiction of colonial desires," which highlight an impending shift in colonial strategy and tactics (Bivona, viii).

As Michael Franklin and Garland Cannon also persuasively argue, Sir William Jones functions as the fount from which this flow takes its shape (in linguistic theory, poetic practice, and administrative orientation), and as Saree Makdisi suggests, "his work on Oriental history and, above all, on the nascent field of Oriental philology was part of a much larger process of 'discovering' and tracing certain linguistic, historical, cultural, and social continuities between the Orient and Europe" (Makdisi, 110). At the least, as Peter J. Kitson argues, his "neoplatonic translations made Hinduism available to the Romantic poets" (16), and canonical writers from Southey to Byron further fuel this syncretic cultural presence, a dynamic of influence traced with energy by C. C. Barfoot ("English," 65–76). When the body of more "interested" information (e.g., political documents informing the considerable "depth of Burke's knowledge of Indian affairs" [Franklin, "Accessing," 51] or internal company memoranda used by Philip Francis in support of "the corruption charges against Hastings" [Makdisi, 112]) is added to this constant current, the depth and breadth of this colonial counterflow becomes apparent. However, what is also readily apparent, this stream of semiosis never distinguishes Buddhism itself as a distinct body of thought from Hinduism, a hermeneutic problem shared by initial and secondary encounters, and I will contextualize this interpretive quandary by briefly mapping the first phase of spiritual colonialism in its European guise.

II. Initial Encounters between Buddhism and the West

The process of encounter between Buddhism and the West was a slow one, perhaps extending back to Alexander the Great and certainly made more complex by Buddhism's virtual eradication in its native home (northern India and Nepal) during several phases of Islamic conquest. Buddhist doctrine and texts, originally recorded in Pali and Sanskrit, were subsequently disseminated via large translation projects throughout Central Asia: northward into Tibet, Nepal, China, Japan, and Mongolia, and eastward into Bhutan, Cambodia, Korea, Thailand, and Vietnam. The first recorded contact between a European and "the Buddhocratic government of Tibet" occurred in a remarkable interfaith gathering at the Karakorum court of the Khans in May 1254 (Batchelor, 93). The occasion was somewhat straightforward; the Khans sought presentations from all the world's religions to assess which one they would endorse in support of their empire, and as Stephen Batchelor indicates, "Both Christians and Buddhists had similar motives for being there: to persuade Mönge Khan—at the time the world's most powerful man—to convert to their religion" (Batchelor, 82). The Franciscan friar William of Rubruck represented the Western view in this dialogue, but after only eight months, he was quite likely expelled from the city, having only gathered a few converts to Christianity, when knowledge of his report to Louis IX— where he "preach[ed] war against them" (Batchelor, 91)—became known to his host. Mönge Khan ultimately converted to Mahayana Buddhism in its Tibetan form, giving rise to the authority of Tantric Buddhism across the high Himalayas as discussed by John Drew.[1] This brief contact between Christianity and Buddhism was followed by the encounters recorded by Marco Polo near the end of the century, yet both Friar William and Marco Polo provided rather poor analyses of the thrust of Buddhist doctrines and their importance throughout the Central Asian region.

The efforts of Friar William and Marco Polo became the first eastward gestures in a vigorous period of spiritual colonialism pursued by the Catholic Church throughout the East, especially by Portugal. However, internal division in Europe complicated this effort, which gained new intensity with the conclusion of the Council of Trent and the imperatives issuing from it. The most important figure in this spiritual colonialism, the Jesuit Francis Xavier (who trained in Paris under Ignatius Loyola), led the effort "to evangelize the newly acquired territories of south India" (Batchelor, 161), arriving in Japan in August 1549. Unlike Friar William, Xavier had considerable success in converting Buddhists to Christianity during his stay in Goa, India, in 1545, and after he traveled to Japan from India, "a period of comradeship between the Jesuits and Shingon priests" (Batchelor, 167) ensued, but the collaboration was based on misrecognition and thus was short-lived.[2] Having successfully established the foundation of a Jesuit mission in Japan, Xavier returned to Goa and subsequently sailed for China in April 1552. However, denied entry by the Peking government, Xavier was forced to languish on the bleak island of Sancian off Canton, where he finally died on December 3, 1552.

Other Jesuits followed Xavier's lead, with the formidable Matteo Ricci arriving in Goa in 1578 and then settling at the new Portuguese outpost of Macao in 1582. Ricci perfectly embodied the Jesuit ideal: he was thoroughly versed in the arts and sciences; he was gifted in the acquisition of languages and dialects; he was totally dedicated to papal authority, and he was physically capable of withstanding the rigorousness of spiritual colonialism. Ricci successfully studied Confucian and Buddhist literature and doctrine, but whereas he saw in Confucius "nothing contrary to the essence of Catholic faith," he believed that Buddhism provided the major hindrance to the continued expansion of Christianity across the East.[3] Even as Ricci was dying in Peking in May 1610, Christovao Ferreira was sailing from Macao ultimately to assume authority of Xavier's mission in Japan, yet the very success of the Jesuit effort raised the suspicions of the Tokugawa Shogunate. The third Shogun Iemitsu enforced a 1608 expulsion edict, and Ferreira, after being captured and tortured, apostatized, becoming the first European convert to Zen Buddhism (Batchelor, 178–82). Thus, at the close of the first stage of encounter, one defined primarily by spiritual colonialism, Japan and China closed its borders to the disruptive Europeans and the Jesuit shock troops.

Perhaps most relevant to this discussion, the Jesuits had already briefly moved into Tibet, establishing an early mission in Guge and, by 1628, penetrating as far as Shigatse before being expelled "on the advice of the 10th Karmapa" (Batchelor, 190). This closed state of affairs continued into the opening decade of the eighteenth century, as geopolitical realignments among Tibet, China, and Japan solidified the conservative attitude toward European intrusion into various regions throughout Asia, a situation that shifted relative to the arrival of the Jesuit Ippolito Desideri in Lhasa in 1716. Desideri's journey to Tibet anticipates in several details the journey later undertaken by Alexander Csoma (discussed later in this essay), although unlike Csoma, Desideri received his charge directly from the papal authority of Clement XI. Upon his arrival, the Jesuit was presented to Lhazang Khan, who instead of expelling him encouraged his cultivation of Tibetan (and for reasons precisely parallel to the interfaith conference arranged by Mönge Khan in 1254), and within nine months the intrepid Desideri had completed an exposition of Christianity in Tibetan. He subsequently took a six-year plunge into the canonical elaborations of Tibetan Buddhism titled the *Kangyur* and *Tengyur* (Tibetan translations of the Buddha's sutras and of major Indian Buddhist commentaries on those sutras respectively), yet as Batchelor notes, the effort was odd in that "Desideri never realized that what he was studying was Buddhism" (193). In a final irony, the geopolitics of Europe, rather than overt hostility from indigenous political regimes, disrupted Desideri's spiritual colonialism and returned him to Rome in 1728, when "his memoirs remained lost . . . until 1875 and were not published until 1904" (Batchelor, 192). At this time, actual Tibetan texts began to arrive in Europe, although these did not emerge from the copious textual materials accumulated by the Vatican as might be expected, but flowed directly from the contact zone between Russian imperialism and the Eastern Other. I have written on this particular aspect of textual encounter elsewhere, yet the slow counterflow of Tibetan texts provided a catalyst that set the stage for the British movement northward from Calcutta and into Tibet near the end of the eighteenth century.

III. The First British Delegation to Tibet

Well before Sir William Jones arrived in India, British colonial authorities were already responding to various "internal and external pressures" emerging from administrative strategies of containment and control, especially as these pressures were applied by Russian imperial efforts in the trans-Himalayan regions directly north of British control. Indeed, even before Jones arrived in India, one can detect a tension in colonial attitudes, and only one decade prior to his arrival, first contact between Tibet and the British government in Bengal was inaugurated by the third Panchen Lama (then known as "the Teshoo Lama"), who was acting at the time as regent for the very young Dalai Lama.[4] On March 29, 1774, Warren Hastings received a somewhat poorly translated letter from Teshoo Lama seeking to resolve a border dispute that erupted in 1772 and which brought British military force to the borders of Tibet. A Bhutanese "desi" or lord named Zhidar (one of the Lama's subjects) created the conflict when he attacked the autonomous country named Cooch Behar.

When he invaded this "small state on Bengal's northern borders," Zhidar unwittingly created the conditions that turned the British colonial gaze northward and that led, ultimately, to the expansion of "British influence in the Himalayan region" (Teltscher, 91). The complexities involved in and evolving out of this communiqué require quoting it at some length:

> I have been repeatedly informed, that you have engaged in hostilities against the Dêh Terria, to which, it is said, the Dêh's own criminal conduct, in committing ravages and other outrages on your frontiers, gave rise. As he is of a rude and ignorant race, past times are not destitute of instances of the like faults. . . . Nevertheless his party has been defeated, many of his people have been killed, three forts have been taken from him, and he has met with the punishment he deserved. It is evident as the sun, that your army has been victorious . . . should you persist in offering further molestations to the Dêh Terria's country, it will irritate both the Lama and all his subjects against you. Therefore, from a regard to our religion and customs, I request you will cease from all hostilities against him; and in doing this, you will confer the greatest favour and friendship upon me.[5]

As Kate Teltscher notes, the deposed raja of Cooch Behar, appealing for and receiving "military assistance from the British," ceded by necessity the "sovereignty of the state to the East India Company" in exchange for direct intervention, and with the British success in defeating Zhidar came the potential threat, from the Tibetan point of view, of further northward expansion, upon which the Panchen Lama sought to foreclose through his function as "mediator" (Turner, xi). The letter, while self-effacing and humble, graceful and loquacious, and filled with solicitude and salutation, also carried with it the implied threat of overt hostilities and widespread rebellion in its view that British failure to end military activity would rouse the resistance of "both the Lama and all his subjects against you" (Turner, xi).

Following receipt of the letter and after a period of consideration, the governor-general responded with a letter requesting that a delegation led by the Scotsman George Bogle be received in Lhasa to formalize relations, and this request, although initially rejected, was finally accepted, granting British access to Bhutan and Tibet. Upon his arrival in Desheripgay, Tibet, on October 12, 1774, George Bogle became "the first British traveler to enter the region" (Teltscher, 91), and he remained with the Teshoo Lama for almost seven months (returning to Bengal on April 8 of the following year). Again as noted by Teltscher, Hastings certainly had imperial reasons for the mission, since he was "motivated by a desire for information, the kind of empirical evidence favored by theorists of the Scottish Enlightenment. The mission was both an exercise in reconnaissance and an intellectual project" (Teltscher, 94). Yet just as clearly, Bogle and Hastings both viewed the delegation functioning beyond purely venal colonial aspirations, since Hastings argued that the mission "was as much textual as commercial or diplomatic" and further hoped to "imprint on the hearts of our own countrymen the sense and obligation of benevolence" (quoted in Teltscher, 94, 95) through such texts. Bogle shared this new view of indigenous literature and culture as well, an attitude articulated much later in a letter to his brother, when he characterized these aspirations as to provide "to the whole world an Account of a Country hitherto little known" (Teltscher, 95).

While Bogle's narrative offered an enlightened and generous appraisal of the Teshoo Lama, another narrative offered by Captain Samuel Turner very much highlights the colonial and imperial imperatives at work in the background. While Bogle and the Lama established a warm personal relationship, the machinations of Turner achieved material advantages for the East India Company and the British government in Calcutta:

> I have obtained the Regent Chanjoo Cooshoo's promise of encouragement to all merchants, natives of India, that may be sent to traffic in Tibet, on behalf of the government of Bengal. No impediment, therefore, now remains in the way of merchants, to prevent their carrying their commercial concerns into Tartary. (Turner, 374)

The appendices attached to Turner's *Narrative* are equally illuminating of the somewhat contradictory aspects of this first delegation, since within these attachments one can see the play of a more familiar colonial agenda. The first appendix offers "views taken on the spot" (Turner, "Title Page") compiled by Lieutenant Samuel Davis, which assessed the military, political, and social conditions defining Tibetan cultural processes and which, therein, provided the type of intelligence sought by the government in Calcutta. As well, in a summation offered by the naturalist Robert Saunders ("Observations Botanical, Mineralogical, and Medical"), one can clearly see the type of calculation of material resources at the core of colonial endeavors across the Indian subcontinent in its older guise. Indeed, Saunders's tables of commodities (Turner, 381–84) are organized by Tibetan imports and exports with its surrounding countries and foreground items like "gold dust, diamonds, pearls, coral, musk, and wool" (Turner, 381).

Strangely, given the rather successful outcome of this first mission, the collapse of colonial pretensions was occasioned by a personal situation. All narratives, letters, and reports agree that during his seven-month stay at Desheripgay, George Bogle developed a warm and close relationship with the Panchen Lama based on mutual respect, which clearly clashes with the view of Tibetan lamas as "little better than shamans of superior dignity" offered much earlier by the Scottish doctor John Bell—who much earlier had accompanied a Russian delegation through Mongolia and China (Teltscher, 100). Bogle's attitude much more closely resembles that to be pursued by Jones, and as Turner reports, "Mr Bogle so ingratiated himself into [the Teshoo Lama's] confidence, as to be intrusted [*sic*], some time after, with considerable remittance in money, for the purpose of building a temple and a dwelling house, for the accommodation of his votaries to Bengal" (Turner, xv), which was accomplished by 1779. However, the hope of establishing permanent ties between the governments of Bengal and Lhasa ended somewhat abruptly, once Bogle returned to India. When the Panchen Lama agreed, several years later and after long solicitation, to visit the emperor of China, he actually invited Bogle to join him in Peking (quite likely hoping to use British influence as a buffer against Chinese control), yet the potential long-term relationship, founded upon the personal rather than imperial, collapsed in a curious synchronicity:

> Unfortunately, however, the death of the Lama [upon arriving in Peking] and that of Mr. Bogle, which happened at nearly the same time, clouded this fair prospect, and completely frustrated every expectation which had been formed. I am sorry to add too, that events, of a much more recent date, have concurred to throw almost insuperable difficulties in the way of re-establishing our intercourse with Tibet, at least for some considerable time to come. (Turner, xvi)

With these two deaths, the hopes for establishing formal relations with Tibet collapsed just as Turner predicted, and particular knowledge of Tibet as the repository of Buddhist texts would await the efforts of a solitary figure, Alexander Csoma, who compiled and published the first Tibetan-English dictionary with the help of the Asiatick Society of Bengal, founded by Sir William Jones the same year as Csoma's birth.

IV. Jones and Colonial Counterflow

When Sir William Jones was appointed to the judgeship that carried him to India, he welcomed the opportunity to escape "the seemingly insoluble problems of England" and to seek his "wealth" in a locale allowing him to combine "law and Oriental studies" (Cannon, *Oriental Jones*, 194). Yet somewhat surprisingly, Jones manifested from the beginning of his relocation a rather "startling [additional] motivation" (Cannon, 194) for one so deeply embedded in the colonialist enterprise—one actually linked to his endorsement of the "Enlightenment principle of association" and the application of "new scientific techniques" (Franklin, *Jones*, 84, 120). Jones's arrival created the conditions shifting Orientalism into a phase not solely governed by crass commercialism but newly tinged with a positive passion for "the dynamism and diversity of Indian culture."[6] Fired by an intuitive "cultural empathy" (Franklin, *Jones*, 120) ignited during his initial engagement with Indian literature (even before mastering Sanskrit) and informed by a "respectful and sympathetic response to Hindu culture" (Franklin, *Jones*, 118) upon his arrival, Jones thought "he could really serve people . . . [and] serve humanity, a goal requiring his return to Orientalism" (Cannon, 194, 195).

In spite of such motives, which upon occasion eerily echo the sense of "white burden" articulated late in the Romantic period and codified across the Victorian Age (the specific shift from Romantic to Modern modes of Orientalism), Jones nonetheless remained embedded in the power structure of the colonizer and deeply implicated in the imperial process. After all, his primary function, through his judiciary activities, literally established Jones as its arm of law. Nonetheless, his arrival made official a type of administrative revaluation reflective of an essential change. One of Jones's first acts, the establishment of the Asiatick Society of Bengal and its influential and widely disseminated journal the following year, created a vehicle for the intellectual and scholarly pursuit of ideas, rather than material goods, and in the process, through its journal, created a linguistic and textual counterflow through which Buddhism—as a distinct body of thought and practice from Hinduism—slowly emerged into European consciousness.

As Franklin argues with considerable force, Jones ingeniously applied the comparativist dimension of Enlightenment epistemology to establish direct connections between Indian and European cultural forms, crafting a cultural circumstance wherein the colonized "subject" provided a vehicle to critique the abundant colonial abuses "of British oppression in India" (Cannon, 194):

> Orientalism might operate as a cultural counter-sphere to attack classical orthodoxy and Eurocentric prejudice. . . . The appropriation of Indian culture as opposed to Indian loot would not only help reform of colonial administration, but also question Western assumptions concerning the automatic cultural superiority of the colonizing power. (Franklin, *Jones*, 84–85)

Jones's notion, again noted by Franklin, "was in many respects a revolutionary idea," since such a view would recognize "that servants of colonial power might prove moral agents of administrative reform and cultural renaissance" (*Jones*, 118). The arrival of Jones crystallized a rather dramatic shift in Britain's view of the Orient (as metonymized by India), a shift from one paradigm (the development and economic exploitation of the East) to another (the understanding and intellectual importation of the East). Saree Makdisi argues in similar fashion in *Romantic Imperialism*, with "the romantic period mark[ing] a transitional moment between . . . opposed sets of colonial projects" (101). As discussed later in this essay, the "transitional moment," especially as embodied in the institutional establishment of the Asiatick Society, proved crucial for the "reemergence" of Buddhism into European consciousness.

Obviously, given such a change in imperial administrative direction, the engagement with and representation of indigenous materials across the Indian subcontinent cannot be reduced, as Edward Said seems to propose in *Orientalism*, to a problematic "form of antihumanism" (Otterspeer, 195). Said's influential text proposes that the primary ideological aspect of Orientalist practice reifies "the sense of Western power over the Orient" (46), yet this view becomes untenable relative to the emergence of Buddhism itself, which capably exerts a broad counterinfluence in Europe across the nineteenth century. Quite clearly, given the paucity of attention paid to Buddhism in most critical analyses of historical Orientalism from Said to the present, this aspect of Orientalism needs scholarly attention, especially since it coincides with shifts in British imperial goals and the explosive emergence of what is now termed "Romanticism." Furthermore, unlike almost all other Eastern religions and systems of thought, Buddhism has cast long shadows across the West, even—in the case of Tibetan Buddhism—taking up residence within it.

Jones himself seems to propose using Indian literary and cultural forms in a deconstructive fashion to critique British imperial pretensions and intentions (expressive of a deconstructive element as one dimension of modern Orientalism itself), and as Leask has argued, "the internal and external pressures determining and undermining such representations are more various than Said's thesis will allow" (2). Indeed, in Franklin's assessment, Said, in ignoring the dynamic and far-reaching alterations inaugurated by Jones, actually places under erasure "co-operative process and the rich opportunities it presented for transculturation" (Franklin, *Jones*, 119), and this very transcultural exchange—linguistically driven and textually embodied—demarcates a significant shift in the British view of the Orient.

In the solid assessment offered by Peter J. Kitson, "Jones's Orientalism did not *simply* impose a colonialist discourse upon India, facilitating British administration. It also partially fostered Indian nationalism by helping in the process of liberating its writing from Brahman control" (16). In the apt expression offered by Tzvetan Todorov, "it is only through talking to the Other (as opposed to issuing orders), that the Other is granted a subjectivity comparable to the Self" (quoted in Teltscher, 92), and Jones, and to a lesser extent Warren Hastings (immediately prior to his trial and ultimate acquittal before Parliament), seem to embody this new dialogic relationship and provide physical mechanisms to bring the Other home through the counterflow of textual translations, appropriations, and transmutations. Equally relevant to this discussion of the emergence of Buddhism into the West, again as proposed by Kitson, is that this "new system of British imperialism appears to have been emerging at roughly the same time as what we know as Romanticism began to appear" (13), and those direct epistemic convergences will shape the conclusion of this essay.[7]

V. The Solitary Sojourn of Alexander Csoma

Briefly comparing the spiritual colonialism of the Jesuits and the material colonialism of the East India Company, one discerns the shift from the theological to the Enlightenment episteme at the core of colonial process. The positivistic operated as the epistemic foundation for European views, and I would argue that this positivistic strain of the Enlightenment, based on reason and rationality, precisely found its Eastern Other in Buddhism, a view later taken by Friedrich Nietzsche. Thus far, the process of Buddhist emergence has been viewed somewhat collectively by examining points of contact and the colonial implications of those encounters. However, the context would be incomplete without looking at the individual, remarkable achievements of the father of Tibetan studies, the Hungarian Alexander Csoma. Csoma's work revolutionized Oriental studies by providing the first systematic study of Tibetan grammar and the first systematic organization of the entire system of Buddhist thought and practice. As well, although supported in his travels by British colonial agents like William Moorcroft and benefited by his relationship with the Asiatick Society of Bengal, Csoma's sojourn was undertaken for completely "Romantic" rather than "Colonial" reasons, since his was a search for linguistic and cultural origins, as he states directly in his preface to his other major linguistic achievement—the first *Tibetan-English Dictionary:* "The study of the Tibetan language did not form part of my original plan but . . . I cheerfully engaged in the study of it, hoping that it might serve me as a vehicle to my immediate purpose, namely, my researches in respect to the origins and language of the Hungarians" (Csoma, preface, vi).

Upon completion of his university training in Göttingen, where he studied under Eichhorn and Blumenbach, Csoma returned to the small village of Köros and the offer of a professorship, but during his stay Csoma and two other students swore an oath to undertake the search for origins (typically Csoma alone honored this vow). In February 1819, "before the snows" melted and "only lightly clad as if he intended merely taking a walk," Csoma departed for his trek to Tibet with only "a stick in his hand and a small bundle" of food and paper under his arm (Mukerjee, 15, 16). His biographer Hirendra Nath Mukerjee describes his passage as "an epic journey" (16), an apt characterization for one of the most arduous trips ever undertaken without official sponsorship or support. During his four-year passage to the Zangla Monastery in Tibet, Csoma traveled through Thrace, Chios, Rhodes, Alexandria, Constantinople, Aleppo (in Syria), Baghdad, Teheran, Meshed (in Khurason), Bokhara, Kabul, Lahore, Leh, and Kashmir.

Arriving at the Kashmiri border with his financial resources depleted, Csoma met the English adventurer William Moorcroft, "an agent of the East India Company intent on securing British influence in Central Asia as a means of thwarting the southward advance of imperial Russia" (Batchelor, 235). Moorcroft offered "some money and letters of introduction" (Mukerjee, 19), and in June 1823 Csoma entered the Zangla Monastery to begin his Tibetan studies with the head lama, Sangye Puntsog:

> On June 26, 1823 . . . a strange wanderer arrived at the Tibetan Lamaist Monastery of Zangla, situated in the Himalayas 3,500 meters up, and far from the routes used by tradesmen and pilgrims. He had come from Leh, the capital of Western Tibet, or Ladakh. . . . His name was Skander Beg. . . . There was something strange about his face . . . but only the lama who received him, Sangye Puntsog, knew what it was. He was a European. The first, the very first one[,] to reach that place. (Terjék, vii)

During his passage into Tibet, Csoma traveled primarily by foot, and he initially spent seventeen months under the tutelage of Sangye Puntsog, studying in conditions hardly less rigorous than encountered in his passage from Europe to Asia:

> The conditions in which [Csoma] worked are difficult even to imagine. . . . At that altitude [well over 10,000 feet] the cold was always intense. . . . During winter, the doorways were blocked with snow, the temperature constantly below zero. With his lama, he would sit in a cell no more than nine feet square, with no heating, no light after dark, neither of the two venturing to leave the "closet"[,] with the bare floor to sleep on and nothing but the stone walls keeping out the cruel cold. (Mukerjee, 20)

Lama Puntsog, who had served "as a government dignitary with the Dalai Lama" (Mukerjee, 25) and was a renowned physician, was erudite and accomplished, knowing the full range of Buddhist sutras, tantras, and techniques. The texts Lama Puntsog used to tutor his rather uncharacteristic European student was, simply put, the entire Buddhist canon available in Tibet at the time, which preserved Sanskrit texts no longer extant in India.

Following this initial period of rigorous study, Csoma departed to make his findings known to the British government in Bengal, arriving in Sabathu (an Anglo-Indian enclave) in May 1825, where his mission was communicated to Captain Kennedy and his results first made known. Remarkably, given the conditions of production, Csoma arrived with both his *Tibetan-English Dictionary* and *Tibetan Grammar in English* completed, and he had also compiled a summation of the 320 volumes (of the Tibetan *Kagyur*), which included a survey of all major Buddhist concepts and is now known as the *Mahavayutpatti*. Thanks to the intervention of the Asiatick Society of Bengal, Csoma's dictionary and grammar were published immediately (since they were viewed as having colonial value), while the *Mahavayutpatti* was not published until the twentieth century, following World War II (when the manuscript was discovered intact, somewhat miraculously, in the paper-devouring basement of the society itself).

Across the next nine years, Csoma returned to Tibet to study with two other lamas, but he finally settled in Calcutta, taking up residence in the Asiatick Society (ironically founded the year of his birth). Once settled, his life and work habits reflected his monastic experience, and for his entire stay Csoma lived in a nine-foot square formed by boxes of books and manuscripts in the basement of the society, where he slept and ate all meals. He was elected an honorary member of the society, often functioning as its cataloguer and librarian, and in 1832 he began publishing a veritable torrent of germinal scholarly work in the society's journal. While space precludes an exhaustive discussion of these publications, Csoma's published works—beginning in 1832 and extending well beyond his death—analyze almost ever aspect of "the great compilation of the Tibetan Sacred Books, in one hundred volumes . . . styled Ka-gyur," including discussions of "The Four Noble Truths" (Buddha), "The Middle Way" (Nagarjuna), "The Way of the Bodhisattva" (Shantideva), and "The Path of Enlightenment" (Atisha) and explanations of compassion, suffering, emptiness, reincarnation, samsara, and nirvana.

At the age of fifty-five, after a ten-year stay in Calcutta, Csoma again turned his thoughts toward Lhasa, which he had never seen and where he believed the secret of the origin of the Hungarians could be discovered. He reached Darjeeling on March 24, 1842, but he succumbed to fever and died on April 11. Appropriately, the body of Alexander Csoma was buried there, resting at the crossroads through which Buddhist learning, in several great waves, flowed to the north and east. As well, unlike almost all other Europeans present on the Indian subcontinent and active in the trans-Himalayan region, his reputation among those indigenous to the region has never wavered, perhaps because during his years in Central Asia (again as reported in his preface to the dictionary) he never once sealed his correspondences, since he sought to provide "transparency" regarding his motives and efforts. Less than a century following his death, "On 22 February 1933, Csoma was officially canonized as a bodhisattva in the grand hall of Taisho Buddhist University in Tokyo and a statue of him in meditation posture, donated by the Hungarian Oriental Society, was installed in the Japanese Imperial Museum" (Batchelor, 237). As Mukerjee notes, this is "the highest praise a man can get in Buddhist terms" (74), since the term "bodhisattva" literally means an "awakened one" and designates one who strives for enlightenment for the sake of all sentient beings, rather than one working toward individual release from the circle of transmigration (which defines the chief doctrinal difference between Mahayana and Theravada schools of Buddhism).

VI. The Flowering of the Dharma

Once Csoma's work appeared in the *Journal of the Asiatick Society of Bengal* and once the *Tibetan-English Dictionary* and *Tibetan Grammar* circulated out of Calcutta into the centers of Oriental studies in Europe, the stage was set for the full flowering of the dharma in the West. Csoma's Tibetan studies, along with a cache of Sanskrit manuscripts from the British agent Brian Hodgson in Nepal, circulated into the hands of the "man best equipped to make sense of them: the brilliant French philologist Eugene Burnouf" (Batchelor, 239). Burnouf's mastery of both Pali and Sanskrit, supplemented by Csoma's Tibetan work, allowed him to recognize in Hodgson's textual materials the original texts from which the Chinese, Tibetan, and Mongolian Buddhist canons were constructed. Burnouf, prior to the emergence of his translation work, published a definitive history of Buddhism (to provide a context for European reception), which was followed by his translation of the *Lotus Sutra*, which appeared in 1852 and which became "the first full-length translation of a Buddhist sutra from Sanskrit into a European language" (Batchelor, 241).[8]

The increasingly positive reception accorded Buddhism during the latter half of the nineteenth century would surely have horrified Xavier, Ricci, or Desideri (and most especially Friar William), yet European commitment to its own epistemic form of enlightenment, albeit in its positivistic aspect, could not but become fascinated with a religion without dogma and committed to deconstruction. The first major philosophical engagement occurred through Arthur Schopenhauer, who often evoked Buddhism in later (post-1844) editions of his masterwork *The World as Will and Representation*. Schopenhauer's interest, stimulated by what Friedrich Schlegel termed the "Oriental Renaissance" and mindful of his admonition that the "highest Romanticism" would emerge from the "Orient," saw in emerging Buddhist texts "a reconciling vision of wholeness" (Batchelor, 253) well matched to the continued refinement of epistemologies of the Western Enlightenment. Of course, Schopenhauer himself admits that his knowledge of Buddhism was partial (in at least two senses of the term), as a casual perusal of the references to Buddhism in his work clearly confirms. For example, his emphasis on the will, which provided such a strong attraction to Friedrich Nietzsche, tends to condition his understanding of crucial Buddhist concepts like "empty nothingness" and "nirvana," from which he swerves, but these very concepts also attract him, since they tend to push toward "the point where subject and object no longer exist" (1:412). This type of resistance to dualism, as any number of critical analyses have established, represents one major aspect of Romanticism's challenge to scientific forms of Enlightenment epistemology predicated on a Cartesian divide. Equally appealing to Schopenhauer was Buddhism's rejection of "theism" (1:487), a strain of thinking again particularly attractive to Nietzsche as the last Romantic, and he returns to this understanding in one of the last references to Buddhist thought in *World as Will* when conceding that "Buddhism [has] pre-eminence over the other [religions]" as the forerunner of his thinking. On that same page, he also acknowledges the influence of "Csoma Körösi" (Alexander Csoma), whose untimely death delayed the emergence of Buddhism itself into Europe. And so, by midcentury, thanks to the historical and philological efforts of Eugene Burnouf (a classmate of Auguste Wilhelm Schlegel) and his colleagues across Europe, as these are filtered through Schopenhauer's massively influential work, knowledge of Buddhism flooded into European consciousness.

Richard Wagner, while working on his opera *The Valkyrie* (ca. 1854), received a copy of Schopenhauer's masterwork as a gift and "proceeded to read it five times in the following nine months" (Batchelor, 259). The work awakened in Wagner an abiding interest in Buddhism, and two years later, he cited Burnouf's *Introduction to the History of Indian Buddhism* as exerting the strongest influence on him during this period. Indeed, the composer conceived and sought to execute an operatic work based on the life of the Buddha, entitled *The Victors*, yet when he died in exile in Venice in 1883, the work remained unfinished. In spite of such failures, Buddhism emerged with clarity and force in the closing decades of the nineteenth century, with centers of Orientalism in Russia, France, Germany, and England offering a widening flow of translations that served to solidify Buddhism as a viable alternative to the perceived logocentric excesses of European cultural forms and its emphasis on "sin."

Few would argue that no philosopher promoted this view more energetically than Friedrich Nietzsche, who was exposed relatively early to Orientalism in its philological form via his roommate at university. Shortly afterward (ca. 1865), Nietzsche, at the age of twenty-one, encountered Schopenhauer's work and its salutary passages on Buddhism, which intersected the hammering philosopher's growing suspicion of the debilitating effects of renunciation and detachment as vehicles of enlightenment. However, in spite of grouping the Buddha with other religious "preachers of death," Nietzsche did intimate that the practice of Buddhism, predicated on an ethical shift away from "sin" and toward "suffering" as the primary cultural condition in need of assuaging (a philosophical reorientation explicit in Schopenhauer), offered significant analogies to emerging Western epistemologies sans Christianity:

> Buddhism is a hundred times more realistic than Christianity—it has the heritage of a cool and objective posing of problems in its composition, it arrives *after* a philosophical movement lasting hundreds of years; the concept "God" is already abolished by the time it arrives. Buddhism is the only really *positivistic* religion history has to show us . . . it no longer speaks of "the struggle against *sin*," but quite in accordance with actuality, "the struggle against *suffering*." It already has . . . the self-deception of moral concepts behind it—it stands, in my language, *beyond* good and evil. (*The Anti-Christ*, 129; original emphasis)

Immediately prior to this famous passage, Nietzsche links Christianity and Buddhism as "nihilistic religions" (129), yet he takes great care to differentiate them ("With my condemnation of Christianity, I should not like to have wronged a kindred religion which preponderates in the number of its believers: *Buddhism*" [129]) even as he sees them as poles of a spectrum of religiosity. Where Christianity "had need of *barbarous* concepts and values," hence for Nietzsche is a primitive religion predicated on "desires to dominate *beasts of prey*," Buddhism "is a religion for *late* human beings . . . a religion for the end and fatigue of a civilization" (132). And in his estimation, Eurocentric culture had arrived at such a state of exhaustion by the end of the nineteenth century. The comparative dimension of Western Enlightenment epistemology, the very practices through which Sir William Jones sought to alter Orientalist scholarship and British administrative tendencies simultaneously, underwrites Nietzsche's efforts, as he explicitly acknowledges in the passing phrase "that one is now able to *compare*" (129) various religious traditions. After a century of increasingly intense engagement, Buddhism finally emerged into European consciousness as "the only really positivistic religion" seen in history, a spiritual "anti-system" without theism capable of dialogically engaging Enlightenment epistemology from the sense of shared ethics founded in suffering rather than sin.

NOTES

1. Of course, the heir of the Mönge Khan was none other than Kublai, the subject of the most famous poetic fragment in English literature, Coleridge's "Kubla Khan." See Drew, 183–229.

2. "When the Buddhist monks heard that Xavier had come from India, they assumed that he practised [*sic*] a form of Buddhism as yet unknown in Japan. Likewise, Xavier initially thought that Buddhism was a modified form of Christianity" (Batchelor, 167).

3. Stephen Batchelor reports that, "Upon hearing of the doctrines of non-self and transparency, he concluded that Buddhism was nihilistic and devoid of positive values" (171).

4. I operate relative to the position articulated by Fulford and Kitson in the introduction to *Romanticism and Colonialism*: "From a post-Althusserian position it is also possible to discriminate between colonialism, as the material system of conquest and control, and imperialism as a form of colonialism buttressed by hegemonic cultural ideological imperatives" (3).

5. As Captain Samuel Turner states in the introduction to *An Account of an Embassy to the Court of the Teshoo Lama in Tibet*, "Teshoo Lama was at that time the Regent of Tibet, and the guardian of Dalai Lama, his superior in religious rank, who was yet in his minority" (viii).

6. The translation of this letter was inserted in Samuel Turner's *Account*, which provides a fascinating glimpse into the calculating imagination at the core of the colonial drive, since the "narrative" (complete with letters exchanged between the Lama and Hasting, as well as "[Cultural, Social, and Political] Views Taken on the Spot" offered by Lieutenant Samuel Davis and "Observations Botanical, Mineralogical, and Medical" provided by Mr. Robert Saunders) actually reads more like a blueprint for assimilation.

7. Michael J. Franklin, "Accessing India: Orientalism, Anti-'Indianism' and the Rhetoric of Jones and Burke," in Fulford and Kitson, 62.

8. The Russian Isaac Jakob Schmidt published a French translation of the *Diamond Sutra* in 1837, but like the translations offered by Csoma, it was based on Tibetan.

CHAPTER 5

Homoerotics and Orientalism in William Beckford's *Vathek*

Liberalism and the Problem of Pederasty

JEFFREY CASS

The postcolonial perspective forces us to rethink the profound limitations of a con-
sensual and collusive "liberal" sense of cultural community. It insists that cultural and
political identity are constructed through a process of alterity. Questions of race and
cultural difference overlay issues of sexuality and gender and overdetermine the social
alliances of class and democratic socialism. The time for "assimilating" minorities to
holistic and organic notions of cultural value has dramatically passed. (251)
    —Homi Bhabha, *The Location of Culture*

Bhabha's challenging remarks (1994) about the intersections of postcolonial
theory and sexuality have resulted in some notable studies about the "alterity" of the sexual other. Hawley's *Postcolonial, Queer* (2001), Patton and Sanchez-Eppler's *Queer Diasporas* (2000), and Jan Campbell's *Arguing with the
Phallus: Feminist, Queer and Postcolonial Theory* (2000) begin to address the
"questions" Bhabha raises in his "postcolonial perspective" by demonstrating
how the "liberal sense of cultural community" has largely failed to achieve
its intended end—constructing and maintaining a communitarian ideology
that emphasizes unity among disparate groups and de-emphasizes their differences. Far from achieving a homegrown, heterogeneous, yet harmonious
group of subalterns who subscribe to what Bhabha identifies as "the holistic
and organic notions of cultural values" and then joyfully merge into the
collective, this heterosexist utopianism ironically illustrates the unconscious
dread and discomfort many "liberals" feel with the actual lives and histories
of marginalized groups. Accepting "alternative lifestyles" into the "cultural
community"—giving GLBT citizens a place at the table—becomes such
a leavening outcome that the queer body (and its interpretive sites) actually disappears into the larger body politic. "Alternative lifestyle" becomes

a polite characterization, a periphrasis for a life whose true sexual realities and activities are alien and off-putting and disturbingly different, even for Rainbow Coalition liberals. After all, in common parlance, *deviation* from social and cultural norms all too easily slips into *deviance*. Analogously, for queer theorists who appropriate a postcolonial critique, conventional representational strategies are frustrating precisely because they result from "liberal" attempts at wide-ranging inclusiveness and cultural assimilation. Rather than affirming and celebrating "queerness," the very differences that distinguish "alternative" sexualities in the first place, these strategies have contributed to the erasure of queer desire and difference, awarding them an undifferentiated place within the harmonious universe of human desire.

Not coincidentally, the postcolonial critique of liberalism coincides with its equally cogent critique of Saidian Orientalism, for sexual deviance also underwrites the stereotypical expectations evoked by the "Oriental Other." As many readers of *Orientalism* have noted, because colonial discourse was so powerful, the Orient remains forever fixed, static, and inert, rather than, as Ania Loomba remarks in her book *Colonialism/Postcolonialism*, relationally dependent (178). She writes: "Colonial identities—on both sides of the divide—are unstable, agonized, and in constant flux" (178). Of course, in a Saidian context, colonial sexual identity emerges from a form of stereotyping. Orientalist texts, in this view, reify the sensuality and exoticism of the female body, which never changes position or shifts its focus back to the colonizer because it is always the object of imperial desire. Likewise, Western expectations of the Oriental text also inscribe a version of the homosexual man, but the beauty of the male body is feminized, open to secret queer inspection, but never explicitly the object of desire. The relationship between effeminacy and beauty also suggests close ties to camp, particularly in dress, because its exaggerated otherness is permitted and even expected in the public display of the Orientalized male body.[1] Unfortunately, Orientalizing the homosexual male in this fashion still underscores an essentialist view of sexual identity. Such desire may indeed be transgressive, but the breaking of sexual taboo is well within the logics of Saidian Orientalism; in fact, it is "embedded within a myth of reciprocity" (158). According to this "myth," sexual relations between the colonizer and the colonized are "reciprocal," comprising a "transaction" to which both parties agree. These relations are necessary to the development of social and cultural harmony though, as Loomba also claims, "colonial sexual encounters, both heterosexual and homosexual, often exploited inequities of class, age, gender, race, and power" (158). Orientalism tends to minimize the force of these "inequities" by naturalizing—making them appear eternal and timeless and standing in place. By contrast, Sánchez-Eppler and Patton suggest in *Queer Diasporas,* "Sexuality is not only not essence, not timeless, it is also not fixed in place; sexuality is on the move" (2). They make this argument in order to emphasize that sexual identity (as is the case with race, gender, and class) is not essential, though typical Orientalized representations of sexuality might so indicate, nor is it "a succession of strategic moves" (4). Sexual identity is, in fact, a "cluster of claims to self that appear and transmogrify in and of place" (4), largely confirming Loomba's arguments about the "flux" of colonial sexual identities and undercutting Said's views about the hegemony of the West and the powerlessness of the East within Orientalist representations.

While Sánchez-Eppler and Patton transform sexual identity into something presently active rather than eternally passive, precisely the positioning of the Saidian Oriental Other, whether female or male, a postcolonial critique of arch-Orientalist texts such as William Beckford's *Vathek* actually makes "deviant" sexual practice visible and conventional readings of homoerotic representations quaint and perhaps even homophobic. Whether on the supportive liberal Left or the discriminatory conservative Right, both sets of readers wish that the reality of queer sexual practices would simply go away. *Vathek* becomes an interesting test case for "liberal" ideology because the author's biography, which hints darkly at a subterranean sexuality that lies beneath his heterosexual cover story (Beckford was married and had a daughter), so easily fuses with the persistently Orientalized sexualities contained in the novel. For *Vathek* admirers, uneasiness about the novel derives from the conflation of homosexuality and pederasty, a connection most liberals go to great lengths to avoid because the social and political anger (rightly) vented against child molestation can all too easily spill over into antigay sentiment. Called "the great Apostle of Paederasty" by Byron (Eisler, 176–77), Beckford becomes a problematic author to engage openly, for he uses the novel's hyper-Orientalism to disguise, displace, and diffuse his scandalous life, which includes a perhaps chaste affair with thirteen-year-old William Courtenay and a whole bevy of boy servants whom he spies on from his tower at Fonthill. One is even tempted to say that Beckford's fascination with Orientalist tropes (and much of his knowledge is authentic, coming directly from sources in the French; Beckford originally even composes *Vathek* in French) is the source of his corruption. Even more outrageously, however, and this is the real source of critical unease, Beckford enjoys his corruption, which, as we shall see, he coyly embeds in the narrative.

And a sampling of critical opinion over the last sixty years reveals an entrenched desire to cleanse Beckford from a squeamish form of sexuality by burying its details within the larger (and acceptable) spectrum of human desire. Eagleton writes that "it is characteristic of liberalism to find names and definitions restrictive" (*Illusions*, 68), and so critics of Beckford, asserting his rightful place in the literary canon, but not wishing to outline his (or any other) "alternative" sexual practice too definitely, tend to make Beckford's pederasty vanish while permitting traces of Beckford's homo-sexuality to survive. As Fuery and Mansfield claim in their book, "[T]he cultural real contains elements that much of the social order refuses to acknowledge as being part of its systems" (34). Representatives of a profes-sion prone to attack by cultural conservatives, Beckford's academic critics, as Foucault might suggest in *Discipline and Punish*, attempt to manage Beck-ford's "body" so that they do not appear to approve of or tacitly support any specific behaviors or actions. And because Beckford has so ably contrived arch-Orientalist landscapes in which "deviant" desire can safely inhabit and even invisibly flourish (with the collusive help of his "liberal" critics), Beck-ford neatly avoids the messiness of his pederasty. Many of his critics divert attention away from Beckford's pederastic practices and direct the focus toward his presumed psychosexual guilt for homosexuality. A dirty old man becomes a tragic closet case. Thus, several critics assume the podium of heterosexist moralizing in order to create a cleaner, more sexually hygienic Beckford. They often emphasize the Orientalized "sensuous desires" and the "intoxicating joys" in *Vathek* while at the same time projecting *Vathek's* ulti-mate doom on Beckford's psychic life. In other words, the (straight) caliph atones for the (queer) author's crimes, confirming moral judgment against *Vathek* while dissipating moral outrage against Beckford. Though not alone in this version of *Vathek's* relationship to Beckford, Mohammed Sharafud-din, one of the most important recent critics of Romantic Orientalism, suc-cinctly summarizes this interpretation of Beckford's novel: "*Vathek* is part of [Beckford's] inner world. It is a projection of an amoral, secret life into the public domain; it gives the rein for the first time to what could well be called the outlawed self" (1).[2]

One of the most insightful of Beckford's critics, Adam Potkay, rightly identifies the novel's emphasis on "male reciprocity, unlimited mutuality, [and] the communion of kind" as forming the basis for the "heaven of boys" that concludes the novel. Yet Potkay sees this pubescent homosociety as faintly misogynistic. Potkay drolly sums up his argument: "*Vathek* relies, in part, on the all-too-familiar logic that when someone must take the blame, *cherchez la femme*" (297). Moreover, he argues, "the attraction of a segregated paradise [at the end of the novel] attests to, even as it rejects, the increasing sexual integration of polite society" (303–4). While Beckford's novel does indeed reflect the anxiety of British society toward its altered sexual land-scapes, this reading of *Vathek* neatly sidesteps the issue of Beckford's traf-ficking in homosexual pleasure and loudly ignores his complacent and smug consumerism. Closer to the mark than other critics of the novel, therefore, is Diego Saglia who observes that for Beckford, the East "is more and more readily available in a metropolitan space which sees a burgeoning consumption of the oriental in the shape of products, objects, visual experiences and literary texts" (76). In the end, most critics prefer to avoid Beckford's hoggish and shameless appetites, reducing his bothersome *jouissance* to safe and pious epithets.

Though not intentional, the more seriously critics take Vathek's fate as a reification of Beckford's "tormented soul," the more glaringly they misread the exuberance of both Beckford's novel and its homoerotic imaginings. An implicit judgment of high moral seriousness underlies such persnickety, sermonizing critical strategies, but such strategies also raise the red flag of homosexual panic, thereby illustrating what Eve Kosofsky Sedgewick refers to as the "Gothic unspeakable" of the Romantic period (95), that public abhorrence of aristocratic representations of homoerotic desire (pederastic desire even more) that might actually "wash through" and infect the "middle classes" (95). If Beckford really does have all those pederastic dreams (or occasional homosexual couplings, and with boys), then the conclusion to his novel represents his justifiable fear of divine "retribution," the worried resolution to the psychic conflicts inherent in all lustful deviates, the understandable anxiety at the activities of sexual predators. And if Beckford, the married proprietor of Fonthill and father of two, actually enjoys his fantasies and occasional homosexual couplings, then, at the very least, he should make no overt displays of desire or love of pleasure that lead the unsuspecting public back to his indiscretions. Although Beckford outrageously indulges in hyperbole when he describes Vathek's fickleness and fecklessness, as well as his uncontrollable appetites and terrifying gothic eye, critics eagerly see an opening that moves the reader away from pederastic desire and toward psychosexual guilt, thus pushing the suggestion that Beckford self-identifies with or can be linked to a psychologically impaired and morally damaged Vathek. In so doing, these critics posit a strange bricolage, for readers must refashion the homosexually combustible, real-life Beckford into the heterosexually conflicted but doomed, fictional Vathek. This process advances a moral whitewash, but it does have the advantage of preserving a liberal commitment to homosexual desire without also having to connect that desire to a discomfiting pederasty.

R. B. Gill makes much the same point in his essay "The Author in the Novel: Creating Beckford in *Vathek*." He interrogates the performativity of Beckford's public image, postulating that the apparent contradiction between Beckford's public and private personae produces "many Beckfords, some he himself created and many created by his various critics" (242). Gill continues: "*Vathek* is a clear case of a novel especially in need of a biographical centre to resolve its ambiguities" (242). Yet Beckford ultimately thwarts the resolution of the novel's "ambiguities," the tantalizing journey of critical ambition provoked by the novel's dazzling exoticism and the novelist's equally exotic biography. Beckford thus hides in open sight his unrestrained glee at creating a queer fantasy under the noses of an audience that simultaneously embraces puritanical sexual mores yet indulges in imaginative "alternative" sexual practices. "Beckford is eager," Gill writes, "that we see him laughing and manipulating the diverse attitudes of Vathek without being compromised by naïve commitment to them" (253).

Readings of *Vathek* that stress the moralistic connections between Beckford's and Vathek's character and actions are, of course, not entirely inaccurate, for one cannot say that Beckford does not at all resemble Vathek. Like Vathek, he is whimsical in his interests, fanciful in his desires, and extravagant in their planning and execution. And like Vathek, Beckford (from a very early age) has the financial resources to be as whimsical, fanciful, and extravagant as he imagines. Finally, and perhaps most tellingly, like Vathek, Beckford can generally afford to resist public disapproval (or at least separate himself from it). Despite a publicly sullied heterosexual reputation, Beckford manages for almost eighty-five years to live the luscious "Oriental" life he is able to purchase, eluding his constrictive, draining family; jealous enemies; sycophantic hangers-on; and titillated, pseudo-ardent admirers (such as Byron). Forcing Beckford to emerge as an author who perceives he is a moral reprobate confirms a critical view that takes Beckford's psychosexual guilt seriously. But if one decouples the seriousness of the novel's ending with Beckford's more playful attitudes toward his title character, the critical field shifts away from inescapable homosexual tragedy and tilts instead toward homoerotic farce. As Malcolm Jack indicates, *Vathek* "shows distinct touches of humour in its . . . bathetic contrast between drama and absurdity" (xxii). Properly contextualized, the "bathetic" mordancy of the novel lies in humorously pitching the caliph from his own heterosexual pedestal, puncturing the traditional sexual norms he represents by lampooning him as a petulant "Mama's boy" who knows nothing of sacrifice, courage, or self-denial, but only omnivorous self-gratification.

In the final analysis, even Byron's Sardanapalus, who spontaneously transforms himself from feminized Oriental despot to glorious and masculine warrior, is more convincing as a serious character than Vathek because, at the last, love and honor form the basis of Sardanapalus's commitment to his country, Byron's last-ditch effort at genuine dramatic pathos. The bathos of Beckford's Orientalized protagonist stems, in part, from Vathek's utter inability to maintain a single idea, to conform to a single standard of predictable public behavior, reasonable or not. In effect, Beckford deliberately exaggerates Vathek's despotism, making him more despotic than other despots in eighteenth-century Oriental tales, precisely because he cannot master or control his appetites at all; he fails to subsume them under any sort of over-arching plan of action that he himself conceives.

In a very real sense, Vathek is a boy expected to rule in an adult world, a very dangerous and intelligent boy who dresses up as a caliph and who can-not possibly meet the social, political, and cultural obligations expected of him. As a religious leader, for example, Vathek fails to listen to or abide by any orthodox sentiments. Though Vathek has a "predilection for theological controversy" (3), he nonetheless ruthlessly persecutes those who contest his heterodoxy, imprisoning them "to cool their blood" (5). His desire to build his own tower that imitates Nimrod so inflames the ire of Mahomet that the Prophet curiously commands his own servants, the "genii," to assist Vathek in its completion in order to see how far Vathek will go in his impieties. But Vathek is no mere dark servant for Eblis, the Islamic equivalent of Lucifer, for Vathek undermines the gravity of his own moral blasphemy. Since he does not appreciate fully his own "irreligious conduct" (4), we cannot regard his inflated, exaggerated desire to enter Eblis's dark kingdom as a serious threat to traditional cultural norms. At best, Vathek parodies a satanic figure, pathetically oblivious to the consequences of his and his mother's caprices or to the damage that his violent rage may cause to his reputation. After the Indian (not yet identified as the Giaour) escapes from Vathek's prison, he kills the guards. Infuriated, Vathek kicks their dead carcasses "till evening without intermission" (7), convincing his subjects he has gone mad. After an old man can only translate the runes on Vathek's magical sabers for one day because the runes themselves change daily, Vathek mercifully orders that only half his beard be burnt. When "reverend Moullahs" bring Vathek a besom (broom) that had been used "to sweep the sacred Cahaba" (39), Vathek takes the besom and brushes away cobwebs from the ceiling as if it were a common cleaning implement, causing two Moslem clerics to die "on the spot" (41). Finally, never truly her adult equal, Vathek says nothing admonitory to Carathis. Ferreting out the hiding place of Gulchenrouz, his mother conspires with her evil camel Alboufaki, uses her necromantic pow-ers to resurrect ghouls, steals mummies from catacombs to supply herself with magical rhinoceros horns and oil of venomous serpents, and ritualisti-cally slaughters Vathek's loyal subjects as fiery oblations to the Giaour. Yet Vathek remains aloof from her actions, even as he grows ever more depen-dent on her powerful magic and on her brilliant public relations.

Although Islamic bees loyal to Allah on one occasion attempt to sting Vathek for his brutal treatment of clerics, no subject ever reproves his deca-dence or attacks his overindulgence. So committed is he to see the banquet halls and riches of the Underworld that he even lapses into the homoerotic to seal his relationship to the Giaour. For example, during a bout with a virulent form of dipsomania, the Indian/Giaour cures him with a draught that finally quenches his thirst. His health restored, Vathek "leap[s] upon the neck of the frightful Indian, and kiss[es] his horrid mouth and hollow cheeks, as though they had been the coral lips and the lilies and the roses of his most beautiful wives" (15). This amazingly unsexy kiss confirms their unholy union, their unbreakable bond. When Vathek treats the Giaour to a lover's kiss, however, he unwittingly makes a lover's promise. Soon after Vathek makes his journey onto the plains outside Samarah, the Indian reveals himself as the Giaour, gives Vathek a glimpse of the Palace of Subterranean Fire, and demands the blood sacrifice of fifty sons as a "libation" he must drink ("Where are they?—Where are they?—perceivest not how my mouth waters?" 26), suggesting perhaps that Vathek's previously insatiable thirst was actually a symptom of the Giaour's authority over Vathek.

To cure the Giaour's thirst, Vathek proposes a contest for fifty of the "handsomest" boys among his subjects, and the proud parents celebrate the Caliph's sudden generosity:

> The lovely innocents destined for the sacrifice, added not a little to the hilarity of the scene. They approached the plain full of sportiveness, some coursing butterflies, others culling flowers, or picking up the shiny little pebbles that attracted their notice. At intervals they nimbly started from each other for the sake of being caught again, and mutually imparting a thousand caresses. (25)

The "cavalcade" of boys, not yet weaned from the feminized ways of the harem and of inconstant women, "sport" with one another and, despite the fact they are contesting for the caliph's favor, impart affection to one another. Blissfully unaware that Vathek intends to sacrifice them to the Giaour by throwing them into a chasm that magically appears behind Vathek, the boys in turn approach Vathek one by one, unable to see the danger ahead of them. In a horrifying striptease, Vathek "undresses himself by degrees" (27), taking off items of clothing and jewelry as prizes for the youthful combatants:

> To the first, I will give my diamond bracelet; to the second, my collar of emeralds; to the third, my aigret of rubies; to the fourth, my girdle of topazes; and to the rest, each a part of my dress, even down to my slippers. (26)

As each child comes forward, Vathek tempts each one with a piece of his ensemble and then "pushes" the unsuspecting boy into the "gulph" and the waiting mouth of the Giaour (27). While Vathek feels compassion for the boys, appreciating their "beauty" even as the Giaour salivates over his victims, Vathek does not intuit his homoerotic connection with the Giaour, not even when he himself becomes ravenously hungry after the sacrifice of the boys, eating everything he can find. In fact, Vathek's stripping itself is a mirage. The more clothing and valuable baubles Vathek removes from his body, the less one discerns his body or true motivations. As with the Giaour, physical proximity and intimacy breed blindness and ignorance. Nakedness becomes a metaphor for secrecy, kissing a metonymy for suspicion and deceit.

In addition, the Giaour's presumed pedophagia literally incarnates a typical form of Orientalized discourse that "constructs the Orient as a passive, childlike entity that can be lover and abused, shaped and contained, managed and consumed" (Sardar, 6). Of this passage, Alan Richardson aptly concludes: "Beckford's private sexual fantasies cannot be disentangled from the cultural fantasy of a supine, infantile, inviting East" (10). But fantasy and consumption are separate realities—an "inviting East" is not the same as an "abused, shaped and contained, managed and consumed" Orient. *Vathek* certainly parodies the Caliph's overindulgence and hyperconsumption, but that parodic representation does not necessarily entail feelings of pederastic guilt. Indeed, it is dangerous to equate Vathek's use of young boys for his infernal purposes and Beckford's exuberance for boys for his domestic ones. Beckford's almost giddy desire for prepubescent males may not amount to a sexual practice; instead, Beckford's pederasty—occluded within Orientalized landscapes—may actually become a scarcely concealed sexual politics that, in the end, is almost too unbearable to contemplate, for it challenges both heteronormative and homonormative categories of acceptable sexual expression.

Indeed, Beckford revels in his outrageousness, basks in his defiance of social norms and expectations. He writes: " . . . I am determined to enjoy my dreams, my phantasies and all my singularities, however discordant to the worldlings around . . ." (quoted in Richardson, 8). That determination helps to explain why Eblis, the Giaour's residence of Orientalized evil, remains so "discordant" to Beckford's "wordling" critics and why those same critics attempt to align the shape of the narrative with their own moralist expectations. While Vathek's travails within the halls of Eblis ultimately do result in the proper punishment of all in service to the Giaour, a predictable conclusion for all literary works of the period that employ satanic tropes, the end matter of Beckford's novel does not presuppose that Beckford feels he is in personal moral jeopardy or that he identifies at all with the justice of its conclusions. In fact, the Eblis scenes in *Vathek* principally serve to reinforce the self-indulgence that drives his Orientalism. In effect, Eblis constitutes a revenge fantasy that challenges the basis of British heterosexist politics in the late eighteenth and early nineteenth centuries. From Beckford's perspective, it is a politics that demands his social and cultural expulsion for his own deviance while refusing to examine its own ideological inconsistencies and sexual foibles.

Familiar with both Christian and Islamic traditions, Beckford cleverly transforms Milton's Satan into the Giaour, Milton's Pandaemonium into Eblis. But whereas Milton emphasizes both the internal agony of Hell's dominion ("The mind is its own place, and itself / Can make a heaven of hell, a hell of heaven," *PL* 1.254–55) and the internal relief of spiritual redemption (" . . . but shalt possess / A paradise within thee, happier far," *PL* 12.586–87), Beckford delightedly gloats over the horrifying physical torments of the (heterosexual) damned and glosses over the internal spiritual agony that must ensue when a soul is utterly separated from the divine. Beckford also parodies perhaps the most famous religious trope of Milton and seventeenth-century metaphysical poetry, the flaming heart. Beckford appropriates the flaming heart by literally rendering the passion and desire that kindle spiritual desire and Orientalizing it through one of the most famous exponents of sexual excess, Soliman ben Daoud. No longer Solomonic in wisdom and judiciousness, Soliman displays his allegiance to the Koranic, not the biblical, traditions. He had been able to conjure genii and other spirits—that was his divine gift or talent, which, like Vathek, he squanders in the service of licentiousness ("I forsook the holy city, and commanded the Genii to rear the stupendous palace of Istakar. . . . There, for a while, I enjoyed myself in the zenith of glory and pleasure," 113). Soliman's belief that his punishment is merely purgatorial underscores the scope of his torment. He deludes himself into hoping that the "cataract" will eventually cease flowing and his enflamed heart will be extinguished. Vathek and Nouronihar immediately recognize not only the horrific nature of his physical torment, but that it will eventually engulf them as well, making valueless the genii's offer of riches, banquets, and honors. More importantly, however, once the hellish flames do engulf their hearts, Beckford stresses their physical revulsion for one another (" . . . all testified their horror for each other by the most ghastly convulsions," 119). Even in Milton's Hell, Satan and the rebel angels can, in some measure, still take pleasure in their physical presence and physical transformations, which helps explain Milton's catalog of demons marching into the Hall of Pandaemonium, as well as Satan's ability to morph into a beautiful angel, the illusion of which only Ithuriel's spear can break. In Beckford's novel, Eblis becomes the imagined place of torment for his deluded tormentors, where the trappings of socially validated and culturally embraced heterosexual passion reveals itself for what it is—sexual colonialism—comprised of vacuous preaching, empty moralizing, vain consumption, and gratuitous threats to achieve worldly mastery and authority.

Interestingly, however, Beckford gives the last word in his novel not to Vathek, but to Vathek's pubescent, hyperfeminized rival, Gulchenrouz (and by extension the "good old genius" who miraculously saves him from Vathek and Carathis, as well as the fifty boys from the bloodlust of the Giaour). Beckford gleefully concludes that the "humble, the despised Gulchenrouz passed whole ages in undisturbed tranquility, and in the pure happiness of childhood" (120). Or, to paraphrase Adam Potkay, Gulchenrouz forever dwells in boy heaven. The pouty boy-consort to Princess Nouronihar escapes Vathek's vindictive whimsy and Carathis's obsession with diabolic power, but not to take his rightful and manly place as head of a kingdom and an arranged marriage. Rather, Gulchenrouz's happy fate is to consort "undisturbed" with other boy-men who may now frolic and play with Gulchenrouz, free of the very adult privileges and responsibilities that should have normally attended them. And the "good old genius" brings the boys to Roc nests "higher than the clouds" (97), where he himself "fixes" his own "abode," "in a . . . nest more capacious than the rest" (97). In the campiest (and, from the Islamic perspective, the most blasphemous) passage in the novel, Allah himself and the Prophet inscribe their names on waving streamers, flashing like lightning and guarding these pederastic but "inviolable asylums" against any magical intrusions from afrits, zombies, or Carathis's potent incantations. For his part, Gulchenrouz receives the accolades of all the boys who "vie[. . .] with each other in kissing his serene forehead and beautiful eye-lids" (97). Beckford continues: "Remote from the inquietudes of the world; the impertinence of harems, the brutality of eunuchs, and the inconstancy of women; there [Gulchenrouz] found a place truly congenial to the delights of *his* soul" (97; emphasis added). For the first time in the novel, Gulchenrouz is free to act as he wishes, and not as the result of the dubious plans of Fakreddin, the faithlessness of Nouronihar, the untrammeled and dark desires of Carathis, or Vathek's unabated search for absolute power. The "good old genius" ironically saves the other boys *from* the fires of Hell by taking them away from Vathek as he is about to make them a blood sacrifice to the Giaour. In addition, however, the "genius" removes the endangered boys from the burden and duty of propagation. They no longer have to endure a harem's "inconstant" women, nor must they face the sexual uselessness of castrated men. In carving out a niche among the Roc nests for his charges, the "good old genius" has firmly established a pederastic oasis among the clouds, a pleasant and eternal homosociety that need never confront the social and cultural exigencies of conventionally Orientalized manhood. In fact, the homoerotics of this boy heaven, its innocent attractiveness (though perhaps it might appear sinister from our contemporary perspective), lies in the boys never becoming fully sexualized, "for the genius, instead of bur-thening his pupils with perishable and vain sciences, conferred upon them the boon of perpetual childhood" (98). In the words of Adam Potkay, the novel is an antibildungsroman, with Beckford's boy heaven becoming "an allegory of infancy" that always and everywhere preempts the unavoidable dissatisfactions that come with adult maturity, in particular sexual segrega-tion and propriety (301).

Diego Saglia points to Beckford's heaven of boys as an Orientalist simu-lacrum, in which "actual and imaginary orients intersect in a nexus of real-ity and fiction, legality, desire and visual attraction, [are] all encapsulated in Beckford's observation 'I have still sparks of Orientalism about me to catch fire at such a sight'"(80). But this simulacrum exhibits slippage even as it feigns representational and moral fixity. Beckford uses this simula-crum to construct his Orientalized queerness, a refuge for his homoerotic desire (and submerged pederasty). Beckford's readership accepts his outra-geous campiness because camp often underlies the Gothic, as it does in the works of Matthew Lewis, Ann Radcliffe, or Charlotte Dacre, and because the Gothic is ultimately a conservative genre, often confirming a culture's ethological underpinnings even as it appears to explode them. Beckford can, therefore, easily hide his homoerotics—his "sparks of Orientalism"—in plain sight because he aligns the fate of his title character with the conven-tions and expectations of most eighteenth- and nineteenth-century literary figures who truck with the sexually satanic. In other words, despite the resemblances between Vathek and Beckford, it would be a mistake to equate them. The man who in his letters salaciously refers to his boy servants by wicked epithets—"Pale Ambrose," "Cadaverous Nicobuse," "Miss Long," "Miss Butterfly," "Countess Pox," or "Mr. Prudent Well-Sealed Up" (Norton, 2)—can hardly be said to rue his homoerotic/pederastic passions or truly identify with Vathek's doom. After his return to England from an exile originally urged by a family terrified of scandal (but perhaps equally upset that they would receive no peerage), Beckford, though married and a father, still aspires to the status of the "good old genius" in the novel of his youth. Dwelling within the panoptic fortress of Fonthill and free from prying scrutiny, Beckford magnanimously reviews his Orientalized estates, at the head of women whose fear of public exposure and ridicule makes them ulti-mately complicit with his psychosexual proclivities, and in charge of a large group of boy servants who incarnate his fictional male harem. In a very real sense, Beckford's own guiltless and shameless terrestrial paradise is, mutatis mutandis, the "heaven of boys" in Vathek.

Robert Mack may be right when he suggests that "Homosexual writers are at home in the oriental tale . . . it is a place to be free of the restrictions of the mundane realism tied to the demands of the market-place and the goings on of 'real' society" (xvii). But *Vathek* is no mere escapist fantasy that briefly distracts the reader from the exigencies of the world and its commercial realities. Nor is its Orientalism the exuberant screen through which Beckford secretes his tragic sexual identity; or, as El Habib Benrahhal Serghini likens it, "Beckford's orientalism has permitted the self to show off its glories, but it has also linked the luxuriance of surface with the sad opulence of the condemned soul" (63). Rather, Beckford's Orientalist tale not only reifies the moralistic expectations inherent to much eighteenth- and nineteenth-century Oriental literature, it also cheerfully undermines them by refusing to acknowledge sexual perversion, licentiousness, or personal embarrassment of any kind. That Beckford may have embraced his own pederastic desires makes him challenging to critics who wish to recontextualize him within a more manageable heterosexist ideology. They then can more readily pass comfortable (and comforting) moral judgments, and critics frequently do so because the "chilling" (to use Haggerty's word) homoerotics of Beckford's writing makes many heterosexual readers uneasy, calling into question any encoded prescriptions about sexuality or the identity politics of the social and cultural status quo. Beckford's Orientalist homoerotics perhaps even threaten the legitimacy of such readers to pass these judgments. In the end, however, the novel may just as easily make gay readers queasy because it shamelessly conflates pederasty and homosexuality, an absolute distinction that activists have recently gone to great lengths to make in order to establish, to the extent possible, a mainstream sexual politics that permits gay men a place at the table (to use Bruce Bawer's clichéd phrase). Long gone are the pre-AIDS, sexual outlawry of John Rechy; the shocking yet titillating fetishism of leather queens; and the winking presence of NAMBLA (North American Man-Boy Love Association) in gay pride parades. Now "queers" find themselves in the astonishing position of recommending lifestyle changes to hapless heterosexual men, of making them over, of transforming them into better and improved versions of their own masculinity. As a result, being mainstreamed means rejecting any kind of separation, especially a sexual separation that promises or justifies pedophilic play within the fantastic landscapes that Beckford conjures. Being mainstreamed signifies normalization, a jettisoning of the closeted but fanciful ghettoes contained by Orientalized discourse. Heterosexual and homosexual readers of *Vathek* thus find themselves ironically bound and committed to an ideology that uncovers Beckford's presumed psychosexual guilt within the text, for without this shame, Beckford's heaven of boys becomes the panicked, postmodern hell of liberals.

✿

NOTES

1. Adrienne McLean makes this case in her essay "The Thousand Ways There Are to Move: Camp and Oriental Dance in the Hollywood Musicals of Jack Cole." McLean cites the important work of Michael Moon, who also makes use of Said's *Orientalism*, in order to argue that despite the campy flamboyancy of Orientalist representations, Orientalism is homophobic because it fixes homosexuality within a heterosexist system, rendering it powerless within such a dominant paradigm. In his work "Flaming Closets," Moon connects the subjugating practices of Orientalism to racist sexual fantasies in which "masters" can freely couple with "the dominated bodies of others" (58).

2. In an unwittingly amusing application of Freudian theory, Brian Fothergill writes that Beckford's trip to Switzerland had quite failed to instill "manly attributes" (62). Indeed, Fothergill melodramatically continues, "Even worse was happening . . . in the city where Calvin's shadow seemed to offer so little protection against the temptations of the world and the flesh if not of the very Devil himself; for by the shores of the lake of Geneva [Beckford's mother's] son found himself involved in a romantic entanglement with another youth" (62). For Fothergill, the problem is not that Beckford had a homosexual dalliance but that "the intensity of his responses to any stimulation of the senses, be it personal or artistic in origin," never diminishes. Beckford assigns too much emotional meaning "to what was in reality no more than an adolescent infatuation" (63). The tragedy of being eternally stuck in a homosexual phase also occurs to Robert Gemmett as well, for in his description of Beckford's relationship to Courtenay, Gemmett reluctantly affirms the hermeneutic circle between Beckford's life and his book: "It is the frustration of this great effort in the Kingdom of Eblis that provides the best image of Beckford, the artist-voluptuary, who, subjected inexorably to the furies of time and reason, must witness a failure of imagination and the ultimate collapse of his palace of art" (117). Even much more recent readings of Vathek rely on the absolute identity between Beckford's psychology and Vathek's retributive fate. Sounding much like Ernest Bernbaum, Marilyn Gaull writes, "But just as the ending, a conventional one of symbolic retribution, conflicted with the novel itself, so Beckford's conventional side—the one who would marry the loyal and agreeable Lady Margaret Gordon, serve in Parliament, and father two daughters who were devoted to him—seemed constantly in conflict with the *deviate*" (234–35; emphasis added). In "Beckford's Paederasty," George E. Haggerty more explicitly ties Beckford's life with the horrifying end of Vathek in Eblis: "[Beckford] grappled throughout his life with a sexual instinct that made him a criminal in his own desire" (137). Eric Meyer views *Vathek* in postcolonial terms, whereby Beckford embodies the colonized East and the imperial West: "The structure of narrative in *Vathek* . . . closely approximates Teresa de Lauretis's Oedipal paradigm, although with a more obviously politically overdetermined subtext: the Orient becomes a feminized passive object that is subject to male desire . . ." (668). Vathek becomes, in this view, the Orientalist penetrator who is himself penetrated or "subject to male desire."

CHAPTER 6

Orientalism in Disraeli's *Alroy*

SHEILA A. SPECTOR

Alroy is usually dismissed as the only "Jewish" novel written by Benjamin Disraeli (1804–1881). It is true that as a fictionalized account of the failed twelfth-century messiah, David Alroy, *The Wondrous Tale of Alroy* is probably the first Jewish historical novel[1]; however, the action is set in the Middle East, and the conflict is between the Jews and various West Asian tribes, in the period between the first two Crusades, before the Ottomans consolidated the Turkish Empire. Consequently, to ignore the presence of Orientalism in the novel is to overlook not only an important component of the book Disraeli would write while deciding to enter politics, but equally as important, to miss significant information about his decision to become a Tory several years later, and his conduct of Britain's foreign policy when he served as prime minister, not to mention the part he played in the purchase of the Suez Canal. Therefore, in order to understand the full implications of this underestimated novel, it is necessary to place the central conflict between Jew and Muslim in the broader context that goes by the name of Orientalism, that is, the Western version of the relationship between the Christians and the so-called infidels of the East.[2]

The political implications of Disraeli's other fiction have long been recognized. Although his initial forays into politics (1832, 1834, and 1835) were unsuccessful, in 1837, Disraeli switched parties and was elected Tory MP for Maidstone, and then in 1841 for Shrewsbury. With the change of government, however, he would be out of office for most of the early 1840s; but in 1847, he was elected Tory MP for Buckinghamshire, an office he would hold until 1876. During that period, he would rise through the ranks, eventually to become prime minister, first from February to December 1868, and then again from February 1874 until April 1880, when he was defeated in a general election and resigned. While out of office in the early 1840s, Disraeli worked out the "Young England" policies that he would pursue when he returned to government, and part of his thinking process was accomplished through his composition of the so-called "Young England" trilogy—*Coningsby* (1844), *Sybil* (1845), and *Tancred* (1847)—a series of novels that present his political theories in a fictionalized form.[3]

As with these novels, *Alroy* should also be viewed as a component of Disraeli's political thought, and therefore, should be approached from the perspective of its broader cultural context, particularly regarding Britain's attitude toward the Middle East and the Jews in the early nineteenth century.[4] Not surprisingly, Napoleon was the catalyst for British involvement in the Middle East. Hoping both to glorify a blatant attempt to establish a sphere of influence in the area, and to gain the financial assistance of supposedly wealthy and influential Jews, in 1799 Napoleon proclaimed his intention of restoring the Jews to their homeland. Although he would be stopped by British naval forces at Acre, Napoleon's incursion into Palestine would have two lasting effects: the British would from that time on have a military base in the area; and they would appropriate Jewish Zionism as a justification for their own imperial aspirations in the Middle East.

Not simply a facet of foreign policy, Zionism had a significant role in the consolidation of British nationalism as well. Dating back to the sixteenth century, the English had defined themselves as a Protestant, and hence, a tolerant nation, as opposed to the intolerant Roman Catholic countries that had fostered the Inquisition. By the second half of the eighteenth century, however, the British had been confronted by their own hypocrisy, in the anti-Semitic and anti-Catholic riots of 1753 and 1780, respectively. In 1800, with the Act of Union that incorporated Ireland into Great Britain, it would be only a matter of time—twenty-nine years, to be precise—before the Catholics would be emancipated. But while Englishmen might consider it acceptable to shift the national identity from a Protestant to a more generalized Christian orientation, many felt that emancipation of the Jews would threaten the fundamental religious identity of the country. As a compromise, they turned to Zionism as a political expedient, establishing the Palestine Association in 1804, with the mission of exploring the Holy Land, and, if possible, of exporting the "Jewish problem" to the Middle East where, it was assumed, the Jews would live under the protection of the British. Thus, British imperialism and nationalism could both be served by Zionism.

Religious support came from the evangelical movements that proliferated in response to the French Revolution.[5] Believing that the apocalypse was at hand, millenarians considered the return of the Jews to the Holy Land and their conversion to Christianity an indispensable prerequisite to the Second Coming. These fundamentalists formalized their interest in 1809, with the establishment of the London Society for Promoting Christianity amongst the Jews. Although far from successful in persuading the Jews to abandon their faith, the evangelicals were instrumental in persuading the British government to establish a consulate in Jerusalem in 1838, the basis through which the British would expand their sphere of influence under Victoria, in preparation for their role in the political Zionist movement of the twentieth century.[6]

Disraeli's biography and, concomitantly, his politics, were to a large extent determined by this history. As a third-generation Englishman, Disraeli was raised in a fully assimilated family, his father, Isaac D'Israeli, being a writer who, if not rated among the best, was certainly one of the most prolific, and who counted Byron and Scott among his admirers.[7] After the death of his own father, Isaac baptized Benjamin, as well as his other three children, to afford them all the educational and political opportunities he himself had been denied because of his faith. For Benjamin, this meant that he could—although he did not—attend university, and later, that he could stand for political office. Even though he was eligible, still the decision to enter politics was complicated by his ethnicity, for despite the fact that he remained a professing Anglican throughout his life, political opponents still attacked him with anti-Semitic slurs. Thus, the "Young England" trilogy, in addition to working out his political policies, was also the vehicle through which Disraeli tried to accommodate his Protestant faith with his Jewish heritage; and before that, at the point when he decided to enter politics, he used *Alroy*, among other things, to justify his conversion to Christianity.[8]

From the political perspective, *Alroy,* written in the late 1820s and early 1830s, can be viewed as part of the process through which Disraeli decided to enter politics. According to popular opinion, the young Disraeli was little more than an opportunistic dilettante. After writing a series of "silver fork" society novels in the 1820s, in 1830–31, he toured Spain, the Mediterranean, and the Near East.[9] Upon his return, in 1831, he published *The Young Duke;* in 1832, he published *Contarini Fleming* and twice lost Wycombe; in 1833, he published *Alroy* and *The Rise of Iskander* together; in 1834, he published "a new edition" of *Alroy*, and again lost Wycombe; in 1835, he lost Taunton, and published *Vindication of the English Constitution,* a political treatise; in 1836, he published *Henrietta Temple;* in 1837, he published *Venetia*, and he switched parties and won as a Tory. To many of his detractors, Disraeli's novel writing undermined his seriousness as a politician. In addition, his conversion to Conservatism and almost simultaneous publication of his *Vindication of the English Constitution*—an argument in favor of retaining Britain's constitutionally established relationship between church and state—were viewed as craven attempts to curry favor with the dominant party. To some, Disraeli's shift suggested that he had sacrificed political integrity for election. However, when *Alroy* is read from the perspective of his *Vindication of the English Constitution,* Disraeli's choice is revealed to have been much more thoughtful and principled than he has been given credit for. Specifically, in *Alroy,* he uses the Middle East as a kind of negative laboratory in which to explore the deleterious effects of a government that could not be predicated on the kinds of principles laid out in the *Vindication.*[10]

Historically, from the sixteenth century on, the strength and dominance of the British Empire had been attributed largely to the constitutionally established relationship between throne and altar.[11] When the Tudors first broke with Rome, their propagandists touted the superiority of the home-grown religion over the Church of Rome, whose pomp and mystery, it was said, usurped the role of the national government. In time, certainly by the end of the eighteenth century, the British had become fairly well convinced that their strength lay to a great extent in their national church, to which many attributed their defeat of Napoleon in 1815. Still, with the repeal of the Test and Corporation Acts in 1828 and Catholic emancipation in 1829, the hegemony of Anglicanism was threatened, leading latitudinarians to demand religious equality for all denominations. In their most extreme forms, the utilitarians would demand that the relationship between church and state be disestablished entirely, while the "Oxford Tractarians" would advocate returning Anglicanism to its high-church, that is, Catholic origins.

Disraeli addressed both of these positions in his *Vindication of the English Constitution,* arguing that the unique relationship between the government and the Anglican Church was an essential component of British identity. Refocusing the debate away from the more conventional perspective of an argument between high church and low, Disraeli approached the question politically, demonstrating how neither form of government advocated by reformers was viable. On the one hand, a theocracy would deteriorate into zealous tyranny, while on the other, a purely secular government would degenerate into amoral utilitarianism. As the golden mean, England's representative Protestant government, according to Disraeli, avoided the dangers of both extremes. Being a Protestant form of government, Anglicanism had liberated itself from the external control of Rome, and being directed by representatives from the entire country, the church could respond to the changing needs of the people. Beyond that, because the church did have a constitutional relationship with the government, religion could be used to help the English generate what Disraeli called their "sovereign principle," that sense of patriotism through which the aggregate of peoples populating Great Britain could be consolidated into a single empire.[12] As an early attempt to explore these ideas, *Alroy* displaces the political theory onto a historical episode culled from Jewish history.

The historical record upon which Disraeli predicated his novel is fairly sparse.[13] One Menahem b. Solomon, born in the twelfth century during the time of the Crusades, was a charismatic leader who convinced his followers, and, it seems likely, himself, that he was the messiah. Changing his name to David Al-Ro'i to imply an association with the House of David, Alroy gathered the Jews of Kurdistan in an attempt to defeat the Seljuk Turks, conquer Edessa, and, finally, the Holy Land. Although he gained an initial following, in time many became disenchanted and, according to one report, his father-in-law was eventually bribed to assassinate him. Disraeli was first attracted to what we now know to be a spurious account, found in David Ben Solomon Gans (1541–1613), *Zemah David* (*Offspring of David*, Prague, 1592). As Disraeli quotes Gans in the novel's last footnote, Alroy, when captured by the Muslims, is supposed to have claimed that as messiah, he would rise again after death, thus hoping to provoke his beheading, rather than be slowly and painfully eviscerated, as was the more usual practice.

In his novel, Disraeli transplants the Jewish tale onto a truncated version of the British national myth, as generated by the Tudor historians and consolidated most notably by Spenser in the first book of *The Faerie Queene*. Spenser's allegory has the linear structure of a quest myth, in which the inexperienced hero undergoes a series of tests that prepare him for the ultimate moral *agon* in which good defeats evil and, as a reward, the hero marries the beautiful heroine, symbolizing the regeneration of his society. In the explicitly Protestant *Faerie Queene,* the Red Crosse Knight (the true Christian hero) volunteers to rescue Adam and Eve from the Dragon (Original Sin), his prize being marriage to the beautiful Una (the true church). On his quest, he must confront Archimago, the evil magician (hypocrisy), who tempts Red Crosse with Fidessa/Duessa (the false faith). Although he follows Duessa to the House of Pride, Red Crosse eventually recognizes his error and escapes, ultimately to arrive at the House of Holiness, where he is schooled to the true faith. Morally strengthened, he is then able to rescue Adam and Eve, unmask Archimago, and having chased off Duessa, marry Una. In Disraeli's inversion of the myth, Alroy undergoes the same process as the Red Crosse Knight; however, lacking the true Protestant faith, his stint at the House of Holiness—the moribund Jerusalem of the twelfth century—cannot provide the armor necessary for his ultimate *agon* against the evil Turks, and as a result, Alroy's spiritual progress is stunted, as he succumbs to the hypocrisy of his Archimago and marries his version of Duessa. Instead of regenerating his society, he thus places his entire empire in jeopardy, concluding not with the victory of good over evil, but with the triumph of the Muslim infidel over the feckless Jew.

As a microcosm of the novel as a whole, the first part delineates the procedure by which Disraeli would imply by its absence the need for a representative Protestant form of government. Both initiating and foreshadowing the further development of the novel, the section involves the confrontation between the Jewish hero and Turkish villain, each depicted from the perspective of the Christian myth: Alroy with good intentions, but without the moral fortitude of the true Christian; and Alschiroch as the Christian transformation of the Muslim into the apotheosis of evil. As the Jewish hero, Alroy is depicted as a good man whose potential is limited. In contrast to Red Crosse, Alroy, who can only dream of restoring the House of David, seems incapable of initiating the action. He is loath to assume his responsibilities as "prince of the captivity," and instead of opposing the Turks, he abdicates to his uncle the obligation to pay tribute, and he stays away from the national festival. After he has wandered off, Hamlet-like, outside the gates of the city, he is taunted by Alschiroch, and soon thereafter, when Alschiroch physically attacks Alroy's sister Miriam, Alroy defends his sister and slays the villain. In Spenser's version, the Red Crosse Knight is inexperienced and naive; yet, he has faith that his quest is just and that he will triumph. In contrast, Alroy, who is more intellectual than his Spenserian prototype, is passive, reacting to external threats but not really acting on his dream of a restored Jewish kingdom. Conversely, Alschiroch, Alroy's antagonist, is the epitome of the Orientalized villain, that is, a Muslim on whom the characteristics of the British stereotype of evil has been imposed.

In this initial conflict, Disraeli conflates several versions of a common trope of Middle Eastern culture, the slaying of an unjust overseer, an action that forces the insubordinate to flee his home. In Exodus (2:11–15), Moses slays an Egyptian who is beating a Hebrew, and fearing retribution, flees to Midian, where he receives his call. In a Persian version, one Shirkuh I b. Ayyub Abu Salah al-Din ("the lion of the mountain"; ca. 1169), the uncle of Saladin, slew a high-born man who had insulted an unprotected female. As a result, both Saladin and his uncle were forced to flee to Egypt (Malcolm, 1:379). In *Alroy*, Disraeli retains the sexual attack of the Persian version, but inverts its tenor, transforming the heroic Shirkuh into the lascivious bully, Alschiroch, and displacing the heroic defense onto the Jew. In this way, he can simultaneously amplify Alroy's heroism and demonize the infidel.

Disraeli's account of the incident is replete with cultural stereotypes. In this first part of the novel, the hero has wandered off to the tomb of Esther and Mordecai, when he hears some shouting:

He looked up, and recognised the youthful and voluptuous Alschiroch, the governor of the city, and brother of the sultan of the Seljuks. He was attended only by a single running footman, an Arab, a detested favourite, and notorious minister of his pleasures.

"Dog!" exclaimed the irritated Alschiroch, "art thou deaf, or obstinate, or both? Are we to call twice to our slaves? Unlock that gate!"

"Wherefore?" inquired Alroy.

"Wherefore! By the holy Prophet he bandies questions with us! Unlock that gate, or thy head shall answer for it!"

"Who art thou," inquired Alroy, "whose voice is so loud? Art thou some holiday Turk, who hath transgressed the orders of thy Prophet, and drunken aught but water? Go to, or I will summon thee before thy Cadi;" and, so saying, he turned towards the tomb.

"By the eyes of my mother, the dog jeers us! But that we are already late, and this horse is like an untamed tiger, I would impale him on the spot. Speak to the dog, Mustapha! manage him!"

About an hour later, Alroy passes by the fountain where a group of maidens is making the daily oblations. Their songs in praise of God are interrupted: "A scream, a shriek, a long wild shriek, confusion, flight, despair! Behold! from out the woods a turbaned man rushes, and seizes the leader of the chorus. Her companions fly on all sides, Miriam alone is left in the arms of Alschiroch." Finally, Alroy acts.

In this opening episode, Disraeli attributes to the Turk most of the negative qualities the British associated with the Oriental antagonist. Alschiroch is vain, arrogant, proud, vicious, likely gluttonous and greedy; he abuses his authority, probably violates Muslim injunctions against alcohol, and, most of all, he is lecherous, attacking not just any women, but votaries performing their evening oblations. Thus, Disraeli provides a muted version of the anticipated idealized dénouement: the hero has slain the villain in defense of the girl. Like Moses before him, he will flee to the wilderness where he will be schooled in his obligations to his people. In contrast to the British prototype, however, his text will be the Old Testament, not the New; as a result, as Disraeli's Christian audience would anticipate, although Alroy might have easily disposed of the governor of the city, he will never be capable of defeating Alschiroch's brother, the Turkish sultan.

Despite this early victory, Disraeli emphasizes in the next section the fact that Alroy is decidedly not a Christ figure and, therefore, is destined to fail. Emulating the Jewish prototype, Alroy flees to the wilderness where he is schooled by his teacher, Jabaster, explicitly identified as a Kabbalist.

Although not explained in the text, the narrator/author includes a footnote that differentiates between the Christian prototype emulated by Red Crosse, and Alroy's Jewish antecedent, the failed messiah Bar Kokhba (mid-second century CE). Citing William Enfield's *History of Philosophy* (which is misidentified as *Philosophy of the Jews*), the narrator explicitly foreshadows Alroy's ultimate failure:

> the famous impostor Barchochebas, who, under the character of the Messiah, promised to deliver his countrymen from the power of the Emperor Adrian. Akibha espoused his cause, and afforded him the protection and support of his name, and an army of two hundred thousand men repaired to his standard. The Romans at first slighted the insurrection; but when they found the insurgents spread slaughter and rapine wherever they came, they sent out a military force against them. At first, the issue of the contest was doubtful. The Messiah himself was not taken until the end of four years. (Author's note 10)[14]

The association with the biblical Zealots by implication characterizes Jabaster in terms of those contemporary religious fundamentalists who wish to make England a strict theocracy. To complicate matters, Jabaster himself had earlier entertained fantasies of being the messiah, and although he has accepted the reality of his own limitations, he is still jealous of Alroy, whose leadership he will ultimately challenge and undermine.

What is portrayed as the inadequacy of Alroy's Jewish education is revealed in his first adventure. Like the inexperienced Red Crosse Knight, Alroy encounters his own version of the Cave of Error, and triumphing with an easy victory, he overestimates his ability to complete his task, leaving himself vulnerable to Archimago, the evil magician. Specifically, having been instructed on his messianic mission and having been given the talismanic ring by Jabaster, Alroy is told to

> Follow the track of the caravan, he was to make his way to Babylon, or Bagdad. From the capital of the caliphs, his journey to Jerusalem was one comparatively easy; but to reach Bagdad he must encounter hardship and danger, the prospect of which would have divested any one of hope, who did not conceive himself the object of an omnipotent and particular Providence. (4:1)

Like the Red Crosse Knight, Alroy chooses the beaten path, in this case the well-traveled caravan route, admiring the sights: "A magnificent city, of an architecture with which he was unacquainted" (followed by detailed description); and as "He gaze[s] with wonder and admiration upon the strange and fascinating scene" (4:1), he is captured by a multicultural group of bandits, including an Islamic Kurd, a Zoroastrian Persian, a Buddhist Indian, a godless African, and their leader, the half-Jewish half-Islamic Scherirah. The one thing these Orientals have in common is that they hate Christians: "[W]e are all against them" (4:4).

More like Enfield's description of the Zealots than Robin Hood's band of merry men, these brigands are all antisocial outlaws, flouting the religious and ethnic customs of their birth, ready to kill Alroy except for Scherirah's sentimental attachment to his mother, for which reason Scherirah makes Alroy his blood brother, promising: "'My troth is pledged,' said the bandit; 'I can never betray him in whose veins my own blood is flowing'" (4:3). By this point, only Alroy is naive enough to believe that the immoral outlaw will honor his pledge. Like Red Crosse's encounter with Error, Alroy overestimates his judgment, leaving him vulnerable for future betrayals. Still, he does have enough presence of mind to escape from the outlaws as soon as he can.

From there, in part 5, Alroy is brought to his House of Pride, by "the Mecca caravan returning to Bagdad" (5:1), where he meets his Archimago— Honain, physician to the caliph, and, it turns out, brother to Jabaster. Like the Spenserian prototype, Honain is actually an amoral hypocrite, in this case a crypto-Jew, who attempts to undermine Alroy's faith with sermons on religious relativism and utilitarianism, and tempts him sexually with an introduction to the novel's Duessa, Schirene. Comparable to the process followed with Alschiroch, Disraeli transforms the Persian Shereen, symbol of "all that is beautiful and delightful in the female sex" (Malcolm, 1:162), into Schirene, the Oriental siren. As the half-Christian half-Muslim daughter of the caliph, Schirene (Duessa/Fidessa) lives in a lavish palace, has exquisite clothes, is stunningly beautiful, but slothfully bored, having nothing to do with her time except read the Persian poetry Honain provides her. Ostensibly serving as her physician, Honain panders her to whatever military leader is victorious at a particular time. For now, it is Alp Arslan, the king of the Karasmé, the up-and-coming tribe of Turks destined to defeat the Seljuks. Still, hedging his bets, Honain introduces Alroy to Schirene, just in case the messianic prophecy actually does come true.

At this, the low point of *The Faerie Queene*, the Red Crosse Knight finds himself completely under the spell of the duplicitous Duessa. However, learning from the instinctive dwarf the truth about the House of Pride, Red Crosse escapes, to begin his long journey of spiritual regeneration in preparation for the ultimate battle. As a Jew, Alroy lacks the intuitions represented by the Christian dwarf. Instead, obeying Honain's instructions, he himself assumes the disguise of a deaf-mute eunuch, and having thus subverted both his senses and his manhood, he finds himself powerless to resist the allure of Schirene. After he reverts to his masculine state, he recognizes the dangers inherent in the Orientalized version of the House of Pride, and he resumes his journey. However, in contrast to Red Crosse, his is a retrograde quest, leading backward to the Tomb of Solomon, as opposed to forward to the Protestant House of Holiness.

In contrast to Spenser's House of Holiness, symbol of the true Protestant faith, twelfth-century Jerusalem is depicted as a destitute slum, the perfect setting for what Christians considered the moribund remnant of an atavistic faith that rejects the new dispensation. Lacking the necessary Christian virtues, the old Jews just keep reworking the same old texts, marveling at specious nonsense, like "Hillel proves that there are two Tombs of the Kings, . . . and that neither of them are the right ones"; or "The first chapter makes equal sense, read backward or forward" (6:3). Their synagogue is located beneath a cemetery, and when an African pilgrim poses a riddle to the congregation, no one can solve it, not even the rabbi. In a fairly overt allusion to the Jews' refusal to accept the Divinity of Christ, no one, except the pilgrim, recognizes that Alroy is the messiah, and when the African indicates that he wishes to talk, an old Jew holds Alroy back, thus replicating, from the Christian perspective, the Jewish rejection of Christ. Alroy must leave both the city and its people before he can be transported to the Temple, where he gains the scepter of Solomon, symbol of his election.

Thanks to his sojourn at the House of Holiness, Red Crosse progresses to the point where he is capable of completing his mission as the Christian knight: after a three-day battle, he defeats the dragon and liberates Adam and Eve; and he returns home betrothed to Una. At the wedding, Archimago arrives with a letter falsely claiming that Red Crosse is already betrothed to Fidessa/Duessa, but Archimago is revealed for the hypocrite he is and is thrown in a dungeon; and Duessa, having been revealed for the hag she is, has run away. Still, although the ceremony is completed, Red Crosse cannot stay home because, as the Christian knight, he must complete his work in preparation for the Second Coming. As a Jew, Alroy is denied this option, and his attempt to consolidate his empire is doomed to failure. Not only will its zealous religious base refuse to adapt to contemporary exigencies, but also his untrustworthy Muslim connections will betray him to Alp Arslan.

Once he has gained the sceptre of Solomon, Alroy attempts to establish a Jewish empire, though his efforts, as part 7 demonstrates, are doomed to failure because they will be undermined by Jabaster's zealotry. In order to defeat the Turks, Alroy consolidates a multicultural army, including Jabaster and the Jews, as supported by Esther the prophetess, but also requiring the assistance of Scherirah and his band of ethnically diverse mercenaries without whom, it is emphasized, the Jews would have been defeated. Still, Alroy does attempt to fulfill his religious obligations, as the detailed description of the Sabbath in chapter 16 indicates; and the religious devotion pays off, as the easy route to Bagdad seems to indicate. Yet, despite the apparent triumph, the account is strewn with indications that the religious crusade will fail.

To begin with, Jabaster's troops cannot hold their own, and require Scherirah's support during battle. In addition, Jabaster, like Bar Kokhba a millennium earlier, intends to return to Jerusalem where he will reestablish the biblical kingdom. As for Esther, as long as she believes Alroy will follow Jabaster's lead, her prophecies are encouraging. However, when she suspects that he will, instead, go to Bagdad, her omens turn ominous. Significantly, even though Alroy requires the aid of non-Jewish soldiers, Jabaster and his followers still advocate a strict theocracy that will deny equal rights to those of other faiths. Alroy's own instinct is to institute a British-style government, with a constitutionally established religion but with religious freedom for others. As soon as Alroy conquers the Seljuks, he attempts to guarantee the emir of Bagdad protection for all Muslims:

> "Noble emir," replied Alroy, "return to Bagdad, and tell your fellow-subjects that the King of Israel grants protection to their persons, and security to their property."
>
> "And for their faith?" enquired the emir, in a lower voice.
>
> "Toleration," replied Alroy, turning to Jabaster.

But the words are no sooner out of his mouth than Jabaster adds the proviso: "Until further regulations" (7:18). When Jabaster pressures for the appointment of his own partisans, that is, religious zealots, to high posts in the government, Alroy resists: "I'll have no dreamers in authority. I must have practical men about me, practical men" (8:1). Alroy's problem, from a British perspective, is that without a representative Protestant government, in which throne determines the appropriate role of altar, Jabaster has no compunction about confronting Alroy with alternative interpretations of the religious imperative. The conflict comes to a head when Alroy and Jabaster argue over the fate of some Jewish soldiers who have desecrated mosques. Jabaster has freed them, despite Alroy's belief that they should be hanged. Although Alroy advocates what Disraeli will identify as the primary strength of the established church, its ability to evolve and adapt to the exigencies of the time, the stiff-necked Jabaster remains mired in an ancient, apparently obsolete religion, becoming so zealous that he plots subversion and assassination.

Without a solid Jewish base of support, Alroy turns away from Jabaster and toward the pragmatic Honain. Comparable, in effect, to the Red Crosse Knight's turning to Archimago for advice, the shift from Jabaster to his brother Honain reflects the ultimate loss of judgment that will cost Alroy everything, including his empire, his family, and his life. As a crypto-Jew pretending to be a Muslim, Honain is the apotheosis of danger represented by the Oriental villain: he is extremely intelligent and highly educated, but he is also wily and duplicitous, and ultimately pragmatic and utilitarian. Without any true loyalty to anything or anyone other than himself, he cannot be trusted. Unfortunately, lacking any other alternative, Alroy places his faith in Honain.

If his reliance in Honain is equivalent to Red Crosse's turning to Archimago, Alroy's marriage to Schirene is tantamount to having Red Crosse reject Una in favor of Duessa, the Whore of Babylon. While still in the process of consolidating his Jewish empire, Alroy is supported by Esther, the prophetess, whose omens all support his endeavors. Obvious to everyone except for Alroy, who seems too obtuse to realize the truth, Esther is in love with the Jewish messiah, and from a narrowly sectarian perspective, she would make the ideal wife. However, Alroy is not in love with her, and once he chooses Schirene, Esther's prophecies turn dark, as she warns him of the dire consequences to follow. Ironically, she is right, for she herself will attempt to kill him. Still, given the ease with which her prophecies alter to conform to her love life, her visions seem to be instigated less by divine inspiration than by sexual desire, and as was the case with Jabaster before her, Alroy is left to rely on his own flawed judgment.

Yet, in marrying Schirene, Alroy gradually actualizes the disguise of deaf-mute eunuch he had assumed on his symbolic visit to his House of Pride. After his initial thoughts about shifting his trust from Jabaster to Honain, Alroy wanders around his newly conquered palace, and recognizing it from the earlier visit, decides to disguise himself and explore further:

> Could I but reach the private portal by the river side, unseen or undetected! 'Tis not impossible. Here are many dresses. I will disguise myself. Trusty scimetar, thou hast done thy duty, rest awhile. 'Tis lucky I am beardless. I shall make a capital eunuch. So! a handsome robe. One dagger for a pinch, slippers powdered with pearls, a caftan of cloth of gold, a Cashmere girdle, and a pelisse of sables. One glance at the mirror. Good! I begin to look like the conqueror of the world! (8:1)

Quite literally unsexing himself again, he dons the eunuch's wardrobe, and in the very next scene, he encounters Schirene. Having already fallen in love with her, he does not take long to propose marriage, thus alienating Jabaster and other Jewish supporters. The courtship and marriage seem taken straight from the Oriental literature prevalent at the time. Schirene is not only beautiful, but she is intelligent and talented, and the "marriage between the King of the Hebrews and the Princess of Bagdad," which takes almost ten pages to describe, would seem to confirm the narrator's apparent exuberance:

> Now what a glorious man was David Alroy, lord of the mightiest empire in the world, and wedded to the most beautiful princess, surrounded by a prosperous and obedient people, guarded by invincible armies, one on whom Earth showered all its fortune, and Heaven all its favour; and all by the power of his own genius! (8:8)

Only most of that is untrue. The people were neither prosperous nor obedient; the army would prove neither invincible nor loyal; Alroy possessed the favor of neither earth nor heaven; and certainly, his accomplishments had not resulted strictly from his own genius. Instead, as the remaining ninety pages of the novel will demonstrate, lacking the true faith, the feckless Jewish messiah will inevitably be brought down by the perfidious Turks. Lacking a "sovereign principle," his empire will disintegrate.

The last two sections of the novel trace the unraveling of Alroy's empire. Jabaster's zealots, realizing that Alroy will never reestablish the Jewish kingdom in Jerusalem, with the help of Scherirah, the mercenary whose loyalty to his blood brother lasted about as long as it took him to make the original pledge, plot sedition. Without his Jewish base, Alroy is forced to rely on the Muslim faction under the leadership of Honain. True to her Spenserian prototype and Oriental stereotype, Schirene's loyalty was not to her husband, but to her hypocritical adviser, so she persuaded Alroy to relinquish the royal seal so that Honain could murder his brother, the only viable threat to his own power. Honain and Schirene then join up with Alp Arslan, her original suitor and, as the king of the Karasmé, the Turk destined to defeat Alroy. The two of them claim that, as an unwilling concubine, Schirene had no choice but to marry Alroy, having been seduced by his witchcraft. After Alroy is captured, Honain tries to manipulate him into confirming her story publicly, so that the marriage can be annulled and she will be free to marry Alp Arslan. At the public trial, however, Alroy, like a tragic hero who has experienced a cathartic recognition of his flaws, proclaims, instead, his Jewish identity:

> King of Karasmé! I stand here accused, of many crimes. Now hear my answers. 'Tis said I am a rebel. My answer is, I am a Prince as thou art, of a sacred race, and far more ancient. I owe fealty to no one but to my God, and

if I have broken that I am yet to learn that Alp Arslan is the avenger of His power. As for thy God and Prophet, I know not them, though they acknowledge mine. 'Tis well understood in every polity, my people stand apart from other nations, and ever will, in spite of suffering. . . . I raised the standard of my faith by the direct commandment of my God, the great Creator of the universe. My magic was His inspiration. . . . The time will come when from out our ancient seed, a worthier chief will rise, not to be quelled even by thee, Sire. (10:22)

Needless to say, the Turks judge him a sorcerer; so rather than show penitence, Alroy provokes Alp Arslan, claiming that if killed, he will rise again. Enraged, the Turk "took off the head of Alroy at a stroke. It fell, and, as it fell, a smile of triumphant derision seemed to play upon the dying features of the hero, and to ask of his enemies, 'Where now are all your tortures?'" (10:22). With this conclusion, Alroy assumes the only role open to the pre-Protestant hero: though defeated, he has still outsmarted the dull-witted infidel.

When read from the perspective of Orientalism, *Alroy* helps clarify British Middle Eastern policy during the nineteenth century, especially as it led up to Anglo-American attitudes of the twentieth. "The Great Game," as the original policy begun before 1829 was known, was designed to protect India by supporting the Ottoman Empire as a buffer to prevent Russia from making inroads into Afghanistan.[15] This attempt to use the Islamic regimes of Asia to protect British interests would be consolidated culturally at the end of the century by "The White Man's Burden," in which Rudyard Kipling exhorts the Americans to take up what the British had considered their obligation of tending "[Their] new-caught, sullen peoples, / Half-devil and half-child" (11.7–8). As pawns in the game, the Jews were viewed as "hapless exiles" who required British protection in their attempt to regain their ancient homeland (Adler, 133).[16] To buttress these Byzantine policies, the British drew on the cultural stereotypes that had been cultivated centuries earlier, in order to convince themselves that their actions were just: they were protecting the helpless Jews against the evil infidels. As late as the 1880s, William Gladstone would defend his decision to withdraw British support because he considered the Ottoman Empire "a bottomless pit of fraud and falsehood"; and even in the twenty-first century, at a time when, as I write today, President George W. Bush is reportedly preparing to use Israel to help expand his "war against terrorism," these attitudes are manifest in the Anglo-American tilt in favor of tiny Israel, the only, as we are frequently reminded, democracy in the area, trying to survive in the midst of the many Islamic tyrannies that surround it. As one reads this neglected novel written in the early 1830s, one cannot help but be struck by Disraeli's prescience, ranging from his descriptions of what today we refer to as "the Arab street," on through the complications of establishing a viable government among competing religious and secular interests. Clearly, the implications of *The Wondrous Tale of Alroy* transcend its narrow identification as Disraeli's "Jewish" novel.

⚜

NOTES

1. It was only in 1913 that Israel Abrahams first associated *Alroy* explicitly with the Anglo-Jewish community; after that, in 1952, Cecil Roth identified it as the first Jewish historical novel (61). More recently, John Vincent has asserted that "*Alroy* is important because of its Jewishness" (68). In the nineteenth century, however, reviewers consid- ered *Alroy* as a combination of an Oriental and Byronic novel, reviews in the *American Monthly Review* comparing Alroy to Robert Southey's *The Curse of Kehama* (1810), the *Court Journal* to Isaac D'Israeli's "Mejnoun and Leila, A Persian Romance," and the *Lon- don Literary Gazette* to William Beckford's *Vathek, an Arabian Tale*. The *Court Journal* also compared *Alroy* to Byron's *Siege of Corinth*. First published in 1833 under the title *The Wondrous Tale of Alroy*, subsequent editions—a "new edition" in 1834, a revised edition in 1846, and the final edition overseen by Disraeli, the Longmans of 1871—were issued under the short title *Alroy*. References in this paper are to my electronic edition, paren- thetical citations indicating section and chapter. In addition to a critical introduction, annotations, and bibliography, the edition also includes reprints of Disraeli's sources, early reviews, and later criticism.

2. Despite the controversy surrounding Edward Said's delineation of Orientalism as the West's projection of a specific identity onto the Muslim world, in this case, Said is particularly apposite, given the fact that Disraeli's foreign policy both derived from and perpetuated the very attitudes Said documents.

3. The first biography of Disraeli, Monypenny and Buckle's six-volume *The Life of Benjamin Disraeli Earl of Beaconsfield*, published between 1910 and 1920, has been super- seded by Stanley Weintraub's *Disraeli: A Biography* (1993).

4. For an overview of British attitudes toward the Jews in the Middle East during the early nineteenth century, see Reeva Spector Simon, "Commerce, Concern, and Christian- ity: Britain and Middle-Eastern Jewry in the Mid-Nineteenth Century."

5. On conversionism, see Michael Ragussis, *Figures of Conversion: "The Jewish Ques- tion" and English National Identity*.

6. In the second half of the century, Disraeli was a strong advocate of British imperi- alism, strengthening the empire in India and arranging for the purchase of the Suez Canal in 1875. Earlier in the century, Lord Palmerston, as foreign secretary and prime minister, among other positions, was instrumental in establishing the British base in the Middle East (see "Lord Palmerston and the Jewish Question," chapter 15 of Adler's *Restoring the Jews to Their Homeland: Nineteen Centuries in the Quest for Zion*, 132–38).

7. In *Radical Assimilation in English Jewish History 1656–1945*, Todd M. Endelman argues that the D'Israeli family (Benjamin removed the apostrophe from the name) was not unique in that respect (see pp. 28–31). On Isaac's biography, see James Ogden, *Isaac*

D'Israeli; and on his work, see the essays by Stuart Peterfreund, "Not for 'Antiquaries,' but for 'Philosophers': Isaac D'Israeli's Talmudic Critique and His Talmudical Way with Literature," and "Identity, Diaspora, and the Secular Voice in the Works of Isaac D'Israeli."

8. On *Alroy* as a justification for Disraeli's conversion, see my "*Alroy* as Disraeli's 'Ideal Ambition.'"

9. Details about Disraeli's travels in the Levant can be found in Robert Blake's *Disraeli's Grand Tour: Benjamin Disraeli and the Holy Land, 1830–31.*

10. For a basic introduction to the novel, including a discussion of how Disraeli adapted Muslim history for fictional purposes, see the critical introduction to my electronic edition.

11. This summary is written from the perspective of Edwin Jones, *The English Nation: The Great Myth.*

12. Not insignificantly, Disraeli's concept of a "sovereign principle" anticipates Benedict Anderson's definition of a nation as "an imagined political community—and imagined as both inherently limited and sovereign" (6).

13. Poliak's entry to the *Encyclopædia Judaica* provides a good overview to the history of David Alroy, while Benjamin ben Jonah of Tudela's diary account, reprinted in my edition, is probably the most detailed. For information about the Turkish background, see Kempiners, Boyle, and Leiser.

14. Bar Kokhba (d. 135 CE) was the leader of the Zealots who defended Masada; Rabbi Akiva (ca. 50–135 CE) was one of the greatest scholars of his age. Although the footnote is punctuated with quotation marks, it is actually a rough paraphrase that incorporates material taken from other sources, some fact, some not. In significant contrast to Jewish sources, both Enfield and Disraeli deride the Zealots.

15. The label, "the Great Game," was apparently coined by one Arthur Conolly, a British officer. This summary of "the Great Game" is from "The Legacy of the Great Game in Asia," the second chapter of David Fromkin's *A Peace to End All Peace* (26–32). The quotation by Gladstone is from Fromkin (30). For basic information about the Middle East, see the *Encyclopedia of the Modern Middle East,* edited by Reeva S. Simon, Philip Mattar, and Richard W. Bulliet.

16. For discussions of the process, begun around 1830, by which the British hoped to gain recognition of the Jews as de facto British protégés, in order to establish a foothold in the Middle East, see Simon, "Commerce, Concern, and Christianity," and Adler, "Lord Palmerston and the Jewish Question."

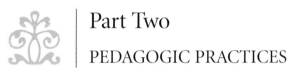

Part Two

PEDAGOGIC PRACTICES

CHAPTER 7

Teaching the Quintessential Turkish Tale

Montagu's Turkish Embassy Letters

JEANNE DUBINO

Lady Mary Wortley Montagu's *Turkish Embassy Letters* have come to represent the "quintessential Turkish Tale." "They are both a telos toward which the dozens of previous books about Turkey lead and a point of reference for the hundreds of travel books that follow. In *The Turkish Embassy Letters*, Montagu indicates a strong awareness of what earlier Western travelers had written about Turkey. Since their publication in 1763, they, too, have become one of the most significant sources on Turkey for subsequent travel writers, on par even, as Billie Melman writes, with Antoine Galland's famous translation of *The Arabian Nights*.[1] John Cam Hobhouse wrote in 1813, fifty years after the publication of the *Letters*, that Montagu "is so commonly read that you will scarcely pardon me for quoting rather than referring to it" (quoted in Chung, 111). *The Turkish Embassy Letters* continue to be one of the most popular travel books about Turkey, as the abundance of critical references alone indicates.[2] It is notable that *Letters* has never been out of print.[3]

In calling the *Letters* a "Turkish Tale," I am playing on the term "traveler's tale." A traveler's tale is a narrative of slightly dubious authenticity, and here, I would add, written by a Westerner. Indeed, "traveler's tale" is an apt synonym of what Edward Said would later call "Orientalism," or the European invention of the East (*Orientalism*, 1). With their descriptions of life at court, in the baths, and in the harems, Montagu's *Letters* certainly fit within the tradition of a European's representation of the East. It is no wonder, then, that *The Turkish Embassy Letters* have become canonical in classes about Orientalism.

The Turkish Embassy Letters are ideal to teach for other reasons as well, particularly for the attractive picture they paint of Montagu herself. Readers, particularly students, are drawn to her; as they travel along with Montagu in her eastward journey, they come to like their travel companion, and they readily identify with her perspectives and her insights. They are, as Louis Althusser writes (170–77), interpellated into the world of the *Letters*. As teachers of literature, especially autobiographical texts such as Montagu's *Letters*, we want to encourage the delight and appreciation that accompany the pleasures of identification. We are happy that students can connect to writers who have written in other worlds, other times. It is hard to argue against the power of empathy. Biographies—and certainly travel writing is a form of biography—are one of the best routes into history; the lives of individuals make the eras during which they lived come alive, especially for students. As teachers, we want students to imaginatively immerse themselves into other places, other eras.

At the same time, however, we want students to resist easy and immediate identification, particularly when they are reading travel writing, which risks, as Jeanne Moskal states, "confirm[ing] rather than challeng[ing] students' expectations, stereotypes, and prejudices." For students to adopt Montagu's vision is for them to accept the beliefs and prejudices that underlie Orientalism. In the world of Orientalism, the Westerner, generally unconsciously, constructs herself at the expense of the Eastern Other. This self-construction "has less to do with the Orient than it does with 'our' world" (Said, *Orientalism*, 12). In a class on Orientalism, instructors seek to have their students recognize and critique this process of construction in an effort to resist interpellation.

How then do we encourage our students to challenge the assumptions underlying Orientalism? By having them examine the world that Montagu creates, and the pictures she paints of herself in this world, as a discursive construction, a representation, rather than a truth (Said, *Orientalism*, 21). Those teaching the *Letters* can point to how these representations and self-representations are not fixed, but ever shifting, involving "the construction of opposites and 'others' whose actuality is always subject to the continuous interpretation and re-interpretation of their differences from 'us'" (Said, "Afterword," 332). There are three stages, then, in teaching the *Letters* as an Orientalist construction, and "Teaching the Quintessential Turkish Tale" outlines each of these stages.[4]

First, a discussion of the epistolary genre of the *Letters* allows us to understand how Montagu, especially in her position as an aristocratic woman writer, enacts her varying identities. Second, "Teaching the Quintessential Turkish Tale" primarily addresses how instructors and students can examine the multiple selves that Montagu creates as a result of these interactions: feminist, aristocrat, colonialist/imperialist, aesthetician, and ethnographer. As we examine these different selves, we regard them as constructed and not natural, and we come to see the role we ourselves play in constructing Montagu. After all, the only identity Montagu would have applied to herself was aristocratic.[5] In connection with Montagu's role as an ethnographer, one needs to examine the different ways she interacts with the other in an ongoing process of "interpretation and re-interpretation," and how her interactions are represented as variable, fluid, and multiple.

When students first read *The Turkish Embassy Letters*, they easily identify with Montagu's persona in her manifold interactions. Certainly, the epistolary form encourages identification, and allows readers to feel as if they are in immediate contact with the writer. As Ian Watt writes, "letters are the most direct material evidence for the inner life of their writers that exist" (191). Even when it is fictionalized, "the letter form in general creates a more personal and private appearance" (Secor, 4). However, like the epistolary novel *Clarissa*, the *Letters* were also written for a wide audience, and as such are a public form of writing as well as private. Apart from its translation into novel writing, letter writing in the eighteenth century became a public endeavor and to that end "a carefully crafted art, refined not only for the particular audience of one but attuned to a potential public readership as well. . . . Lady Mary's familiar letters, then, are poised rather precariously between the private and public realms of personal talk and literary art" (Gardner, 2).

The epistolary form, furthermore, was one appropriate to her social class and gender.[6] In my teaching of the *Letters*, I reminded students that their writing history indicates that Montagu very much had publication in mind, though, as Robert Halsband notes, not in her lifetime (Lowe, 35). Knowing that her daughter Lady Bute would not want to see her letters in print, Montagu left a copy with the Reverend Benjamin Sowden in Rotterdam for safekeeping (Epstein, 8). From 1718–1763, the *Letters* were "revised throughout her life" (Kietzman, 1), "from actual letters to a limited readership, to pseudo-letters to fictive addressees, being aimed at a wider, more varied audience" (Melman, 79). Over the course of this revision, the narrative voice "developed into a fictional narrator, assuming diverse voices and different masks to convey to her audience different points of view, in accordance with the person (or character) she addressed. And the recipients of the letters were no longer merely 'real' readers, but 'implied' ones as well as . . . characterised and fictionalised" (Melman, 79). Other features that point toward Montagu's having publication in mind include the conversational quality (Gardner, 2); the "idealized descriptions of meetings with beautiful people, . . . fairly typical of eighteenth-century letters written with an eye to posthumous publication" (Aravamudan, 81); and "the style and page layout of the collected book of familiar letters" (Chung, 123).

I asked students to think about Montagu in terms of her multiple self-constructions, to consider the kinds of personae she assumes before her different audience members. How does she constitute herself before her various addressees?[7] We compared the letters written to her sister Lady Mar to those written to Alexander Pope. With Lady Mar, Montagu is more intimate and gossipy. She describes her encounters with individual women, such as Fatima, and reports on the events in her private life such as, for example, the birth of her daughter (113). With Alexander Pope, she is more deliberately erudite and witty. She fills her letters to him with classical allusions, and points out how accomplished she is in her Turkish: "[I am] studying the Turkish language (in which, by the way, I am already very learned)" (103). To the Abbe Conti she writes about religious matters (62–63). "[A]ssuming diverse voices and different masks to convey to her audience different points of view, in accordance with the person (or character) she addressed" (Melman, 79), Montagu knew what would please her audience.[8] As students and instructors deconstruct her rhetorical skill, it would almost seem as if she knew what would please even audiences today. Within the range of these letters we can see how Montagu emerges, to contemporary readers, as feminist, aristocrat, colonialist/imperialist, aesthetician, and ethnographer, and how these identities cut across addressees, and intersect, overlap, and sometimes contradict each other. As we discuss each of these identities, I ask students to define them, and to complicate their definitions.

We started with feminist, because that was the most attractive (though, unfortunately, the word itself is not: most students will acknowledge, "I am not a feminist, but . . ."), the most identifiable, and the most complicated. What makes Montagu seem to be a feminist, I asked? First of all, they noted, because she went to Turkey at all in an age when few Western men traveled the width of Europe and far fewer women. Next, while there, she had access to places where "no man has gone before," as she proudly proclaims about her visit to the baths: "'tis no less than death for a man to be found in one of these places" (60). We discussed her tone of "oneupwomanship" here[9] in her report on what no man was able to see: the private lives of women. She was permitted access by virtue of her gender. Students and I kept in mind as well that the *Letters* are truly remarkable because they are indeed the first secular book about the Middle East written by a Western woman (Melman, 78).[10] Coming from a society that values firsts, North American students, like Western critics before them,[11] applauded Montagu for her adventurousness, her pioneering spirit.

I asked students to consider other reasons for why the *Letters* are a work of feminism. They are from a woman's point of view, and they are about women's experiences. As Anna Secor notes, we do not have a masculine conquering voice, but rather a "gendered discourse of emotional response" (10).[12] The emotional response, one born of personal experience and "not external authorities, make[s] a report accurate" (Melman, 84).[13] Throughout the *Letters*, Montagu "takes pains to dim national and religious attributes" and instead "consciously emphasises gender" (Melman, 84). Moreover, in her focus on women's manners and customs, Montagu, as Emily Cooley writes, is defining culture as feminine (8). Her comments on seemingly frivolous topics such as fashion and grooming; social events, such as operas; on the Turkish language of social interaction, or, to cite Woolf, "a little language such as lovers use" (295); and festivals, such as carnivals, explore "several cross-cultural constructions of femininity" (Aravamudan, 75). Montagu's attention to the details of her trip make the *Letters* an important social document, if not an exceptional example of eighteenth-century feminism. If, as Naomi Schor has written, the detail, in the eighteenth century, is the feminine, then the *Letters* are a kind of feminist history.[14]

Students and I studied two of the most famous passages in the *Letters* in an effort to understand how Montagu's vision is a feminist one: the Sophia bath and the harem scenes. We looked at these two scenes as celebrations of women's spaces. Montagu announces at the beginning of the bath scene, "I am now got into a new world, where everything I see appears to me a change of scene" (57). Born into this new world, like Shakespeare's Miranda, or Milton's Eve, Montagu approaches this scene, and the following harem scene, with awe and wonder: "[I] could not help fancying I had been some time in Mohammed's paradise, so much was I charmed with what I had seen" (91). Ruth Bernard Yeazell applies Mary Louise Pratt's concept of "feminotopia" to these women's spaces; "feminotopias" are episodes "that present idealized worlds of female autonomy, empowerment, and pleasure" (122). Montagu's feminotopia is a "female heaven" void of men (Cooley, 14), and is at the very least suggestive of "the possibility of an erotic universe in which there are no men, a site of social and sexual practices that are not organized around the phallus or a central male authority" (Lowe, 48). Aravamudan remarks on its inclusivity (82),[15] and Cooley on its atmosphere of equality (12).[16]

In idealizing Turkish women's space, I asked students, is Montagu avoiding Orientalist tropes, or is she instead evoking them? We discussed "the Orientalist topos of the female harem, and the specter of what Malek Alloula calls 'oriental sapphism'" (Lowe, 47–48). Like other travelers before and after her, Montagu "tended to glorify the terrestrial sensual paradise of noble savages" (Melman, 97). Yet, as Melman also points out, "[t]he *haremlik* is not a microcosmic state but rather the reverse of the state. . . . Montagu's harem is neither a merely exotic place, nor a philosopher's Utopia. It is in fact not dissimilar to the aristocratic household in Britain, at that time. In other words: the harem is neither different nor foreign" (97). Chung insists that Montagu supplants an Orientalist universe with Milton's paradise, and in merging East with West, "Turk with Christian, the Arabian Nights with the Fountain of Domestic Sweets, prose with poetry, and Other with self" (116), Montagu's relationship with the "Turkish women around her changes to alterity from identity, to threat from salvation, to paradise lost from paradise, to tempting Other from loving Mother" (116).

I culled quotations from the critics whose articles and books are cited here. Students addressed the following questions: In writing about the bath as a "new world," is Montagu's perspective a colonialist one? Or, in reference to Pratt's "feminotopia," is she writing about a nonplace—literally, a utopia?[17] Could one regard the bath as more mundane, a female version of a man's sphere, such as the coffeehouse,[18] a place where ordinary conversations took place, "where all the news of the town is told, scandal invented etc." (Montagu, 59)? Just as Turkish women are sober conversationalists, Turkish men, writes Montagu, are as ordinary as their English brothers. Or is the bath, where the dressing of hair takes place, an eighteenth-century version of a women's space, the beauty salon? Is Montagu reproducing Orientalist stereotypes by recreating a female version of the harem? Is the bath a microcosmic state, or is it a reverse of the state? Does Montagu construct the bath as an aristocratic household? Are the baths all of this and more, a symbol of plentitude and totality? Certainly, students could see, in the question of women's space alone, a wide range of critical opinions.

We moved on to the way Montagu does not just describe the meaning of this space to her, but imagines what she must mean to the women who occupy it. We considered how Montagu does not just position herself as the subject, but as the object. She imagines that she must have "certainly appeared very extraordinary" (58) to the women in her riding dress. She perceives that it is the Turkish women who tolerate her: "not one of them that showed the least surprise or impertinent curiosity, but received me with all the obliging civility possible. I know no European court where the ladies would have behaved themselves in so polite a manner to a stranger" (58). In contrast to the two hundred naked women, who implore her to undress, she keeps her clothes on, but eventually relents to some degree by opening her shirt[19] and showing them her stays. To the Turkish women, Montagu's stays are a chastity belt to which only her husband has the key: "I saw they believed I was so locked up in that machine, that it was not in my own power to open it, which contrivance they attributed to my husband" (Montagu, 59–60). In addition to showing herself as the object of the gaze, and to representing the Turkish women as adopting the subject position, Montagu shows herself to be imprisoned by her culture, in contrast to the freely moving Turkish women.[20]

Students noted that Montagu regards naked Turkish women as freer than their clothed Western counterparts. They saw, a few pages later, that Montagu also considers Turkish women to be freer when they are clothed, and more particularly, when they are veiled. For Montagu, the stays are a clear symbol of imprisonment; on the other hand, the veil, regarded by the West as a symbol of subjugation even to this day,[21] in fact enables women's liberty: "This perpetual masquerade gives them entire liberty of following their inclinations without danger of discovery" (Montagu, 71). The veiled woman can indulge in her own sexual proclivities without being identified. As Aravamudan writes, "[t]he interplay between nudity and masking will fascinate [Montagu], especially because it will be seen as providing aristocratic Turkish women—and ought, she thinks, to provide all women—with an escape from social ties by means of negativity and anonymity" (79). In escaping these restrictive social ties, ties that turn women into objects for others' uses, aristocratic Turkish women have greater subjectivity than Englishwomen do.[22]

In her defense of the veil, Montagu is attempting to offset the worst of the stereotypes about Turkish women: that they are imprisoned by despotic Turkish men, and that the veil is a symbol of their imprisonment. She expresses her exasperation with such stereotypes: "I cannot forbear admiring either the exemplary discretion or extreme stupidity of all the writers that have given accounts of them" (Montagu, 71). Montagu admires the way the veil obscured class differences, so that the mistress and her slave could not be distinguished from one another, and the way it also allowed women to have extramarital affairs. Students and I debated whether or not Montagu was demonstrating proto-Marxist, liberal feminism here, or whether, in her comparison of the veil to a masquerade, she was perpetuating classic Orientalism. I brought in an excerpt from Lisa Lowe, who critiqued Montagu's application of the westernized notion of the masquerade to the veil, and in doing so, projected onto Turkish women her desire for sexual freedom:

> The characterization of Turkish women's comportment as a "Masquerade" also assimilates Turkish culture to English terms and modes of cultural expression. . . . For Montagu to call the Turkish woman's veil a masquerade is to transfer these specifically English associations to Turkish women's society, to interpret the Turkish context by means of an ideologically charged English classification, and to attribute to Turkish women a powerful ability to subvert the traditional cultural systems of sexuality and class relations. . . . Implying that Turkish women are the site of a variety of subversive actions, that veiled they are protected by an anonymity that allows them sexual and social license, Montagu makes of Turkish women a sign of liberty and freedom in

a manner not unlike Dumont's earlier rendering of Turkish women as a sign
of enslavement and barbarism. (45)

We contrasted Lowe to Aravamudan, who more positively reads Montagu's use of masquerade in performative terms: "Masquerade will come to
be the 'perpetual practise' that suggests a model of female subjectivity for
Montagu, one that will come to be structurally related to a kind of freedom
that suspends truth" (78).

Students concluded that Montagu challenged eighteenth-century restrictions placed on women. Did she also question the privileges she enjoyed
as an aristocrat, I asked students? No; on the contrary, Montagu sought to
preserve class boundaries. We looked at the following passage in which she
boasts that her class position makes her account more accurate than those
of previous travel writers, who were "only" merchants: "'Tis certain we have
but very imperfect relations of the manners and religion of these people, this
part of the world being seldom visited but by merchants, who mind little but
their own affairs" (60).[23] She can speak of what she knows because she, as an
aristocrat, was admitted to the houses of people of quality, unlike the "common voyage writers," who were denied access:

> You will perhaps be surprised at an account so different from what you have
> been entertained with by the common voyage writers, who are very fond
> of speaking of what they don't know. It must be under a very particular
> character, or on some extraordinary occasion when a Christian is admitted
> into the house of a man of quality, and their harems are always forbidden
> ground. (85)[24]

Students furthermore noticed that Montagu praises Turks who hold the
same class position that she does; like her, they will not speak with someone
whom they perceive to be from a lower class: "The Turks are very proud and
will not converse with a stranger they are not assured is considerable in his
own country. I speak of the men of distinction, for as to the ordinary fellows,
you may imagine what ideas their conversation can give of the general genius
of the people" (104). Montagu, however, holds the same class prejudices
against "common" Turks that she holds against commoners in general. She
applauds Achmed Bey, a Turkish *effendi* (gentleman and scholar), for his
interpretation of the Koran that allows for "those that knew how to use it
with moderation" (e.g., gentlemen such as himself) and prohibits it "for the
common people" (Montagu, 62–63). Montagu believes that generosity "is
very often found amongst Turks of rank" (Montagu, 137).

Montagu belonged to the most powerful class in one of the most powerful countries in the world. I wanted students to understand the context for her travels to the East in 1717. In addition to being a great sea power, Britiain emerged, following the Peace of Utrecht in 1713, as a major imperial power. Having been one of the superpowers in the sixteenth century, the Ottoman Empire, on the other hand, was on the way toward losing its ascendancy. It had recently lost significant territory, marked by the Treaty of Karlowitz in 1699. Furthermore, the capitulations—trade treaties that allowed the West "free and unrestricted trade in the [Ottoman] Empire" (Secor, 5)—enacted in the sixteenth century became even more entrenched, leading to an increasing imbalance of trade relations between Turkey and the West (Secor, 6). Into this climate Montagu's husband, Edward, was sent, as Ambassador Extraordinary to Constantinople and also as a representative for the Levant Company, which held the charter for trade in the Near East (Desai, xv). Thus, Edward Montagu was serving England both in a diplomatic and in a commercial capacity (Lowe, 37), and Mary was along for the ride.

And ride she did, literally, on "a little white favourite" that, she writes, "I would not part with on any terms" (83). Students and I examined the scene in which she appears on horseback. In her letter to her friend Anne Thistlethwayte, she boasts, "My side saddle is the first was ever seen in this part of the world and is gazed at with as much wonder as the ship of Columbus was in America" (83). Here, we noted, she is not only aligning herself with a famous explorer, she is emphasizing her whiteness. As Donna Landry notes, "This scene is a festival of whiteness put on for darker foreign faces to gape at" (471). Even if Lady Montagu "may be only an accessory to the British mercantile and political interests represented by her husband's embassy, . . . she exhibits the confluence of imperial ambitions and personal imperiousness characteristic of English people abroad during this period" (Landry, 471).[25] Though, as we have seen above in her role as a champion for aristocratic Turkish women, and as we shall see even more below in her role as ethnographer, Montagu urges against conventional colonialist attitudes, she does slip into them in scenes such as this one, and even more when she is outside aristocratic circles. In a later moment more redolent of obvious racism, students and I examined Montagu's comparison of Tunisians to baboons in which she concludes, "'tis hard to fancy them a distinct race" (151). Few students would want to identify with Montagu in such instances. On the other hand, as Jennifer Thorn writes, "[i]t is fatally easy for students to criticize earlier eras for their benighted attitudes and limited knowledge. Even as I want students to grapple with the material force of bias, I want not to reinforce inadvertently a bias that is arguably as pernicious, a smug complacency that simply by recognizing others' shortcomings, we escape them in ourselves" (3).

We have seen how the *Letters* allow us to regard Montagu as a feminist, aristocrat, and colonialist/imperialist. The epistolary genre also allows her to represent herself as an "aesthetic subject" (vs. as an aesthetic object). As Elizabeth Bohls writes, in the eighteenth century, the gaze belonged to the male, and the discourse of the gaze—more particularly, the discourse of aesthetics—was "written by men from a perspective textually marked as masculine" (Bohls, 3). Notably, "the painters of Montagu's days were [also] almost all men" (Bohls, 36)—the aesthetic subjects—, and the nudes they painted—the aesthetic objects,—almost all women (Bohls, 36). Women writers like Montagu had to struggle "to appropriate the powerful language of aesthetics" (Bohls, 3), and as such, "also challenged its most basic assumptions" (Bohls, 3). It was not Montagu's gender, but rather her aristocratic class[26] that entitled her to the authority of an aesthetician (Bohls, 19).

I asked students to consider the interplay between Montagu as an aesthetic subject, and the objects of her art, most notably, the women in the baths and the harem. Did Montagu regard the women with an aesthetic eye, a desiring eye, or both? Is it possible to separate the two? Students and I looked closely at the following passage:

> I perceived that the ladies with finest skins and most delicate shapes had the greatest share of my admiration, though their faces were sometimes less beautiful than those of their companions. To tell you the truth, I had wickedness enough to wish secretly that Mr Gervase [a contemporary painter] could have been there invisible. (Montagu, 59)

How could we read this first sentence? It expresses a genuinely aesthetic appreciation of beauty. This appreciation is confirmed when Montagu also writes that the women in the bath are "as exactly proportioned as ever any goddess was drawn by the pencil of Guido or Titian" (59), and Fatima, the Sultana whom Montagu later meets in the harem, more beautiful than what the great ancient Greek court painter "Apelles is said to have essayed, by a collection of the most exact features, to form a perfect face" (89). How does the second sentence, however, in the passage set off above, alter our perception of Montagu's aesthetic intentions? One might argue that it tips the balance into the erotic. I brought in a handout of excerpts of critical analyses of this scene, many of which are cited in this discussion. Students and I debated whether, in displacing her desire onto a male painter, Montagu is admitting to a wicked desire—a homoerotic desire—within herself. "Could the imagined male gazers be surrogates onto whom Montagu displaces her homoerotic attraction to the beautiful bathers?" Bohls asks (36). For Landry, Montagu's homoeroticism is not even a question; Landry directly translates the "wickedness" here into a "homoeroticism that requires switching to a masculine point of view to manifest itself" (478). Yeğenoğlu interprets this scene as a clear-cut instance of Orientalism: "in her relation with the Orient, she attaches a phallus to herself so that she can enter into the domain of the other, to the origin of all civilizations, to the 'mother-nature-Orient,' and thereby *be*" (93).[27] When several of my male students read this scene, they openly admitted their own heterosexual desires through their identification with Montagu's homosexual ones, and, indeed, were quicker than the women in the class were to call Montagu a "lesbian." It is no wonder, additionally, that this scene should have been used by painters such as Ingres in his celebrated *Le Bain Turc* (Turkish bath)[28]; it is telling to see the way some men will appropriate Montagu's homoerotic gaze, a gaze she herself attempts to appropriate from male painters herself.

Indeed, in her attempt to appropriate the gaze of male painters—and not just that of the contemporary Charles Jervas, but those of the Early Modern artists Guido Reni and Titian—Montagu is attempting to aestheticize what is ordinarily eroticized. Montagu "substitutes for the crass power differential of Orientalism the subtler inequalities of aesthetic discourse" (Bohls, 42). Bohls argues that "[t]he language of aesthetics does not just mute the baths' erotic appeal, but, more important, raises its tone to a refinement commensurate with the status of these Turkish aristocrats" (33).[29] Where Bohls emphasizes the aesthetics of the bath scene, Secor focuses on the way Montagu attempts to desexualize this scene: Montagu's "description of the women's baths challenges discourses of Oriental sensuality by desexualizing this supposedly voluptuous space" (Secor, 11). The reference to the imagined "wickedness" of the painter Charles Jervas does not negate, Secor insists, "the simultaneous rejection of typical Orientalist themes regarding the all-female space of the bath" (Secor, 12). Secor sees further desexualization in Montagu's refusal to color the skin of the women she sees—in her whitewashing, her "claims to racial similarity in reference to the 'shineingly white' skins of the naked women" (Secor, 12).[30] Yet, however Montagu may see the Turkish women with an aesthetic eye, her comparison of Turkish women to works of art nevertheless "casts them as objects, rather than subjects" (34–35). Bohls continues, Montagu's "apparent concern to present 'Oriental' women as peers of Europeans is partially undercut by her aesthetic strategy. Blocking their portrayal as erotic objects, she renders them instead as another kind of object—aesthetic objects to her own aesthetic subject" (39–40).

As an aesthetic subject, was Montagu a voyeur? I asked students to consider whether her form of engagement stopped in the act of looking. Did she just stand back and look appreciatively and longingly? Or was her engagement a more active one? Students noted her role as a participant. I brought in Mary Jo Kietzman, who redefines aesthetic appreciation to include participation. Kietzman's argument is that, as a participant, Montagu offers us a new way of seeing, a new epistemology.[31] In her role of a participant, Montagu does not foreground her own powers of creation, but rather the scene itself. Indeed, Kietzman writes, one of the most basic assumptions that Montagu challenged was the very epistemology of aesthetics. Montagu was empowered to make this challenge by entering women's spaces, such as the bath or harem, where she feels more like a participant than a voyeur. She "stands back to allow the 'objects' of her gaze, as well as the atmosphere and subtle action within the spaces she describes, to occupy the readers' attention" (Kietzman, 3–4).

One could also describe this kind of activity as that befitting an ethnographer. Apart from the one anthropology major, most students were not familiar with ethnography; we briefly clarified how ethnography is similar to what we would now call cultural anthropology,[32] and enumerated how Montagu performed as an ethnographer. Rather than emphasizing her own responses and reactions, Montagu foregrounds the scenes that she witnesses, as we have seen above. When she can, she attempts to let the people she meets speak for themselves. When she is not aiming toward straight empirical reporting, she is often engaging in cultural relativism. Finally, in the spirit of contemporary anthropology, Montagu, to some extent, undergoes a transformation herself as a result of her intercultural contact. This question of self-transformation, however, takes us back to the central critique of Orientalism: the construction of the Western self in relation to the other. The class ended with a consideration of the question, what does it mean to engage with the other?

Montagu's desire to give voice to the other is particularly evident in her several references to hair braiding in her visit to the Sophia baths; in the following passages, Montagu writes, the women were "only adorned by their beautiful hair divided into many tresses, hanging on their shoulders, braided either with pearl or ribbon" (59).[33] This braiding is performed by slaves, who, writes Montagu, "were employed in braiding their hair in several pretty manners" (59). Inge Boer describes in detail the way "[t]he braiding of hair can be analyzed as a means of communication, as something that women perform on each other in their own spaces" (61).[34] Though, as Teresa Heffernan writes, the shifting balance of power meant that the "West assert[ed] its dominance by speaking for and producing a silenced Orient" (204), in the instance of this hair-braiding scene, as Boer insists, Montagu is attempting to let Turkish women speak for themselves.[35]

Montagu strives to avoid judging another's culture by her own standards. Instead, she "replaces the existing bias of a simple ethnocentrism in favor of the observer's culture with an eclectic relativism" (Aravamudan, 70–71). As an ethnographer, Montagu strives to adhere to a central tenet of cultural relativism, examining "the culture only from within the culture itself" (Cooley, 9). For example, Montagu writes to Lady Bristol,

> I know you'll expect I should say something particular of that of the slaves, and you will imagine me half a Turk when I don't speak of it with the same horror other Christians have done before me, but I cannot forbear applauding the humanity of the Turks to those creatures. They are never ill used and their slavery is in my opinion no worse than servitude all over the world. (130)

Even at the risk of becoming "half a Turk," Montagu will not condemn the Turkish practice of keeping slaves, but, indeed, will rather defend it. Her willingness to assimilate is in keeping with her role as an ethnographer, which, as part of its methodology, can require some cultural immersion, and at the very least, an engagement with another culture. Montagu is delighted to submerge herself in Turkish culture; she is proud of wearing Turkish clothing—of "turning Turk."[36] Montagu's adoption of Turkish dress symbolizes an internal alteration as well; she undergoes "the transformation of identity that occurs when an individual from one culture is psychically and physiologically absorbed into another" (Aravamudan, 71). If she could have, Montagu would have literally inoculated herself with Turkish culture—with a Turkish culture, namely a small dose of smallpox.[37] Indeed, Montagu is famous for introducing the idea of a smallpox vaccine to England; she would not limit transformation to herself, but would become "patriot enough to take pains to bring this useful invention into fashion in England" (Montagu, 81).

For Montagu, Turkey is, at the very least, on a par with England: after she tells her sister that Turkish men are no more rakish than Englishmen, Montagu declares, "the manners of mankind do not differ so widely as our voyage writers would make us believe" (72). Ultimately, we are all alike, and, additionally, as Montagu writes in the next citation, difference does not mean wrongness: "As to their morality or good conduct, I can say, like Harlequin, that 'tis just as 'tis with you, and the Turkish ladies don't commit one sin the less for not being Christians" (71). Indeed, in the following example and elsewhere, Montagu praises Turkey over England, for its greater sense of justice; in this case, for its punishment of convicted liars. In England, liars are "triumphant criminals"; in Turkey, they "are burnt in the forehead with a hot iron." Montagu writes, "I am also charmed with many points of the Turkish law, to our shame be it spoken, better designed and better executed than ours, particularly the punishment of convicted liars" (108).

However, as students pointed out, even as Montagu attempts to be a fair-minded, if not celebratory, ethnographer, she cannot altogether avoid the tropes of Orientalism. In the example cited immediately above, she is expressing her charm over a law that other travel writers would likely have regarded as brutal. In her preference for the justice of this law, she is countering her predecessors. However, her sheer reportage of the law certainly gives the reader pause.[38] In another instance, Montagu declares,

> these people are not so unpolished as we represent them. 'Tis true their magnificence is of a different taste from ours, and perhaps of a better. I am almost of opinion they have a right notion of life; while they consume it in music, gardens, wine and delicate eating, while we are tormenting our brains with some scheme of politics or studying some science to which we can never attain. . . . I allow you to laugh at me for the sensual declaration that I had rather be a rich effendi with all his ignorance than Sir Isaac Newton with all his knowledge. (142)

As vigorously as Montagu may assert her preference to be a "rich effendi," she asserts, as Secor writes,

> the veracity of another Orientalist trope: Orientals have an ignorant, sensual, hedonistic "notion of life," while Europeans are represented by Sir Isaac Newton.
> . . . Furthermore, her professed willingness to switch places is couched in terms of class, in that she sees the life of the "rich Effendi" (a title of respect) as the embodiment of this Oriental life of pleasure of which she dreams (8).

Critics, such as Meyda Yeğenoğlu, would insist that with the return to the focus on Western identity construction, we are returning to classic Orientalism. For Yeğenoğlu, the East remains a place in which a Westerner forges her or his identity. Yeğenoğlu writes, "[T]he 'inner' space of the Orient, . . . its women, . . . its harem, . . . is the very ground upon which [a Western woman's] identity is anchored and founded" (93). Students noted that there seemed to be no way, according to Yeğenoğlu, for a Westerner to be in the East, or even to talk about the East, without being an "Orientalist." Were all of us also Orientalists because we made the East the subject of our class? According to Yeğenoğlu, yes. Following Said,[39] Yeğenoğlu defines Orientalism by its citationary quality. She argues that it is through the "citationary process" that Orientalism "anchors its hegemony" (91). For Yeğenoğlu, the symbolic universe of Orientalism is *not* without any contradictions, displacements, or contestations. Orientalism establishes its *unity* despite the polymorphous nature of the texts that constitute it. The Orientalist universe, in its unity, is a multifarious or voluminous textuality, but these characteristics [. . .] do not in any simple way constitute a subversive challenge to its power and unity. On the contrary, they enrich the Orientalist discourse. (81; original emphasis)

The students and I considered Yeğenoğlu's insistence that Orientalism establishes its unity through its ubiquity. In her many references to earlier writers on Turkey,[40] is Montagu offering a "subversive challenge to [Orientalism's] power and unity," or is she increasing the "multifarious or voluminous textuality" of the world of Orientalist discourse? Whether Montagu echoes the Orientalism of her forebears by, for example, exoticizing the other,[41] or whether she tries to set the record straight by claiming, for example, that "these people are not so unpolished as we represent them" (142),[42] is she being Orientalist either way? Is Montagu's positive portrayal of Islam anti-Orientalist, or is she using Islam as a way to register her anti-Catholicism?[43]

Other critics, however, define Orientalism less broadly. How is it possible to engage in intercultural contact without orientalizing? Engaging with the other—as one does in travel—and changing as a result of that engagement does not automatically turn one into an Orientalist, as several critics note,[44] including Mary Jo Kietzman, who, along with Secor and Aravamudan, define Orientalism more narrowly than Yeğenoğlu. For Kietzman, Orientalism specifically involves fixing the other. Kietzman argues for another metaphor of exchange besides one based on fixity; hers is based on equality and mutuality. As she writes that the "paradigm of colonizing subject and objectified Other" (Kietzman, 1) is an Orientalist one, she implies that another paradigm, such as hers, which emphasizes fluidity, is not. For Kietzman, the dislocation effected by travel produces a "contingent and circumscribed" (1) set of responses that in turn constitute identity. When identity is cross-culturally constituted it is inherently unstable and hybrid (5–6). Secor describes "intercultural contact" as a negotiating one, ultimately serving to "create the 'domestic subject'" (2; the phrase "domestic self" is from Mary Louise Pratt). For Aravamudan, the subject is performatively dispersed "into several identificatory positions. The subject inhabits the position of both desiring subject and object, thereby reconfiguring itself" (69). Thus, we see how Kietzman, with her emphasis on fluidity and hybridity; Secor, with hers on negotiation; and Aravamudan, with his on multiple identification, including identification with the desired object—all characterize Montagu's cultural confrontation as flexible to some degree. These critics read reciprocity in

Montagu's cultural encounters. For them, her *Letters* represent "moments of cultural confrontation in which self and Other do not remain fixed in polarized positions but are rewritten through discursive and social interaction" (Kietzman, 2).

When students initially read *The Turkish Embassy Letters*, they like them for their protagonist and hero Lady Montagu herself. They, like many readers of travel writing, particularly epistolary travel writing, become swept up in her point of view, and are drawn to her sympathetic representation of the Turks whom she meets. Certainly, as instructors, we want to encourage students to enter into others' perspectives. At the same time, in a class on Orientalism, we want students to challenge those perspectives as well. In critiquing Montagu's worldview, they will become more aware of their own. In understanding her identity as a shifting, variable, and complex construct, they will come to realize that identity itself is fluid and overdetermined. If we, as instructors, can show our students how *The Turkish Embassy Letters* are a "Turkish Tale" of a Westerner who constitutes herself in relation to the East, we can help them both to appreciate Montagu's artistry and her insights, and to understand the ideological underpinnings of Orientalism.

NOTES

1. "Those readers who documented their reactions were, themselves, travel-writers, who in their own turn, described the harem. And in the alternative system of information about and interpretation of the Middle East, the 'Embassy Letters' acquired a status and authority comparable with those of Galland's *Nights*, in the more traditional discourse" (Melman, 82).

2. In addition to the sources cited in this essay, other important works on *The Turkish Embassy Letters* include Cynthia Lowenthal, "The Veil of Romance: Lady Mary's Embassy Letters," 66–82; Felicity Nussbaum, *Torrid Zones: Maternity, Sexuality and Empire in Eighteenth-Century English Narratives;* Robert Halsband, ed., *The Life of Lady Mary Wortley Montagu;* and Isobel Grundy, "'Trash, Trumpery, and Idle Time': Lady Mary Wortley Montagu and Fiction," 293–310.

3. "*The Turkish Embassy Letters* has remained continuously in print since its publication, and Lady Mary's letter to her sister in which she extols the liberty of Turkish women has become a staple in anthologies of women's travel writing" (Secor, 4–5).

4. I taught *The Turkish Embassy Letters* in an upper-division English Department Special Topics course, The Middle East and West in Literature.

5. The other terms did not come into use until the following century.

6. Writes Kevin Gardner, "Lady Mary, rarely stooping, as it were, to the business of producing literature in the standard genres, and likewise unfettered by the rigorous

demands of writing 'true' history, found the letter to be the perfect medium for expressing [her] creativity" (2). See also Chung, who writes that the *Letters* "need to be read accurately as the consequence of aristocratic birth and education, yet Montagu used her semiotic inheritances resourcefully for the purposes of anti-patriarchal feminist critique" (Chung, 119).

7. See Kevin Gardner's "The Aesthetics of Intimacy: Lady Mary Wortley Montagu and Her Readers" for a discussion of epistolary quality of *The Turkish Embassy Letters* and the effect of this genre of Montagu's contemporary readers and on her twenty-first-century readers.

8. See also Lowe, 49.

9. See Aravamudan, who writes, "The incompetence of previous writers on Turkey—all of them male—is a result of their lack of access to the information they pretend to have garnered, and their naïve repetition of second-hand fantastical accounts received from unreliable informants. Montagu's criticisms are obviously intended to demonstrate her superior erudition, contemporaneity, and novelty. Along with the emphasis laid on this being a first-hand female account, it is not difficult to discern a healthy tone of one-upwomanship" (74). Bohls would add that for Montagu, men "are the truly superficial travelers" (25).

10. Melman dates "the female literature on the harem from 1763, the year of the posthumous publication of Lady Mary Wortley Montagu's famous *Turkish Embassy Letters*" (78). She argues that "Lady Montagu's letters, in short, may be appropriately designated a key text, the corner-stone in the new, alternative discourse that developed in the West on the Middle East" (Melman, 78).

11. Such as Anna Secor, who writes that "Montagu's life and letters are a testimony to her own tenacious quest for a personal sort of liberty, both intellectual and sensual in nature, which was difficult for her to achieve within the constraints of her society" (2).

12. See Wheatcroft, who, while praising Montagu for her "unequalled" testimony, also accuses her of, among other things, turning a blind eye to "manifest cruelties and injustice": "The Ottomans whom Lady Mary met represented a society already changing, and one about to undergo even greater transformations. She largely ignored the manifest cruelties and injustice implicit in the system, but, as a corrective to the highly coloured or ill-willed imaginings of most male commentators, her testimony is unequalled. She wrote as the narrow opening-up to the Western world was beginning under Ahmet II" (219–20).

13. Melman writes, "The reliable representation of the private, becomes the *litmus-test* to the travellers' credibility and his or her tolerance towards the more public areas of life: the government, the administration, economy and public (as against private) religion" (84).

14. And a discourse on feminist aesthetics, as will be explained further below. For now, it is worth noting that, as Bohls writes, "The patriotic traveler (presumptively male) was expected to collect useful information for country and sovereign, to note geography and fortifications. But Montagu leaves such pursuits to 'learned' men and turns instead to pretty walks and fine prospects, the beauty of visible surfaces—in short, to aesthetics. She steps mock-apologetically into the position of the aesthetic subject" (25). Montagu judges the customs that she sees, such as sumptuary laws, "from an aesthetic perspective" (25).

15. "Montagu visualizes an inclusive women's sphere at the bath, a gynaecium of unselfconscious but interactive female nudity that she may be contrasting implicitly with

the exclusionary masculine preserve of the Greek gymnasium, whose masculine participants were also naked while demonstrating their athletic prowess" (82).

16. "[S]tripping the women of clothes levels by stripping them of rank" (Cooley, 12).

17. Yeazell also calls this fantasy a "dream of cosmopolitanism." She elaborates: "[P]erhaps the most exhilarating aspect of travel was the prospect of belonging wholly to no country—of wandering at liberty through the world, free to pick and choose one's 'customs' at will" (123). See Kietzman, who finds this reading belittling (6).

18. According to Jurgen Habermas, in 1710, there were three thousand coffeehouses in London alone (32). They became a fad in Turkey as well, until they were shut down "as notorious centres of unrest" (Goodwin, 247). Other critics, including Aravamudan, note that "the bathhouse is the Turkish woman's riposte to the Englishman's coffee house.... This Turkish bagnio perhaps simulates the Habermasian sphere of the development of communicative freedom" (81–82).

19. Or skirt; see Chung.

20. Teresa Heffernan writes that Montagu's refusal to open her stays "interrupts the binary of veiled and unveiled, the slave and the free woman, religion and reason, which structures the travel accounts of her predecessors. Lady Mary's undressing or unveiling does not naively assume an unfettered freedom but rather displays a gendered social order that underlies the very rhetoric of Western freedom" (211). Aravamudan considers another interrupted binary; he notes that Montagu, in full dress, is caught between the "dignified and ridiculous" (83).

21. Sanjukta Ghosh recently delivered a harsh denunciation of white liberal feminists for associating the veil with oppression.

22. As Bohls points out, Montagu objects to women turning themselves into aesthetic objects; "the mincing Saxon beauties [whom Montagu had met earlier, and whom she characterizes as dolled-up objects] seem to warn Montagu that her position as an aesthetic subject is a compromised prerogative" (27).

23. Anna Secor connects this class-bound rhetoric to Montagu's refutation of earlier writers on Turkey, whom Secor refers to here as Orientalists: "both the Orientalists themselves and the people of whom they write are of the lower classes, and therefore not able to authentically represent or be representative of Oriental culture" (11).

24. "Montagu's identification with the wives and mistress of Turkish dignitaries also makes use of the existing discourse of class distinction, and an established identity of aristocratic privilege across cultures" (Lowe, 32).

25. Landry addresses the significance of Lady Montagu on horseback. Her article, "Horsy and Persistently Queer: Imperialism, Feminism, Bestiality," considers the way Montagu, among other British travelers to Turkey, "becomes, by dint of being mounted on a horse, the embodiment of an imperial race, a warrior class, a nation destined for global superiority and far-flung rule. The horse represents an extension of the self, but nobler" (475). See also Lowe, who writes, "Just as Montagu's *Letters* occasionally resonate with the dominant British orientalist discourse, so the social context that produces *The Turkish Embassy Letters*—the diplomatic presence of Montagu's husband, Ambassador Wortley Montagu, in early-eighteenth-century Turkey—locates her text as part of England's colonial discourse about Great Britain's foreign commercial interests and colonies" (50–51). Critics of Orientalism focus, as students noted, on the way the West makes use of the knowledge derived from all these activities to construct its own identity. As Lisa Lowe writes, "[B]y figuring travelers in foreign lands encountering strange and disorient-

ing customs and practices, the trope of travel allegorized the problems of maintaining cultural institutions amidst challenging othernesses, of establishing cultural standards and norms in the context of heterogeneity and difference. . . . [T]he utopian geographic expansion implied by travel literature addressed national anxieties about maintaining hegemony in an age of rapidly changing boundaries and territories" (31).

26. Hunt's "Racism, Imperialism, and the Traveler's Gaze in Eighteenth-Century England" explores the way the gaze was becoming, by the middle of the eighteenth century, a middle-class one.

27. See also Secor, who writes, "[T]he scene is sexualized by the invisible male painter because his mention reiterates the 'forbidden' nature of the space, and this prohibition is itself linked through the discursive chains of Orientalism to the supposed sensual hedonism of the women" (12).

28. According to Ruth Bernard Yeazell, Ingres took notes on the bath scene, not the harem scene. However, that Ingres's "first biographer could refer to Lady Mary's letters as themselves describing 'les moeurs intérieures du harem' [the best harem interior] suggests just how easily such a fantasy may override the evidence" (116).

29. Additionally, as Lisa Lowe notes, "it appears that Montagu is able to articulate her affection for Fatima only by means of the established literary tradition that exists for the praise and regard of female beauty, a male tradition of courtly love poetry exemplified by the sonnets of Shakespeare, Sidney, and Spenser" (48).

30. Certainly, elsewhere, we can see how Montagu desexualizes Turkish women by, for example, declaiming against their constant state of pregnancy. For Montagu, bearing a child every year of one's life is not a sign of sexual proclivity, or even desirable fertility, but rather, vanity (107). Kietzman regards this disagreement as a sign of respect: "While the impulse to identify suggests a desire to find the common ground necessary for any dialogue, disagreement is just as important—evidence that the participants take the subject of inquiry seriously?" (5).

31. See also Madeleine Dobie, who writes that the voyeurism of the *Letters*, "generated by the absolute seclusion of women and reflecting male control, is in fact the locus of a destabilization of the series of oppositions and power structures which initially seem to govern the western depiction of oriental women" ("Embodying," 51).

32. The online journal *Ethnography* describes itself as "[b]ridging the chasm between sociology and anthropology" (*Ethnography*).

33. Montagu makes other references; see also 70.

34. Boer goes on to explain the way that hair braiding does not just function as a means of communication, but as a form of business (63), and "a part of a process of production of knowledge, information, and pleasure" (64).

35. Students and I compared Montagu's second visit with Fatima, wife of the vizier's second-in-command, with the first visit. In the first visit, Montagu spends a great deal of time on physical description; in the second, however, she lets Fatima speak for herself. See Kietzman, 4–5, for a good discussion on the way Montagu represents Fatima's complex subjectivity. See also Heffernan, who discusses the way Montagu avoids the trap of Western feminism of speaking *for* the other, but rather learns how to speak *to* the other (210).

36. She expressly announces to her sister, "I will try to awaken your gratitude by giving you a full and true relation of the novelties of this place, none of which would surprise you more than a sight of my person, as I am now in my Turkish habit, though I believe you would be of my opinion that 'tis admirably becoming" (69).

37. She didn't because she had already contracted smallpox, and been disfigured by it. However, she did have her son "engrafted" (81) when she was in Turkey.

38. But Montagu does arrive, of course, at greater degrees of success elsewhere in offsetting stereotypes about Turkish ferocity. She writes about a murder that had recently taken place: "One would imagine this defect in their government [in not typically investigating murders] should make such tragedies very frequent, yet they are extremely rare, which is enough to prove the people not naturally cruel, neither do I think in many other particulars they deserve the barbarous character we give them" (*Letters*, 136).

39. Writes Said, "Orientalism is after all a system for citing works and authors" (*Orientalism*, 23).

40. Including Paul Rycaut (62, 133, 138, 140), Jean Dumont (104), Richard Knolles (133), Aaron Hill (134), and George Sandys (145, 146).

41. See Secor, 7–8. Yeazell also notes the way Montagu shares "the common belief of the period that in traveling east she had traveled back in time as well" (114).

42. See Aravamudan, who writes that Montagu's "travels appear as a tentative ideological step that levies 'positive' orientalist empiricism against the romantic and gothic extravagances more typical of eighteenth-century English orientalisms" (91).

43. Montagu makes her anti-Catholicism clear in passages such as the following where she refers to the "farce of relics"; in one instance, she writes, the Roman Catholics "have dressed up an image of our Saviour over the altar, in a fair full-bottomed wig, very well powdered" (9–10; see also Melman, 94).

44. See also Heffernan and Chung. Even Said noted, years after the publication of *Orientalism*, that his "book had the unfortunate effect of making it almost impossible to use the term 'Orientalism' in a neutral sense, so much had it become a term of abuse" (Afterword, 340).

CHAPTER 8

Representing India in Drawing-Room and Classroom;

or, Miss Owenson and "Those Gay Gentlemen, Brahma, Vishnu, and Co."

MICHAEL J. FRANKLIN

The taste for this kind of reading is so various, that what pleases one, another will throw away in disgust. The lady, who would delight in the description of a masked ball, given by the Lady Ann, So and So, or the elegant and fashionable attentions of my Lord—, will find but little interest in the account of traversing a burning waste where the dry and hot air parches the lip and the feet tread, as in a channel of burning lava, or in perusing the horrors of an auto da fé.[1]

No one will deny Miss Owenson the praise of a lively fancy, and most prolific invention, but surely every reader must agree that this lady has still to cultivate the sober qualities of judgment, without which, alas! her productions will pass in rapid succession from the shelves of the circulating library, to far less agreeable places and purposes.[2]

Sidney Owenson's *The Missionary: An Indian Tale* (1811) was an influential text; receiving four London editions and a New York edition in its year of publication, it became an important source for some of the great "Oriental" poetry of both Byron and Shelley.[3] The novel has a major claim on critical attention now: it deserves to be read and it repays close study in university classrooms, especially in the context of its historical significance for Orientalism and Romanticism; and in the specific climate of current debate over issues of women's writing, race, colonialism, and nationhood.

It is as a mediating text that *The Missionary* is profoundly useful in today's classroom, introducing a very wide range of issues central to the study of literature and its history, including: the complexities of social and political alignments in the Romantic period literature and criticism; the conception of female genius and the function of the female artist within constricting gender ideologies; questions of canon-construction and genre status; the urgent need for post-Saidian analysis to discriminate between

differing Orientalisms; the colonial debate between Anglicists and Orientalists; the continuing relevance of syncreticism and pluralism; and the attempt
to identify similitude rather than difference in the "otherness" of Ireland or
India.

Had dust jackets or publisher's blurbs been in vogue, subsequent editions of *The Missionary* would doubtlessly have borne this Shelleyan sound
bite: "Since I have read this book I have read no other—but I have thought
strangely."[4] Unsurprisingly, however, the initial reception of the novel
which simultaneously arrested Percy Shelley's reading, liberated his poetic
imagination, and inspired his version of the Indian sublime was predictably
marked by that blend of gentle head patting and ironic condescension which
characterized the appearance of her earlier "productions."

In the extracts cited above we can note the somewhat dismissive tone
and the attempt to impugn the intellectual capacities of "lady" author and
"lady" readers by recourse to the binaries of pleasure and disgust; of imagination and reason; of "agreeable places" and unsavory destinations—both
in terms of reader (firmly gendered as female) expectations (the celebrity of
a fashionable rout or the burning deserts of Lahore), and textual teleology
(its leaves serving as pie-wrappings or suffering an excremental fate). Indeed,
The Missionary might be introduced into the classroom as an exemplary case
study in *Rezeptionsaesthetik*, and a paramount concern must be to consider
exactly how earlier generations of critics and readers have shaped our conceptions of this text and its author.

In this novel Sydney Owenson was making a timely political intervention
in a current debate concerning the nature of imperial government, and it is
instructive to examine the imaginative demands made of its readers in the
second decade of the nineteenth century or in the opening decade of the
twenty-first century with its specter of resurgent neo-imperialism. To read
with or against the grain of this text's particular agenda is to create some
species of dialogue between past and present postcolonialisms in which
anxieties of authorship and reception are dwarfed by anxieties of empire. We
must first contextualize the "masculine" authority implicit in the discursive
strategies of the critics of these two Tory periodicals in their de/dif/fusing of
a "feminine" polemic of colonialism, by considering Owenson's reputation
as a heroine of colonized Ireland.

This was a role that she wrote herself into and performed with a loving
and self-publicizing attention to detail; certainly her originality is not to be
questioned. Before Walter Scott took the credit for establishing the genre
of the historical novel, or indeed the publishing sensation of Germaine de
Staël's *Corinne, or Italy* (1807), Sydney Owenson's construction of national
identities pioneered a powerfully political Irish-based historical fiction. In

The Wild Irish Girl: A National Tale (1806), an intelligent romantic heroine figures a conquered nation, focusing a people's pride in national culture and autonomy.[5]

Owenson created in *The Wild Irish Girl* a romanticized and feminized Ireland united in its past and present. Owenson wrote herself into the literary, philosophical, and political public sphere, utilizing an eighteenth-century discourse of sentiment to develop emergent nineteenth-century concepts of the nation. Simultaneously addressing questions of European imperialism and issues of "internal colonialism" with a direct bearing upon Ireland, she "internalizes" the Otherness of the subaltern. She was acutely aware that the subjugated race, like the subjugated sex, must compensate by means of subtler or more subversive means of representation for its lack of political representation.[6]

Anticipating a critical reaction that would marginalize her contribution to the political debate, she defiantly asserts that what might, in the estimation of a largely male public sphere, seem to devalue her representation of Irish history—her gender and her choice of genre—were in fact validating and authorizing elements. Predictably, the *Monthly Review*, though sympathetic to her cause, disagreed: "the best friend of that gallant nation would not quote a novel as authority." Exasperated by the blend of truth and fiction in *The Wild Irish Girl*, the reviewer asserted:

> [O]ne good memorial is worth twenty romances. It must be the statistical man who will essentially benefit Ireland, and not the professed writer of fiction. The latter may reach to the private drawing-room, but the former will obtain attention in senates and councils.[7]

Despite his anxiousness to shape and guide the taste of middle-class readers, the reviewerfails fully to appreciate the affective capacity of public opinion that might be swayed even—or especially—by a work of fiction. "The appeal to public opinion," wrote Owenson, "belongs to the age in which we live," and she used her national tales to air the politics of empire in the public domain of the reviews and the domestic sphere of the drawing room.[8]

Although in announcing: "Politics can never be a woman's science; but patriotism must naturally be a woman's sentiment"[9] she seemed to produce a gendered distinction between the spheres of politics and patriotism, actually her novels blurred that distinction, confirming that both patriotism and politics could be a woman's art:

> I shall be accused of unfeminine presumption in "meddling with politics"; but while so many of my countrywomen "meddle" with subjects of much

higher importance;—while missionary misses and proselyting peeresses affect to "stand instead of God, amongst the children of men," may I not be permitted, under the influence of merely human sympathies, to interest myself for human wrongs; to preach in my way on the "evil that hath come upon my people," and to "fight with gentle words, till time brings friends," in that cause, which made Esther eloquent, and Judith brave? For love of country is of no sex.[10]

Few writers, however, have used sex so effectively in reflecting and initiating "love of country" through producing texts of eroticized nationalism.[11] Having textualized and distanced in the "national, natural character" of Glorvina her own erotic, auto-erotic, and (to borrow Leerssen's useful term) "auto-exotic" desires of self-representation, she effectively merged her authorial Self with the textual Other.[12] Though bluestocking in her footnotes, her theatrical self-fashioning continued with the purchase of an Irish harp and a romantic black cloak, under which she naturally assumed the diaphanous mantle of Glorvina. Ireland, Glorvina, and Owenson thus became a triune heroine of sensibility. Her readers were encouraged to engage if not in sexual tourism then in a heavily eroticized cultural tourism, and the appeal of this formula might be extended far beyond colonial Ireland to colonized Greece in *Woman: or, Ida of Athens* (1809), a novel that ought to be essential reading for students of Byron; or further east to colonized India.[13] While dismissive of "missionary misses," this miss's *Missionary* was to produce a heroine who was to play a key role in the romantic representation of India. Owenson effectively eroticized Romantic nationalism, for if *The Wild Irish Girl* had "made Ireland romantic," *The Missionary* made a major contribution toward the romancing of India.[14]

Having accommodated the strangeness of Ireland to Regency British drawing rooms, introducing the Otherness of India might have seemed a more difficult task. Hinduism could present a substantial challenge for Owenson's cultural relativism, but if the Irish had Oriental Phoenician roots (as Father John, Glorvina's preceptor in *The Wild Irish Girl*, maintains), she contemplated an "Indian Tale" in a spirit of Indo-European, or even Indo-Hibernian, solidarity.[15] Furthermore, she had considerable help: firstly and most importantly in the shape of that most respectable Celtic forerunner, Sir William Jones, whose series of hymns to Indian deities and translations of Sanskrit classics had first domesticated Hinduism in metropolitan drawing rooms of the 1780s and 1790s; second, she was writing out of her own experience of sentimentalizing the subcontinent in aristocratic drawing rooms.[16]

It is in this context that we must consider the interrelated questions of the specific circumstances of the textual production of *The Missionary* and the social circumstances of Sydney Owenson as its author. Since early 1809 she had been a fashionable cultural accessory, a sort of Glorvina in residence, to the influential household of the high-Tory John Hamilton, Marquis of Abercorn. In a contemptuous review of *Woman: or, Ida of Athens* (1809), the bilious satirist John Wilson Croker had described the situation with a certain perceptiveness; "This young lady . . . is the *enfant gâté* of a particular circle, who see, in her constitutional sprightliness, marks of genius, and encourage her dangerous propensity to publication."[17]

The Missionary was composed during lengthy stays with the Abercorn household at their secluded Northern Ireland mansion of Baron's Court and their imposing residence of Stanmore Priory near London. When the *Critical* reviewer had opined that the "lady" reader "would delight in the description of a masked ball, given by the Lady Ann, *so and so*," he was making a knowing reference to Lady Anne Jane Gore Hamilton, Marchioness of Abercorn, the dedicatee of *The Missionary*. But Owenson's dramatic skills were not limited to masquerade on the dance floor; the protective and collaborative ambience of the Abercorns' drawing room provided a captive and captivated audience in which she could imaginatively extend her autoerotic and "auto-exotic" repertoire to include the radiant Otherness of Luxima. Between the culturally produced poles of a self-deprecation and self-celebration, Owenson performs and manipulates a subversive celebrity feminism wherein the author becomes not Glorvina with harp, but a version of akuntal with fawn. At Baron's Court her day's writing, relayed in almost Shahrazad fashion, would be subjected to postprandial dissection:

> [S]he used to read aloud, after dinner, to the Marquis and Marchioness, what she had written in the morning. She said . . . that the Marquis used to quiz her most unmercifully, declaring that the story was "the greatest nonsense he had ever heard in his life," which did not, however, prevent him from listening to it with great amusement.[18]

In Stanmore Priory, where the company included celebrities of both parties and aristocrats such as the Duke of Devonshire, Lord Aberdeen, Lord Castlereagh, Lord Ripon, the Princess of Wales, the Duc de Berri, and the ex-king of Sweden, the level of audience participation was even greater: "not a few grave statesmen, disenthralled for a few weeks, from the cares and turmoils of office, loungingly abandoned themselves to the luxury of listening to Miss Owenson, as she read aloud her exciting and wildly romantic story." Indeed, accordingly to Fitzpatrick, many narrative improbabilities and stylistic excesses might well be laid at the door of her beau-monde auditors:

The Missionary is open to objection, but is so improbable that it can hardly be deemed a dangerous novel. It is, in many parts, very rhapsodical; but the fault is, to some degree, attributable to the motley suggestions which the distinguished guests at Stanmore urged, and many of which the authoress, in compliment to her influential friends, laughingly adopted.[19]

Such insights help situate the author between the scholarly demands of her Indological studies and the performative expectations of her aristocratic audience. Whatever the extent of audience-inspired interpolation, the novel was composed in the library to provide luxurious listening in the drawing room, confirming Owenson's characteristic blend of the creative and the theatrical, and aiming ultimately at a drawing-room readership for whom Orientalism might prove congenial amusement.

That *The Missionary* was not "a dangerous novel" had less to do with its implausibility than with its exposure of Iberian rather than British imperialism and its seventeenth-century setting in Kashmir, beyond the territorial acquisitions of the East India Company. Its topical resonance, however, was indisputable, and, if we remember that politicians were beginning to recognize the power of narrative fiction in the shaping of public opinion, we can begin to appreciate some of the reasons why at least one of her statesman listeners was anxious that the novel should be published.

Of course, Lord Castlereagh's interest in the novel might well have been inspired simply by his fascination with its author.[20] As Fitzpatrick asserts: "The good nature of this distinguished statesman was the more remarkable as Lady Morgan had repeatedly, and forcibly, denounced the Legislative Union, of which he was the chief director, as corrupt and calamitous, atrocious in its principle, and abominable in its means."[21] Like many powerful men, he had a practiced line in disarming comments, evaporating her initial hostility with his reported remark: "No one cares for Ireland but Miss Owenson and I," and he presumably made much of their mutual concern for India. Ultimately the politician whom Byron was to label an "intellectual eunuch" was delighted at Sydney Owenson's apparent willingness to accompany him in his tuneless renditions of airs from his favorite *The Beggar's Opera*.

Castlereagh's interest in India was a long-standing one. His years as President of the Board of Control had taught him the difficulties of handling the complexities of his government's relationships with both the East India Company and the Governor-General in India. In supporting the Marquess Wellesley's establishment of Fort William College for the training of writers sent out to India, Castlereagh had indicated his position in the Orientalist-Anglicist controversy. This debate concerning how and to what extent India should be modernized became heated in the years up to the renewal of the company's charter in 1813. The Orientalists, on the one hand, who respected Indian traditions and argued for an acculturated civil service, were opposed by the Westernizing tendencies of the Anglicists and evangelicals, brought into an uneasy alliance through their fear that cultural pluralism might lead to the "Indianization" of British youth.[22]

The participation of Viscount Castlereagh, architect of the 1800 Act of Union by which Ireland's Parliament had voted itself out of existence, in the negotiations for the publication of *The Missionary* is replete with political ironies. Ten years later Percy Bysshe Shelley was to depict Murder masked like Castlereagh and accompanied by seven bloodhounds, but in late 1809 the viscount drove this Jacobin novelist, wild Irish patriot, republican sympathizer, and "radical slut" to a meeting with her publisher John Joseph Stockdale at his Cabinet Office, where Owenson sold her manuscript for four hundred pounds.[23] What the Secretary of State for War and the Colonies and the author of *The Missionary* had in common was a belief in the East India Company's policy of noninterference with the religious "prejudices" of the Indian races.[24] Castlereagh, having witnessed Sydney Owenson's performances in the private sphere of the Abercorns' drawing room, shrewdly realized how the romancing of India and the comparative and sympathetic representation of Hinduism might prove useful in the manipulation of public opinion. Certainly, the editor of Owenson's memoirs thought Castlereagh "perhaps, the greatest admirer the *Missionary* ever found," and early in 1810 its author, with a characteristic interweaving of the political, the professional, and the personal, was writing to her patron Alicia Lefanu, the well-connected Bluestocking sister of Sheridan:

> What will please *you* more than anything is that I have *sold my book, The Missionary, famously*. That I am now correcting the proof sheets, and that I have sat to the celebrated Sir Thomas Lawrence for my picture, from which an engraving is done for my work. (original emphasis)[25]

Having considered the social circumstances of its production, it is instructive to return to the critical reception of *The Missionary*, first advertised in the *Morning Chronicle* of January 21, 1811. As we have seen, reviewers, earnest in their attempts to police the British public sphere by regulating its tastes and reading habits, irritated by the generic hybridity of the national tale and its complex negotiation between fiction and history, dismissed her productions as "romantic" novels of sensibility. Despite a somewhat playfully patronizing tone, however, the representative of the *Critical Review* emerged as something of a fan: "Miss Owenson has such a fanciful and happy facility in her comparisons, her descriptions of persons, &c. as often makes us stare with amaze."[26]

Surprisingly, considering Owenson's political reputation, the *Anti-Jacobin Review* was even more positive about her talents as an author. There has been a notable improvement; *The Missionary* contains "nothing of that grossness for which her *Ida of Athens* was justly censured," but the same emphasis is placed upon the need for restraint.[27] The reviewer stresses the heat of Owenson's performance: her "too ardent feelings," "warm imagination," "glowing language," "her descriptions are traced with a pencil of fire."[28] These sentimental excesses and superheated desires are dictated by her reliance upon "the language of passion, the rude offspring of nature, unregulated by prudence, unchastened by duty." In this way her lack of stylistic restraint is made to imply a corresponding lack of moral restraint as if she displayed an inherently Celtic subjectivity or Oriental sensibility that required a greater familiarity with British moral discipline and English grammar.[29]

What annoyed the *Anti-Jacobin* reviewer was the outpouring of an "Orientalized" profuseness and the unleashing of a feminine subjectivity. Western women should be subject to control and especially to self-control; where the novel proved "defective in point of taste," "offensive to modesty," or lacking in "that sensitive delicacy, which is the eminent characteristic, and the best ornament, of the female mind," the reviewer announces: "[W]e were tempted to refer to the title-page to convince ourselves that the pages before us are really the production of a female and a spinster" (378).

The response of these workaday, and presumably male, critics to *The Missionary* perfectly illustrates Terry Eagleton's characterization of the reception of her Irish tales:

> [R]omance, however strained and febrile, always bears such a utopian impulse within it; and if the visions it generates seem idle it is because the workaday world fashioned by men have rendered them so. [. . .] The very forms of her fiction, with their scandalously flaunted play of fantasy, are thus an implicit rebuke to the mean-spirited jobbers and brokers of the male Ascendancy.[30]

In an important article, Ina Ferris has shown that Owenson's extravagant and romantic theatricality "functioned in large part parodically and polemically as a form of cover or critique, allowing intervention in areas generally outside the feminine sphere and enabling her to write herself as an author in the public realm."[31] Significantly, the *Anti-Jacobin* reviewer refers to Owenson not only as "an experienced novel writer," but also as "a public writer," and she must have valued such an acknowledgment. An endorsement of her cultural and religious relativism had also come from the *Critical Review,* which recognized, if rather archly, her success in representing the Hindu pantheon in a sympathetic light: "And, what is more, she makes us as familiar and sociable with those gay gentlemen, Brahma, Vishnu, and Co. as if we had been brought up under the same firm all our lives; as well as with Monsieur Camdeo, the god of mystic love, and a long *et cetera* of personages which make up the Indian mythology."[32]

This had been the task of cultural translation which Jones had set himself thirty years earlier by means of scholarly articles in *Asiatick Researches,* such as "On the Gods of Greece, Italy, and India" (1784), or through the syncretic poetic of his "Hymns to Hindu Deities" (1784–88). Where Jones had used Pindaric and Miltonic resonances to lend a classical dignity and respectability to his subjects in the minds of his drawing-room readers, Owenson used a hybridized genre of romance/historical tale to cater to a more extensive novel-reading public. Sydney Owenson, in her concern to use sentimental fiction to dispel prejudice, had observed how effectively the literary and linguistic researches of Sir William Jones had succeeded in adjusting metropolitan stereotypes of India. Jones had introduced to Occidental drawing rooms the beautiful daughter of a Brahman sage and a heavenly courtesan, an Indian heroine with whom the West promptly fell in love. Blending a perfumed exoticism and a divine eroticism, Sakuntala embodied the earthly and vegetal paradise of the India of the imagination. Jones had published his translation of Kālidāsa's *Sacontalá* in Calcutta in 1789, and Mary Wollstonecraft, reviewing the London edition of 1790, discovered delicacy, refinement, and a pure morality in *Sacontalá,* the very qualities Jones was anxious to stress in his representation of Hindu culture. Here was a sentimental heroine who immediately appealed, in Wollstonecraft's words, to both "the man of taste" and "the philosopher," and here was a complete model for Owenson's Luxima.[33] If reviewers in Britain fell under her spell, in Germany she caused a sensation. The play was for Herder his *indische Blume;* Schiller rhapsodized about Sacontalá as the ideal of feminine beauty; Novalis loving addressed his fiancée as "Sakontala"; Friedrich Schlegel pronounced India as the source of all human wisdom; and Goethe captured the essence of *Sacontalá* fever in the line: "Nenn ich, Sakontala, dich, und so ist Alles gesagt" ("When I name you, Śakuntalā, everything is said").

This enraptured European response to the blend of the divine and the erotic in the narrative which Kālidāsa had adapted from the *Mahabharata,* mediated by Jones in his dual roles of translator and interpreter of Asian culture, established *Sacontalá* as not merely evidence, but as the representational icon, of Indian civilization.[34] The plot concerns the aesthetic and erotic entrancement of King Dushmanta by the beauty of Śakuntalā and the enthrallment of these German men of letters not only represented a remarkable level of Western audience identification with this Indian king, but even more surprisingly, marked a response completely in accord with classical Indian aesthetics in the shape of *rasa* theory.[35]

What made Owenson's commercial and political achievement even timelier was that *The Missionary* was published within a year of Robert Southey's *The Curse of Kehama* (1810), which portrayed Hinduism as a cesspool of monstrous gods and demonic devotees.[36] The politics of Southey's poem aligned him with the evangelical lobby, and the delightful horror of its Oriental Gothic impressed the young Percy Shelley. Ultimately, however, it was not a poem designed to Gothicize India in support of missionary activity, but a novel that Romanticized India, opposing interventionist cultural and religious policies that reignited Shelley's poetic imagination. Reading and rereading *The Missionary* proved a revelation for Shelley. While the periodical critics were suggesting that Owenson should "curb her imagination, discipline her feelings, and regulate her language," the imaginative power of *The Missionary*, "a book," according to William Fitzpatrick, "worthy only of the Minerva Press," was operating upon the superior genius of Shelley.[37] Shelley reacted to Luxima with the same rapture as the German Romantics had idolized Śakuntalā. His desire to bring Luxima to life is never totally achieved, but etherealized versions of this Indian Maid reappear in his poetry from *Alastor* onward:

> Will you read it, it is really a divine thing. Luxima the Indian is an Angel. What a pity that we cannot incorporate these creatures of Fancy; the very thought of them thrills the soul. Since I have read this book I have read no other—but I have thought strangely.[38]

What particularly fascinated Shelley was the way in which Owenson "uses Kashmir as a paradisal image for that ideal interior landscape of the fulfilled psyche."[39] Furthermore, the skeptical immaterialism of Vedantic philosophy that she had absorbed from Jones and sympathetically handled in *The Missionary* clearly had some influence upon the growth of the poet's mind. The immediate effect of the poet's reading may be traced in the Indian Gothic of "Zeinab and Kathema," but the enduring and more central influence of the novel is demonstrated when, in spite of Shelley's immersion in the classics, it is in the Vale of Kashmir that the young poet in *Alastor* experiences his vision of the epipsyche. Shelley's voluptuous veiled maiden sings the European revolutionary themes of liberty and virtue rather than Hindu hymns to Camdeo, but she is a vision and version of the seraphic Luxima.

For Shelley, Owenson's domestication of the Indian sublime was sufficiently effective to produce a preoccupation with India that lasted throughout his poetic career. He ordered Jones's complete *Works* in December 1812, and John Drew's detailed critique of Shelley's image of India, which reads *Prometheus Unbound* (1820) in terms of Kashmiri mythology, has convincingly demonstrated that Jones and Owenson were the mediating figures for his imagination.

Luxima the ethereal and entrancing Vedanta priestess, in her nature worship and exquisite sensibility, and with her pet fawn, her wreath of delicate buchampaca flowers, and her hymns to Camdeo, represents Owenson's attempt to reheat *Sacontalá* fever. Her name is based on the beautiful wife of Vishnu, the Hindu goddess Lakshmī, whom Jones had portrayed as an Indian Venus emerging Botticelli-like from an ocean of milk.[40] The Latinized version mingles suggestions of Eastern luxuriance and luxury with a sense of *ex Orient lux*. Her hero, Hilarion, the energetic Portuguese aristocrat and Franciscan missionary, bears the name of one of the most austere of the desert fathers, whose delicate frame endured both the physical extremes of heat and cold and the burning fires of lust. Hilarion, like his sainted namesake, will endure both cave dwelling and climatic extremes, but his sensual trials are undergone in the spiced air of the Edenic Vale of Kashmir. The encounter of Brahman priestess and Catholic missionary mingles Miltonic and imperialistic resonances, figured as it is in the oppositional binaries of geography, race, and gender:

> Silently gazing, in wonder, upon each other, they stood finely opposed, the noblest specimens of the human species as it appears in the most opposite regions of the earth; she, like the East, lovely and luxuriant; he, like the West, lofty and commanding: the one, radiant in all the lustre, attractive in all the softness which distinguishes her native regions; the other, towering in all the energy, imposing in all the vigour, which marks his ruder latitudes: she, looking like a creature formed to feel and submit; he, like a being created to resist and to command: while both appeared as the ministers and representatives of the two most powerful religions of the earth; the one no less enthusiastic in her brilliant errors, than the other confident in his immutable truth.[41]

This static tableau would seem to show Owenson as complicit in colonialist gendering, using the hypermasculinity of imperialist discourse that conventionally gendered the Hindu as lethargic, soft, and feminine. Luxima figures the perfumed allure of the subcontinent if not the forbidden attractions of miscegenation. Owenson's representation of Hinduism, however, contrasts with this portrayal of yielding submission, for Luxima's religion "unites the most boundless toleration to the most obstinate faith; the most perfect indifference to proselytism, to the most unvanquishable conviction of its own supreme excellence" (125). Hilarion's self-confident powers of command and resistance are seen to be undermined not solely through the agency of romantic love, but via the Enlightenment processes, derived from Jones's scholarly Orientalism, of comparative religion and ideological relativism. The mutual sympathy of Hindu and Christian, which Owenson proceeds to illustrate within a Kashmiri frame, has the power to disconcert and disorientate the reader, and it derives that power from Jones's discoveries of similitude.

Europe sat up and paid attention when Jones, in his "Third Anniversary Discourse" (1786), found in Sanskrit a "more refined" sister of Greek and Latin. This introduced alarming ideas of linguistic and familial relationship between the colonial rulers and their "black" subjects. In the same discourse, he concluded that it is not possible "to read the *Védánta*, or the many fine compositions in illustration of it, without believing, that PYTHAGORAS and PLATO derived their sublime theories from the same fountain with the sages of *India*."[42] Indian philosophy possessed the reassuring familiarity of Platonic thought and each might be apprehended equally by the twice-born Brahman or the Enlightened rationalist, by Vedanta priestess or Franciscan monk.

Owenson, well versed in the didactic functions of enlightened sentimentalism, refined her Orientalism by means of a close reading of Jones's important essay "On the Mystical Poetry of the Persians and Hindus" (1791). Here Jones had quoted from Isaac Barrow, the teacher of Newton and "deepest theologian of his age," to demonstrate that Barrow's conception of divine love "differs only from the mystical theology of the *Súfis* and *Yógis*, as the flowers and fruit of *Europe* differ in scent and flavour from those of *Asia*."[43] In characteristic popularizing and performative mode, Sydney Owenson ventriloquizes Barrow's words by placing them on the fragrant lips of Luxima. Delighted to find common ground between Vedantic and Christian concepts of mystic love, she exclaims enthusiastically: "We cannot cling to the hope of infinite felicity, without rejoicing in the first daughter of love to God, which is charity towards man" (140).[44] Similarly, Hilarion's native informant, a Kashmiri Brahman pandit, when expounding the tenets of Luxima's religion, sounds remarkably like *Sri* William Jones: "That matter has no essence, independent of mental perception; and that external sensation would vanish into nothing, if the divine energy for a moment subsided" (89).[45] In this way the pandit—in his "confirmed deism" (88)—is literally rendered a mouthpiece of Jonesian syncretism as Owenson artfully deconstructs the binarisms of colonialist prejudice.

Focusing and dramatizing such syncretic reflection for European readers of romance Owenson successfully dissolves the Otherness of Hinduism, "mak[ing] us as familiar and sociable with those gay gentlemen, Brahma, Vishnu, and Co. as if we had been brought up under the same firm all our lives." When students, having been exposed to the dramatic sensuality of Śakuntalā and the romantic radiance of Luxima, become aware of exactly what Owenson is about, many opportunities for heuristic investigations are made available and such possibilities are increased exponentially by the availability of digital resources.[46] It thus becomes possible to track Owenson's antiquarian footsteps through the Oriental library of her friend and former lover, the Dublin barrister Sir Charles Ormsby.[47]

At least seventeen Orientalist tomes are cited in Owenson's footnotes, but frequent unacknowledged borrowings from Jones and other authorities ensure the authenticity of Kashmiri "costume." Students can discover that on a single page of Owenson's text (121), interspersed between dignifying quotations from *Paradise Lost*, and colorful references from Jones's "Hymn to Camdeo" (Kāma: the Hindu god of love), two scented descriptions are drawn from facing pages of Jones's "Botanical Observations on Select Indian Plants." The lattices of Luxima's pavilion "were composed of the aromatic verani, whose property it is, to allay a feverish heat; and which, by being dashed by the waters of an artificial fountain, bestowed a fragrant coolness on the air." The following paragraph depicts the priestess offering as incense to Camdeo "leaves of the sacred sami-tree."[48]

In this way students can appreciate the detailed attention given by Owenson both to matters of theology and cultural distinctiveness, and begin to comprehend exactly how the Enlightenment blend of sentimentalism and scholarship she made very much her own might well have irritated male critical preconceptions of gender and genre, even while the popularity of this novel reinforced, disseminated, and made assimilable the political and pluralistic significance of syncretism.

That Sydney Owenson, despite her celebrity posturing, was no "air-head" becomes clearly apparent through detailed consideration of some recent secondary criticism, especially in its underestimation of the thoroughness of her research. Julia Wright, in her useful edition of *The Missionary*, fails to disguise condescension toward both the scholarship of "Romantic-era Orientalists" and the use Owenson made of their research.[49] When Luxima wishes she had thrown herself on her husband's pyre, thereby to "have enjoyed the bliss of Heaven while fourteen Indras reign" (150), this reference is not erroneous, as Wright asserts, but a most apposite quotation from Henry Colebrooke's paper on *satī*.[50] Balachandra Rajan, in a valuable consideration of *The Missionary*, emphasizes Owenson's thoughtful remembering of Milton, but Luxima's use of the phrase "*a dark-spotted flower in the garden of love*" (275, n.102; original emphasis) in her dying words does not recall *Comus,* but is a most apt borrowing from the narrative of Mejnún and Lailì: "He had seen the depredations of Grief through absence from his beloved object: he had plucked many a black-spotted flower from *the garden of love,*" which again she had found in Jones.[51]

Rajan also asserts that when Luxima "accepts Christianity and prefers a platonic life with Hilarion to a fuller one with Suleiman Sheikh (with whom she would not have done any better) she surrenders herself to victimization."[52] Arguably Luxima never does "accept Christianity," for the repeated name of "Brahma!" (258–59) is on her dying lips. Furthermore Rajan's parenthetical remark presumably refers to the fact that the handsome young Islamic prince, who also falls under Luxima's spell and offers her "to become the empress of thine own people" (167), was shortly to share his father Dārā Shikūh's fate, murdered at the hands of Dārā Shikūh's brother Aurangzeb. What Rajan fails to consider is that the introduction of the Mughal prince Suleiman Shikūh to establish a love triangle reconfigures the binaries of imperialism in a most subtle fashion. On the simplest level it reminds the reader that India had successfully absorbed and assimilated a series of imperial conquests. On the subtler level of Owenson's Orientalism, however, it can be seen that introducing an Islamic hero of Suleiman's parentage represented a significant Jonesian touch. His father, the scholar-prince Dārā Shikūh, had inherited the syncretic mantle of his great-grandfather, Akbar; had translated some of the *Upanishads*; and composed a Persian text entitled *Majma 'al-bahrayn* or "The Mingling of the Two Oceans," which maintained that the fundamental tenets of Hinduism were essentially monotheistic and stressed the connections between Sufism and Vedantic thought. Jones had recommended this "pleasing essay . . . by that amiable and unfortunate prince," and Owenson was similarly alert to the pluralistic prospects of ultimate harmony between the two (or indeed three) great religions of India.[53]

The dimensions of her antiquarian "Indian venture" reveal just how deeply Sydney Owenson had "waded through" Ormsby's Orientalist library. Whereas many contemporary literati considered the Hastings circle and the Asiatick Society to be exclusively interested in Sanskrit literature, Owenson underscores Jones's commitment to the liberal syncretic tradition developed by Dārā Shikūh. A certain fascination with metaphysics may be discerned in her consideration of the religious discussion in the Hindu temple where a disciple considers "the fifth element, or subtle spirit, which causes universal attraction" (93), an element that interconnects the theology and metaphysics of Newton, Vedic thought, and Sufism.[54]

Moving from this metaphysical fifth element to the third element of the Hindu trinity or *trimurti* (the "& Co." of the *Critical* reviewer's enterprising "'firm" of "Brahma Vishnu & Co."), namely Śiva, the terrible Lord of Sleep, Time, and Destruction, the difficulties of introducing Hinduism into either drawing room or classroom become all too apparent; Śiva is no "gay gentleman." A classic study of Śiva by Wendy Doniger O'Flaherty is subtitled *The Erotic Ascetic,* chapter 9 of which contains successive sections titled "The Dangers of Śiva's Excessive Chastity," and "The Dangers of Śiva's Excessive Sexuality"; self-evidently "The road of excess leads to the palace of wisdom."[55]

The problem in pedagogical terms is where to start on this dangerous road of excess, always assuming, of course, that one's students are not already halfway along it! Whereas Shelley came to Jones via Southey's *Curse of Kehama* and *The Missionary,* my students, proceeding chronologically through a module shamelessly entitled "The Erotics and Exotics of Romantic Orientalism," come to Owenson's representation of Hinduism in the same way as Owenson herself did, by means of the more demanding path of Jones's translations and hymns. There are, however, advantages to this route. A consideration of Jones's "Hymn to Camdeo" and "Hymn to Durgá" introduces students to the strained relationship between Śiva and his erotic alter ego Kāma, which culminates in the latter's being reduced to "silver ashes" by the fire-flashing third eye of Siva for daring to rouse the ascetic god from his profoundly dangerous meditation to make him fall in love with Durgá in her aspect of Pārvatī, the beautiful daughter of Himalaya.[56]

In Hinduism there coexist two forms of heat, apparently mutually opposed, but actually profoundly interwoven: *kāma,* the heat of sexual desire, and *tapas,* the heat generated by deep meditation and ascetic practices, especially chastity. The interaction of these two forces represented by Śiva and Kāma is fundamental in Hindu culture; the gods can feel threatened by the spiritual power generated through devoted asceticism. This idea is at the heart of the tale of *Śakuntalā*; the gods sent the beautiful nymph Menakā to seduce the ascetic *rishi* Visvamitra; Menaka diffused his heat and subsequently gave birth to Sakuntala. The notion of *tapas,* as productive of God-defying powers, is also the originary idea of *The Curse of Kehama,* but whereas Southey was concerned only to display the monstrosity of Hinduism in its potential to produce the "Man-Almighty," Owenson's more subtle treatment of the interrelationship between *kāma* and *tapas* demonstrated an informed and empathic participation in the multivalent nature of Hindu mythology.[57]

While we have seen the contemporary critics commenting upon the heat of Owenson's "pencil of fire," what they fail to understand is that the "superheated" tensions between *kāma* and *tapas* provide an ideal sentimentalist and Indocentric medium for depicting the sensual encounter between the austerities of "brachmachira" (*brahmacārin*: devoted to chastity) and the Franciscan monk. Like his sainted namesake, the young Hilarion, "sighed to retire to some boundless desert, to live superior to nature, and to nature's laws, beyond the power of temptation, and the possibility of error; to subdue, alike, the human weakness and the human passion" (73).[58] Hilarion is described as a "soul of fire" (81), and associated with the enlightening power of the sun.[59] In India, "the Christian wanderer" is frequently taken for "a sanaissee, or pilgrim, of some distant nation, performing tupesya [i.e., *tapas*] in a strange land" (106).[60] The novel thus provides an Indian "take" upon the dangers inherent in the restraint of huge energies, and students can come to appreciate how the binaries of climate, culture, gender, and religion are reconfigured by means of detailed study of Owenson's treatment of the heats of passion and of self-restraint.

Students can also investigate the gothic use Owenson makes of the "blue light of the subterraneous fire (burning naphtha) flashed on an image of Camdeo her tutelary deity" (191), which both reflects Kāma being reduced to "silver ashes" by the fire-flashing third eye of Śiva, and anticipates the ultimate fiery immolation of the Inquisition's auto-da-fé.[61] The sources of Owenson's description of the burning wastes can be traced in François Bernier; the significant variations made to the incident in the *Mahābhārata* narrative of Rajah Nala separated from his beloved Damayantī by a bamboo forest fire may also be placed under scrutiny, as may the related details of the natural asbestos and naphtha bandage.[62] By using the Internet students can discover that Owenson's "*grotto of congelations*" (named "from the splendour of the stalactites that hung like glittering icicles from its shining roof"), the cave in which Hilarion constructs a rude altar with his golden crucifix, does not necessarily represent a cooling respite; it is actually the sacred Kashmiri shrine at Amarnāth where pilgrims to this day assemble to witness an impressive ice stalagmite in the phallic shape of a *Śivalinga*.

Whereas Southey's evangelical bias opens *The Curse of Kehama* with the widow-burning ritual of *satī*, Owenson's climacteric features the auto-da-fé of the Christian Inquisition; thus she subjects the crude despotisms of Oriental and Occidental superstitions to a species of Enlightenment relativism. Throughout the novel Luxima is cast in the role of active ministrant and savior as she tends and heals the injured missionary. By contrast Hilarion, although he had earlier rescued Luxima's fawn from the jaws of a wolf, proves unable to "save" either her body or her soul. Her distracted and dramatic intervention in the Goan Inquisition saves Hilarion's life at the cost of her own—a case, *pace* Gayatri Spivak, of a brown woman saving a white man from white men—and sparks off a native insurrection.[63] Relativity here is again underscored by an informed awareness of the tenets of Hinduism, for while the Christians, fixing their eyes upon the cross which Hilarion had placed upon her breast, see in Luxima a miraculous savior, the Hindus, observing the Brahminical mark on her forehead, "beheld the fancied *herald* of the tenth *Avatar,* announcing vengeance to the enemies of their religion" (249; original emphasis).[64] While Luxima brandishes no blazing sword (indeed, she interposes her body between Hilarion and the knife of one of the Inquisition guards, or "officers of the bow-string" [249] as Owenson, undermining the stereotypes of Asiatic despotism, terms them), her intervention disrupts the gendered passivity of the Oriental female while representing a profoundly nonviolent Hindu intervention.

Following Luxima's death, Hilarion, formerly "lofty and commanding" and confident in the "immutable truth of his mission, returns to Śiva's *"grotto of congelations"* in the hills of Srinagar, effectively "feminized" as a Hindu *sannyāsin* (ascetic devotee of Śiva), for though "his religion was unknown," at dawn and dusk he "prayed at the confluence of rivers" (260) (*tirtha*: an especially sacred place, often where rivers meet). So the seducer (in the final sentence of the novel Hilarion is described as having "seduced [Luxima] from the altar of the god she served") is ultimately seduced if not by "those gay gentlemen, Brahma, Vishnu, and Co.," then by the enlightened lessons in devotional syncretism that Luxima had taught. As recent events confirm with painful clarity, there is still much room in today's world for such pluralism.

NOTES

1. Review of *The Missionary, Critical Review* 23 (June 1811): 183.
2. Review of *The Missionary, British Critic* 37 (June 1811): 631.
3. A French translation followed in 1812, and a German one in 1825.
4. *Letters of Percy Bysshe Shelley,* ed. Frederick Jones, 1:107.
5. Thirty years later Owenson reflected: "At the moment *The Wild Irish Girl* appeared it was dangerous to write on Ireland, hazardous to praise her, and difficult to find a publisher for an Irish tale which had a political tendency. For even ballads sung in the streets of Dublin had been denounced by government spies, and hushed by the Castle "sbirri" because the old Irish refrain of *Erin go bragh* awakened the cheers of the ragged, starving audience" (preface to the 1836 edition).
6. "I came to the self-devoted task with a diffidence proportioned to the ardour which instigated me to the attempt; for as a *woman*, a *young woman*, and an *Irishwoman*, I felt all the delicacy of undertaking a work which had for its professed theme of its discussion, circumstances of national import, and national interest." (original emphasis). *Lady*

Morgan's Memoirs: Autobiography, Diaries, Correspondence, ed. W. Hepworth Dixon and Geraldine Jewsbury,1:48–50; henceforth cited as *Memoirs*.

7. *Monthly Review* 57 (December 1808): 381.

8. Advertisement to *Florence Macarthy: An Irish Tale*, iii.

9. Preface to *Patriotic Sketches of Ireland*, x.

10. Preface to *The O'Briens and the O'Flahertys; A National Tale*, vi.

11. In some respects the eroticizing of Owenson's discourse might be seen as complicit in what Edward Said saw as Orientalism's predilection for exoticizing and eroticizing the Other, but far from the colonialist (male) fantasy of passive sexual availability legitimizing Western imperial control; she eroticizes individual rational women empowered by their cultural claim to authority and agency within their own societies.

12. Joep Leerssen defines auto-exoticism as "a mode of seeing, presenting and representing oneself in one's otherness (in this case: one's non-Englishness)." *Remembrance and Imagination: Patterns in the Historical and Literary Representation of Ireland in the Nineteenth Century*, 37–38.

13. In a lively article Malcolm Kelsall indicates that "Byron's put down of Owenson [in the notes to *Childe Harold* II] is a snub to a competitor. [. . .] One may reasonably conclude that Byron had no need to endure the fatigues of travel to write his romances, but might have drawn all he needed from Sydney Owenson. Indeed, the parallels [with *Ida of Athens*] in some respects are so close that it may be said that he ravished the text without compunction." This having been said, Kelsall, with all the patriarchal gusto of a *British Critic* contributor, puts down Owenson's Orientalist novels as "superheated female pulp fiction fit only for Catherine Morland in a tedious spell of rainy weather." See "Reading Orientalism: *Woman: or Ida of Athens*," 12–14. Cf. n. 28 below.

14. J. Th. Leerssen, "How *The Wild Irish Girl* Made Ireland Romantic," in *The Clash of Ireland: Literary Contrasts and Connections*, ed. C. C. Barfoot and Theo D'Haen, 98–117.

15. See my "Passion's Empire: Sydney Owensen's Indian Venture, Phoenicianism, Orientalism, and Binarism," in *Studies in Romanticism* (2007).

16. It is uncertain whether Owenson knew Phebe Gibbes's *Hartly House, Calcutta*, which used the affective potential of the sentimental letter to introduce Hinduism in a sympathetic fashion to the drawing rooms of the novel-reading public. Gibbes foregrounds a developing love affair between the novel's English heroine and her Brahman tutor. Bored by the dominating masculine discourse of the colonizer, Sophia embraces what she views as the gentle and sensitive religion of the subject Hindu. This sympathetic reaction to Hinduism is intensified by her irritation at the boorish attentions of European suitors to the extent that only the author's apparent belief that Brahmans are necessarily celibate, and more conclusively the Brahman's death of a fever, save metropolitan sensibilities from the specter of miscegenation.

17. *Quarterly Review* 1 (1809): 52. Croker, of course, was later to savage "Cockney" Keats.

18. *Memoirs*, 1:407.

19. William Fitzpatrick, *Lady Morgan, Her Career, Literary and Personal*, 160.

20. The Marchioness of Abercorn, for example, wrote to Owenson: "Have you sent the *Luxima* to England yet? Pray tell me, for though I never wished to hear it read ten pages at a time, I am very impatient to see it all together, and sincerely anxious for its success" (undated letter), *Memoirs*, 1:410.

21. Fitzpatrick, *Lady Morgan*, 159–60.

22. See David Kopf, *British Orientalism and the Bengal Renaissance: The Dynamics of Indian Modernization 1773–1835*, 43–64. Governor-General Wellesley, in the tradition of

the Orientalist regime established by Hastings, had discouraged missionary activity in Bengal, and this was largely Castlereagh's position. According to Ainslie Embree: "Lord Castlereagh, who was handling the Charter Bill for the Government, thought that while this would satisfy the enthusiasts, it would do no harm, since he was convinced that despite the number of petitions, very few Englishmen were really anxious to go out to India as missionaries" (*Charles Grant and British Rule in India*, 272). For a consideration of Owenson's friend Thomas Moore's satire on the making of "Company's Christians" in India, see my "The Building of Empire and the Building of Babel: Sir William Jones, Lord Byron, and Their Productions of the Orient," in *Byron East and West*, ed. Martin Prochazka, 74–75.

23. In response to the "Peterloo massacre" of August 16, 1819, Shelley was to write: "I met Murder on the way— / He had a mask like Castlereagh— / Very smooth he looked, yet grim; / Seven blood-hounds followed him" (*The Mask of Anarchy*, ll. 5–8. It was Owenson's own sister, Olivia, who in a satirical verse described Sydney as "an elegant artist, a radical slut, and a right Bonapartist"; see Mary Campbell, *Lady Morgan: The Life and Times of Sydney Owenson*, 150. Jane Austen was pleased to receive profits of 140 pounds from her *Sense and Sensibility*, published in the same year as *The Missionary*.

24. In the final analysis, perhaps the most significant circumstance of the publication negotiations for *The Missionary* was her choice of J. J. Stockdale. John Drew has asserted that "*The Missionary* may be read as a perfectly extraordinary fictionalization of the psyche of William Jones" (*India and the Romantic Imagination*, 242), and it is interesting to note that Stockdale had been the joint publisher of Lady Anna Maria Jones's thirteen-volume edition of her husband's complete works three years earlier, *The Works of Sir William Jones*, ed. Anna Maria Jones, 13 vols., henceforth cited as *Works*.

25. Letter of January 18, 1810, *Memoirs*, 1.395.

26. *Critical Review* 23 (June 1811): 195.

27. "The author has displayed strong marks of genius in this production, and has convinced us, that, if she will consent to curb her imagination, to discipline her feelings, and to regulate her language; she is very competent to produce works which will place her high indeed, on the list of the best novel-writers of the present day," *Anti-Jacobin Review* 38 (April 1811): 384.

28. "If the warmth of her language could affect the Body it [*Ida of Athens*] might be worth reading in this weather," wrote Jane Austen to Cassandra on a chilly January 17, 1809; see *Jane Austen's Letters*, ed. R. W. Chapman, 251.

29. In this grammatical emphasis the critics were, of course, following the lead of Croker, whose review of *Ida of Athens* suggested its author should purchase a spelling book and a pocket dictionary; *Quarterly Review* 1 (1809): 52.

30. Terry Eagleton, *Heathcliff and the Great Hunger: Studies in Irish Culture*, 184. Two modern critics, whom I would hesitate to label either "mean-spirited" or part of a critical "male Ascendancy," have experienced even greater difficulties in coming to terms with *The Missionary*: Martin Jarrett-Kerr describes it as "a farrago of extravagant nonsense," "Indian Religion in English Literature 1675–1967," 94, and James Newcomer sees the novel as one in which "she went totally astray," *Lady Morgan the Novelist*, 22.

31. Ina Ferris, "Writing on the Border: The National Tale, Female Writing, and the Public Sphere," in Rajan and Wright, 86–106, 86.

32. *Critical Review* 23 (June 1811): 183. Jones's *A Discourse on the Institution of a Society*, together with his "First Charge to the Grand Jury at Calcutta" and his "Hymn to Camdeo" [note the three *separate* genres of scholarly article, legal discourse, and Pindaric ode], was published in London in 1784, whetting metropolitan appetites for what was to

come from Calcutta. The inclusion of his hymn to the Hindu god of love signals not so much his affirmation of the power of knowledge as his commitment to the knowledge of power, and to the sources of power in Indian culture. One reviewer commented: "How grand and stupendous is the following plan! [. . .] We may reasonably expect to enlarge our stock of poetical imagery, as well as of history, from the labors of the Asiatic Society . . . to combine the useful and the pleasing" (*Critical Review* 59 [1785]: 19–21).

33. *Analytical Review* 7 (August 1790): 361. See *Sir William Jones: Selected Poetical and Prose Works*, ed. Michael J. Franklin, 213–97; henceforth cited as *Selected Works*. Kālidāsa's *Sacontalá* received, in the century following its publication, no fewer than forty-six translations in twelve different languages.

34. This exactly mirrored the judgment of the Indian poetic tradition itself, according to which "the *Sakuntala* is the validating aesthetic creation of a civilization" (Edwin Gerow, "Plot Structure and the Development of *Rasa* in the *Śakuntalā*," *Journal of the American Oriental Society*, pt. 1, 99 (1979): 559–72, and pt. 2, 100 (1980): 267–82; 1:564.

35. I have argued elsewhere that the European cult of Sensibility rendered European Romanticism particularly susceptible to the Sanskrit literary concept of *rasa*, with its emphasis upon the cultivation of the emotions, as displayed par excellence in *Śakuntalā* (see my *The European Discovery of India: Key Indological Sources of Romanticism*, 3: xiv–xvi). In this context it is important to remember the symbiotic relationship between popular and academic Orientalisms. Jones had learned Arabic with a Syrian named Mirza who had helped him translate the *Arabian Nights* back into its original tongue; his *Persian Grammar* had proved popular through its incorporation of substantial selections from Hāfiz; and he showed little reluctance to employ the language of sensibility in communicating the revelation of Sanskrit literature: "I am in love with the *Gopia*, charmed with *Crishen*, an enthusiastick admirer of *Rām*, and a devout adorer of *Brimha-bishen-mehais*: not to mention that *Judishteir, Arjen, Corno*, and the other warriors of the *M'hab'harat* appear greater in my eyes than Agamemnon, Ajax, and Achilles appeared, when I first read the Iliad" (letter of June 22, 1784 to Charles Wilkins, *The Letters of Sir William Jones*, ed. Garland Cannon, 2:652).

36. "[T]he religion of the Hindoos, which of all false religions is the most monstrous in its fables, and the most fatal in its effects," preface to *The Curse of Kehama: The Poetical Works of Robert Southey*, 8:xxiii.

37. *Anti-Jacobin Review* 38 (April 1811): 384; Fitzpatrick, *Lady Morgan*, 160–61.

38. *Letters of Percy Bysshe Shelley*, 1:107. In another letter to Thomas Jefferson Hogg, apparently of the following day, June 20, 1811, Shelley reiterates: "Have you read a new novel, the Missionary by Miss Owenson. It is a divine thing. Luxima the Indian Princess, were it possible to embody such a character, is *perfect*. The Missionary has been my companion for some time. I advise you to read it" (ibid., 1;112). In a third letter to Hogg [July 28, 1811?], Shelley again questions: "Have you read the Missionary. It is a beautiful thing. It is here & I cd not help reading it again—or do you not read novels" (ibid., 1:130).

39. Drew, *India and the Romantic Imagination*, 254.

40. "A Hymn to Lacshmī," *Selected Works*, 153–63.

41. *The Missionary: An Indian Tale*, ed. Julia M. Wright, 109; subsequent references will appear parenthetically in the text.

42. *Selected Works*, 361–63.

43. "On the Mystical Poetry of the Persians and Hindus," *Works*, 4:216.

44. "[W]e cannot cleave to infinite felicity, without also perpetually rejoicing in the first daughter of Love to GOD, Charity toward men," "On the Mystical Poetry of the Persians and Hindus," *Works*, 4:215. These are not isolated examples; what they reveal on

Owenson's part is a commendable commitment to syncretic method, if not to scholarly discipline. On Owenson's assimilation of Jones, see Drew, *India and the Romantic Imagination*, 241–42.

45. "[T]hat it [matter] has no essence independent of mental perception, [. . .] that external appearances and sensations are illusory, and would vanish into nothing, if the divine energy, which alone sustains them, were suspended but for a moment" (*Works*, 3:239). In her edition, Julia Wright seriously underplays the influence of Jones; despite Owenson's use of key French texts, her representation of India is certainly not "de(anglo)centered" as Wright claims (51). Apart from footnoted references, and, of course, the facilitating inspiration of the *Sacontalá*, unacknowledged but inherently relevant borrowings from Sir William Jones's essays are extremely frequent.

46. My teaching of *The Missionary* last semester adventitiously coincided with a library trial of the invaluable resource "Eighteenth-Century Collections Online."

47. "I have at last, waded through your *Oriental Library*, and it is impossible *you* can ever feel the weight of the obligation I owe you, except you turn author, and some kind friend supplies you with rare books that give the sanction of authority to your own wild and improbable visions. Your Indian histories place me upon the fairy ground you know I love to tread, 'where nothing is but what is not,' and you have contributed so largely and efficiently to my Indian venture, that you have a right to share in the profits, and a claim to be considered a silent partner in the firm," undated letter to Ormsby, *Memoirs*, 2:388.

48. "68. VIRANI [. . .] implies a power of allaying feverish heat; [. . .] among the innocent luxuries of this climate, we may assign the first rank to the coolness and fragrance, which the large hurdles or screens in which they are interwoven, impart to the hottest air, by the means of water dashed through them; while the strong southern wind spreads the scent before it, and the quick evaporation contributes to cool the atmosphere. [. . .] 69. ŚAMĪ [. . .] used by the Bráhmens to kindle their sacred fire" (*Works*, 5:154–55). The following page of *The Missionary* has Hilarion, while pondering the similarities between Oriental and Occidental traditions of mysticism, involuntarily repeating "The true object of soul and mind is the glory of a union with our beloved" (122). Cf. Jones's illustration of Sufi doctrine from Háfiz: "The true object of heart and soul is the glory of a union with our beloved" ("On the Mystical Poetry of the Persians and Hindus," *Works*, 3:225).

49. "Readers should keep in mind that Orientalist materials of Owenson's day are often contradictory, and tend to fall rather short of the standards of twentieth-century scholarship" (Wright, ed., *The Missionary*, 263).

50. *The Missionary*, 271. "Such a wife, adoring her husband, in celestial felicity with him, greatest, most admired, with him shall enjoy the delights of heaven while fourteen INDRAS reign" (Angiras, cited in H. T. Colebrooke, "On the Duties of a Faithful Hindu Widow," 212).

51. Rajan, *Under Western Eyes: India from Milton to Macaulay*, 133; "On the Orthography of Asiatick Words," *Works*, 3:313.

52. Rajan, 133.

53. Aurangzeb, an austerely orthodox Sunni, effectively ended such syncretic investigation. Akbar S. Ahmed has argued that dominion over the Muslims of South Asia has always moved between the contrasting leadership styles of Dārā Shikūh's Sufi-inspired syncretism and Aurangzeb's fundamentalism, this polarity being reflected in Zulfikar Ali Bhutto and General Zia respectively (see *Pakistan Society: Islam, Ethnicity and Leadership in South Asia*).

54. "That *most subtil spirit*, which he suspected to pervade natural bodies, and lying

concealed in them, to cause attraction and repulsion; the emission, reflection, and refraction of light; electricity, calefaction, sensation, and muscular motion, is described by the *Hindus* as a *fifth element*" ("Eleventh Anniversary Discourse: On the Philosophy of the Asiaticks," *Works*, 3:246; original emphasis).

55. Wendy Doniger, *Asceticism and Eroticism in the Mythology of Śiva*. Blake had read Charles Wilkins's *Bhăgvăt-Gēētā* (1785) and, fascinated by the Brahmans as guardians of hermetic wisdom, completed a drawing, now sadly lost, listed as No. X in *A Descriptive Catalogue*, titled "The Bramins": "The subject is Mr. Wilkin[s] translating the Geeta; an ideal design, suggested by the first publication of that party of Hindu Scriptures translated by Mr. Wilkin[s]. I understand that my Costume is incorrect, but in this I plead the authority of the ancients, who often deviated from the Habits, to preserve the Manners, as in the instance of Laocoon, who, though a priest, is represented naked" (*William Blake: Complete Writings*, ed. Geoffrey Keynes, 583).

56. "But, when thy daring arm untam'd / At Mahadeo [Śiva] a loveshaft aim'd, / Heav'n shook, and, smit with stony wonder, / Told his deep dread in bursts of thunder, / Whilst on thy beauteous limbs an azure fire / Blaz'd forth, which never must expire" ("A Hymn to Camdeo," ll. 65–70, *Selected Works*, 103; cf. "Hymn to Durgá," *Selected Works*, 168–78; esp. 2.3–3.3, 103, 171–72. On the difficulties of introducing Durgá into the drawing room, see my "Cultural Possession, Imperial Control, and Comparative Religion: The Calcutta Perspectives of Sir William Jones and Nathaniel Brassey Halhed."

57. I have marshaled evidence for this reading in "Passion's Empire" (see n. 15 above).

58. It is instructive to compare the Occidental example of the legend of St. Keiven which Owenson inserted into the 1812 third edition of *St Clair*. The saint unsuccessfully attempts to seek "an asylum against the power of woman" in the scenic "*Glendilough*, or the Valley of *Two Lakes*"; the beautiful chieftain's daughter finds his cave, and the saint, in trying to drive her away, accidentally pushes her to her death in the lake far below; *St Clair*, reprinted in *The Romantics: Women Novelists*, ed. Caroline Franklin and Peter Garside, 12; 1:32–47.

59. This is imaged in terms anticipatory of the syncretism which he is ultimately to espouse: "He pursued, with an eagle glance, the sun's majestic course: 'Today,' he said, 'it rose upon the Pagoda of Brahma; it hastens to gild, with equal rays, the temple once dedicated to its own divinity, in the deserts of Palmyra; to illumine the Caaba of Mecca; and to shine upon the tabernacle of Jerusalem!'" (81).

60. Jonathan Duncan considers "*Tupisya* or modes of devotional discipline," in "An Account of Two Fakeers, with Their Portraits," 38.

61 Owenson could have read of naphtha springs in *Asiatick Researches* 3 (1792): 297; vol. 4 (1795): 378; 5 (1798): 41. Significantly she describes Hilarion's self-sacrificial vow to renounce his physical love for Luxima as "the great immolation" (182).

62. Bernier, *Travels in the Mogul Empire*, trans. Archibald Constable, 2nd ed., 403–4. Rajah Nala rescues from the flames "a prodigious snake"—who turns out to be Agni, the god of fire. See "The History of the Nella-Rajah," in Nathaniel Edward Kindersley, *Specimens of Hindoo Literature*, 224–25. In *The Missionary*, Hilarion finds "a serpent of immense size" ready to strike at the sleeping Luxima's head. Without prejudice to the substantially different employment of the snake in Hebrew and Sanskrit texts, every symbolic/Miltonic Eden narrative would seem to require a serpent, and Hilarion's resolution to dispatch it with his crosier is rendered redundant when an Indian "vesper hymn" charms it away.

63. Owenson had stressed the contemporary relevance of her historical analogue by

glossing this passage with a footnote concerning the 1806 Sepoy Revolt at Vellore. This aligns Sydney Owenson with the (substantially) Whig opposition to missionary activity in India as illustrated by the Reverend Sydney Smith's weighty *Edinburgh Review* article of 1808 contextualizing the mutiny. Smith warned that the inevitable loss of caste among Indian converts to Christianity would destabilize Hindu society, threatening economic and political control in the subcontinent: "Brother Ringletaube may write home that he makes a Christian, when, in reality, he ought only to state that he has destroyed a Hindoo" (*Edinburgh Review* 12 [April 1808]: 177).

64. The tenth *avatara* of Vishnu, Kalki, will appear riding a white horse and brandishing a blazing sword to destroy the universal depravity of the Kali Yug (Age of Kali), an all-too-familiar world in which, according to the seventh-century (or earlier) *Vishnu Purāna*, "monarchs will be ever addicted to falsehood and wickedness [. . .] property alone will confer rank; wealth will be the only source of devotion; [. . .] women will be objects merely of sensual gratification. Earth will be venerated [not for its *tirthas* or sacred places] but for its mineral treasures," *European Discovery of India*, 5:482–83. Thomas Campbell depicts the tenth Avatar as follows: "Heaven's fiery horse, beneath his warrior form, / Paws the light clouds, and gallops on the storm! / Wide waves his flickering sword; his bright arms glow / Like summer suns, and light the world below! [. . .] To pour redress on India's injured realm, / The oppressor to dethrone, the proud to whelm; / To chase destruction from her plundered shore / With arts and arms that triumphed once before, / The tenth Avatar comes!" *The Pleasures of Hope*, ll. 589–92, 595–99).

CHAPTER 9

"Unlettered Tartars" and "Torpid Barbarians"

*Teaching the Figure of the Turk in
Shelley and De Quincey*

FILIZ TURHAN

Much contemporary scholarship has given us an increased appreciation for the role of colonialism and imperialism within the cultural movement we call Romanticism. This compelling body of scholarship has naturally provided instructors with a particularly rich way of conceiving and developing their courses. Perhaps the only pedagogical "disadvantage" to this critical output is the exponential increase in potential course material (literary, historical, and theoretical) from which the teacher must select to create a nuanced course in Romanticism. In particular, the ongoing interest in Orientalism has suggested that class time be devoted to such once-considered marginal works of the "big six" such as "The Giaour" or *The Revolt of Islam* as well as Orientalist works of other writers such as Sydney Owenson and William Beckford.

I want to suggest that a productive way to organize the material for students is to focus on one theme or trope as it is utilized in two texts produced very nearly simultaneously, but for very different purposes and to very different results. This process affords one the opportunity to present a single critical issue in all its complexity and difference and to demonstrate the fact that writers were not univocal on these matters. In this case, I am thinking of two texts written in 1821: Percy Shelley's *Hellas* and Thomas De Quincey's *Confessions of an English Opium Eater*, and most specifically, how each defines an English Self against a Turkish Other. A classroom reading of these texts can illustrate how they both rely on a presentation of the Turks as a trope for racial difference, which, in turn, has implications for Britain as an imperial power. While the focus on the figure of the Turk may initially seem to be rather narrow, several key reasons justify it: there is an increasingly important discourse of race as the British come into contact with different peoples, and the racial difference of the Turks provides an opportunity to explore this development; the proximity of Turkey to Europe made for its lengthy history in English literature; and its special role as the oppressors of the Greeks, who were increasingly seen to be the progenitors of European culture, made it an especially virulent foe. In addition, a visual comparison of the Ottoman and British Empires can be drawn quickly in class, and doing so helps in establishing the size and dimensions of the British Empire at this time. Moreover, both *Hellas* and the *Confessions* can be adapted to different level courses: although they both warrant complete readings, they can be easily excerpted, should the scope of the class demand it. Lastly, the specific juxtaposition of these texts is especially handy given that *Hellas* represents the near end of Shelley's writing career, whereas the *Confessions* marks (more or less) the start of De Quincey's. Because De Quincey's career ran well into the midcentury, such a juxtaposition can provide an opportunity to discuss the evolution of Orientalist discourse from about 1809 (Shelley's juvenilia) to the 1850s. In doing so, a variety of pertinent related issues can be discussed: for example, republicanism, Philhellenism, Indian colonization, the China trade in opium, the distinction of genres, and the uses of biographical criticism. In what follows, I provide a very brief outline of key Turkish-British facts, followed by close readings of passages of the two texts, and suggestions for student research and writing.

By the early nineteenth century, the Turkish and British Empires had approximately a 240-year diplomatic and trade history behind them, with a concomitant textual record of histories, plays, poetry, and travels to represent it. As a result, British Romantic writers inherited a whole constellation of images, associations, and attitudes about the Turks that was quite familiar to their readers. Overwhelmingly, the Turks were perceived to be the active oppressors of women and Christians, the wielders of a false religion, and the hypocritical indulgers in sexuality, drink, and opium. Furthermore, because the Ottoman Empire itself was a consolidated, familiar imperial power, its role as a political, military, and moral counterimage of empire was particularly powerful for Britons during these important years of British imperial expansion. Indeed, it is a noteworthy aspect of literary depictions of the Ottoman Empire that conservative and liberal writers alike utilized it as a means to criticize or defend practices at home; either way, they depicted the Ottoman Empire as a hideous model of oppression to avoid at all costs.

In the early stages of Turkish-British relations, the Turks were clearly the superior power—granting the Capitulations (trade rights) in the year 1580 and allowing Britain to establish the Turkey Company in 1581. By the early nineteenth century the reverse was true: while the Turks still retained control over much of southeast Europe, Anatolia, the Middle East, and northern Africa, their political power was being challenged by popular uprisings and their commercial development was significantly curtailed by outmoded economic and banking policies. In contrast, the British were successfully infiltrating India, China, and parts of Africa, primarily as a trade entity. In short, Turkish strength was fast diminishing in proportion to Britain's expanding economic, military, and political global power and this image of decline was especially useful to writers seeking to represent British imperial growth.

As Britain's power in the area increased, so, theoretically, did its ability to influence Turkish policy with regard to its domains and the subject peoples living within them. As a result, the moral pressure on British authorities to implement anti-Turkish policies in favor of their Christian subjects was great. As an aggressive Eastern-Muslim imperial power, the Ottoman Empire drew odium and moral outrage from Western Christians for centuries, but the political will to act on these motivations to defend eastern European Christendom was always slowed by economic considerations. Sir Paul Rycaut, a former consul of Smyrna, provides an early example of this impulse in *The History of the Present State of the Ottoman Empire* (1682): "And some study several ways, and prescribe Rules by which a War may be most advantageously managed against the Turk, I on the contrary, am more inclinable to give my judgement in what manner our Peace and Trade may best be secured and maintained; knowing that so considerable a welfare of our Nation depends upon it" (405–6). Rycaut's notion may not have seemed morally defensible, but the argument was certainly economically sound. Nearly two centuries later, the hesitation to challenge the Ottoman Empire in southeastern Europe was especially strong in the wake of the Napoleonic wars and the resulting Holy Alliance (November 20, 1815), a treaty that sought to reestablish a strong monarchist order throughout Europe. Thus, various republican, revolutionary movements from Spain, to Naples, to the Ottoman Empire, were especially unpalatable to many conservatives. Precisely for this reason, the Greek uprising of 1821 was particularly challenging to Western Christian powers: although it was morally unpopular to favor the Muslim oppressor over the Christian Greeks, the potential political instability in the region was unacceptably dangerous. The Philhellenes, aesthetically and politically minded supporters of Greek independence, especially utilized both the associations of classical civilization and Christianity to criticize politicians who were not explicitly in favor of supporting the Greek cause.[1]

Considering the long and complex relationship between the Ottoman and British Empires, it is no wonder that Western writers have repeatedly depicted the Turks in literature. In many ways, the Turkish Other is remarkably consistent over time: writers working in a variety of forms frequently used it in a self-defining racial binary whose stability is undercut specifically because of an intervening third racial category. For instance, in *Othello* (1604), the Moor strives to maintain his identification with the Venetians, and indeed he is seen by many to be *the* stalwart barricade between them and the "general enemy Ottoman" (1.3.57). At the end of the play, Othello reinforces the contrast between Venetian and Turk, but he now aligns himself rhetorically with the Other, by slaying himself in the same manner as he narrates once having done to the enemy Turk: "in Aleppo once, / Where a malignant and turbanned Turk / Beat a Venetian and traduced the state, / I took by the throat th' circumcised dog and smote him, thus" (5.2.414–18). Two hundred years later, Mary Shelley uses the Turk in a similar racial triangle in *Frankenstein* (1818): Safie is firmly identified throughout the text as "the Arabian," having been surreptitiously taught Christianity by her Arabian mother, and having wholly disavowed the Muslim identity she inherits from her Turkish father. This reprehensible Turkish father is established as the enemy of both the French De Laceys and the Arabian Safie, although clearly as his daughter there is an undeniable alliance between them. In both cases, the Turk is the active enemy of the state, Christianity, and domesticity.

This racial binary turned unstable triangle is similarly visible in *Hellas* and *Confessions of an English Opium Eater,* even though the texts have significant formal differences: one is a lyrical drama modeled on Aeschylus's *Persians*, the other is a memoir, avowedly *not* modeled on Rousseau's *Confessions*. While Shelley's *Hellas* conforms strictly to the Aristotelian unities, De Quincey's *Confessions* begins in a loose format and eventually unravels into a disparate collection of dream narratives. Although Shelley's play has an overtly political goal, De Quincey's magazine piece has an entertaining, if not admonitory one. While *Hellas*, issued by Ollier in a small edition in early 1822, failed to attract much popular or critical attention, the *Confessions*, first printed in the *London Magazine* in October and November 1821, enjoyed immense popularity, was widely reviewed, imitated, reprinted in book form in 1822, and revised and expanded in 1856. Although De Quincey uses the Turkish figure in the *Confessions* primarily for the purpose of individual self-definition, Shelley broadens this within *Hellas* to challenge British imperial policy with regard to Greek independence.

Nevertheless, some similarities in their writing approaches are evident. Despite the fact that travel into Ottoman domains had become a relatively common experience (particularly during the Napoleonic wars when European travel was not well advised), neither Shelley nor De Quincey had ever traveled to the East. As a result, both were more or less ignorant of realities of the area about which they were writing: Shelley was working from what he called in the preface to *Hellas* "newspaper erudition" about the Greek War of Independence and De Quincey was proceeding from his readings and his personal views on Turkish opium eaters, culture, and manners (and subsequently of those of China and Egypt), evidently made more intense from his personal demons (see Barrell, Simmons). Moreover, both texts are sensational for very practical reasons: they are given to descriptions that shock and titillate through the narration of explicit horror and violence—Shelley to gain sympathy for a revolution, and De Quincey to sell magazines and earn much-needed cash. Most important for our purposes, both texts take the reader into a territory implicated as Turkish, dangerously aligning the English Self with that Turkish Other, yet going to great lengths to maintain a distance that secures the integrity of the Western subject. However, both lose control of the distance, and forge similarities that are stylistically manifest. As in the texts cited above, stable racial binaries fall apart when each figure inevitably wiggles out of its initial characterization. The close readings that follow show how this happens in *Hellas* through the portrayal of the sultan and the Greek chorus and in the *Confessions* through the depiction of De Quincey's increasingly torpid condition as his opium habit persists over the years. For both writers, the disintegration of the individual racial distinction in turn inflects their visions of British imperial power: for De Quincey this becomes evident in his later writings, but for Shelley the repercussions are palpable in *Hellas* itself.

De Quincey's infamous Oriental Others include Turks, Chinese, Egyptians, and Afghans. His characteristic attitude toward these figures, their cultures, and their governments is notably vitriolic, jingoistic, and nationalistic, tinged frequently with a vicious humor and sense of personal outrage.[2] Students are frequently at a loss to determine when De Quincey is being serious and when he is deliberately exaggerating for comic effect; at the risk of admitting ambiguity it's interesting to show that it's a little of both, not because he's a bad writer, but as a reaction to a particular psychic pressure. John Barrell and others have connected elements of De Quincey's early biography (most notably, the death of his sister Elizabeth and the infamous colonial games played by him and his bully-brother William) to his anxious denunciation of various Eastern cultures. In these memories, De Quincey is associated with passivity and girlishness, associations that are simultaneously warm and reassuring but also embarrassing. Because of this painfully ambivalent attitude, we see an identification with the Other that is reconfigured into exaggerated disavowal. Utilizing theories of Narcissism, Diane Simmons has recently explained De Quincey's characteristic use of Asians as a "socially acceptable, if irrational, outlet for the rage and sadistic desire for revenge" associated with the narcissistic damage inflicted upon him as a child (182). Furthermore, Simmons follows Ronald Hyam and others in noting that this kind of close connection between troubled childhood experiences and adult attitudes toward the East is a characteristic shared by many "rulers of empire" (Hyam, 49).

In order to illustrate De Quincey's characteristic brand of Orientalism, class discussion can focus on his direct references to the Turks; such a reading illustrates the specifically vexed attitude borne of the fact that opium implicates him (and by extension other English opium eaters) as Turkish in spirit. As we will see later, Shelley typically forges similarities between British and Turkish despots as a specific rhetorical tool to achieve a specific political and poetical message; however, De Quincey's identification with the Turkish Other is an inadvertent by-product of his use of opium and in strong need of rhetorical control so as to qualify or break the disturbing connection. Although his rhetoric of qualification and carefully crafted disclaimers serve to deny the association, as his habit increases, the distinction collapses and similarities are forged. De Quincey's rhetorical construction of the Turk is a harbinger of the overwhelmingly disturbing figure of the "Southern Asians" who haunt his dreams and the outskirts of the *Confessions*.

At the close of part 1, De Quincey refers to Turks within a context of both moral and personal superiority. In discussing the medical profession's handling of opium, De Quincey introduces Awsiter, the apothecary to Greenwich hospital, who speculates as to why no predecessor of his has fully described the effects of opium: "for there are so many properties in it, if universally known, that would habituate the use, and make it more in request with us than the Turks themselves" (32). De Quincey disputes this claim by developing two related themes in the text. First, he juxtaposes English attitudes, abilities, let us say, spirit, with that of the Turks; and second, he introduces his superior knowledge. Opium constitutes a secret world of information, experience, and knowledge, for which the user trades his freedom. De Quincey, by first asserting that he has gained this knowledge, while yet possessing his freedom, justifies his disagreement with the doctor. The doctor says, in effect, if the English knew all there really was to know of opium, we would have more opium eaters in England than in Turkey. De Quincey suggests the opposite, that the English, combining their innate good sense with the proper scientific knowledge of the drug, would master it, and it is *he*, De Quincey, who will provide this knowledge. Unfortunately, by the end of "The Pains of Opium," he will describe his uncontrollable addiction and admit his woeful lack of medical knowledge in general, without acknowledging the wrongheadedness of this initial claim; in fact, the irony of this misconception seems to be wholly lost on him.

De Quincey intensifies his focus on these issues in "The Pleasures of Opium," which contains an awful paradox, if not a stunning example of racial hypocrisy. In his goal to dispel the myths that surround the effects of opium, De Quincey juxtaposes those lying "travellers to Turkey" (72) who misrepresent the bodily effects of opium, with himself, an authentic arm-chair Orientalist whose authority is based on opium-eating experience in England. After distinguishing between opium and alcohol, he moves quickly to disprove two related, common misconceptions of opium: that "the eleva-tion of spirits produced by opium is *necessarily* followed by a proportionate depression, and that the *natural and even immediate* consequence of opium is torpor and stagnation, animal and mental" (77; emphasis added). The qualifiers "necessarily" and "natural and even immediate" make it clear that what he is saying is not always the case, despite his strong condemnation of such beliefs. It is particularly ironic because by the end of the chapter he admits that solitude and silence *are* the most appropriate environments in which to enjoy one's trances; he alludes to the terrifying nightmares and total humiliation he experiences as a result of his opium eating in later years. In other words, the attempt to dispel those myths of the "bodily effects of opium" is rather quickly supplanted by an admission that those very quali-ties *are* ultimately the true result of the drug. However, the subtlety of the rhetoric stops the passage from being blatantly hypocritical, for those quali-fiers "necessarily" and "immediate consequence" restrict the applicability of the statement, and allow for the seemingly contradictory vision of the opium eater at the end of the section.

Having established that torpor and depression do not necessarily accom-pany the use of opium, De Quincey is able to contrast the novel image of the opium-eating Englishmen and the seminal image of the opium-eating Turk. Here again, his rhetoric subtly renders his accusations against the Turks contingent. In the three references to torpid Turks which immediately follow, each assertion is prefaced with the proper rhetorical device to qualify the message: "With respect to the torpor *supposed* to follow, or rather, (*if we were to* credit the numerous pictures of Turkish opium-eaters) to accompany the practice of opium eating. . . . Turkish Opium eaters, *it seems*, are absurd enough to sit, like so many equestrian statues, on logs of wood as stupid as themselves. . . . It will be seen that at least opium did not move me to seek solitude, and much less to seek inactivity, or the torpid state of self-involu-tion *ascribed to* the Turks" (77; emphasis added). The use of qualifiers works to distance the image from De Quincey's immediate experience to such a degree as to make them seem not only beyond his notice, but also beyond contempt.

The distinction between Turkish torpor and English perseverance is amplified when De Quincey subsequently sets the stage for an old-fashioned drinking contest: "But that the reader may judge of the degree in which opium is likely to stupefy the faculties of an Englishman." One of the ways he maintains a position of superiority is that his motive for taking the opium at this stage of his life was intellectual: "I was a hard student, and at severe studies for all the rest of my time: and certainly I had a right occasionally to recreations as well as other people" (77). While the Turks are likened to wood, this Englishman is an active, hardworking student who is merely indulging in a little hard-earned rest and relaxation. And when he does indulge in his naughty pleasure, he takes himself to the opera where the stimulation of the mind through opium is put to good use. It is here that the most outlandish Turkish reference occurs:

> I question whether any Turk, of all that ever entered the paradise of opium-eaters, can have had the pleasure I had. But indeed, I honour the Barbarian too much by supposing them capable of any pleasure approaching to the intellectual ones of an Englishman. For music is an intellectual or a sensual pleasure, according to the temperament of him who hears it. (78)

Here he is clearly asserting that the ability to appreciate music is an intellectual and a racial quality, and has nothing to do with opium, because only certain minds are capable of hearing music, for although musical notation is (ironically) "like a collection of Arabic characters" to him (79), like opium, he knows music through the natural faculty of a mind in communion with an external object. Thus, although his rhetoric above suggests that he cannot substantiate his opinions regarding Turkish torpor, his description of appreciating music does in fact assert the truth of those reports.

In the final section, "The Pains of Opium," De Quincey admits the depths to which he has sunk as a result of his opium addiction; indeed, his self-portrait in this section shows the total breakdown of the rhetorical distinction between the English Self (the hard student) and the Turkish Other (the torpid barbarian): "I have thus described and illustrated my intellectual *torpor*, in terms that apply, more or less, to every part of the four years during which I was under the *Circean* spells of opium. But for misery and suffering, I might, indeed, be said to have existed in a dormant state" (101; emphasis added). The use of the word "torpor" to describe himself after its close association with the Turkish opium eater collapses the careful distinction earlier established; moreover, the use of the adjective "Circean" even implicates his Greek identity as Other. In other places De Quincey's oft-invoked self-image as a superior Greek scholar works to set him above nearly anyone with whom he comes into contact (most notably his teachers at the Manchester Grammar School) and yet here something Greek is as seductive and torpidity-inducing as its counterpart, the Turk. Like Shelley's claim that "we are all Greeks," from the preface to *Hellas,* De Quincey's sense of superiority is undercut when "Greekness" is associated with the Turkish qualities of torpidity, intellectual passivity, and dissipation.

Thus, the scathingly humorous portrait of the torpid Turk is a concise way for De Quincey to establish his authority as the *English* opium eater. His superior knowledge of the drug, borne in part from his possessing "the superior faculties of an Englishman," debunks the misconceptions widely available to the uninitiated through such sources as pictures of indolent Turks. However, his presentation of the patently inferior Turk seen in "numerous pictures . . . sitting on Logs of wood as stupid as themselves," breaks down when the superior Englishman assumes the inevitable stance of torpidity; De Quincey even invites the reader to draw his own counterpicture of the tormented English opium eater as the "criminal at the bar" (96). The two pictures side by side show just how his opium knowledge has overwhelmed and changed him, a change that becomes increasingly clear at the close of the text.

Having modeled through intensive close readings the way De Quincey utilizes the Turkish Other as a trope for racial difference, one can invite the students to list the other figures that are present in the text, such as Ann of Oxford Street, the Malay, and the various Asians in the dream visions. Students can then compose their own essays that trace the rhetorical patterns of identification and denial at work in De Quincey's presentation of these others. For example, as negative as the image of the Turk is here, the rhetorical construction of the Chinese (and other "Southern Asians") in the dream section of May 1818 is intensified to an unbearable degree. Just as the distinction between Englishman and Turk disintegrates, so does De Quincey's interaction with the Asian. On one hand he is wholly alien: "In China, over and above what it has in common with the rest of Southern Asia, I am terrified by the modes of life, by the manners, and the barrier of utter abhorrence, and want of sympathy placed between us by feelings deeper than I can analyze. I could sooner live with lunatics, or brute animals" (109). On the other hand, he identifies only too fully: "I was the idol; I was the priest; I was worshipped; I was sacrificed" (109). The fear and loathing traceable in the language of China in the *Confessions* is in turn a harbinger of the extremely negative treatment he will give them, as a cultural, political, and trade entity in the two so-called Opium essays of 1840 and 1857, pertinent passages of which can be provided to students in handouts. In the essay of 1840 he describes China as "incapable of a true civilization, semi-refined in manners and mechanic arts, but incurably savage in the moral sense" (Masson, 14:193). De Quincey's wholehearted support of Britain's right to sell opium in China is thus based partly on the fact that the Chinese are racially distinct and notably inferior to the British. Hence, their government's incorrect actions are commensurate with their moral status.[3]

Although De Quincey's conservative approach to politics and empire sharply contrasts with Shelley's liberal convictions, they both use the Turk as a figure of racial distinction which in turn has implications for the image of the British Empire. Although a long and sometimes trying read for students (especially its narrative sections), *Hellas* provides for the opportunity to discuss two key Shelleyan issues: Philhellenism and the doctrine of perfectability. Given his intense interest in classical studies, as well as his support of republican movements throughout Europe, Shelley took an active interest in the contemporary situation of the Greeks, as well as their oppressors, the Turks. Poems depicting the Ottoman Empire occur at key moments in Shelley's career and in each case Shelley characteristically represents the Ottoman sphere as a place of political strife on the verge of utter destruction.[4] One of his most illuminating and damning comments on the Turkish Empire appears in the prose treatise *A Philosophical View of Reform* (1820) where Shelley describes the flow of liberty from Greece throughout the Western world; in addition, he describes the inevitable liberation of the Indians, the Persians, and the Negroes. However, he very notably excludes the Turks from the renovating winds of change:

> The Turkish Empire is in its last stage of ruin, and it cannot be doubted but that the time is approaching when the deserts of Asia Minor and Greece will be colonized by the overflowing population of countries less enslaved and debased, and that the climate and the scenery which was birthplace of all that is wise and beautiful will not remain forever the spoil of wild beasts and unlettered Tartars. (18)

In this passage Shelley reduces the Turks to "wild beasts and unlettered Tartars" because they have no advanced social institutions which would suggest that any vestige of their empire could be renovated into a liberated, modern government. Instead, he envisions the land wholly emptied of its people and ripe for colonization by those worthy of it. Considering his inclusion of such non-European "Others" as Indians, Persians, and Negroes, this exclusion of Turks suggests that he categorized them as hopelessly irredeemable and would heartily applaud their fall.

Indeed, in 1821 it did seem as if the "last stage" of Turkish ruin was finally at hand. At this time, the Shelleys were following with great interest the Greek uprising against the Turkish oppressors as well as other republican movements throughout Europe. In her note to *Hellas* written for the edition of 1839, Mary Shelley devotes considerable space to a delineation of the "great political excitement at the beginning of the year 1821" that inspired Shelley (480). Living in Italy, the Shelleys had little direct knowledge of the situation in the Ottoman Empire, but they did have contact with various important men (most notably Prince Alexander Mavrocordatos, to whom the poem is dedicated) who provided them with information and helped inspire them with the belief that radical improvement for the Greeks was imminent.[5] In his enthusiastic faith that there would be real change for the people living in these realms, Shelley was moved to write one of his most explicitly political and least allegorical long poems. In contrast with elements of his earlier poem *The Revolt of Islam* (1818), Shelley knew that the real Greece would not free itself from the yoke of Ottoman oppression with a poetry-inspired Festival of Brotherhood outside Constantinople or a former odalisque walking through the city streets preaching gender equality. Instead, freedom would have to be achieved with guns and blood, and British support for the cause would be indispensable. Shelley therefore sought a form for his poem which would express his own philosophical hopes and also convince the "despot" at home that "the independence of Greece [should be maintained] both against Russia and the Turks" (448). Shelley's sense of the urgency of his revolutionary message is borne out in his letter of November 11 urging Ollier to publish the poem at once because "what little interest this poem may ever excite, depends upon its immediate publication" (*Letters*, 335). In the text, therefore, we can trace a strong utopian language within a narrative of the actual temporal events unfolding in 1821. In fact, scholars are not at all in agreement as to the success of Shelley's effort to wed these two elements in *Hellas*.[6] Far from being a problem, this critical argument can provide the class with a useful writing exercise: students can join the community of scholars in dialogue, weighing in on the argument, with each student determining how to balance close readings of the text with material from outside the text as a way to judge Shelley's intentions and results.

Throughout his career, Shelley struggled to conceive and articulate a history of humanity that would both acknowledge the seemingly endless recurrence of eras of intense human misery while still demonstrating the overall upward trajectory of history. The paradoxical pull between eternal ideals and actual human misery is evident in the early *Queen Mab* (1813) as well as the late *Hellas*, where the tension between actual war and philosophical ideal would seem to be easily managed because the two entities at war are so clearly identified as right (Greece) and wrong (Turkey). Since Turkey has no claim to modern ideals, its violent fall can be portrayed not as a decline in civilization but a great lurch forward, even if the period of its fall is marked by intense human suffering and social chaos. In *Hellas*, the Greek-born spirit of Liberty has traveled the world, and is finally returning home, thereby revitalizing the ideal of "Hellas." Shelley dramatizes this historical notion by emphasizing the fundamental, ontological split between Hellas and Turkey. Turkey is associated with transience, error, and war because of the way it was first established: "Inheritor of glory, / Conceived in darkness, born in blood, and nourished / With tears and toil, thou seest the mortal throes / Of that whose birth was but the same" (ll. 849–52). Shelley's notion of historical progress inspires him to show that Turkey as a world power is only a temporal and temporary oppressor because its power is based on oppression and force of arms; its empire has been as one long, dark night. In contrast, Hellas is of a wholly different make; it embodies the eternal concept of Liberty: "[built] below the tide of war, / Based on the crystalline sea / Of thought and its eternity" (ll. 697–99). Shelley envisions Hellas as a portion of eternity, not subject to the flux of the temporal, for it is at the foundation of life. Thus are the two entities, Hellas and Turkey, set up in what initially seems a solid binary opposition ostensibly in the hope that this philosophical fact would inspire enthusiastic political, economic, and military support for the Greek cause.

However, Shelley's own awareness of the difficulties facing any group of people in seeking freedom from their oppressors makes his effort to present the "series of lyric pictures" (as he described *Hellas*) in stark terms nearly impossible. One of the main problems is the undeniable gap between Greece the temporal and Hellas the ideal, which Shelley himself acknowledges in the preface when he describes the "degraded" state of the contemporary Greeks (see Roessel, 13–41 and Turhan, 112–18). Therefore, over the course of the poem, complexities and contradictions creep in and undercut the stability of the binary, despite Shelley's overt goal to express his sympathy for the Greeks and condemnation of the Turks. Oddly enough, the Turks become more "Greek" and the Greeks become more "Turkish." As if this weren't dangerous enough, the instability is made even worse considering the tricky position of the British in the poem. In the preface and the poem itself, Shelley deliberately posits a connection between the British power structure and the Turks, thereby implicating the British as "Turkish." Conversely, in the preface he famously asserts that "We are all Greeks," with the "we" referring to the British people. However, the subsequently ambiguous images of the Greeks and the reformed Turkish sultan not only suggest how they break out of their reliable categories of good and bad, but also threaten the ideal upon which British identification with the Greeks is based.

Borrowing from Aeschylus's *Persians*, Shelley places us directly in the imperial harem along with the contemporary Turkish sultan, Mahmud II, and shows us his moment-by-moment reaction to the war news. In the beginning, he is concerned with the perpetuation of his rule, and commands his men to new heights of violence: "Go! Bid [the Janissaries] pay themselves / With Christian blood! Are there no Grecian virgins / Whose shrieks and spasms and tears they may enjoy? / No infidel children to impale on spears?" (ll. 241–45). Despite the fact that Mahmud is a tyrant with blood on his hands, he also desires the philosophical education that will give him the ability to act well, and so he sends for Ahaseurus, Shelley's ubiquitous Wandering Jew. Over the course of the three dialogue scenes, Mahmud experiences a fundamental recognition about the nature of human reality and history, which in effect "cures" him of his Turkish tyranny.

Upon his arrival, Ahaseurus shows Mahmud the illusory nature of material reality. Mahmud understands the error of his ways, but is debarred from acting upon this realization. Although he is the all-powerful sultan, his place in history was determined long ago: because Turkey was born in the strife and violence of war, it must die that way. Remarkably, Shelley's Mahmud is an apt pupil who immediately accepts the lesson that empire is no more: "The chalice of destruction full, and all / Thirsting to drink, and who among us dares / To dash it from his lips? And where is hope?" (ll. 270–72). As the final messengers report the defeat of the Greeks, Mahmud is left in the vexed position of allowing the carnage to continue, although he knows both that the fall of his empire is inevitable, and, even worse, that his ancestors have been guilty of the cruelest forms of despotic repression from the very beginning. Ironically, Mahmud's exit lines show him to be on the verge of relinquishing power, but powerless to do so: "I must rebuke / This drunkenness of triumph ere it die / And dying bring despair. Victory? Poor slaves!" (ll. 928–30). While this may at first appear to be a commendable attempt to imagine Mahmud as a sympathetic, flawed human tyrant, within the scope of the play, such a portrayal opens up possibilities of change that Shelley is unwilling to pursue. Although the scene mirrors Xerxes' return from war in *The Persians,* the critical difference between the two is that Xerxes' defeat is final; his recognition and reversal occur simultaneously and are inextricably bound. In contrast, Mahmud's recognition of wrong is not accompanied by a reversal of fortune; instead, his forces are overpowering the Greeks. At the moment, however, that the sultan exchanges his identity as a bloody tyrant for that of a Western-educated philosopher, Shelley writes him out of the play. After all, given that one of the goals of the poem is to foment British support for the war, presenting Mahmud as a recognizably humane and reformed ruler would be counterproductive.

Just as the Turkish Other comes dangerously close to renovation and reform, compromising his image as a bloody tyrant, the Greek chorus introduces dangerous problems into the play that undercut the rhetorical construction of Greece. For instance, in the second lyrical passage Shelley (like many Philhellenes) utilizes Christianity as a justification for Western support for the war, even though he himself harbored such critical views of it; thus, he mitigates the persuasiveness of the message by qualifying his presentation of the universal aspect of Christianity. This split purpose is more pronounced in the chorus's reflections on the ideal of Liberty: the problem is that if Shelley too firmly insists on the ontological identification of Greece and Liberty, then there is little need to drum up support for the enterprise because the Greek victory would be inevitable. On the other hand, to point out the difficulties of the war effort would seem to contradict the utopian language closely associated with Greece. From the start of the poem, victory is presented to be both inevitable and only potentially the apotheosis of Hellas, for Freedom may leave a "desert or a Paradise" depending on the contingencies of experience. This image delivers the message that, although it may be inevitable for Greece to be free one day, without outside support, that day will be long delayed and the interim suffering may be excessive. In the third choral song, the difficult goal of positing the ideal of Hellas and the reality of Greece culminates: just as he vividly paints the violent images of the current war and invokes the names of places associated with intense battles, "Thermae, Asopos and Persia" (ll. 688–89), Shelley also puts forth the seemingly opposite assertion that "Athens arose" from the sea with Light and Liberty. The philosophical position that Hellas is ontologically based on an ideal of eternal Liberty, which nevertheless falls victim to contingency, is a paradox that becomes increasingly difficult to sustain. This becomes finally visible in the assertion that, although "Pity's altar" resides in Sacred Athens, the Greeks may yet succumb to the hideous perils of bloodlust and revenge against their oppressors, in effect, to become "Turkish" by adopting the very qualities of violence associated with the Turks. Just how is it possible for the two to coexist? The likelihood and indeed, the advisability of pity for the Turkish oppressor becomes even more paradoxical toward the end of the play when the voices from outside raise the pitch of sensational violence to its zenith; for example, in their new victory, partially secured through the aid of the Europeans, the Turks cry out: "Oh, keep holy / This jubilee of unrevenged blood! / Kill! Crush! Despoil! Let not a Greek escape!" (ll. 1020–22).

Although the Greeks are losing the war at the poem's end, an idealistic hope yet lingers, for the chorus asserts that Greece may now be a wreck, but that it will eventually be built again "above the idle foam of Time" (l. 1007), that "another Athens shall arise, / And to remoter time / Bequeath, like sunset to the skies, / The splendour of its prime" (ll. 1084–87). However, by this time the question as to the source of this paradoxical faith has become increasingly palpable. One wonders how the ideal of Liberty can go into hibernation and come out again in real time. The chorus's position is a philosophical conundrum that it does not solve, and so the warring goals of political contingency and philosophical idealism sputter and falter at the end of the poem. Just as Mahmud walks off stage ready to stop the war but unable to, the chorus relinquishes its position and disavows its role: "Cease! Drain not to its dregs the urn / Of bitter prophecy. / The world is weary of the past, / O might it die or rest at last!" (ll. 1097–1101).

To acknowledge that *Hellas*'s weaving together of utopian, political philosophy with a real political, military event of 1821 is problematic does not at all detract from its powerful position in Shelley's body of work or from its usefulness in characterizing discourses of Orientalism. Read in conjunction with others such as "Ode to Liberty" (1820) and the *Defense of Poetry* (1820), *Hellas* testifies to the power and the paradox inherent in Shelley's belief in historical progressivism, as well as its particular challenge to the conservative, reactionary politics of the Holy Alliance. It is only because Shelley attempts to base the legitimacy of the Greek fight for independence on a tenuous racial distinction between Turks and Greeks that fissures in the poem's surface appear. Moreover, the contrast between Shelley's identification of the British *leader* with the Turks but the British *people* with the Greeks introduces another ambiguity into the poem's structure, one which notably reflects the complicated reactions among Westerners to the Greek and other republican movements.

Over the centuries of Turkish-British relations, writers of various political persuasions took advantage of the familiar negative characteristics of wastefulness, hypocrisy, and gratuitous violence of the Turk to help define a sense of the self. De Quincey and Shelley both depict the Turk as a figure of racial difference whose Otherness is first posited as fundamentally, positively distinct, but whose distinctiveness is revealed to be illusory. In the *Confessions of an English Opium Eater*, De Quincey's self-association with the weak, effeminate, uncivilized East (Turks et al.) inspires him to heights of sarcastic, humorous, and vitriolic denunciations of the East. In *Hellas,* Shelley's strategy to place Greece and Turkey at opposite ends of a spectrum, with Britain in the middle, both associated with Greece and Turkey, falls apart when he tries to incorporate recognition of realistic contingencies associated with a real war. Whether the Turk is seen as De Quincey's "torpid barbarian" or Shelley's "unlettered Tartar," it is an image well established over the centuries, which is nonetheless unstable and ambiguous. The comforting belief that "we" are not only different from, but inherently superior to, "them," becomes increasingly difficult to maintain, as the human reality of the Other is established through the intimate contact that is an inescapable correlative of empire building. Thus, as the growth of the British Empire rapidly increased throughout the nineteenth century, British interaction with different cultures necessarily became more intimate and complex and as a result, the ability to maintain cultural and racial distinctions was also challenged. The unstable presentation of the Turks marks an early and common example of this difficulty.

A look at these texts produced almost simultaneously gives us a great insight into the ways in which English writers envisioned the English self during a time when world politics, commerce, and empire-building were expanding exponentially. Just such a juxtaposition of texts, drawing out consistencies and varieties, provides students of Romanticism, Orientalism, and imperialism with a concise and meaningful way to see just how the challenges of global expansion could reflect upon self-image.

NOTES

1. While Castlereagh had followed a strict policy of supporting the Ottoman Empire against any rebel activities, his successor, Canning, attempted to steer a middle ground in which England would offer mediation services between its ally the Turks and the upstart Greeks (see St. Claire).

2. Although most scholars agree that De Quincey's political leanings were quite conservative, Robert Morrison has argued that the level of his rhetoric is frequently tied to the publishing venue in which specific pieces appear. It is also noteworthy that De Quincey admired and favorably reviewed Shelley's *The Revolt of Islam*, a very radical, reform-minded text.

3. It is noteworthy that De Quincey's insistence on Britain's unassailable right to sell opium to the Chinese was not prevalent, even among British conservatives (see McDonaugh).

4. Other poems that do so include Shelley's first long poem, "Henry and Louisa" (1809), and *The Revolt of Islam* (1818), in which the mighty struggle between the Greeks and Turks took on nearly cosmic dimension.

5. In December 1820, the Shelleys made the acquaintance of Mavrocordatos, the de facto leader of the exiled Greek patriots in Europe. In April 1821, his cousin, General Ypsilanti, raised a Greek army in Wallachia and in May Mavrocordatos departed Italy to join in the fighting (Holmes, 624, 646). The Shelleys continued to get information from his cousin, the Prince Argyropli, and from the Greek patriots who passed through the port cities of Tuscany both on the way to and returning from Wallachia.

6. Critical appraisal of Shelley's *Hellas* tends to fall into two schools of thought: that which sees the poem's overall focus on history as positive and hopeful, and that which sees it as fundamentally ambivalent, and by extension, negative and hopeless. For a full survey of the critical terrain, see Turhan (94–105).

CHAPTER 10

"Boundless Thoughts and Free Souls"

Teaching Byron's Sardanapalus, Lara, *and* The Corsair

G. TODD DAVIS

O'er the glad waters of the dark blue sea,
Our thoughts as boundless, and our souls as free,
Far as the breeze can bear, the billows foam,
Survey our empire, and behold our home!
These are our realms, no limit to their sway,—
Our flag the sceptre all who meet obey.
　　—Byron, *The Corsair*

My students often find Byron irresistible. Works such as *Manfred* and *The Corsair* appeal to their love of the Byronic hero—his "boundless" thoughts and limitless freedoms—even though most students have yet to learn why Byron or the Byronic hero exemplifies these qualities or why they already have such familiarity with Byron and the Byronic. Students are less enamored of *Childe Harold's Pilgrimage*, finding it plodding, maudlin, and, to use their ubiquitous word, "boring." *Don Juan* brings them no end of pleasure, especially after hearing various snippets of Byron's biography, which they can intersperse within the text itself. They find the bedroom scene between Donna Julia, Don Alfonso, and Don Juan extraordinarily funny, although the dark humor of the shipwreck scene often remains opaque to them. I have used "Darkness" quite successfully in my introductory composition and literature classes; its compact and concise structure, intense sentiments, and pervasive gloominess poignantly speak to them in a post-9/11 world. Repeatedly, though, they have balked at the Oriental tales, finding the language and context too difficult and foreign to fathom. (Incidentally, they dislike William Beckford's *Vathek* for the same reasons.) As a result, I have been forced to find or create inventive means by which to help them understand not only the prose and stylistics but the historical context as well of Byron's *Oriental Tales.*

Invariably, my students carp about relevance: Why is this work important? How does it relate to our lives? How will reading it help us get better jobs? Leaving that last question for another time and place, I find their first two concerns notable but often ambiguous. After all, we can talk extensively about canonization, about literary histories, about authorial intentions and objectives, but I believe these questions belie their deeper concerns, the basis of which underscores their uncertainty about their place in the world and the importance of their response to how we make meaning in texts. As such, I introduce my students to Reception Theory, which allows them to better understand not only their own responses but also the importance of those responses to the academic community at large.

For help in understanding Reception Theory, I often introduce my students to Hans Robert Jauss, who investigates the synergistic give-and-take among audience, text, and author, formulating the construct as a three-sided figure connected at each focal point. In *Toward an Aesthetic of Reception*, Jauss says:

> In the triangle of author, work, and public the last is no passive part, no chain of mere reactions, but rather itself an energy formative of history. The historical life of a literary work is unthinkable without the active participation of its addressees. For it is only through the process of its mediation that the work enters into the changing horizon-of-experience of a continuity in which the perpetual inversion occurs from simple reception to critical understanding, from passive to active reception, from recognized aesthetic norms to a new production that surpasses them. (19)

According to Jauss, addressees actively create the text while they are simultaneously limited by the text's horizons. A complex mediation results, whereby the audience actively engages the text and develops a critical understanding of it, a process that crystallizes into a new production "through negation of familiar experience or through raising newly articulated experiences to the level of consciousness" (25). Jauss stipulates how the text regulates and influences readers' interpretations by emphasizing a series of expectations against which readers can distinguish the text. This "dynamic process" actively articulates the audience and the work, which can be "objectified historically along the spectrum of the audience's reactions and criticism's judgment" (25). The work and audience create continually renewing "horizons-of experience," the ever-broadening landscapes of critical and perceptual understanding, through which "recognized aesthetic norms" are transformed into "new productions" that surpass or efface their originals but also retain enough of the former material to be recognizable in each incarnation. To put it another way: "These changing expectations, coupled with knowledge of (and reaction to) past readers' responses, combine to produce for each literary work a critical 'tradition' that is continuously enriched and modified as new generations of readers emphasize different points or see old ones in a new light" (Murfin and Ray, 332). In general, the audience consumes material and transforms it into critical discourse, thereby augmenting and enhancing the constantly expanding horizon for future generations. As Jauss says, the "next work can solve formal and moral problems left behind by the last work, and present new problems in turn" (32).

Jauss can be easily allied with Edward Said through the "horizon-of-experience." Said defines Orientalism as a "way of coming to terms with the Orient that is based on the Orient's special place in European Western experience" (1). As such, Orientalism works within a horizon that has been mediated by the audience's presumption of knowledge and familiarity of European explorers and travelers. This continuity persists because it hasn't been limited by an explicitly defined understanding of places and cultures. Said defines the Orient as an "invention" and a "created consistency," a constructed simulacra that has no origin except through the embellished tales of authors and ambassadors. Said suggests that Orientalism has "less to do with the Orient than it does with 'our' world" (12). Consequently, as Jauss would say, we can see how the landscape of critical and perpetual understanding has remained within a passive construction, never moving beyond this compliance with the myth to an active engagement with the object itself. With no "negation" of the "familiar experience," the Orient continues to exist as the romantic, exotic world with which Europeans had become comfortable.

The European reading audience, which had long been devouring material about the Orient, incessantly refashioned and perpetuated this landscape through their own writing and conversation. Said has observed that "Beckford, Byron, Goethe, and Hugo restructured the Orient by their art and made its colors, lights, and people visible through their images, rhythms, and motifs. At most, the 'real' Orient provoked a writer to his vision; it very rarely guided it" (22). I suggest to my students that this fascination with and construction of the Orient continues today and that they are an integral part of this continuing process. I provide such filmic examples as *Crouching Tiger, Hidden Dragon; The Matrix Trilogy*; and *Kill Bill, Volume 1* and *Volume 2* as evidence of our unrelenting fascination with the myth and fantasy of the Orient. They begin to see how we as audience members manifestly construct the view that most easily and comfortably fits within our own "horizon-of-experience."

Byron, as both author and audience, remains, while he writes within a liminal state between author and audience through the mediation of the text. In his elucidation of Gadamer, Jauss stipulates, "the producer of a text becomes also a recipient when he sets out to write" ("Changing Horizon," 148). By filling this doubled and mediated role, Byron varies the scope and alters the boundaries of the horizon of experience and expectation. However, this dialogue between author and audience generates an alterity that prefigures and influences the relationship between producer and consumer. Jauss continues: "A dialogue consists not only of two interlocutors, but also of the willingness of one to recognize and accept the other in his otherness" ("Changing Horizon," 148). As a writer, one sees oneself as both the subject and the object, as both the self and the other. Consequently, an author always remains in both an empathetic and an antagonistic relationship with his/her audience, even through a visualization of him/herself as audience.

This, I argue, is Byron's objective in creating the vampiric curse in *The Giaour:* he ultimately transforms his reception anxiety into an Orientalist trope that assaults and preys upon the audience that would consume him. Since the predatory and supernatural vampire can be seen as the superlative "Other," it becomes an apt metaphor to describe the writing process and linguistic relationships. Byron characterizes his reading audience as an entity that consumes him through the medium of his work: they drain it of its content and meaning, and then introduce an appropriated approximation back into the mediation. A new creation emerges, not the original but not distinct either: effectively, it emerges as an amalgamation of old and new, reformulated and reinvigorated. The production, consumption, and reproduction of the linguistic relationship are analyzed from a synchronic perspective within a historical diachrony. To this end, a "representation of literature in the historical succession of such systems would be possible through a series of arbitrary points of intersection between diachrony and synchrony" (*Aesthetic,* 39). Consequently, the audience receives and consumes Byron's works, then mediates between the text and the next generation of audience members. The "evolution" continues with this mediation of past and present, which must be viewed through synchronic points of intersection that eventually produce a diachronic literary history. Individual representations of the Byronic vampire evoke question-and-answer formulations of previously consumed texts, which in turn sustain the tropes that inform the subsequent fictional representations, thereby perpetuating their reproducibility.

This metaphor of reproducibility informs not only the way Byron and his audience serve as reciprocal interlocutors, but also how the audience reconfigures Byron as the Orientalized vampire. Ghislaine McDayter theorizes Byron's audience as parasitical and ties Byron's discomfort over production to the literary commodification so prevalent during the late eighteenth and early nineteenth centuries. Byron would not "be the slave to any appetite," she says and extrapolates: "While that included the appetites of his lovers, it referred more particularly to his adoring 'fans,' who were always assumed to be female (or at least feminized), and who the poet came increasingly to regard as insatiable beings who fed upon his literary corpus to satisfy their taste for the Byronic" (43). The exaggerated gendering of Byron's audience generates an insidious heterosexism by asserting that Byron's "lovers" and "fans," and by extension his insatiably voracious consumers, were always assumed female or feminized. Moreover, by appending sex, this gendering intensifies Orientalized vampirism as well. Byron thus keeps the vampires and victims, much as Stoker does in *Dracula,* explicitly heterosexual. I would argue that Byron's readers and lovers were both male and female, and that the vampiric trope that weaves its way through this Byronic intertextuality also bespeaks a homoerotic articulation.

McDayter rightly suggests that Byron came to see his audience as increasingly and ravenously consuming, always clamoring for more of what he had previously provided. Byron says to John Murray: "I knew the precise worth of popular applause—for few Scribblers have had more of it." While always appreciating an enthusiastic audience, Byron lamented the relentless necessity of continually playing to its wants and fancies for works that resembled his previous compositions: "If I chose to swerve into their paths—I could retain it or resume it—or increase it—but I neither love ye—nor fear ye—and though I buy with ye—and sell with ye—and talk with ye—I will neither eat with ye—drink with ye—nor pray with ye" (*Byron's Letters & Journals* [hereinafter *BLJ*] 6:108, April 6, 1819). Byron's quotation from Shakespeare's *Merchant of Venice* is telling, not only because he acknowledged the inevitability of bartering his goods for fame and applause despite his denials to the contrary, but also because he recognized the thankless and exhausting nature of writing. On the one hand, Byron needed his audience but, on the other, loathed their voracious appetites. Playing to them while mocking them, he implicitly asked for their acceptance while he explicitly castigated them for their constant clamor.

This public cacophony for all things Byronic established dissonance for Byron rather than harmony. He privileged his writing, demeaned his audience, and alluded to the Bible when he said that he had been throwing his "pearls to Swine." He continues: "[A]s long as I wrote the exaggerated nonsense which has corrupted the public taste—they applauded to the very echo—and now that I have really composed within these three or four years some things which should 'not willingly be let die'—the whole herd snort and grumble and return to wallow in their mire" (*BLJ* 9:160–61, May 20, 1822). Somewhat late in his writing career, Byron debases his early Gothic and Oriental writing as "exaggerated nonsense" with which he has "corrupted" the public view and ruined his audience for anything that he might write later in a different genre or fashion. "It is fit that I should pay the penalty of spoiling them—as no man has contributed more than me in my earlier compositions to produce that exaggerated & false taste—it is a fit retribution that anything [like a?] classical production should be received as these plays have been treated." The sympathetic and antagonistic attitudes clash here, inasmuch as the Gothic and Oriental genres that had produced so much fame and cachet for Byron had become a horizon that was no longer secure. The exotic and fanciful productions had fashioned an "exaggerated" and "false taste," a horizon of experience and expectation that Byron would have to contest with any new text.

I inevitably suggest to my students that Byron appears somewhat disingenuous here. He demeans his adoring public but never long forgets its powerful influence on his writing. In a letter to Douglas Kinnaird, Byron asserts: "I *never courted* the public—and I never will *yield* to it" (*BLJ* 9:93–94, January 26, 1822). Byron belies his desire for public approval here, but the notion that an audience may be courted and a writer yield to its wishes reiterates the sympathetic and antagonistic as well as erotic conflict. McDayter asserts, "[A]ll of the Romantics repeatedly used metaphors of parasitic consumption and alienation to describe their perceived loss of cultural and interpretive authority" (44). Byron writes within a horizon of experience already primed for his "parasitic" creation. In *The Giaour*, Byron transformed his anxiety and anger over his text's reception into a fictionalized vampiric curse. In the *Oriental Tales*, Byron transforms his extensive knowledge of Oriental mores and culture into credible characters and compelling narratives; his characters represent the Eastern milieu rather than merely evoke it.

Returning to the work of Said, I intimate that while his theories work quite well on a continental scale, they might not so easily function for specific individuals, especially Byron.[1] Said suggests that Europeans reiterated their "superiority over Oriental backwardness" (7). I would argue that, if anything, Byron establishes an Oriental superiority against which he measures the English and often finds them lacking. After all, Byron did not "invent" the Orient—he characterized and embodied it. In his *Compendium of Eastern Elements in Byron's Oriental Tales,* Naji B. Oueijan concurs: "In his Oriental tales, Byron's major concern is studying the Object to present as it was and not as it was imagined" (11). Oueijan distinguishes a "genuine" Oriental work from a "false" one as follows:

First, the Oriental ingredients found in the genuine literature are essential to the creation of local color of the East and for the enhancement of the Eastern ideas of the works, while the Oriental elements in the inauthentic literature are merely present for decorative effect; second, the authors of the first type of works consciously present in their works authentic pictures of the East motivated by pure scholarly interests, while those of the second type sometimes consciously and sometimes unconsciously exhibit in their works highly imaginative and distorted images. (12)

While I caution my students that black-and-white designations such as "genuine" and "false" often demonstrate a more complex grayness and fluid representation, I do agree with Oueijan that Byron tends more toward the "genuine" and less toward the "false" because of his extensive travels and his remarkable tendency toward assimilation and adaptation. Still, Byron was working within a horizon of Orientalism that had been constructed long before his "Grand Tour"; as such, he was surely influenced by his culture's obsession with the constructed mythology and fantasy.

Having thus explained the intricacies of Jauss and his connection to Said, I then emphasize and employ their theories to help my students better understand how to read and understand Byron's *Oriental Tales*. The triangular functioning of author, text, and audience presents itself as a tool by which to formulate not only the active mediation within the horizons of experience and expectation, but also the synchronic and diachronic literary histories. For the author aspect, I use excerpts from Byron's letters and journals to elucidate key moments in Byron's life and creative process; for the context and historical nuances of the text, I supplement Byron's *Oriental Tales* with excerpts from Oueijan's *Compendium*, his articles in *Prism(s)*, Daniel P. Watkins's *Social Relations in Byron's Eastern Tales*, Jerome J. McGann's notes from *Byron: The Complete Poetical Works* (hereinafter *CPW*), and Nigel Leask's *British Romantic Writers and the East*; for the audience component, I draw upon excerpts from Donald H. Reiman's *The Romantics Reviewed* as well as my students' personal responses to the texts. Obviously, these are not the only sources one might exploit, but I find them invaluable for expanding and complicating Jauss's triangle as it relates to Byron's *Oriental Tales*.

Byron's letters and journals provide extensive background and contextual information relating to his Grand Tour and his mental disposition during the composition of the various tales. His lively writing style and dry-witted humor appeal to my students where other sources, such as biographies or criticisms, might fall on deaf ears. For example, after arriving in Lisbon, Portugal, he writes to Hodgson on July 16, 1809: "I am very happy here because I love oranges, and talks bad Latin to the monks, who understand it, as it is like their own,—and I goes into society (with my pocket pistols), and I swims in the Tagus all across at once, and I rides on an ass or a mule, and swears Portuguese, and have got a diarrhoea and bites from the mosquitoes. But what of that? Comfort must not be expected by folks that go a pleasuring" (*BLJ,* 1:215). Students enjoy his unceremonious yet expressive narration and cavalier attitude about traditionally personal subjects. They come to feel as if they know this Byron, as if he is speaking to them across the ages. Consequently, students have expressed during discussions the heightened sense of relevance and immediacy his poetry brings to them as a result of knowing more about his life and his viewpoints.

I take advantage of the episode with the Ali Pasha to introduce issues regarding sexuality, even though I have to caution my students that what we today would understand as a sexual orientation would not have existed in the same form during the early nineteenth century. In a letter to his mother on November 12, 1809, Byron recounts the meeting as follows:

> I was dressed in a full suit of Staff uniform with a very magnificent saber . . . he received me *standing,* a wonderful compliment from a Mussulman, & made me sit down on his right hand. . . . He said he was certain I was a man of birth because I had small ears, curling hair, & little white hands, and expressed himself pleased with my appearance & garb.—He told me to consider him as a father whilst I was in Turkey, & said he looked on me as his son. . . . He begged me to visit him often and at night when he was more at leisure. (*BLJ,* 1:227–28; original emphasis)

In his biography, Marchand suggests that Byron "recognized more fully when he had reflected upon the interview and had seen more of Turkish manners, that Ali's observation of his handsome features had a particular meaning more personal and sensuous than an interest in his noble birth or rank would have elicited" (210). I would argue that the implicit meaning behind these invitations didn't require too much of Byron's self-reflection at a later period. He would have fully recognized the implied suggestion at the moment it was made to him. This was, after all, one of the main reasons he had chosen to visit Turkey: to explore sexual avenues that were trodden far more openly in the East and that were illegal and punishable by death in England. Interestingly, he sends Rushton home because, as he explains to his mother, "*boys* are not *safe* amongst the Turks" (*BLJ,* 1:222; original emphasis); at twenty-one, Byron was hardly more than a boy himself.

Byron's sexuality has received much attention from critics and biographers alike. I don't have the room within this essay to recount the extensive scholarship relating to this subject.[2] I would, however, suggest, as I do with my students, that Byron desired to explore this aspect of his life more fully; one of the only ways to accomplish this was to travel to a place where it was more openly tolerated. To Henry Drury on June 25, 1809, Byron wrote: "I have laid down my pen, but have promised to contribute a chapter on the state of morals, and a further treatise on the same to be entituled 'Sodomy simplified or Paederasty proved to be praiseworthy from ancient authors and modern practice.'—Hobhouse further hopes to indemnify himself in Turkey for a life of exemplary chastity at home by letting out his 'fair bodye' to the whole Divan" (*BLJ*, 1:208). In a letter to Drury dated May 3, 1810, he says: "In England the vices in fashion are whoring & drinking, in Turkey, Sodomy & smoking" (*BLJ*, 1:238). Said suggests that the "Orient was almost a European invention, and had been since antiquity a place of romance, exotic being, haunting memories and landscapes, remarkable experiences" (1). For Byron, the East was indeed a place to unearth these "exotic beings" and experiences, and then recount these "remarkable experiences" to numerous friends and family in England.

Both Crompton and Christensen have commented upon Byron's need to leave England and explore the East within a sexualized context. Crompton's chapter, "To the East," in *Byron and Greek Love* speaks for itself in that Crompton thoroughly explores the various texts and readings that influenced Byron's travel plans. Moreover, he pays particular attention to the codes that permeate Byron's letters and journals as well as the young men (e.g., Eustathius Georgiou or Niccolo Giraud) whom Byron encountered and wooed. In *Lord Byron's Strength*, Christensen says that "Asia Minor" was a "domain where Byron [could] safely indulge his peculiar appetite" (54). Continuing, Christensen asserts that Byron insisted Hobhouse return to England after an extended period so that he could correspond with him about his latest exploits: "The departure of Hobhouse is ultimately less important for allowing Byron to *have* the experience than it is for enabling Byron to *represent* the experience, tantalizingly, as a scene for an audience of intimate male friends" (59; original emphasis). Moreover, Christensen stresses that what they shared was a "*literary* sense of identity . . . formed by the positing of a particular kind of sexual experience as something that, because it cannot meet the eye, underwrites everything that can" (60; original emphasis).

Not only was Byron using the "Grand Tour" to explore these various aspects of his sexuality, but he was also using the letters to his friends in England as a way to solidify his sexual adventures within discourse. Byron was fascinated with language. In a diary entry on November 16, 1813, he recites lines from Shakespeare's *Antony and Cleopatra*, which he had seen with Matthew Lewis at Covent Garden: "and are not '*words things?*' and such '*words*' very pestilent '*things*' too?" (*BLJ*, 3:207; original emphasis). This concept would later appear in *Don Juan:* "But words are things, and a small drop of ink, / Falling like dew, upon a thought, produces /That which makes thousands, perhaps millions, think" (*CPW* 3:793–95). Throughout his writing life, Byron remained poignantly aware of the power of words and his ability to manipulate them to his advantage. As for Byron's relationship with his readership, which I mentioned previously, he acknowledged and appreciated popularity's appeal and his audience's pleasure, but he also feared its all-consuming voraciousness. He became prey to his audience members' incessant demands for travelogues and moody heroes. His new works bumped up against the aesthetic resonance of his established works, thereby creating a dissonance between the expectations of his audience and his own expectations for a new construction. In Jaussian fashion, Byron's new production enters into a horizon of experience that his audience wishes to remain static; however, through the operation of this new production, the horizon of experience changes, leading the contemporary audience to resist or accept the change but allowing future generations to experience an altered horizon of expectation. Consequently, his focus on *words* as *things* lends itself to a heightened awareness of both his prowess as an author and his influence on his audience. Moreover, by disseminating discourse about his sexual exploits, he uses a medium through which language itself solidifies, accentuates, and legitimizes his sexual fluidity. As Christensen observes: "The profession is formed by the positing of a particular kind of sexual experience as something that, because it cannot meet the eye, underwrites everything that can" (*Lord Byron's Strength*, 60).

Once my students and I have examined the ways in which Byron's life, letters and journals, and homoerotic inclinations have influenced the writing of the *Oriental Tales,* we look at the tales themselves in order to focus on Jauss's second component: the text. Rather than spend too little time here detailing my readings of the texts, which differ only slightly from the traditional readings of these works, I will instead focus on the secondary texts I employ to help my students better understand the primary ones. I assign the introduction to Said's *Orientalism,* so that we have a foundation and vocabulary from which to speak about such tales as *The Giaour, Lara,* and *The Corsair.* The initial focus on *Orientalism* allows us to better understand the European construction of the Orient and, as Said says, the "deepest and most recurring images of the Other" (1). Since few of my students have ever visited the lands and people about which Byron speaks and writes, I necessarily incorporate Said in order for them to gain perspective about our cultural representations and relationships "of power, of domination, of varying degrees of a complex hegemony" (5).

I complicate Said's theories, though, with Naji Oueijan's *Compendium of Eastern Elements in Byron's Oriental Tales* as well as his articles from *Prism(s)*. Usually, I place my copy as well as the library's copy on reserve, so that my students can have access to the material as needed. I explain that Oueijan complicates Said's theories about the "East-West relationship" and that the conflict was not necessarily caused by Islamic and Christian fundamentalists but by "world-powers" (8). I also explore Oueijan's suggestion that Said "confuses the Romantics' tendency to medievalize with their earnest proclivity to Orientalize" (10). Still, I must admit that I spend less time on Oueijan's problems with Said and more time on his elaborations of Eastern elements. Since many of my students are unfamiliar with the East's traditions, holy sites, rituals, names, and mythology, I strongly urge them to peruse Oueijan's extensive and detailed explanations for a better understanding of the historical and contextual aspects of the *Oriental Tales*. This allows them to appreciate Byron's symbolism and imagery more immediately. For instance, Oueijan explains that Gulnare's name refers to "pomegranate-flowers," an apt metaphor for "a beautiful Eastern flower, but a flower with thorns that hurt" (109), a definition that provides a nice introduction to a conversation about Gulnare's murderous repayment of Conrad's self-sacrificing rescue of her from the fire.

Depending upon which tales I'm teaching, I assign the pertinent portions from Nigel Leask's *British Romantic Writers and the East* and Daniel P. Watkins's *Social Relations in Byron's Eastern Tales*, as well as the endnotes from McGann's *Byron: Complete Poetical Works*. Both Leask and Watkins incorporate a historical component into their readings of the tales, which allows my students to better understand the time period and context of the works. Leask, much like Oueijan, complicates Said by showing "that the internal and external pressures determining and undermining such representations [of the Oriental Other as a monological construct] are more various than Said's thesis will allow" (2). Here again, though, I spend less time focusing on Leask's problems with Said and more time on how his interpretations help us to better understand the critical tradition and the place these tales inhabit within, as Jauss would say, a literary series. I emphasize how Leask shows Byron reflecting "upon his own culture as the world's dominant colonial power, and upon the significance of his own complicity in that power as a poet of orientalism" (23). This idea helps to initiate a conversation about colonialism in general, and about England's imperial dominance during the nineteenth century. Moreover, we can then discuss Byron's place in this hierarchy, as an aristocrat and as a widely popular poet, and whether or not he was "complicit" within and privileged by this structure of "dominance."

I also use Leask to once again emphasize the sexuality within the *Oriental*

Tales.[3] In addition to suggesting an interesting comparison between the dyad of Lara and Kaled, and Byron and Niccolo, he also establishes homoerotic conventions within the narrative itself: "[T]he focus on Kaled's ambivalent identity at the critical moment of Ezzelin's denunciation of Lara has the effect of foregrounding its importance, creating a climax of mystery and suspense in the replacement of the customary female figure by an object of homosexual desire" (58). I inevitably cite Lady Byron's remembrances of Byron's feelings toward *Lara:* "There's more in *that* than any of them, [said Byron] shuddering and avoiding my eye" (*Astarte;* original emphasis, 20). Not only, I suggest to my students, does Byron's concept of the hero incorporate aspects of the innocent youth with the libertine, of the sacred with the profane, of the condescending with the cursed, but it also incorporates the two disparate and stereotypical views held of same-sex desire: the Platonically heroic and the doctrinally damned. Byron reinterprets and merges this dichotomy into a much more edifying, much less antagonistic view, bringing about a resolution, both for himself and for those around him.

I often move from *Lara* to *Sardanapalus* in order to capitalize on the prevailing sexuality and gender issues within these works. Invariably, I point out to my students that these plays, as Byron himself urged repeatedly, were meant to be imagined in the mind rather than performed on stage. They regularly disagree with this, envisioning directors who could easily translate this material into film; we often cast actors into the parts, which allows them to better visualize the characters and eventually the cinematography. I promote these activities because my students' imaginations are inclined toward the visual rather than the aural or linguistic. Through casting these characters with well-known celebrities, they become more intimately involved in the plot and structure of the play itself. This helps immensely when it comes time to explain the historical or contextual ramifications of the Assyrian monarchy or the Zoroastrian mythology.

Sardanapalus as Oriental despot provides ample opportunities to discuss gender and masculinity. We begin by locating the numerous passages that describe the king as "effeminate," "voluptuous," "man queen," "soft yet beloved," "she-king," and "less than woman." The double entendre of the scepter and its varying stages of tumescence rarely goes unnoticed. Andrew Elfenbein's work on effeminacy from *Romantic Genius: The Prehistory of a Homosexual Role* works quite well here and I assign the introduction and chapter 1 from his text as supplemental reading. He says:

> Effeminacy had a long history in civic humanism as an image of corrupted manliness. An effeminate man gave himself over to intemperance, typically at the cost of neglecting public good for private indulgence. His intemper-

210 / Chapter 10

ance might involve sodomy, because taking the passive position in sex with another man was supposedly an example of immoderation. Yet it might just as well involve subservience to a wife or mistress, lecherousness, or the compulsive pursuit of sexual experience to the neglect of more "manly" activities, excessive attention to fashion and coiffure in an attempt to attract women more effectively, or conversely, such personal vanity and self-absorption as to preclude any but the feeblest interest in sexuality at all. (20)

Sardanapalus fits more comfortably within the latter category than the former. He is denigrated and scorned because he continually exposes himself to sumptuousness, becoming a veritable despot of "vice and luxury." His peaceful and beneficent reign causes uneasiness and malfeasance within the ranks of his advisers and allies. Byron echoes Machiavelli when he says that it is better for a king to be feared than loved. Sardanapalus eventually exonerates himself on the battlefield, fighting with vigor and valor but only after having thoroughly appraised his armored appearance in a full-length mirror.

I often assign the specific chapter from Watkins to supplement whichever of the *Oriental Tales* we are reading. He nicely encapsulates a historical and contextual reading within each section, which allows my students to understand more fully the elaborate and sometimes veiled intertextuality. Watkins underscores the "complex network of relations that defines and ultimately controls social reality. Specifically, the tales describe the pervasive cultural attitudes, practices, and beliefs which, under certain circumstances, not only limit human independence, but in fact support reactionary and morally destitute social systems" (16). My students find these "relations" the most difficult facet of the tales, and so, even though they find Watkins somewhat difficult to comprehend, they inexorably arrive at a greater appreciation of the texts as a result of having read his work. Watkins allows us to discuss how Byron "often placed considerations of human experience within an encompassing social context" (16). As such, we can situate Byron within a larger context of social customs and ethical ameliorations while at the same time seeing his overt disdain for tyrannical dominance and brutality. Along these lines, Watkins focuses upon the "powerful (if submerged) social imagination controlling much of [Byron's] poetry." For my students, this remains essential to understanding the *Oriental Tales* within a larger historical and societal milieu.

As for the audience awareness component of the Jaussian triangle, I begin by focusing on the extraordinary popularity of the *Oriental Tales* during Byron's time. I recount how *The Corsair* sold ten thousand copies on the first day of publication, a notable feat before the advent of industrialized printing. Leask avows: "Byron was encouraged by his publisher John Murray to make the most of the saleability of poetry with an 'oriental flavour,' and the series of *Eastern Tales* produced between 1813 and 1816 made him the most popular poet in Britain and established the 'Byron Myth' as a European phenomenon" (14). For confirmation of this, I usually direct them to Donald H. Reiman's *The Romantics Reviewed,* which I also place on library reserve. With little direction as to which criticism to read, many students surprise the class with different excerpts from numerous sources. This allows them to both confirm the "myth" with glowing reviews or to refute the "myth" with vitriolic censure. They are inevitably surprised yet fascinated by the overt glorification or denunciation within these excerpts, having been raised upon at least an assumption of the media's objectivity. We can then talk about the ways in which criticism has either remained the same or changed over the succeeding one hundred and eighty or so years between these various reviews and our classroom discussions. Reiman's numerous volumes serve as an excellent resource for contemporaneous views on Byron's poetry and how his life became integrated within the concept of the Byronic hero itself.

As an additional emphasis on public writing and audience perceptions, I require my students to submit weekly e-mails that the class Web site distributes to each student. The e-mails act as communal reading journals, becoming progressively more and more intertwined as the semester advances. Once a week, each student receives approximately one-half to three-quarters of a typed page of text from each student in the class detailing the concerns, insights, or problems that are arising. On student/teacher evaluations, they invariably grouse about the weekly necessity and then move on to say how much they learned from the exercise. They move, as Jauss says, "from simple reception to critical understanding, from passive to active reception, from recognized aesthetic norms to a new production that surpasses them." Through actively becoming engaged in their learning process and through developing a shared critical response to the texts at hand, they enter into the "historical life of the literary work" by becoming "active" participants within the "changing horizon-of-experience" (*Aesthetic,* 19).

By providing my students with the aforementioned Jaussian structures, I hope to help them not only to understand more fully Byron's *Oriental Tales* but also to appreciate more comprehensively any literature that they study. Fundamentally, I ask my students to recreate Byron in their own constructed image and situate him within a historical and cultural milieu. Watkins says that his aim in *Social Relations in Byron's Eastern Tales* is to allow the "poems to throw the rich detail of social life into relief, to magnify rather than obscure its active role" (34). I attempt a similar goal with my students by using Jauss as a template for their learning structure, thereby allowing the "rich detail" of the *Oriental Tales* to "magnify" my students' "active roles" as readers, scholars, and critics.

⚜

NOTES

1. Leask suggests a similar reading of Said: "It seems to me that whilst Said is right in asserting the links between knowledge of the East . . . and the history of colonial power, he is wrong in denominating it a 'closed system.' The (plural) anxieties of empire which I will be examining in the works of Byron, Shelley and De Quincey and numerous other British Romantic writers cannot be laid on any such procrustean bed" (2).

2. For further information on Byron, Romanticism, and sexuality, see: Crompton, Christensen, Knight, Moore, Grebanier, Wolfson, Haggerty, Moore, Elfenbein, and Soderholm, among others.

3. Another excellent analysis on the relationship between Byron's work and sexuality can be found in Keegan.

CHAPTER 11

Byron's *The Giaour*

Teaching Orientalism in the Wake of September 11

ALAN RICHARDSON

In January of 2000, during that coveted two-week period between the end of the MLA convention and the beginning of spring term, I began working in earnest on a teaching anthology called *Three Oriental Tales*. The proposal for this volume had grown out of my own teaching needs, as I found myself developing new courses with titles like British Literature and Empire, British Literature in Global Context, and British Romanticism and Imperial Culture. I had long taught William Beckford's *Vathek* in various incarnations of a course on the Gothic and Romantic novel, and this had given me a chance to introduce students to Orientalism and its critique. By the 1990s, however, especially in the aftermath of the first Gulf War, I found myself wanting to provide much more in the way of context for *Vathek*. Orientalist writings from periodicals like the *Spectator*, the *Rambler*, and Goldsmith's "Chinese Letters" series from the *World* would give students a sense of how broadly eighteenth-century British culture became permeated with "Oriental" references, fantasies, and furniture; alternative Orientalist fictions, especially by woman writers, would demonstrate the multiple literary and ideological uses to which this material might be put. At least one Oriental tale in verse from my primary field, the Romantic era, could serve to show how the energies of Orientalist fiction passed from prose to poetic forms in the early nineteenth century. Since there had never been a single volume featuring anything like this range of materials, I decided to propose my own, and so was born *Three Oriental Tales*, with *Vathek*, Sheridan's *History of Nourjahad*, and Byron's *The Giaour*, as well as Maria Edgeworth's "Murad the Unlucky" and a number of shorter works. With some due skepticism regarding the bottom line, the proposal was accepted for Houghton Mifflin's British "New Riversides" series, just then getting underway.

For all the usual reasons, work on the volume did not go nearly as quickly as I'd hoped, which put me in an awkward position with the series editor, who happened to be myself. However, by late spring of 2001 the manuscript was finally ready to go into copyediting, ensuring that it would be out in time for the MLA convention that year and for my own undergraduate seminar on British Literature and Empire scheduled for Spring 2002. When the copyedited manuscript went to the typesetters on August 14, I had no way of knowing that less than a month later an event would occur that would make half-forgotten works of literary Orientalism live in a new way for my students. We can, and perhaps we should, continue to argue about how much and just what really changed on September 11, 2001. But there can be no argument that the conditions for teaching Orientalism changed significantly, and perhaps permanently.

Over the first forty-eight hours or so after the four passenger planes had been transformed into fuel-air bombs, it seemed that the old binaries—East and West, fanatic and secular, Islam and, what, the "free world," Christendom?—were destined to become reasserted as simplistically as ever before. Television commentators began speaking without qualification of a "clash between civilizations"; a radio commentator—on public radio—confessed to wanting to see "the whole Middle East in flames," as though it were one undifferentiated, anti-Western, fanatically Muslim East; Sikhs became targets because their turbans marked them as the stereotypical Oriental Other. Binary thinking was not limited to pro-American zealots. On the day of the suicide bombings, a colleague of mine who is from India worried out loud, as we all gathered in the hall to try to begin making sense of the overwhelming events, that we would soon witness massive mob violence across America amounting to the wholesale "ethnic cleansing" of Muslims. Thousands of Muslims were indeed murdered over the next twelve months in violent mob actions—in India.[1]

In the United States, anti-Muslim hate crimes indeed rose, but not as dramatically as many of us had feared and with nothing like the homicidal mass hysteria my colleague had imagined. Our born-again, conspicuously Texan president surprised us by attending services at a mosque and declaring Islam a religion of peace; copies of the Koran flew off of bookstore shelves across the country; and public and private schools, churches, and television and radio interview programs invited Muslim scholars, clerics, or just neighbors to talk about their traditions and their faith. Virtually every presenter I heard or read about began by cautioning against entertaining any monolithic conception of Islam or of the Islamic world and, by extension, against deploying any simplistic East/West opposition. The distinctions—among various Islamic traditions, among different Islamic states and groups, among a variety of political positions associated with Islam—pointed up by one presenter, commentator, or editorialist after another soon became a staple of the daily news, as the U.S. invasion of Afghanistan, begun on October 7, rapidly progressed. The Muslim, largely non-Pashtun militias of the Northern Alliance, as well as the Muslim state of Pakistan, had suddenly become U.S. allies. Turkish soldiers would be stationed in Kabul by February of the next year, and take control of the International Security Assistance Force—and the Kabul airfield—by June. The most casual reader or viewer of the news couldn't fail to become aware that some Muslim groups were no more fond of Taliban-style theocracy than any Western liberal democrat, that some Muslims lived under a rigorously secularist government, that Osama bin Laden did not typify Islam any more than Jerry Falwell did Christianity.

What, the attentive reader may by now be wondering, does all this have to do with teaching the first of Lord Byron's "Eastern Tales" in verse, *The Giaour*? Not quite everything, but a great deal, as I hope to show in the remainder of this brief essay. *The Giaour* begins much as did the immediate public reaction to the horrors of September 11: by seeming to confirm a simplistically and remorselessly dichotomous view of East and West, Europe and its Oriental Other. The narrator—only one of several, as it will turn out—presents a scrupulously Eurocentric view of Greece under Ottoman dominion: enslaved ("servile offspring of the free") though classically associated with freedom and democracy (111) and debased though once heroic: "Self-abasement pav'd the way / To vilain-bonds and despot-sway" (40–41).[2] In contrast with its intellectual and moral vitality during the classical period, Greece must now be seen even as deathly, a beautiful corpse:

'Tis Greece—but living Greece no more!
So coldly sweet, so deadly fair,
We start—for soul is wanting there.
Hers is the loveliness in death. (91–94)

The metaphorical corpse of Greece under Muslim rule is the first of the series of dead bodies that haunt this text, establishing a rather ghoulish atmosphere from the start that persists to the poem's last line, with its evocation of the Giaour's two inseparable companions, the ghosts of "her he lov'd" and "him he slew" (l. 1334).

The pointed contrast between Ottoman Greece and the Greece of classical times does more, however, than merely to promote a sense of inevitable East/West antagonism, that "clash of civilizations." Byron, or rather his unnamed narrator, deploys the contrast between then and now, a heroically free and a supinely dominated Greece, to imply as well that such antagonisms are ancient and deeply rooted. References to Themistocles ("When will such hero live again?" [6]) and to the battles of Thermopylae (109) and Salamis (113), evoking Athenian and Spartan resistance to the invasion of Greece by Persia in the fifth century BCE, urge the reader to understand Ottoman rule as only the most recent in a series of attempts, successful or not, by Asiatic tyrants to destroy Greece and all it represents. Byron's initial narrator, pro-Hellenic and classically educated like Byron himself, seems committed to a vision of Greece and Asia, Europe and the East that associates the first term with the birth of freedom and democratic aspirations, the second with an essentially despotic character and an endemic hostility toward freedom and self-rule, whether for Greece or for its European heirs.

Byron attempts in advance, however, to forestall any reading of *The Giaour* that naively takes the first narrator as the official voice of the poem. In editing a text, perhaps especially in editing it for the classroom, one becomes hypersensitized to matters of placement. Byron's "Advertisement" to his poem, for example, is sometimes placed *after* the poem, among a mixture of Byron's original notes and material supplied by a modern editor—when not omitted altogether.[3] And yet early editions overseen by Byron himself position the "Advertisement" directly before the opening lines, a placement I followed in my own edition and one that has significant effects on a first reading of the poem. For the "Advertisement," if read at all carefully, functions to instruct the reader in advance to take a more particularized, localized, and historically specific view of the events narrated through the purposefully (and notoriously) disjointed fragments of the poem that follows. That fragmentation itself suggests that the story of the Giaour, Leila, and Hasssan will not lend itself to a single viewpoint or ideological frame, nor willingly cohere into a neat structure built on a binary grid. But, in advance of any of the poem's wrenching and defamiliarizing shifts in speaker, tone, and perspective—all part of what one might call its program of "dis-Orientation"—the "Advertisement" establishes a remarkably different historical and ideological frame than the one that characterizes the poem's introductory lines (1–167), with their marked Orientalist bias.

Byron was, of course, a great admirer of *Vathek*, and Byron's praise of *Vathek* in his notes to this very poem would in fact lead to the republication of Beckford's Oriental tale in 1816 and its eventual reputation as a minor classic. As the "Advertisement" to *The Giaour* makes clear, however, Byron's Orientalist poem is as precisely contextualized, in historical time and in geopolitical space, as Beckford's Orientalist fantasy is decontextualized. What Said famously declared of Orientalism generally—that it "stands forth and away from" the "Orient as such"—applies perfectly to *Vathek* but cannot be said of *The Giaour*, a poem that depends heavily on Byron's firsthand experience in relevant parts of the East and his genuine interest in the Muslim cultures he encountered there. Scholars, most notably Mohammed Sharafuddin and Abdur Raheem Kidwai, in a position to comment authoritatively on Byron's representations of Islamic beliefs, practices, and customs, have been impressed by their accuracy and by Byron's sympathy for a non-Christian, Eastern belief system. Sharafuddin, in particular, credits Byron with a degree of "sympathy" for Islam "amounting to identification," and quotes a remark attributed to Byron (dubiously enough) by his estranged wife, that he "was very *near* becoming a Mussalman" (224–25; original emphasis). Byron had no interest, he writes, in "reinforcing English perspectives, that is, English complacency and supremacy" (243)—no desire, in other terms, to create a work of what would now ordinarily be called "Orientalism." He "wished the full reality of Islam to become perceptible," Sharafuddin continues, "not because he was seeking an alternative authority to the west"—not in order to construct the East as what Raymond Schwab terms the "alter-ego" to the Occident (4)—but "because, as a generous liberal who hated tyranny and believed in national independence, he took delight in racial, social, cultural and religious *variety* and *otherness*" (243). Whether taking a "delight" in otherness can be quite disentangled, in any British Orientalist work, from feelings of "complacency and supremacy" remains very much an open question, but Sharafuddin bears compelling testimony to Byron's refusal to create a phantasmic Orient from whole cloth, or rather from the network of literary, historical, and pseudohistorical materials that Beckford drew upon in concocting the simulated Orient of *Vathek*.

If Byron refuses to create a simulated, pastiche Orient à la *Vathek* (and all the other progeny of the *Arabian Nights*), neither does he care to position the Giaour as the representative of a unified and hegemonic "West." True, he leaves the text open to the temptation of reading it as a staged "political allegory," with the Giaour standing in for a more or less undifferentiated Europe and Hassan for Ottoman Turkey, with Leila (who is, significantly, Circassian) closely associated with Greece (the "natural paradise of the landscape" evoked in the poem's opening section), the "land over which the Turks and the Venetians have been fighting for centuries" (McGann, 156). And critics have sometimes succumbed. To do so, however, means losing a good deal of the ambivalence and, more to the point here, of the pedagogical value of Byron's *Giaour*, not least its value for the present moment.

Teaching *The Giaour* that spring of 2002, then, I encouraged my students to analyze the binaristic structure of its first section, and to comment on Orientalist motifs they could recognize from *Nourjahad* and *Vathek*, before asking them to read carefully with me Byron's "Advertisement" and then, if they wished, to connect it with recent events. It begins, Byronically enough, by evoking a history of sexual relations between the "ladies" of "the East" and the "Christians" fortunate or enterprising enough to enjoy their favors: the exotic as the erotic, one of the most enduring of Orientalist tropes (Praz, 207). Twice Byron insists upon the fragmentary nature of the narrative to follow—"these disjointed fragments," "the story, when entire"—preparing the reader for the kaleidoscopic experience to follow, a matter not so much of shifting as of shattered perspectives. Turning back to the fragmentary narrative itself, Byron then touches on an equally worn trope—Oriental tyranny and barbarity toward women—in introducing Leila as a "female slave," thrown "in the Mussalman manner" into the sea for betraying the lord of the harem. But these stock Orientalist motifs immediately give way to a surprising density of historical specificity as the "Advertisement" goes on to give the setting a precision that I did not fully appreciate until I tried to annotate it:

> The story, when entire, contained the adventures of a female slave, who is thrown, in the Mussalman manner, into the sea for infidelity, and avenged by a young Venetian, her lover, at the time the Seven Islands were possessed by the Republic of Venice, and soon after the Arnauts were beaten back from the Morea, which they had ravaged for some time subsequent to the Russian invasion. The desertion of the Mainotes, on being refused the plunder of Misitra, led to the abandonment of that enterprise, and to the desolation of the Morea, during which the cruelty on all sides was unparalleled even in the annals of the faithful.

By making the Giaour a Venetian rather than some other enterprising European—say, an Englishman—Byron hints at, not the inexorability, but the fragility of Western domination in the East. As Britain's would be, Venice's empire had been a maritime one, depending on strategic islands, like the seven Ionian islands off Greece, and built inward from stretches of coastline. And it had failed. Although the Ottoman Empire was already in decline, its implosion (not to mention the transformation of Turkey into a secular state) can be seen much more easily with historical hindsight than at the time; in 1824, in *The Last Man*, Mary Shelley has the Ottomans hanging on for a last great (and losing) battle with the West as late as the end of the twenty-first century (117). In Byron's poem of 1813, it's the Giaour, not Hassan, who might be taken to represent the "sick man of Europe," representative of a dying empire struggling to hang on to its last few colonial possessions. Such shifts in global domination involve, Byron reminds us at the outset, an enormous human cost, one played out locally in "ravaged" areas like the Morea (the Peloponnesian peninsula) at the time of the poem's fictional events. The ending of Russian occupation followed by a chaotic and brutal period of warring militias, moving in and out of uneasy alliances, could only remind my students of Afghanistan, a daily front-page item in the news throughout the first half of 2002. And Byron's emphasis on the cruelty shown by "*all* sides" and his pointed underdetermination of the "annals of the faithful"—which faith?—helped the discussion turn to how Byron sets up dichotomies only to undermine them throughout the poem. I had guessed that following recent events had unsettled inherited dichotomies for my students, I hoped that this would help them see how Byron unsettles analogous oppositions in *The Giaour*, and at best I wanted my students to become better readers both of nineteenth-century Orientalist poetry and of twenty-first-century news coverage by placing the two into juxtaposition.

Take costume, for example. Many readers of *The Giaour*, on encountering the passage that describes the Venetian adventurer of the title in Albanian ("Arnaut") garb, will likely think in terms of fancy dress (see fig. 3). The portrait of Byron in his own dashing Albanian costume is so well known (it adorns the dust jacket, for example, of Sharafuddin's book, as well as the paperback cover of Louis Crompton's *Byron and Greek Love* and the cover of this book) as to make the connection nearly inevitable. Hassan, however, does not read the Giaour's change of clothing in terms of masquerade or theater; quite the opposite:

> I know him by his jet-black barb,
> Though now array'd in Arnaut garb,
> Apostate from his own vile faith. (614–16)

For Hassan, the change to Albanian dress signifies a change in loyalties, implying that in allying himself with a group of Muslim mercenaries (what we would call today an "unaligned Muslim militia group"), the Giaour has renounced his Christian faith and his European allegiance. And in fact, when the Giaour later turns up as a kind of boarder at a Greek monastery, he refuses to pray and defies classification in terms of "faith and race" (807). There's no option of simply changing back out of this costume and reassuming an unproblematic "Western" identity. My students, in early 2002, had been presented dozens if not hundreds of time, on television, on the covers of newspapers, and on the Internet, with a comparably heterogeneous image: the so-called American Taliban, John Walker Lindh, arrayed in his own Muslim garb, looking anything but ready for a costume party. Lindh's untrimmed beard, his waist-wrap (*wizar*), the various head coverings he sports in one oft-circulated image or another, all speak to his own version of apostasy, his transformation into the other, the enemy, the homegrown mujahadin. Bringing their associations with Lindh's disheveled, alienating image to bear on Byron's poem, my students could much more readily grasp what it might mean for a stray Venetian to make common cause with a group of Muslim bandits, and why Hassan leaps to the conclusion he does. It helped them arrive at a reading of the Giaour, not as a representative of Occidentalism, but of hybridity—not only will he not pray with Christians, but he refers to God (in one of his gentlest moments) as "Alla" (l. 1133). To read the Giaour as representative of an ascendant, imperialist West means losing sight of that hybridity, and the sense of porousness and mutual vulnerability of cultures that goes with it.

The Giaour's status as between cultures, neither Christian nor Muslim, should complicate any reading that casts him and Hassan as binary opposites representing two perennially antagonistic civilizations. More than that, Byron counters the predictable impulse toward such reading by constructing the relation between Hassan and the Giaour with at least as much thematic doubling as opposition. It's not merely that both love the same woman, a relation that may mask as much homoerotic attraction as it displays heterosexual desire.

> But love itself could never pant
> For all that Beauty sights to grant
> With half the fervour Hate bestows
> Upon the last embrace of foes. (647–50)

Although *The Giaour* is not precisely a colonialist text, it exhibits the "predominately homoerotic cast" that Sara Suleri attributes to "narratives of colonialism," participating as well in what Suleri, developing her homoerotic thesis, terms the "dynamic of complicity that renders the colonizer a secret sharer of the imputed cultural characteristics of the other race" (16). These characteristics include a common proclivity for violence and a gaze that others find hard to withstand: of the Giaour, "Oft will his glance the gazer rue" (837); of Hassan, "And glared his eye with fiercer fire" (594), contributing to a look "dreaded more than hostile sword" (600). The Giaour goes so far as to endorse the act—Hassan's murder of his faithless paramour—that supposedly defines "Mussalman" barbarity: "Yet did he but what I had done / Had she been false to more than one" (1062–63). As the recent revelations concerning the torture and sexual humiliation of Iraqi prisoners in U.S. custody in Abu Ghraib, the prison that formerly epitomized Saddam Hussein's tyrannical brutality, reminded a chastened American public, barbarity can never belong exclusively to East or West.

The figure of Leila, third term in the poem's multicultural erotic triangle, also lends itself to a hybrid reading. Leila is from Circassia (which Byron, after Beckford, also calls "Franguestan"), a region of the northern Caucasus sited precisely on the imaginary geopolitical line between Europe and Asia. One could make Circassia a site of the age-old "conflict" between East and West—Christianized in the sixth century CE, Islamized under Ottoman rule in the seventeenth (McGann, 156)—but that again would entail adopting the very bipolarity that Byron's text seeks to undermine. Variously assimilating and resisting the influence of the Greeks, Romans, Khazars, and Mongols, as well as the neighboring Georgians, Russians, and Turks, Circassia represents a commingling of cultures, part of a region where Muslim and Christian traditions had long co-existed (along with customs surviving from pagan times). This cultural ambiguity is underscored by Leila's alleged disguise as a "Georgian page" (456), a reminder that, in the Caucasus, a mile or two south may mean a different religious identity and a markedly different alignment along the ideological East-West axis. In this region of the globe, East and West *do* meet, repeatedly, uncertainly, and in ways always subject to further revision and realignment. (Just ask the Chechens.) In Orientalist discourse, Circassia is associated not only with luxuriousness (because of the fabled beauty of its women) but with hybridity as well, as a region of fair-skinned, blue-eyed Muslims.[4] Viewers of David Lean's film *Lawrence of Arabia* will recall the scene in which the startlingly blue-eyed Peter O'Toole, desperately trying to pass as a Muslim while in Turkish hands, agrees with his captor, the Turkish bey (played with campy homoerotic inflections by Jose Ferrer), that he must be Circassian. The point is not to show that O'Toole's Lawrence is clever enough to "pass" but rather that his disguise, like the Giaour's, like Lindh's, remains so thin, rendering him an icon not of "going native" but of Suleri's "dynamic of complicity," much like Byron's Giaour before him. Lawrence, however, proves able to return to Britain, however uneasily; the Giaour remains in Greece, itself (in 1813) neither securely European nor Oriental, Christian nor Muslim.

The labor of editing and annotating a text like *The Giaour* can involve unusual (or at least unusually sustained) attention to matters of detail, involving everything from variant place names (*Liakura, Franguestan*), to obscure ethnic or tribal designations (*Osmanlie, Mainote*), to classical references (*Thermopylae, Parne's vale*) that have lost their transparency for most contemporary readers. The process of pinning these down can leave one fascinated by an author's blatant disregard for matters of historical or geographical plausibility—as with *Vathek*—or, alternatively, deeply impressed with the geopolitical precision of a text such as *The Giaour*. For Byron, history is a matter not of monolithic, eternally contending cultural blocs but of shifting loyalties and alliances, unstable identities, cultures that interpenetrate as much as they collide. It remains possible to read *The Giaour* as a xenophobic and chauvinistic attack on the Muslim world—his *Eastern Tales* have been characterized as "poems of the gratuitous violence, irrational vengeance, and cold-hearted barbarity of the Turks" (Sardar, 46)—but such readings must repress the very specificity of detail and fragmentation of perspective that, for a critic like Sharafuddin, differentiates Byron's Orientalism from what may be termed the "alteritist" variety. And we are in as great a need of precision in geopolitical specificity, recognition of multiple perspectives, acceptance of cultural hybridity, and distinctions within broadly defined "civilizations" as ever.

Now in the summer of 2004, as I write, a U.S. army of occupation remains entrenched in Iraq while U.S. and allied NATO forces seem as far as ever from successfully stabilizing the military situation in Afghanistan. With the United States engaged in direct political and military intervention in Central Asia and in the Middle East as never before, in the name of a vaguely defined and infinitely extendable "war on terror," teaching Orientalism critically remains one of our important tasks as professors of literature. Monolithic constructions of both "East" and "West" and simplistic oppositions between them have a vexingly insistent way of reasserting themselves again and again. When 70 percent of the American public assumes, for example, despite the lack of any evidence, that Osama bin Laden and Saddam Hussein collaborated with one another, one may reasonably suspect that this has more to do with Orientalist habits of thought than with a clever disinformation campaign; or, put differently, a disinformation campaign to this effect would not need to be very clever.[5] Byron challenged and attempted to disrupt such habits of thought in *The Giaour*, some two centuries ago, much as many writers and speakers, in many different media and formats, attempted to disrupt them in the aftermath of September 11. This is clearly a task not to be accomplished once and for all, but taken up repeatedly. And it is one that we can be doing in our classrooms.

NOTES

1. "In February and March of 2002 more than two thousand Muslims were murdered on the streets of Gujurat . . . women were gang-raped and children were burned alive and 150,000 driven from their homes while the police and administration watched and sometimes actively participated" (Roy, 12). The striking contrast with India does not mean, of course, that there was no reaction against Muslims in the United States, where a large number of individuals, "more than 1,000," nearly all of them Muslim, were detained

in the first two months following September 11, some indefinitely (Denniston, A2).

2. All quotations from *The Giaour* (cited by line) follow my edition included in *Three Oriental Tales*.

3. The Norton "Critical Edition" of *Byron's Poetry*, for example, quotes only two words from the Advertisement in a footnote (84), while the Modern Library edition of Byron's *Selected Poetry* simply omits the Advertisement without comment (539).

4. For a fascinating study of cultural hybridity (and sexual liaisons across ethnic lines) during the Romantic era in British India, see Dalrymple, *White Mughals*.

5. This survey, commissioned by the *Washington Post* and carried out by TNS Intersearch from August 7–11, 2003, was widely reported in the press; see, e.g., Benedetto's report for *USA Today*.

CHAPTER 12

Teaching Nineteenth-Century Orientalist Entertainments

EDWARD ZITER

Our students are immersed in Orientalist imagery. They have grown up on Disney's *Aladdin* and CNN coverage of Gulf wars. However, few students are likely to see patterns of representation uniting media accounts with children's films, and fewer still will have any sense of the genealogy of such representations. Beginning in the eighteenth century, when greater numbers of Europeans began traveling in the Ottoman Empire, both elite and popular entertainment forms have provided highly detailed representations of the people and institutions of the eastern Mediterranean, formulating and disseminating a remarkably consistent and coherent image of the East. The challenge for teaching Orientalism is to encourage students to question and historicize patterns of representation that seem natural and unavoidable, and this is best accomplished when we teach across genres and periods.

Such teaching poses significant challenges for selecting course materials, structuring conversations across periods and genres, and encouraging students to chart genealogies of Orientalist entertainments. Enlist students to create their own archive of Orientalist imagery. Start by spending a class session examining harem painting and Bedouin depictions. If you do not have access to a slide library, go to www.artcyclopedia.com/subjects/Orientalism.html—better yet, send the students to the Web site. Then ask students to find similarly staged images (whether or not Arabs are specifically depicted) in contemporary films or fashion magazines. Any student with access to a video store or newsstand can bring in teaching materials for several class sessions. There is also a long list of action-adventure films with Arab villains. It is similarly simple to make available to one's students Orientalist imagery in elite entertainment forms such as opera and drama. There are several videos of Mozart's *Abduction from the Seraglio* (one of fourteen harem-abduction operas staged in the second half of the eighteenth century) and the 1992 videorecording of the Royal Opera House, Covent Garden production of Strauss's *Salome* is particularly rich in Orientalist imagery. While most of the dozen or so Orientalist ballets of the Romantic period have fallen out of the repertory, there are commercially available videorecordings of several versions of *La Bayadere* and *Le Corsaire*. There are a great number of dramas depicting the eastern Mediterranean that are available in any research library. Working backward from contemporary manifestations, students will begin to see how our entertainment industry repeats tropes that developed over centuries in galleries and theaters.

This leads to a teaching that moves between genres and across periods. The class is free to examine Ida Rubinstein's dancing in *Cléopâtre* as well as Douglas Fairbanks's silent acting in *The Thief of Bagdad*, Verdi's *Aida* and MGM's *Kismet*, French Orientalist painting, and American Orientalist follies. This is not to equate all Orientalists' works from all periods. The meaning of a work exceeds the individual tropes it contains. It would be ludicrous to read Voltaire's *Mahomet the Prophet; or, Fanaticism* and ignore the work's implicit criticism of Christianity. However, it would also be a mistake to ignore the fact that Voltaire makes this critique by recourse to the image of the Oriental despot who conflates religion, sex, and violence—an image that predated the play and continues to circulate in popular culture. Moreover, productions (and the censorship of productions) invariably reflect their social and political context and this, too, needs to be a part of classroom discussion. In the eighteenth century, Voltaire's *Mahomet* was opposed by Jansenist Catholics who recognized the object of Voltaire's criticism. In the contemporary age of immigrant labor, it was Muslim groups who blocked a 1994 production of the play in Geneva.

A student who recognizes Orientalist tropes is not only able to see their perpetuation but also how these tropes are manipulated and resisted. One of the finest examples, Lessing's remarkable *Nathan the Wise*, which at first appears to be a story of Eastern sectarian revenge only to transform into a story of tolerance, continues on the German stage.[1] Arguably, the modernist period saw the most radical manipulation and transformation of Orientalist tropes. While many modernist theater practitioners, in a search for a distinctive voice, turned to Orientalist imagery that was already divorced from a "real" referent (Wilde's *Salome*, Freska's *Sumurun*, Diaghilev's *Schéhérazade*), other modernists were inspired by actual Eastern performances (Brecht's discussion of Mei Lan-fang, Yates's fascination with Noh, Artaud's response to Balinese dance, Growtowski's use of Kathakali methods). The process of theatrical borrowing has itself been examined and problematized by such important contemporary practitioners as Ariane Mnouchkine, Robert Wilson, Elizabeth LeCompte, The Builders Association, motiroti, and Peter Brook, and there has been no shortage of writing on their work. In fact, the MLA bibliography lists twenty-two journal articles on Peter Brook's production of *The Mahabharata.*

As this brief description shows, it is a relatively easy matter to direct students to depictions of the Orient in canonical theater, opera, and dance and depictions in film and contemporary advertising. This can result in a misrepresentation of the history of Orientalism and can reinforce an unhealthy division of classroom labor: past Orientalism appears confined to high art, present Orientalism is confined to popular entertainment; the teacher has access to the past, the student has access to the present. To the contrary, popular entertainment prior to the twentieth century was a principal medium through which images of the Arab world have been formulated and disseminated in Europe and the United States. And if students are to own the genealogies charted in the class, they must be responsible for researching both past and present representations. This is particularly the case as time allows us to more clearly see the entertainment industry's influence on government policy.

I offer an example on which I have written elsewhere.[2] After the loss of Khartoum and the death of Maj. Gen. Charles Gordon at the hands of Sudanese rebels in 1885, music hall songs transformed Prime Minister Gladstone from the G.O.M (Grand Old Man) to the M.O.G. (Murder of Gordon). A number of songs celebrated Col. Fred Burnaby, the popular officer and explorer who died at Abu Klea. The image of Burnaby bravely resisting native onslaught had become such an ingrained image that eight years later when Drury Lane dramatized the British victories in Burma, the stage directions explained that the hero stood "in a conspicuous place à la Captain Burnaby, coolly reloading and picking off the enemy." Of course, the greatest number of music hall songs focused on the death of Gordon, the most famous being G. H. MacDermott's "Too Late! Too Late!" At least one music hall devoted an entire bill to the fall of Khartoum, when the Royal (later known as the Holborn Empire) staged *Shadows of Fate; or, Heroes of the Soudan*, a "Grand Spectacular Entertainment with scenic effects, descriptive war songs, and original music." Several imperial melodramas, unwilling to acknowledge defeat, depicted British victories at Khartoum in defiance of actual events.

Such entertainments not only contributed to the weakening of the Liberal Party and Gladstone's resignation in June 1885, they informed future policy in the region. The entertainment industry translated events of the war into deeply felt and memorable tableaux, act closers in a melodrama in which virtue inevitably vanquished villainy and both were immediately identifiable. Not surprisingly, melodramatic convention would later shape justifications for the reconquest of the Sudan, culminating in the bloody Battle of Omdurman in 1898. As Angela C. Pao has written of French imperial melodrama of the same period, "If dramatic authors did indeed rely heavily, even exclusively, on dispatches and commentaries published in the daily papers for their plot outlines and composition of scenes, journalists just as consistently organized their reportage in terms of dramatic scenarios."[3] In the case of the Sudan, the entertainment industry perpetuated the belief that the expected denouement had been delayed, prompting both the press and the government to present the 1898 war as a long-awaited final act.

Students often recognize the reciprocal influences of Victorian press and popular entertainment but are more inclined to view their own media as an unmediated presentation of events. Nineteenth-century press artists had complete control over the images they created; newspapers could further select or delete elements when creating engravings; theaters and music halls explicitly reproduced images from the illustrated dailies; and types of images common in popular entertainment (such as the last stand) became more frequently and prominently presented in dailies. By contrast, a modern-day embedded reporter, according to some students, is simply recording events as they happen; the camera does not lie. Simply identifying jingoism in past Orientalisms does not necessarily help the student become a more critical media consumer. Our media is much more balanced and objective than theirs, the student may counter, and much less influence by the entertainment industry; our justifications for war are much more legitimate.

However, it is precisely that the grounds for war in the 1880s and 1890s were so compelling to a large portion of the population, and that war reporting was seen as unbiased, that is pertinent to our present situation. In addition to avenging Gordon, the 1898 war was depicted as an attempt to end the slave trade and the persecution of women. Melodramas such as *Freedom* had already made the case that the 1882 occupation of Egypt had been prompted by the desire to protect Arab women from Arab men, and a similar claim was made for the British defense of Khartoum in the 1885 melodrama, *Khartoum! Or, The Star of the Desert*. When the claim that Oriental despots victimized their women was again advanced by the press and entertainment industry in 1898, its aura of authenticity had been bolstered through frequent repetition. The point is not that these claims were groundless, though it is hard to see how the death of eleven thousand Sudanese at Omdurman in a battle that cost forty-eight British lives improved the lot of Sudanese women. (The assertion that the British were liberating Egyptian and Sudanese women is particularly striking given that British women lacked voting rights until 1918 and that, arguably, the British occupation of Egypt created new obstacles to female education.)[4] Instead, the question is why this claim to protect brown women from brown men had (and has) such power even though repeatedly the mission of female uplift quickly recedes once fighting is done.

Of course there is no single answer to this question, nor should a teacher try to provide one. To speak of a psychology of imperialism is to invoke a web of conflicting and shifting desires. Yet, despite this, one can speak of frequent tropes in Orientalist entertainments. Among the most prominent is the depiction of nonproductive excess secluded from view until a hero slips through cave openings, guarded gates, or closed markets. In this sense, the East is a harem inviting intervention. In the repeated depiction of abductions from seraglios in the eighteenth and early nineteenth centuries, Europe rehearsed the role it would play in the Arab world in the following decades. When I teach Orientalist entertainments, harem imagery threads its way through the semester and students are asked to explore the range of media that invoke this phantasm of the imperial imagination. By beginning the class with examinations of Orientalist art and its contemporary echoes, students are introduced to harem imagery and are encouraged to see its repetition and transformation in different media and periods.

A particularly important site for this teaching has been the study of pseudo-ethnographic displays of living exotics, a subject that I encourage students to research on their own. In Britain, this phenomenon grew particularly pronounced in 1851, and prompts us to reread the Great Exhibition of that year. In one class, I directed students to examine the depiction of foreign peoples at the Great Exhibition or in competing venues. I broke students into teams and assigned each team a four-month stretch of either the *Illustrated London News* or the *Times* (both of which are available on microform). A seventh group was asked to examine Henry Mayhew and George Cruikshank's novel, *1851, or, the adventures of Mr. and Mrs. Sandboys and family: who came up to London to "enjoy themselves," and to see the Great Exhibition* (1851). All groups then reported back on particular accounts they encountered and why they found these accounts significant. I gave students this assignment at the same time that I was researching these and other texts for a chapter in my book *The Orient on the Victorian Stage*. As often happens, the teaching and writing fed one another. The writing that follows here is derived from both my memory of a successful teaching and the writing that that teaching helped generate.

Because I was researching the subject matter, I was able to alert students to potentially interesting coverage and augment their research with my own. In the process, students came to understand themselves as historians of popular entertainment, and came to recognize the diffusion of Orientalist imagery in various art and entertainment forms across centuries. Part of the objective of this assignment is to develop a vocabulary for understanding exotic display. I had resisted the temptation to assign theoretical texts at the start of the semester, but instead regularly brought short extracts from theorists such as Edward Said, Franz Fanon, Emily Apter, and Ann Laura Stoler that I thought would be relevant. This is a strategy I regularly use because it helps students see theory as a valuable tool for understanding specific practices. Students are immediately able to access what is, or is not, useful for their analysis. I prefaced this assignment with a discussion of ethnography. Though the term "ethnology" was probably coined in the 1830s, London's Ethnological Society was not founded until 1843 and the first ethnological display probably dates from 1845 when the British Museum's collection of Natural and Artificial Curiosities was reorganized as an "Ethnological Gallery." The term gained greater prominence after the Great Exhibition. Several guidebooks used the term to describe features of the collection, and when the exhibition building was transferred to Sydenham in 1852, an ethnological section was added.

Exotic people were displayed in London well before the exhibition year; however, the significance of such displays changed radically with these new midcentury vocabularies. From the middle of the sixteenth century onward, American and African natives were regularly featured in London exhibits.[5] These peoples were invariably advertised as fantastic and unusual. Far from asserting the characteristic nature of the displayed peoples, showmen more often asserted that their natives were noblemen or paragons of savage conceptions of beauty. Moreover, the uniqueness of the displayed person was not attributed to their behavior or customs. The Inuit people displayed by Capt. George Cartwright in 1772 continued to attract crowds even after trading their skin dresses for broadcloth. The Tahitian youth Omai, who was brought to London after Cook's second voyage, was lauded precisely for his ability to adopt European dress and social manners. Whether displayed peoples were presented as noble savages or as distinct species (as would increasingly be the case), they were valued for a rarity that was defined as immanent to their person. By the Victorian period, however, the objectives and strategies of display had changed. As Tony Bennett has noted, collections in this period "were rearranged in accordance with the principle of representativeness rather than that of rarity."[6] No longer was the collection a place for displaying the wondrous. Instead, the collection served to reveal the structure of the natural world and social institutions through the careful manipulation of commonplace objects. In other words, the collection illuminated the rule and not the exception. As Barbara Kirshenblatt-Gimblett

Figure 10. Snake charmers at Regent's Park Zoo, from the *Illustrated London News,* June 15, 1850. Image courtesy of The Rare Books and Manuscripts Library of The Ohio State University Libraries.

has remarked, nineteenth-century natural historians "were interested in taxonomies of the normal, not in singularities of chance formation."[7]

This evolution in display strategy coincided with the reorientation of Britain's imperial ambitions from the west to the east. The Eastern objects, animals and peoples that became common attractions in entertainment venues at this time, reveal changing ideas on native display. From at least the Romantic period, exotic people were presented not as mere oddities but as performers. This continued into the Victorian period, but increasingly these performances were accompanied by ethnographic analysis. For example, an *Illustrated London News* review of the two Egyptian snake charmers who performed at the Regent's Park Zoo in 1850 contrasted Egyptian and Indian snake charming, explained that the Egyptian snake charmers were of the Rufaiah tribe, that they cited Rufais as the founder of their craft, and that he "appears to have been a Mussulman saint" with a tomb in "Busrah." The paper's accompanying illustration was remarkably untheatrical and seems more interested in delineating the performer's clothing than capturing the performance (fig. 10).

The belief that people present pictures of their native lands through their dress and behavior augmented the attraction of the Great Exhibition. The exhibition (commonly known as the Crystal Palace because of its giant glass and iron exhibition building) was thought to have drawn people—as well as products—from all corners of the globe. Newspapers regularly reported the presence of foreign dignitaries at the exhibition. As Paul Greenhalgh explains in his analysis of the human displays at world's fairs, "the actual presence of peoples at exhibitions went back to 1851, when representatives of most nations of the British Empire were constantly in attendance at the Crystal Palace."[8] Even before the exhibition had opened, the *Times* announced that "the whole world is in our streets" (April 30, 1851, 4). Like other nineteenth-century commentators, John Tallis describes both products and peoples in his three-volume account of the exhibition. Relating the days preceding the opening, Tallis seems to forget which of the two were actually on display: "Now rapidly congregated on British ground the representatives of the different nations, with their respective productions and wares, who had been invited to take their place in the great industrial mart. . . ."[9] In a revealing reversal, foreign people take their place in the "industrial mart," accompanied by productions and wares almost as an afterthought. Even before the exhibition opened its doors, writers commented on the influx of foreigners who accompanied the goods shipped for display. Tallis quotes one writer as explaining that

> not a packet showed its flag on Southampton Water that was not crowded with a living freight of dusky Spaniards, and duskier Portugese; of swarthy Moors, and swarthier Egyptians; of cane-coloured East Indians, and copper-coloured Tartars; of Mulattos, with complexions of a lively brown, and of Haytians, with countenances—such as Solomon loved—of a lovely black. (1:19)

Just as the British arranged their products and industry according to an elaborate typology, the "living freight" that streamed to London was similarly organized in progressively darker hues.

The Mayhew and Cruikshank novel provides students with a similar taxonomy of races at the Great Exhibition. The novel opens with the assertion that the Great Exhibition attracted "the sight-seers of all the world" and then presents a long list of attending peoples. Beginning with the exotic, the novel describes Africans arriving on ostriches, caravans from "Zoolu to Fez," as well as Eskimos, Senegalese, Egyptians, East Indians, and indigenous people from New Zealand and elsewhere. The exhibition's comprehensive

Figure 11. Visitors to the Crystal Palace, from Henry Mayhew–George Cruikshank's *1851, or, The Adventures of Mr. and Mrs. Sandboys and family: who came up to London to "enjoy themselves" and to see the Great Exhibition.* Reproduced with the kind permission of the Trustees of New York University.

displays are mirrored in an equally comprehensive attendance. In fact, from the novel it is not clear what constitutes a "sight-seer" and what constitutes a sight. One of the novel's attendees was a well-known object of display—the Hottentot Venus, a South African woman presented to Piccadilly audiences in 1810—muddying the distinction between viewer and viewed. After completing this confused litany, the novel then explains that St. Paul's and Westminster Abbey had been transformed into theaters for the exhibition of the "Black Band of his Majesty of Tsjaddi" along with:

> The Musicians of Tongoose; the Singers of the Maldives; the Glee Minstrels of Paraguay; the Troubadours of far Vancouver; the Snow Ball Family from the Gold Coast; the Canary of the Samoiedes; the Theban Brothers; and "expressly engaged for the occasion," the celebrated Band of Robbers from the Desert.[10]

The Great Exhibition extends out from Hyde Park to consume the entire city. Even religious monuments became adjunct exhibit rooms, and the dis-

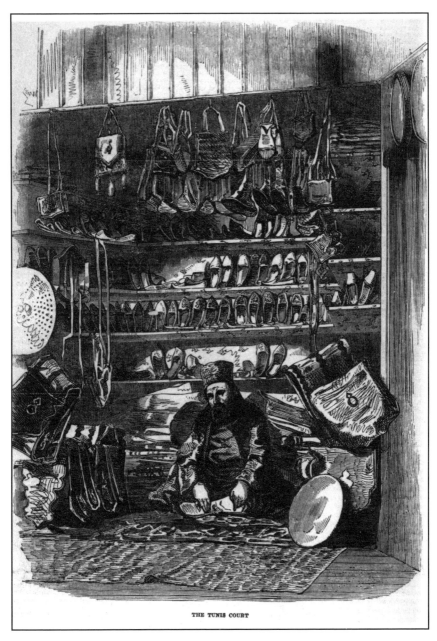

THE TUNIS COURT

Figure 12. Tunisian Court, from the *Illustrated London News,* May 21, 1851. Image courtesy of The Rare Books and Manuscripts Library of The Ohio State University Libraries.

play of the world's industry is complemented by the display of the world's inhabitants.

As a class on popular entertainment, a principal goal is to encourage students to analyze visual representations and the novel's frontispiece provides such an opportunity. The illustration shows the Crystal Palace perched atop the globe as people from every region stream upward. Arabs, Indians, Native Americans, and Africans all make their way up—suggestive of both the perceived internationalism of the exhibition's visitors as well as the belief that the exhibition would raise up the ruder nations (fig. 11).

The *Illustrated London News*'s depiction of the attendant of the Tunisian Court from May 31, 1851, is another interesting image (fig. 12). Heightened attention to exotic people prompted visitors to examine the displays of Eastern nations as ethnographic context, rather than simple examples of industry and manufactures. The Tunisian Court received an award even though most commentators seemed to agree with the *Illustrated London News* that the objects displayed there were "more remarkable as matters of curiosity than for their intrinsic value or importance" (May 31, 1851, 493). However, these same commentators were quick to praise the exhibit's "bazaar-like fittings." More importantly, the feature that set the Tunisian exhibit apart from other "picturesque" displays would appear to be its native attendants. When the *Times* described the objects displayed in the Tunisian Court, its first entry was "Moorish attendants" (May 15, 1851, 5). The *Illustrated London News* implied that the Tunisian Court was required viewing primarily because of its attendant, alternately described as a "good-natured Turk" and an "extremely picturesque and obliging native custodien." The image suggests a natural simplicity, surrounded as he is by objects that the paper described as "of the rudest description, but all admirably calculated to afford illustration of the *ménage* and *convenances* of the North African tribes." In this context, the attendant emerged as a specimen of the North African tribes and the surrounding objects became props intended to heighten the realism of the human display environment.

Ethnographic displays in both the Fine Art Court and the Indian courts further prompted visitors to read certain foreign displays as cultural documents. These courts contained wax models of native North and South Americans and Mexican peasants in "proper costume and displaying their characteristic customs."[11] An even more extensive series of models was displayed in the Indian Court. These clay and plaster models featured elaborate reproductions of village life with rows of wooden houses and shops. One collection cited for praise included upward of sixty groups purportedly illustrating the various castes and professions of the Hindus. While the organizers of the exhibition did not devise an ethnography section, commenta-

Figure 13. Algerian family at Vauxhall Gardens, from the *Illustrated London News*, July 12, 1851. Image courtesy of The Rare Books and Manuscripts Library of The Ohio State University Libraries.

tors like John Tallis adopted this term as a heading when describing the exhibition's collection of human models. In any case, the lack of an ethnology section was corrected when the Crystal Palace was removed from Hyde Park and reerected at Sydenham the following year. *The Illustrated London News* announced that at the new Sydenham Crystal Palace, "one of the most conspicuous and attractive sections will be that of Ethnology" (August 21, 1852, 150). Recognizing that exhibition crowds were interested in racial—as well as industrial—display, the private organizers of the Sydenham exhibit devoted extensive resources to depicting exotic peoples.

While ethnological human display was at most an implied entertainment at the Great Exhibition of 1851, it became a salient attraction at competing venues. My students responded with a combination of intrigue and anger on encountering the *Illustrated London News*'s account of the Algerian family on display at the Vauxhall Gardens. In an attempt to attract exhibition audiences, Robert Wardell of Vauxhall Gardens arranged for an Algerian family to reside at the pleasure garden and to display themselves for a small additional admission price. According to the *Illustrated London News*, "the

World's Fair and the mighty expectations it elicited induced Youssoff [the head of the household] to visit London with his interesting dependents." Here was an example of the streaming horde of natives depicted in Cruikshank's illustration for the *Adventures of Mr. and Mrs. Sandboys*. Though visitors to the Great Exhibition might not be lucky enough to spot one of the visiting exotics, they were assured of seeing an entire family at the Vauxhall Gardens. The family wore "the Arab costume" and were displayed on a "gorgeous divan" specially constructed for their exhibition. As added proof of authenticity, the paper reported that the family professed Islam, though "divested of its fanaticism" (July 12, 1851, 43). Youssoff, the paper explained, had served fifteen years in the French army as a soldier and interpreter. Perhaps it was this Western contact, culminating in a trip to the Great Exhibition, that had civilized the family's religious beliefs. For the exhibitor, however, the native could absorb only so much civilization before losing value as an ethnographic object. This tension is evident in the paper's illustration of the family (fig. 13). Youssof turns to the illustrator in half-profile, flanked by his demurely seated wife and their three children. It is a typical bourgeois family portrait, except for the elaborate "Arab costume." This is the comfortable ethnology of the pleasure garden; natives check any disturbing habits at the entrance and show their receptiveness to Western civilization while retaining the characteristic costumes that conjure the East.

The growing significance of ethnological performance in human displays is illustrated by the troupe of Syrian natives who performed as part of the Holy Land panorama at the Egyptian Hall during the summer of the Great Exhibition. The Middle East had long been a popular panorama subject, and three panoramas of the Holy Land were on view that summer. In response to a competitive market, panorama managers had been incorporating live performance into their exhibitions in recent years. For example, the Egyptian Hall's Nile panorama of 1849 featured "characteristic musical illustrations" including "the famous boat-song, 'Hèy, hèy, hò, Hellèysa,' a barcolle with which the boatman of the Nile cheer their voyage."[12] Originally, the Holy Land panorama of 1851 at the Egyptian Hall was accompanied by Hebrew Melodies; however, as ever larger crowds flooded London, the Egyptian Hall turned to a more compelling illustration of Eastern life. The Syrian troupe that replaced the Hebrew choir clearly had greater ethnological value; as the *Athenaeum* explained, the attraction of the Syrians was simple—they "exhibit[ed] the manners and customs of their country" (August 30, 1851, 932). In a series of scenes and tableaux, the troupe recreated Arab marriage customs, including a musical performance on native instruments and a marriage procession, followed by a scene in a coffeehouse. The *Athenaeum* was particularly impressed that "before the termination of each performance, one of the company of Syrians got up and explained, in very good English, the whole of the matter in hand." It was probably this level of explanation that enabled the *Athenaeum* reviewer to explain the significance of the scenes, provide Arab terms, and include obscure historical details such as the fact that the wax tapers held during the procession replaced the oil lamps used eighteen hundred years ago. Even the review in the *Illustrated London News* included transliterations of the Arabic names of the musical instruments in the performance.

Despite this attention to ethnological detail, human displays in the year of the Crystal Palace preserved a fanciful exoticism and sensuality that had long characterized the East of West-end entertainment. In describing the Algerian family at Vauxhall, the *Illustrated London News* alternated between stressing the quotidian nature of the Algerian family and presenting them as objects of wonder and desire. Their divan was "gorgeous," the Arab costume was "remarkable for its beauty and gorgeousness," and (in a rather suggestive tone) the paper concluded that "the crowds who nightly visit them" all assert that "the personal attractions of the females, with the extreme novelty of their appearance, render the exhibition very gratifying." The family is framed by a sumptuous setting, indication of both visual pleasure and authenticity. The divan, while clearly Wardell's creation, referenced the countless Orientalist fancies of London's theaters and—paradoxically perhaps—gained authenticity in the process.

In discussing examples such as this I sometimes introduce Edward Said's discussion of "the restorative citation of antecedent authority" in order to approach how the entertainment industry, no less than Arabists, derived legitimacy by rewriting and piecing together past performances just as "a restorer of old sketches might put a series of them together for the cumulative picture they might implicitly represent." Newly acquired images of the East were adapted to existing expectations. Said explains, "From these complex rewritings the actualities of the modern Orient were systematically excluded," especially when new details detracted from the sensuality of past representations.[13] The Algerian family's bourgeois configuration was not allowed to undermine their inherent sumptuousness; their gorgeous clothing and setting reveal that they are true Arabs. In the most telling move, the two girls (aged fourteen and sixteen respectively) and their mother were refashioned as "the females" whose "personal attractions" and "novelty of appearance" rendered gratification to the nighttime viewer. This Westernized family was simultaneously an example of an Arabian harem. Contradiction was at the core of these Orientalist displays in which the harem—the space that is, by its name, forbidden—lavishly invited the spectator's gaze.

Prior to this assignment, the class had read William Dimond's *The Bride of Abydos* (a combination of the poem of that title and *The Corsair*, both by Byron) and this 1818 play provides an early precedent for staging the harem:

> Zuliaka's apartment [within the harem]. Female slaves advance joyously, some with musical instruments others employ themselves in disposing strands of flowers. While the center of the stage is occupied by dancers how pursue each other for the bridal veil and by turns possess it. Zuliaka in a glittering habit enters during their sports and reclines herself disconsolately. At the end of the dance the slaves dispose the veil into a canopy above her. (2.2)

Though significantly more chaste than the theatrical harems that would follow, the scene contains tropes that would be seen repeatedly: native instruments and music that intensify the sensualization of female bodies; sapphic play that reads as both innocent and provocative; the careful staging of segregation and enclosure in the midst of public display; and at the center, the languid (here disconsolate) odalisque consumed by secret thoughts.

In the context of this tradition of theatrical Orientalism, not only does the *Illustrated London News*'s description of the Algerian family at Vauxhall suggest harem iconography, even the *Athenaeum*'s self-consciously ethnographic account of the Syrian troupe at the Egyptian Hall conjures a familiar world of Eastern pleasures and excess. The *Athenaeum* explained that bridegroom and mother wore "the richest silks of Damascus" and sat on "a well-furnished divan" as they awaited congratulatory visits. Their female visitors emitted a "gurgling shriek" as the group grew, until the musicians arrived, took their places on the ground, and performed. The *Illustrated London News* added that coffee and pipes were "amply supplied" to the guests throughout. The *Athenaeum* then explained that the scene was followed by a marriage procession, at the end of which the bride finally made her appearance with her attendants. The papers painted images of Eastern luxury; a beautiful setting and costumes combined with shouting women, music, pipes, and coffee to reproduce images of Eastern excess that were common in the theater. At the climax, she enters surrounded by her women—simultaneously chaste bride and odalisque.

These human displays evoked another important element of theatrical Orientalism, the fantastic. *The Thousand and One Nights* (also known as *The Arabian Nights*) enjoyed a huge popularity in England from the time English versions of André Galland's French translation began appearing in London at the start of the eighteenth century. During the Victorian period, Sinbad and Aladdin were regularly featured on the pantomime stage in increasingly lavish productions. It is not surprising, then, that the *Illustrated London News* praised the Syrian troupe for their creation of "a scene in a coffee-house, in which a dwarf tells a tale from the 'Arabian Nights'" all the while "taking whiffs from the pipes of the customers, by way of recompense." The *Athenaeum*, in typically contradictory terms, stated that the storyteller's "gestures and grotesque figure were admirable." The fantastic and the grotesque, as much as the gorgeous and luxurious, were expected features of Eastern displays. Consequently, a sideshow fascination with the storyteller's "grotesque figure" could masquerade as critical assessment of the accuracy of an Eastern display and the presence of fantastic tales served as proof of authenticity.

Students often wish to measure these entertainments according to their adherence to or departure from indigenous practice. "Do storytellers in Syria recite tales from *The Thousand and One Nights?*" students will typically ask. The practice of *hekowati* continues in Syria, though now confined to Ramadan and only in a few venues, and it was much more common before television. However, whether or not these are "real" or invented practices has little to do with the power of such images to the British imagination. These performances facilitated established tropes of Orientalist discourse even as they were framed by presenters and reviewers as examples of ethnographic display. As the *Illustrated London News* explained in its review of the Syrian troupe:

> All this, it must be acknowledged, is as novel as it is genuine; and as we witness these native musicians, singers, and story-tellers in their Oriental costume, we feel that a real addition is made to the knowledge of the fireside tourist, who need not go far from his chimney-corner to behold the very persons and manners of which he reads in books of adventure and modern travel. (*Illustrated London News,* August 30, 1851, 266)

In Orientalist displays, the "novel" and the "genuine" went hand in hand, illustrating a world familiar from both travel narratives and adventure stories. Even as native performance was increasingly seen as a means of re-creating distant places for the fireside tourist, these performances continued to be valued for their exotic playfulness—for their delightful mix of music, singing, and extravagant costume.

Even commentators on the Great Exhibition similarly invoked an East of fantastic and sensual excess when discussing the Eastern courts, often citing *The Arabian Nights* and Oriental romances as illustrations of what visitors could expect. For example, Tallis gave special attention to an apartment in one of the India courts that was furnished like an Indian palace, explaining that it "realised all that the Arabian Nights, and other romances, have detailed with respect to their gorgeous and costly luxury."[14] It was apparently unimportant that *The Arabian Nights* are set Baghdad and not India. *The Nights* authenticate the recreation of Indian architecture at the Crystal Palace, not because the text has any relation to the exhibit, but because *The Nights* had become shorthand for the strategies by which sensual and extravagant displays were contained within the safe parameters of the East. As Tallis himself explained, "Oriental magnificence is still a proverbial mode of describing a degree of splendour and artistical richness, which is not found among ourselves" (1:37).

Just as human displays combined a newer ethnographic vocabulary with an older romantic vocabulary of Eastern sensuality and fantasy, the exhibition similarly reveals a dialectical relation between seemingly antithetical Orientalist discourses. Visitors to the exhibition frequently contrasted the unceasing progression of Western civilization and the perceived stasis of Eastern civilization; however, at the same time, commentators invoked images of Eastern excess in order to praise the bounty of industrialization. British manufacturers were often arranged to illustrate progress and improvements over time. Leaving British manufacturers, visitors found that most of the contributions from the colonies were in the Raw Materials section, with the exception of the separate India courts. Even the Indian displays stood in marked opposition of the story of progress told in the manufacture and machinery sections. A writer for the *Illustrated London News* posed a common question when he asked why, in the Indian agricultural and manufacturing arts, "no advance should be made for centuries." Influenced by theories of environmental determinism then prominent in ethnological and historical thought, the writer turned to climate and geography to explain why "this people have made so little progress" and why "the great bulk of them are in the same condition, moral, social, and intellectual, that they were in 300 years ago" (*Illustrated London News*, May 31, 1851, 489). Outside of Europe, visitors encountered savage lands capable of producing little more than raw materials or the crudest manufactures (a Bedouin tent was a prominent feature of the Tunisian exhibit). Even the relatively civilized peoples of the East (as they were represented by the British) were depicted as frozen in time, their limited industry demonstrating a "moral, social, and intellectual" paralysis.

While the exhibition proclaimed a commitment to "progress," and identified itself as a "rational amusement," its real attraction was an opulence and scale that bordered on excess. In highlighting these qualities, the exhibition turned to tropes associated with the Eastern civilizations that appeared static or declining when framed within the Crystal Palace. In describing the opening of the exhibition, Tallis employed the images of "oriental magnificence" that were supposedly absent from England:

> And, unquestionably, neither Eastern fairy tale, nor *Arabian Night's* wonder, could surpass, or even emulate the gorgeous reality that greeted the delighted gaze of the assembled spectators, as the royal party and brilliant cortège advanced through the bronze and gilded gates that led into this hall of enchantment; fragrant exotics bloomed and shed their soft perfume around, [and] crystal fountains threw up their sparkling waters. . . . [15]

Tallis painted an image of an opulent Eastern palace and not without cause; Owen Jones, who was responsible for the interior decoration of the Crystal Palace, designed the iron railing around the building in a Moorish fretwork and based his paint colors and application on the Alhambra. (Jones had published a study of the Alhambra seven years earlier.) In fact, Jones had wanted to hang large carpets above the mezzanines and arched arabesque paintings over the central aisles, giving "the impression of a bazaar, and . . . further emphasis[ing] the impression of eastern atmosphere" in the opinion of one design historian[16] (Darby, 105). It was perhaps Jones's design that prompted the *Times* to compare the exhibition building to "an *Arabian Night's* structure."[17] The East served as the squalid example against which British plenty was defined; at the same time, however, the East provided the metaphors by which Britain could assess that plenty. While the Eastern exhibits were overshadowed by the displays of British industry in the minds of most commentators, in point of fact, the exhibition ceaselessly presented an East of its own fashioning.

Framed within this lavish architecture, the exhibition fetishized works of industry in much the same way that human displays and theater fetishized Eastern women. The exhibition imagined itself as an elaborate harem. Its array of commodities and machinery posited a world of impossibly endless availability. As Prince Albert said at the opening ceremony, "[T]he products of all quarters of the globe are placed at our disposal, and we have only to choose which is the best and cheapest for our purposes" (quoted in Richards, 28). In this fantasy world of availability, one need only select from a throng that simply awaits his choice. Britain turned to an East of its own creation for the imagery that would give a material form to this idea of availability. The Crystal Palace, with its Moorish fretwork and Alhambresque coloring, was another of London's gorgeous divans and the personal attractions and novelty of the displayed objects similarly promised gratification. Islamic ornament and color were the raw materials from which Britain constructed its monument to surplus. In the process the exhibition referenced the East appearing in the foreign courts and at Vauxhall Gardens, which were read in light of theatrical Orientalism. In pleasure gardens and foreign courts, theater-savvy spectators looked past muslin veils and damask cloth to discover sweetmeats and coffees in the hands of convivial old Turks and alluring Algerians. Here, then, was the "real" East, more tangible than decorative patterns or color combinations, more engaging than a bale of cotton or a sack of dates. This was the East as Eastern body, a world that invited Western industry and intervention with the languid desire of an odalisque.

"These girls were slaves, they are free! England has decreed it, and in England's name I speak." Flash forward to 1882. Shortly after Britain began its occupation of Egypt, Drury Lane mounted the imperial melodrama *Freedom*. Earnest Gascoigne, captain of Her Britannic Majesty's gunboat *Arrow*, makes his entrance preceded by the horde of slave girls he has just liberated from a slave trader's boat (2.2). In the scenes that follow, the villain foments a nationalistic rebellion only so that he may abduct the daughter of a British financier and imprison her in his harem. The financier had come to Egypt looking for open markets, but instead the atavistic Egyptians sought to shield their nation from British "progress" just as they segregate their women (and any unfortunate white women they should get their hands on). Fortunately for both Egyptian women and British financiers, the HMS *Arrow* is on hand bearing freedom. This same promise to liberate women from the practices of Islam marks the melodramas depicting subsequent interventions in the Sudan. Not only do I want my students to examine why this justification was compelling in its day, I want them to examine why similar justifications remain compelling today.

NOTES

1. See Sarah Bryant-Betail, "Theater as Heterotopia: Lessing's *Nathan the Wise*," 91–108.
2. See Edward Ziter, *The Orient on the Victorian Stage*, 164–97.
3. *The Orient of the Boulevards: Exoticism, Empire, and Nineteenth-Century French Theater*, 123.
4. Leila Ahmed, *Women and Gender in Islam: Historical Roots of a Modern Debate*, 153.
5. Richard Daniel Altick, *The Shows of London*, 45–49.
6. Tony Bennett, *The Birth of the Museum: History, Theory, Politics*, 39.
7. Barbara Kirshenblatt-Gimblett, "Objects of Ethnography," in *Exhibiting Cultures*, ed. Karp and Lavine, 392.
8. Paul Greenhalgh, *Ephemeral Vistas: The Expositions Universelles, Great Exhibitions*

and World's Fairs, 1851–1939, 85.

9. John Tallis, *Tallis's History and Description of the Crystal Palace, and the Exhibition of the World's Industry in 1851*, 1:15.

10. Henry Mayhew and George Cruikshank, *1851, or, The Adventures of Mr. and Mrs. Sandboys and family: who came up to London to "enjoy themselves" and to see the Great Exhibition*, 2.

11. Tallis, 2:192.

12. Altick, 209.

13. Edward Said, *Orientalism*, 176–77.

14. Tallis, 1:33.

15. Ibid.

16. Micheal Darby, *The Islamic Perspective: An Aspect of British Architecture and Design in the Nineteenth Century*, 105.

17. Quoted in Tallis, 1:19.

WORKS CITED

Abrahams, Israel. "A Masterpiece for the Week: Disraeli's 'Alroy.'" *Jewish World*, no. 3005 (Tamuz 11, 5673/ July 16, 1913): 9–10. Repr. Disraeli, Benjamin. *Alroy*. Ed. Sheila A. Spector. *Romantic Circles Electronic Editions*. Gen. eds. Neil Fraistat and Steven E. Jones. http://www.rc.umd.edu/editions/alroy.ns.

Adler, Joseph. *Restoring the Jews to Their Homeland: Nineteen Centuries in the Quest for Zion*. Northvale, NJ and Jerusalem: Jason Aronson, 1997.

Ahmed, Akbar S. *Pakistan Society: Islam, Ethnicity and Leadership in South Asia*. Oxford: Oxford University Press, 1987.

Ahmed, Leila. *Women and Gender in Islam: Historical Roots of a Modern Debate*. New Haven, CT: Yale University Press, 1992.

Aiken, M. *Memoirs of Religious Importers from the Seventh to the Nineteenth Century*. London: Longman & Rees, J. Wright, 1799.

Alloulah, Malek. *The Colonial Harem*. Trans. Wlad and Myrna Godzich. Manchester: Manchester University Press, 1986.

Altick, Richard Daniel. *The Shows of London*. Cambridge, MA: Belknap Press, 1978.

Althusser, Louis. *Lenin and Philosophy and Other Essays*. Trans. Ben Brewster. New York: Monthly Review Press, 1971.

Anderson, Benedict. *Imagined Communities: Reflections on the Origin and Spread of Nationalism*. Rev. ed. London and New York: Verso, 1991.

Apter, Emily. "Female Trouble in the Colonial Harem." *Differences* 4 (1992): 203–24.

——. "Global *Translatio*: The 'Invention' of Comparative Literature, Istanbul, 1933." *Debating World Literature*, ed. Christopher Prendergast, 76–109. London and New York: Verso, 2004.

——. "Saidian Orientalism." *boundary 2* 31, no. 2 (2004): 35–53.

Aravamudan, Srivinas. "Lady Mary Wortley Montagu in the *Hammam*: Masquerade, Womanliness, and Levantization." *English Literacry History* 62 (1995): 69–104.

Aubin, Penelope. *The Noble Slaves; or, the lives and adventures of two lords and two ladies, who were Shipwreck'd*. London, 1722.

Auerbach, Erich. *Mimesis: The Representation of Reality in Western Literature*. Princeton, NJ and Oxford: Princeton University Press, 2003 (1953). Trans. Willard R. Trask. Introduction by Edward Said.

Baedeker, K[arl], ed. *Egypt: Handbook for Travellers*. Vol. 1. Leipsic [*sic*]: Karl Baedeker, and London: Duplau, 1878.

Baer, Joel. "Penelope Aubin and the Pirates of Madagascar." *Eighteenth-Century Women: Studies in Their Lives, Work, and Culture* 1 (2001): 49–62.

Bage, Robert. *The Fair Syrian.* 2 vols. Repr. of 1787 ed. New York: Garland, 1979.

Bagchee, Shymal. Course Description for "Discriminating Orientalisms" (ENGL 665). University of Alberta Web site. http://www.humanities.ualberta.ca/english.

"Bakshîsh: Important Notice." Preface. *The Nile: Notes for Travellers in Egypt and in the Egyptian Sudan.* By E. A. Wallis Budge. 12th ed. London: Thomas Cook and Son, 1912.

Bailey-Goldschmidt, Janice, and Martin Kalfakovic. "Sex, Lies and European Hegemony: Travel Literature and Ideology." *Journal of Popular Culture* 26, no. 4 (1993): 141–53. *Academic Search Premier.* EBSCO. Plymouth State University, Lamson Lib. Accessed. November 2, 2003. http://www.epnet.com/.

Barbour, Richmond. *Before Orientalism: London's Theater of the East, 1576–1626.* Cambridge: Cambridge University Press, 2003.

Barrell, John. "Death on the Nile: Fantasy and the Literature of Tourism, 1840–1860." *Essays in Criticism* 41 (1991): 97–127.

———. *The Infection of Thomas De Quincey: A Psychopathology of Imperialism.* New Haven, CT: Yale University Press, 1991.

Barfoot, C. C. "English Romantic Poets and the 'Free-Floating Orient.'" *Oriental Prospects,* 65–96.

———, and Theo D'haen, eds. *Oriental Prospects: Western Literature and the Lure of the East.* Amsterdam-Atlanta: Rodopi, 1998.

Batchelor, Stephen. *The Awakening of the West: The Encounter of Buddhism and Western Culture.* Berkeley: Parallax Press, 1994.

Beaulieu, Jill, and Mary Roberts, eds. *Orientalism's Interlocutors: Painting, Architecture, Photography.* Durham, NC and London: Duke University Press, 2002.

Beck, Brandon. *From the Rising of the Sun: English Images of the Ottoman Empire to 1715.* New York: Peter Lang, 1987.

Beckford, William. *Vathek.* 1980. Ed. Roger Lonsdale. Oxford: Oxford University Press, 1998.

Beers, William. *Women and Sacrifice: Male Narcissism and the Psychology of Religion.* Detroit: Wayne State University Press, 1992.

Behdad, Ali. *Belated Travelers: Orientalism in the Age of Colonial Dissolution.* Durham, NC and London: Duke University Press, 1994.

Benedetto, Richard. "Bush: No Proof of Sadddam Role in 9/11." *USAToday.com.* September 17, 2003. http://www.usatoday.com/news/washington/2003–09–17bush-saddam_x.htm.

Bennett, Tony. *The Birth of the Museum: History, Theory, Politics.* London: Routledge, 1995.

Benthall, Jonathan. "Firstfruits in the *Quran.*" In *Sacrifice in Religious Experience,* ed. Alfred I. Baumgarten, 257–69. Leiden: Brill, 2002.

Bernier, François. *Travels in the Mogul Empire.* Trans. Archibald Constable. 2nd ed. Oxford: Oxford University Press, 1914.

Bernstein, Matthew, and Gaylyn Studlar, eds. *Visions of the East: Orientalism in Film.* New Brunswick, NJ: Rutgers University Press, 1997.

Bevan, Samuel. *Sand and Canvas; a Narrative of Adventures in Egypt, with a Sojourn among the Artists in Rome.* London: Charles Gilpin, 1849.

Bhabha, Homi. "Adagio." In Bhabha and Mitchell, 371–80.

———. "Interrogating Identity." In *The Location of Culture*, 57–93. New York: Routledge, 1994.

———. "The Other Question: Stereotype, Discrimination, and the Discourse of Colonialism." In *The Location of Culture*, 66–92, 102–20. London: Routledge.

Bhabha, Homi, and W. J. T. Mitchell, eds. "Edward Said: Continuing the Conversation." *Critical Inquiry* 31, no. 2 (2005): 365–529.

Bickerstaff, Isaac. *The Sultan, or, a peep into the Seraglio.* London: C. Dilly, 1787.

Bivona, Daniel. *Desire and Contradiction: Imperial Visions and Domestic Debates in Victorian Literature.* Manchester: Manchester University Press, 1990.

Blake, Robert. *Disraeli's Grand Tour: Benjamin Disraeli and the Holy Land, 1830–31.* New York: Oxford University Press, 1982.

Boer, Inge E. *After 'Orientalism': Critical Entanglements, Productive Looks.* Amsterdam: Rodopi, 2004.

———. "Despotism from Under the Veil: Masculine and Feminine Readings of the Despot and the Harem." *Cultural Critique* 32 (1995–96): 43–73.

Bohls, Elizabeth. *Women Travel Writers and the Language of Aesthetics, 1716–1818.* Cambridge: Cambridge University Press, 1995

Bohrer, Frederick N. *Orientalism and Visual Culture: Imagining Mesopotamia in Nineteenth-Century Europe.* Cambridge: Cambridge University Press, 2003.

Boyle, J. A., ed. *The Saljuq and Mongol Periods.* Vol. 5 of *The Cambridge History of Iran.* Cambridge: Cambridge University Press, 1968.

Brantlinger, Patrick. *Dark Vanishings: Discourse on the Extinction of Primitive Races, 1800–1930.* Ithaca, NY and London: Cornell University Press, 2003.

———. *Rule of Darkness: British Literature and Imperialism, 1830–1914.* Ithaca, NY: Cornell University Press, 1988.

Breckenridge, Carol A., and Peter van der Veer. *Orientalism and the Postcolonial Predicament: Perspectives on South Asia.* Philadelphia: University of Pennsylvania Press, 1993.

Brennan, Timothy. "The Illusion of a Future: *Orientalism* as Traveling Theory." *Critical Theory* 26 (Spring 2000): 558–83.

———. "Resolution." In Bhabha and Mitchell, 406–18.

Brettell, Caroline B. "Introduction: Travel Literature, Ethnography, and Ethnohistory." *Ethnohistory* 33.

Plymouth State University, Lamson Lib. Accessed November 2, 2003. http://www.epnet.com/.

Brown, Laura. *Ends of Empire: Women and Ideology in Early Eighteenth-Century English Literature.* Ithaca, NY: Cornell University Press, 1993.

Bryant-Bertail, Sarah. "Theatre as Heterotopia: Lessing's Nathan the Wise." *Assaph: Studies in the Theatre* 16 (2000): 91–108.

Burnham, Michelle. *Captivity and Sentiment: Cultural Exchange in American Literature, 1682–1861.* Hanover, NH: University Press of New England, 1997.

Burton, Richard F. *Personal Narrative of a Pilgrimage to al-Madinah and Meccah.* 1855. Memorial ed. Ed. Isabel Burton. 1893. Vol. 1. New York: Dover, 1964.

———. *Selected Papers on Anthropology, Travel and Exploration.* London: Philpot, 1924.

Buruma, Ian, and Avishai Margalit. *Occidentalism: The West in the Eyes of Its Enemies.* New York: Penguin, 2004.

Butler, Marilyn. "Orientalism." In *The Penguin History of Literature.* Vol. 5, *The Romantic Period.* Ed. David B. Pirie, 395–447. London: Penguin, 1994.

Buzard, James. *The Beaten Track: European Tourism, Literature, and the Ways to Culture, 1800–1918*. Oxford: Clarendon Press, 1993.

Byron, George Gordon, Lord. *The Letters and Journals of Lord Byron*. Ed. Leslie A. Marchand. 12 vols. London: Murray, 1973–1980.

———. *Byron's Poetry*. Ed. Frank D. McConnell. New York: Norton, 1978.

———. *The Giaour*. In *Three Oriental Tales: Frances Sheridan,* History of Nourjahad*; William Beckford,* Vathek*; Lord Byron,* The Giaour. Ed. Alan Richardson, 180–226. Boston: Houghton Mifflin, 2001.

———. *Selected Poetry of Lord Byron*. 2nd ed. Ed. Louis Marchand. New York: Modern Library, 2001.

Campbell, Jan. *Arguing with the Phallus: Feminist Queer and Postcolonial Theory*. New York: St. Martin's Press, 2000.

Campbell, Mary. *Lady Morgan: The Life and Times of Sydney Owenson*. London: Pandora Press, 1988.

Campbell, Thomas. *The Pleasures of hope; in two parts with Other Poems*. Edinburgh: Mundell & Son, 1799.

Cannadine, David. *Ornamentalism: How the British Saw Their Empire*. Oxford: Oxford University Press, 2001.

Cannon, Garland, ed. *The Letters of Sir William Jones*. 2 vols. Oxford: Clarendon Press, 1970.

———. *The Life and Mind of Oriental Jones: Sir William Jones, the Father of Modern Linguistics*. Cambridge: Cambridge University Press, 1991.

Carey, Daniel. "Questioning Incommensurability in Early Modern Cultural Exchange." *Common Knowledge* 6 (1997): 32–50.

Carr, Raymond, ed. *Spain: A History*. Oxford: Oxford University Press, 2000.

Carrier, James, ed. *Occidentalism: Images of the West*. Oxford: Clarendon Press, 1995.

Cass, Jeffrey. "'Egypt on Steroids': Luxor Las Vegas and Postmodern Orientalism." In *Architecture and Tourism: Perception, Performance, and Place*, ed. D. Medina Lasansky and Brian McLaren, 241–63. Oxford and New York: Berg Publishers, 2004.

———. "Miltonic Orientalism: *Jane Eyre* and the Two Dalilas." *Dickens Studies Annual* 33 (2003): 191–213.

———. "'The Scraps, Patches, and Rags of Daily Life': Gaskell's Oriental Other and the Conservation of Cranford." *Papers on Language and Literature* 35, no. 2 (1999): 417–33.

Chapman, R. W., ed. *Jane Austen's Letters*. Oxford: Oxford University Press, 1952.

Chapman, William Ryan. "Arranging Ethnology: A.H.L.F. Pitt Rivers and the Typological Tradition." In *Objects and Others: Essays on Museums and Material Culture*, ed. George W. Stocking Jr., 15–48. Madison: University of Wisconsin Press, 1985.

Chew, Samuel. *The Crescent and the Rose: Islam and England during the Renaissance*. New York: Oxford University Press, 1937.

Christensen, Jerome. *Lord Byron's Strength: Romantic Writing and Commercial Society*. Baltimore: Johns Hopkins University Press, 1993.

Chung, Rebecca. "A Woman Triumphs: From *Travels of an English Lady in Europe, Asia, and Africa* (1763) by Lady Mary Wortley Montagu." In *Travel Knowledge: European "Discoveries" in the Early Modern Period*, ed. Ivo Kamps and Jyotsna G. Singh, 110–24. New York: Palgrave, 2001.

Cirakman, Asli. *From the "Terror of the World" to the 'Sick Man of Europe": European Images of Ottoman Empire and Society from the Sixteenth Century to the Nineteenth*. New York: Peter Lang, 2002.

Clifford, James. "On Orientalism." In *The Predicament of Culture: Twentieth-Century Ethnography, Literature, and Art*, 255–76. *Cambridge*, MA: Harvard University Press, 1988.

———. *Routes: Travel and Translation in the Late Twentieth Century*. Cambridge: Harvard University Press, 1997.

Codell, Julie F., and Dianne Sachko Macleod, eds. *Orientalism Transposed: The Impact of the Colonies on British Culture*. Brookfield, VT: Ashgate, 1998.

Colebrooke, H. T. "On the Duties of a Faithful Hindu Widow." *Asiatick Researches*, IV (1795): 109–19.

Colley, Linda. *Captives: Britain, Empire and the World, 1600–1850*. London: Jonathan Cape, 2002.

———. "The Narrative of Elizabeth Marsh: Barbary, Sex, and Power." In *The Global Eighteenth Century*, ed. Felicity Nussbaum, 138–50. Baltimore: Johns Hopkins University Press, 2003.

Cooley, Emily. "Proto-Feminism and Ethnography in Lady Mary Wortley Montagu's *Turkish Embassy Letters.*" *Publications of the Mississippi Philological Association* (2002): 8–15.

Cowley, Hanah. *A Day in Turkey, or the Russian Slaves*. 4th ed. London: G. G. J. and J. Robinson, 1792.

Crinson, Mark. *Empire Building: Orientalism and Victorian Architecture*. New York: Routledge, 1996.

Crompton, Louis. *Byron and Greek Love: Homophobia in 19th-Century England*. Berkeley: University of California Press, 1985.

Crow, John A. *Spain: The Root and the Flower*. 3rd ed. Berkeley: University of California Press, 1985.

Csoma de Kőrős, Alexander. *Tibetan-English Dictionary*. Budapest: Akadémiai Kiadó, 1984.

Dalrymple, William. *White Mughals: Love and Betrayal in Eighteenth-Century India*. New York: Viking, 2003.

Dallmayr, Fred. *Beyond Orientalism*. Albany: SUNY Press, 1996.

Darby, Micheal. *The Islamic Perspective: An Aspect of British Architecture and Design in the Nineteenth Century*. London: Leighton House Gallery, 1983.

David, Deirdre. *Rule Britannia: Women, Fiction, and Victorian Writing*. Ithaca, NY and London: Cornell University Press, 1995.

Denniston, Lyle. "Supreme Court Rejects Detainee Case." *Boston Globe*. January 13, 2004, A2.

Dennon, Joseph. *Irish Orientalism: A Literary and Intellectual History*. Syracuse, NY: Syracuse University Press, 2004.

De Quincey, Thomas. *Confessions of an English Opium Eater*. Ed. Alethea Hayter. New York: Penguin, 1971.

Desai, Anita. Introduction. *The Turkish Embassy Letters*, by Lady Mary Wortley Montagu, vii–xxxvii. London: Virago, 2000.

Dimond, W. *The Bride of Abydos*. London: T. H. Lacey, [1818].

Disraeli, Benjamin. *Alroy*. Ed. Sheila A. Spector. In *Romantic Circles Electronic Editions*. Gen. eds. Neil Fraistat and Steven E. Jones, 2005. http://www.rc.umd.edu/editions/alroy.ns.

Dixon, W. Hepworth and Geraldine Jewsbury, eds. *Lady Morgan's Memoirs: Autobiography, Diaries Correspondence*. 2 vols. London: W. H. Allen, 1863 (1862).

Dobie, Madeleine. "Embodying Oriental Women: Representation and Voyeurism in Montesquieu, Montagu and Ingres." *Cincinnati Romance Review* 13 (1994): 51–60.

——. *Foreign Bodies: Gender, Language, and Culture in French Orientalism*. Stanford, CA: Stanford University Press, 2001.

Doniger, Wendy. *Asceticism and Eroticism in the Mythology of Siva*. Oxford: Oxford University Press, 1973.

Drew, John. *India and the Romantic Imagination*. Delhi: Oxford University Press, 1987.

Duncan, James, and Derek Gregory. Introduction. *Writes of Passage: Reading Travel Writing*, ed. James Duncan and Derek Gregory, 1–13. London: Routledge, 1999.

Duncan, Jonathan. "An Account of Two Fakeers, with Their Portraits." *Asiatick Researches* 5 (1798): 37–52.

Dutton, Michael, and Peter Williams. "Translating Theories: Edward Said on Orientalism, Imperialism and Alterity." *Southern Review: Literary and Interdisciplinary Essays* 26, no. 3 (November 1993): 314–57.

Eagleton, Terry. *The Great Hunger: Studies in Irish Culture*. London and New York: Verso, 1995.

——. *The Illusions of Postmodernism*. Oxford: Blackwell Publishers, 1996.

Edwards, Amelia B. *A Thousand Miles Up the Nile*. 1877. Rev. ed. 1888. New York: A. L. Burt, n.d.

Edwards, Holly, et al. *Noble Dreams, Wicked Pleasures: Orientalism in America, 1870–1930*. Princeton, NJ: Princeton University Press and the Sterling and Francine Clark Art Institute, 2000.

Eisler, Benita. *Byron—Child of Passion, Fool of Fame*. New York: Knopf, 1999.

Elfenbein, Andrew. *Romantic Genius: The Prehistory of a Homosexual Role*. New York: Columbia University Press, 1999.

Embree, Ainslie. *Charles Grant and British Rule in India*. New York: Columbia University Press, 1962.

Endelman, Todd M. *Radical Assimilation in English Jewish History 1656–1945*. Bloomington: Indiana University Press, 1990.

Enfield, William. *The History of Philosophy from the Earliest Periods: Drawn Up from Brucker's Historia Critica Philosophiæ*. 2 vols. 1971; London, 1837.

Epstein, Joseph. "Wise, Foolish, Enchanting Lady Mary." *New Criterion* 13, no. 5 (1995): 8–17. *Academic Search Premier*. EBSCO. Plymouth State University, Lamson Lib. Accessed January 17, 2004. http://www.epnet.com/.

"Ethnography." Accessed April 15, 2004. http://www.wsu.edu:8001/vcwsu/commons/topics/culture/glossary/ethnography.html.

Ethnography. "Description." Accessed April 15, 2004. http://www.sagepub.com/journal.aspx?pid+157.

Fairholt, F[rederick] W[illiam]. *Up the Nile, and Home Again: A Handbook for Travellers and a Travel-book for the Library*. London: Chapman and Hall, 1862.

Ferguson, Moira. *Colonialism and Gender Relations from Mary Wollstonecraft to Jamaica Kincaid*. New York: Columbia University Press, 1993.

Ferris, Ina. "Writing on the Border: The National Tale, Female Writing, and the Public Sphere." In *Romanticism, History and the Possibilities of Genre*, ed. Tilottama Rajan and Julia H. Wright, 86–106. New York: Cambridge University Press, 1998.

Fitzpatrick, William J. *Lady Morgan: Her Career, Literary and Personal*. London, 1860.

Fleming, K. E. *The Muslim Bonaparte: Diplomacy and Orientalism in Ali Pasha's Greece*. Princeton, NJ: Princeton University Press, 1999.

Fothergill, Brian. *Beckford of Fonthill*. London and Boston: Faber and Faber, 1979.

Foucault, Michel. *Discipline and Punish: The Birth of the Prison*. Trans. Alan Sheridan. New York: Vintage Books, 1995.

Franey, Laura E. *Victorian Travel Writing and Imperial Violence: British Writing on Africa, 1855–1902*. Basingstoke: Palgrave Macmillan, 2003.

Franklin, Michael J. "Accessing India: Orientalism, Anti-'Indianism' and the Rhetoric of Jones and Burke." In Fulford and Kitson, 48–66.

———. "The Building of Empire and the Building of Babel; Sir William Jones, Lord Byron, and the Productions of the Orient." In *Byron East and West*, ed. Martin Prochazka, 63–78. Prague: Charles University, 2000.

———. "Cultural Possession, Imperial Control, and Comparative Religion: The Calcutta Perspectives of Sir William Jones and Nathaniel Brassey Halhed." *Yearbook of English Studies* 32 (2002): 1–18.

———, ed. *The European Discovery of India: Key Indological Texts that Shaped European Romanticism*. 6 vols. London: Ganesha Press, 2001.

———. "Passion's Empire: Sydney Owenson's Indian Venture, Phoenicianism, Orientalism, and Binarism." In *Studies in Romanticism*.

———. *Sir William Jones: Selected Poetical and Prose Works*. Cardiff: University of Wales Press, 1995.

Fromkin, David. *A Peace to End All Peace: The Fall of the Ottoman Empire and the Creation of the Modern Middle East*. New York: Henry Holt, 1989.

Fuery, Patrick, and Nick Mansfield. *Cultural Studies and Critical Theory*. 2nd ed. Oxford: Oxford University Press, 2000.

Fulford, Tim, ed. *Romanticism and Millenarianism*. New York: Palgrave, 2002.

———, and Peter J. Kitson, eds. *Romanticism and Colonialism*. Cambridge: Cambridge University Press, 1998.

———, Debbie Lee, and Peter J. Kitson. *Literature, Science and Exploration in the Romantic Era: Bodies of Knowledge*. Cambridge: Cambridge University Press, 2004.

Gans, David Ben Solomon. *Chronologia Sacra-Profana a Mundi Conditu ad Annum M.5352 vel Christi 1592, dicta [Zemah David] German Davidis*. Trans. Guilielmum Henric Voustium. 1644.

Gardner, Kevin J. "The Aesthetics of Intimacy: Lady Mary Wortley Montagu and Her Readers." *Papers on Language & Literature* 34, no. 2 (1998): 113–33. *Academic Search Premier*. EBSCO. Plymouth State University, Lamson Library. Accessed January 17, 2004. http://www.epnet.com/.

Garside, Peter, and Caroline Franklin. *The Romantics: Women Novelists*. 12 vols. London: Routledge; Bristol: Thoemmes, 1990–1995.

Gaull, Marilyn. *English Romanticism: The Human Context*. New York and London: W. W. Norton, 1988.

Geertz, Clifford. *The Interpretation of Cultures*. New York: Basic, 1973.

Gemmett, Robert J. *William Beckford*. Boston: Twayne Publishers, 1977.

Gerow, Edwin. "Plot Structure and the Development of Rasa in the Sakuntalá." Part 1. *Journal of the American Oriental Society* 99 (1979): 559–72.

———. "Plot Structure and the Development of Rasa in the Sakuntalá." Part 2. *Journal of the American Oriental Society* 100 (1980): 267–82.

Ghosh, Sanjukta. "From Burqas to Bikinis: White Women's Burden and the 'Afghani Woman.'" Paper presented at Race in the 21st Century: Third Biennial World Affairs Symposium. Keene State College, Keene, NH. October 31, 2003.

Gibbes, Phebe. *Hartly House, Calcutta*. London: J. Dodsley, 1789.

Gikandi, Simon. *Maps of Englishness: Writing Identity in the Culture of Colonialism*. New York: Columbia University Press, 1996.

Gilders, William K. *Blood Ritual in the Hebrew Bible*. Baltimore: Johns Hopkins University Press, 2004.

Gill, R. B. "The Author in the Novel: Creating Beckford in *Vathek*." *Eighteenth-Century Fiction* 15, no. 2 (2003): 241–54.

Girardot, Norman J. *The Victorian Translation of China: James Legge's Oriental Pilgrimage*. Berkeley: University of California Press, 2002.

Goodwin, Jason. *Lords of the Horizons: A History of the Ottoman Empire*. New York: Henry Holt, 1998.

Greenfield, Cathy. "Editorial." *Southern Review* 26, no. 3 (1993): 311–13.

Greenhalgh, Paul. *Ephemeral Vistas: The* Expositions Universelles*, Great Exhibitions and World's Fairs, 1851–1939*. Manchester: Manchester University Press, 1988.

Gregory, Derek. "Scripting Egypt: Orientalism and the Cultures of Travel." In *Writes of Passage: Reading Travel Writing*, ed. James Duncan and Derek Gregory, 114–50. London: Routledge, 1999.

Grewal, Inderpal. *Home and Harem: Nation, Gender, Empire, and the Cultures of Travel*. Durham, NC: Duke University Press, 1996.

Grosrichard, Alain. *The Sultan's Court: European Fantasies of the East*. Trans. Liz Heron. New York: Verso, 1998.

Grundy, Isobel. "'Trash, Trumpery, and Idle Time': Lady Mary Wortley Montagu and Fiction." *Eighteenth-Century Fiction* 5, no. 4 (1993): 293–310.

——. *Lady Mary Wortley Montagu*. Oxford: Oxford University Press, 1999.

Habermas, Jurgen. *The Structural Transformation of the Public Sphere: An Inquiry into a Category of Bourgeois Society*. Trans. Thomas Burger. Cambridge, MA: MIT Press, 1989.

Haddad, Emily. *Orientalist Poetics: The Islamic Middle East in Nineteenth-Century English and French Poetry*. Burlington, VT: Ashgate, 2002.

Haggerty, George E. "Beckford's Paederasty." In *Illicit Sex: Identity Politics in Early Modern Culture*. Eds. Thomas DiPiero and Pat Gill, 123–42. Athens and London: University of Georgia Press, 1997. Rpt. *Men in Love: Masculinity and Sexuality in the Eighteenth Century*. New York: Columbia University Press, 1999.

Halsband, Robert, ed. *The Life of Lady Mary Wortley Montagu*. Oxford: Clarendon Press, 1956.

[Hamley, William George]. "The Opening of the Suez Canal. Part III." *Blackwood's Edinburgh Magazine* (March 1870): 356–75.

Harlow, Barbara, and Mia Carter. *Imperialism and Orientalism: A Documentary Sourcebook*. Malden, MA and Oxford: Blackwell Publishers, 1999.

Harlow, Vincent T. *The Founding of the Second British Empire, 1763–1793*. 2 vols. London: Longmans, 1952.

Harootunian, Harry. "Conjunctural Traces: Said's Inventory." In Bhabha and Mitchell, 431–42.

Hawley, John C. C. *Postcolonial, Queer*. Albany: SUNY Press, 2001.

Heffernan, Teresa. "Feminism Against the East/West Divide: Lady Mary's *Turkish Embassy Letters*." *Eighteenth-Century Studies* 33, no. 2 (1999–2000): 201–15.

Heywood, C. J. "Sir Paul Rycaut, a Seventeenth-Century Observer of the Ottoman State: Notes for a Study." In *English and Continental Views of the Ottoman Empire, 1500–1800*, ed. Ezel Kural Shaw and C. J. Heywood, 31–59. Los Angeles: University of California Press, 1972.

Hill, Michael R. "Empiricism and Reason in Harriet Martineau's Sociology." Introduction. *How to Observe Morals and Manners*. By Harriet Martineau.1838. Ed. Michael R. Hill. New Brunswick, NJ: Transaction, 1989.

Hoeveler, Diane Long, and Sarah Davies Cordova. "Gothic Opera in Britain and France: Genre, Nationalism, and Trans-Cultural Angst." In *Romanticism on the Net* 34–35 (May–August 2004). htt://www.erudit.org/revue/ron/2004/v /n34–35/009435ar. html.

Holmes, Richard. *Shelley: The Pursuit*. New York: E. P. Dutton, 1975.

Hourani, Albert. *Europe and the Middle East*. Berkeley: University of California Press, 1980.

Hughes, Merritt Y, ed. *John Milton: The Complete Poetry and Major Prose*. New York: Odyssey, 1957.

Hulme, Peter. *Colonial Encounters: Europe and the Native Caribbean, 1492–1797*. London: Methuen, 1986.

Hunt, Margaret. "Racism, Imperialism, and the Traveler's Gaze in Eighteenth-Century England." *Journal of British Studies* 32 (1993): 333–57.

Hussein, Abdirahman. *Edward Said: Criticism and Society*. London and New York: Verso, 2002.

Hyam, Ronald. *Empire and Sexuality*. Manchester: Manchester University Press, 1990.

Jack, Malcolm. Introduction. *Vathek and Other Stories*. By William Beckford, ix–xxxiii. Harmondsmouth: Penguin Books, 1993.

James, Lawrence. *The Rise and Fall of the British Empire*. 1994. London: Abacus, 1998.

Jarrett-Kerr, Martin. "Indian Religion in English Literature, 1675–1967." *Essays and Studies* 94 (1984): 87–103.

Jauss, Hans Robert. "The Identity of the Poetic Text in the Changing Horizons of Understanding." In *Identity of the Literary Text*. Eds. Mario Valdés, Mario Owen Miller, and Jonathan Culler, 146–74. Toronto: University of Toronto Press, 1985.

——. *Toward an Aesthetic of Reception*. Trans. Timothy Bahti. Minneapolis: University of Minnesota Press, 1982.

Jay, Nancy. "Sacrifice as Remedy for Having Been Born of a Woman." In *Immaculate and Powerful: The Female in Sacred Image and Social Reality*. Ed. C. W. Atkinson. Boston: Beacon, 1985.

Johnson, Robert. *British Imperialism*. New York: Palgrave Macmillan, 2003.

Johnston, Judith. "The Pyramids of Egypt: Monuments to Victorian Desire." *Australasian Victorian Studies Journal* 7 (2001): 71–88.

Jones, Anna Maria, ed. *The Works of William Jones*. 13 vols. London: Stockdale and Walker, 1807.

Jones, Edwin. *The English Nation: The Great Myth*. Phoenix Mill: Sutton, 1998.

Jones, Ted. *The French Riviera: A Literary Guide for Travellers*. London: Tauris, 2004.

Karatani, Kojin. "Uses of Aesthetics: After Orientalism." *boundary 2* 25, no. 2 (1998): 145–60.

Keegan, Abigail F. *Byron's Othered Self and Voice: Contextualizing the Homographic Signature*. New York: Peter Lang, 2003.

Kelly, Gary. "Social Conflict, Nation and Empire: From Gothicism to Romantic Orientalism." *Ariel* 20, no. 2 (1989): 5–18.

Kelsall, Malcolm. "Reading Orientalism: Woman: Or, Ida of Athens." *Review of National Literatures and World Report* 1 (1998): 11–20.

Kempiners, Fussell G., Jr. "Seljuk Dynasty." *Encyclopedia of Asian History*. Ainslie T. Embree, editor in chief, 3:409–11. New York: Scribner's, 1988.

Keynes, Geoffrey, ed. *William Blake: Complete Writings*. Oxford: Oxford University Press, 1971.

Kidwai, Abdur Raheem. *Orientalism in Lord Byron's 'Turkish Tales': The Giaour (1813), The Bride of Abydos (1813), The Corsair (1814), and The Siege of Corinth (1816)*. Lewiston, NY: Mellen University Press, 1995.

Kietzman, Mary Jo. "Montagu's *Turkish Embassy Letters* and Cultural Dislocation." *Studies in English Literature* 38, no. 3 (1998). *Academic Search Premier*. EBSCO. Plymouth State University, Lamson Library. Accessed January 17, 2004. http://www. epnet.com/.

Kindersley, Nathaniel Edward. "The History of the Nella-Rajah." In *Specimens of Hindoo Literature, Consisting of Translations, from the Tamoul Language, of Some Hindoo Works of Morality and Imagination*, 83–328. Rpt. London, 1794.

King, Richard. *Orientalism and Religion: Postcolonial Theory, India, and "The Mystic East."* New York: Routledge, 1999.

Kinross, John Patrick Douglas Balfour. *The Ottoman Centuries: The Rise and Fall of the Turkish Empire*. New York: Morrow Quill, 1977.

Kirshenblatt-Gimblett, Barbara. "Objects of Ethnography." In *Exhibiting Cultures: The Poetics and Politics of Museum Display*, ed. Ivan Karp and Steven D. Lavine, 392. Washington, DC: Smithsonian Institution Press, 1991.

Kitson, Peter J. "Romanticism and Colonialism: Races, Places, Peoples, 1785–1800." In Fulford and Kitson, 13–34.

Kontje, Todd. *German Orientalisms*. Ann Arbor: University of Michigan Press, 2004.

Kopf, David. *British Orientalism and the Bengal: The Dynamics of Indian Modernization, 1773–1835*. Berkeley and Los Angeles: University of California Press, 1969.

Korte, Barbara. *English Travel Writing from Pilgrimages to Postcolonial Explorations*. 1996. Trans. Catherine Matthias. Basingstoke: Macmillan, 2000.

Kushigian, Julia A. *Orientalism in the Hispanic Literary Tradition: In Dialogue with Borges, Paz, and Sarduy*. Albuquerque: University of New Mexico Press, 1991.

Landry, Donna. "Horsy and Persistently Queer: Imperialism, Feminism and Bestiality." *Textual Practice* 15, no. 3 (2001): 467–85.

Lane, Christopher. *The Ruling Passion: British Colonial Allegory and the Paradox of Homosexual Desire*. Durham, NC: Duke University Press, 1995.

Lane, Edward William. *An Account of the Manners and Customs of the Modern Egyptians*. 1836. 5th ed. Ed. Edward Stanley Poole. 1860. Intro. Jon Manchip White. New York: Dover, 1973.

Langer, William L., et al. *Western Civilization 1: Prehistory to Peace of Utrecht*. 2nd ed. New York: Harper & Row, 1975.

Leask, Nigel. *British Romantic Writers and the East: Anxieties of Empire*. Cambridge: Cambridge University Press, 1992.

———. *Curiosity and the Aesthetics of Travel Writing, 1770–1840 "From an Antique Land."* Oxford: Oxford University Press, 2002.

Lee, Anthony W. *Picturing Chinatown: Art and Orientalism in San Francisco*. Berkeley and Los Angeles: University of California Press, 2001.

Leerssen, Joep. "How *The Wild Irish Girl* Made Ireland Romantic." In *The Clash of Ireland: Literary Contrasts and Connections*, ed. C. C. Barfoot and Theo D'Haen, 98–117. Amsterdam and Atlanta, GA: Rodopi, 1989.

———. *Remembrance and Imagination: Patterns in the Historical and Literary Representation of Ireland in the Nineteenth Century*. Cork: Cork University Press, 1996.

Leiser, Gary, trans., ed., and intro. *A History of the Seljuks: Ibrahim Kafesoğlu's Interpretation and the Resulting Controversy*. Carbondale: Southern Illinois University Press, 1988.

Lewis, Reina. *Gendering Orientalism: Race, Femininity, and Representation*. London and New York: Routledge, 1996.

——. "'Only Women Should Go to Turkey': Henriette Browne and the Female Orientalist Gaze." In *Race-ing Art History: Critical Readings in Race and Art History*, ed. Kymberly N. Pinder, 87–118. New York: Routledge, 2002.

——. *Rethinking Orientalism: Women, Travel, and the Ottoman Harem*. New Brunswick, NJ: Rutgers University Press, 2004.

Loftie, W[illiam] J[ohn]. *A Ride in Egypt from Sioot to Luxor in 1879*. London: Macmillan, 1879.

Longino, Michele. *Orientalism in French Classical Drama*. Cambridge: Cambridge University Press, 2002.

Loomba, Ania. *Colonialism/Postcolonialism*. New York: Routledge, 1998.

Lorcin, Patricia M. E. "Women's Travel Writing." In World History Sources. Accessed January 16, 2004. http://chnm.gmu.edu/worldhistorysources/searchwhm.php?function=print&whmid=146.

Lovell, Mary S. *A Rage to Live: Richard and Isabel Burton*. New York: Norton, 1998.

Lowe, Lisa. *Critical Terrains: French and British Orientalisms*. Ithaca, NY and London: Cornell University Press, 1991.

Lowenthal, Cynthia. "The Veil of Romance: Lady Mary's Embassy Letters." *Eighteenth-Century Life* 14, no. 1 (1990): 66–82.

MacCarthy, Fiona. *Byron: Life and Legend*. New York: Farrar, Straus, and Giroux, 2002.

Macfie, A. L. *Orientalism*. Edinburgh and London: Pearson Education (Longman), 2002.

——. *Orientalism: A Reader*. Washington Square: NYU Press, 2000.

Mack, Robert E. Introduction. *Oriental Tales*, xvii–xlix. Oxford: Oxford University Press, 1992.

Mackenzie, John M. *Orientalism: History, Theory, and the Arts*. Manchester and New York: Manchester University Press, 1995.

Majeed, Javed. *Ungoverned Imaginings: James Mill: The History of British India and Orientalism*. New York: Oxford, 1992.

Makdisi, Saree. *Romantic Imperialism: Universal Empire and the Culture of Modernity*. Cambridge: Cambridge University Press, 1998.

Malcolm, John. *The History of Persia, from the Most Early Period to the Present Time: Containing an Account of the Religion, Government, Usages, and Character of the Inhabitants of that Kingdom*. 2 vols. London: Murray, 1815.

Malcolm, Noel. Rev. of The Rise of Oriental Travel: English Visitors to the Ottoman Empire, 1580–1720, by Gerald M. MacLean. Telegraph Newspaper, May 2, 2004. Accessed May 10, 2004. http://www.telegraph.co.uk/arts/main.jhtml?xml=%2Farts%2F2004%2F05%2F02%2Fbopa102.xml&secureRefresh=true&_requestid=24827.

Manning, Samuel. *The Land of the Pharaohs: Egypt and Sinai; Illustrated by Pen and Pencil*. London: Religious Tract Society, [1875?].

Marchand, Leslie A. *Byron: A Biography*. New York: Knopf, 1957.

——. *Byron's Letters and Journals*. 13 vols. Cambridge, MA: Harvard University Press, 1982.

Marrouchi, Mustapha. *Edward Said at the Limits*. Albany: SUNY Press, 2004.

Marsh, Elizabeth. *The Female Captive*. 2 vols. London: C. Bathurst, 1769. Rpt. Rabat: Ketabook, 2003.

———. "Narrative of Her Captivity in Barbary." MS Item 170/604. Charles E. Young Research Library, University of California, Los Angeles.

Martineau, Harriet. *Eastern Life, Present and Past*. 1848. 2nd ed. Boston: Roberts Brothers, 1876.

———. *How to Observe Morals and Manners*. Ed. Michael R. Hill. New Brunswick, NJ: Transaction, 1989. Repr. of *How to Observe: Morals and Manners*. 1838.

Masson, David, ed. *De Quincey's Collected Writings*. Vol. 14. London: A & C Black, 1897.

Matar, Nabil. *Turks, Moors, and Englishmen in the Age of Discovery*. New York: Columbia University Press, 1999.

Mayhew, Henry, and George Cruikshank. *1851, or, The Adventures of Mr. And Mrs. Sandboys, Their Son and Daughter: Who Came Up to London to Enjoy Themselves and see the Great Exhibition*. New York: Stringer and Townsend, 1851.

McClintock, Anne. *Imperial Leather: Race, Gender, and Sexuality in the Colonial Context*. New York: Routledge, 1995.

McDayter, Ghislaine. "Conjuring Byron: Byromania, Literary Commodification and the Birth of Celebrity." In *Byromania: Portraits of the Artist in Nineteenth- and Twentieth-Century Culture*, ed. Frances Wilson, 43–62. New York: St. Martin's, 1999.

McDonagh, Josephine. "Opium and the Imperial Imagination." In *Reviewing Romanticism*, ed. Philip W. Martin and Robin Jarvis, 116–33. London: Macmillan, 1992.

McGann, Jerome. *Fiery Dust: Byron's Poetic Development*. Chicago: University of Chicago Press, 1968.

——— ed. *Lord Byron: The Complete Poetical Works*. Oxford: Clarendon Press, 1980–1986.

Mellor, Anne K. *Mothers of the Nation: Women's Political Writing in England, 1780–1830*. Bloomington: Indiana University Press, 2000.

McLean, Adrienne. "The Thousand Ways There Are to Move: Camp and Oriental Dance in the Hollywood Musicals of Jack Cole." In *Visions of the East: Orientalism in Film*, ed. Bernstein M. and G. Studlar, 130–57. New Brunswick, NJ: Rutgers University Press, 1997.

Melman, Billie. *Women's Orients: English Women and the Middle East, 1718–1918*. Ann Arbor: University of Michigan Press, 1992.

Meyer, Eric. "'I Know Thee Not, I Loathe Thy Race': Romantic Orientalism in the Eye of the Other." *English Literary History* 58, no. 3 (1991): 657–99.

Millbanke, Ralph, Earl of Lovelace. *Astarte: A Fragment of Truth . . . Concerning Lord Byron*. Ed. Mary, Countess of Lovelace. London: Christophers, 1921.

Mills, Sarah. *Discourses of Difference: An Analysis of Women's Travel Writing and Colonialism*. London: Routledge, 1991.

Mitchell, Timothy. *Colonizing Egypt*. 1988. Berkeley: University of California Press, 1991.

Mitchell, W. J. T. "Secular Divination: Edward Said's Humanism." *Critical Inquiry* 31, no. 2 (2005): 462–71.

Monypenny, William Flavelle, and George Earle Buckle. *The Life of Benjamin Disraeli Earl of Beaconsfield*. 6 vols. London: Murray, 1910–20.

Montagu, Lady Mary Wortley. *The Complete Letters of Lady Mary Wortley Montagu*. Vol. 1 (1708–1720). Ed. Robert Halsband. Oxford: Clarendon Press, 1965.

———. *The Turkish Embassy Letters*. 1763. London: Virago, 2000.

Moon, Michael. "Flaming Closets." In *Bodies of the Text: Dance as Theory, Literature as Dance*, ed. Ellen G. Goellner and Jacqueline Shea Murphy, 57–78. New Brunswick, NJ: Rutgers University Press, 1995.

Moore-Gilbert, Bart. *Kipling and "Orientalism."* New York: St. Martin's Press, 1986.

——, Gareth Stanton, and Willy Maley. Introduction. *Postcolonial Criticism*, 1–72. London: Longman, 1997.

Morrison, Robert. "Red De Quincey." *Wordsworth Circle* 29, no. 2 (1998): 131–36.

Moskal, Jeanne. "Reversing Travel Books." Paper presented at MLA Convention, San Diego. December 29, 2003.

Mufti, Aamir. "Auerbach in Istanbul: Edward Said, Secular Criticism, and the Question of Minority Culture." In *Edward Said and the Work of the Critic: Speaking Truth to Power*, ed. Paul A. Bové, 229–56. Durham, NC: Duke University Press, 2000.

——. "Global Comparativism." In Bhabha and Mitchell, 472–89.

Mukerjee, Hirendra Nath. *The Great Tibetologist Alexander Csoma De Koros: Hermit-Hero from Hungary.* New Dehli: Sterling Publications, 1984.

Mullen, Bill V. *Afro-Orientalism.* University of Minnesota Press, 2004.

Mulvey, Laura. "Visual Pleasure and Narrative Cinema." *Screen* 16 (1975): 6–18.

Murfin, Ross C., and Supryia M. Ray, eds. *The Bedford Glossary of Critical and Literary Terms.* Boston: Bedford Books, 1997.

Netton, Ian Richard. "The Mysteries of Islam." In *Exoticism in the Enlightenment.* Ed. G. S. Rousseau and Roy Porter, 23–45. New York: Manchester University Press, 1986.

Newcomer, James. *Lady Morgan the Novelist.* Lewisburg, PA and London: Bucknell University Press, 1990.

Nietzsche, Friedrich. *The Twilight of the Idols/The Anti-Christ.* Trans. R. J. Hollingdale. Harmondsworth: Penguin Books, 1968.

Niro, Brian. *Race.* New York: Palgrave Macmillan, 2003.

Nochlin, Linda. "The Imaginary Orient." In *The Politics of Vision: Essays on Nineteenth-Century Art and Society*, 33–59. New York: Harper and Row, 1989.

Norton, Rictor. "William Beckford: The Fool of Fonthill." In *The Great Queens of History*. Updated November 16, 1999. http://www.infopt.demon.co.uk/beckf01.htm.

Nussbaum, Felicity. *Torrid Zones: Maternity, Sexuality and Empire in Eighteenth-Century English Narratives.* Baltimore: Johns Hopkins University Press, 1995.

Ogden, James. *Isaac D'Israeli.* Oxford: Clarendon Press, 1969.

O'Connor, Erin. "Preface for a Post-Postcolonial Criticism." *Victorian Studies* 45, no. 2 (2003): 217–46.

O'Quinn, Daniel. "Hannah Cowley's *A Day in Turkey* and the Political Efficacy of Charles James Fox." *European Romantic Review* 14 (2003): 17–30.

Otterspeer, Willem. "The Vulnerabilities of an Honest Broker: Edward Said and the Problems of Theory." *Oriental Prospects: Western Literature and the Lure of the East.* In Barfoot and D'haen, 189–98.

Oueijan, Naji B. *A Compendium of Eastern Elements in Byron's Oriental Tales.* New York: Peter Lang Publishing, 1999.

Owenseon, Sydney (Lady Morgan). Advertisement to *Florence Macarthy: An Irish Tale.* 1819.

——. *The Missionary: An Indian Tale.* Ed. Julia M. Wright. Petersborough, ON and Orchard Park, NY: Broadview Press, 2002.

——. Preface to *The O'Briens and the O'Flahertys.* 1827. London: Pandora Press, 1988.

——. Preface to *Patriotic Sketches of Ireland. Written in Connaught.* 2 vols. London: Phillips, 1807.

——. Preface to *The Wild Irish Girl: A National Tale.* 1836 edition.

——. *St. Clair. The Romantics: Women Novelists.* 12 vols. Boxed. Introduction by Peter

Garside and Caroline Franklin. London: Routledge; Bristol: Thoemmes, 1994.

Pao, Angela. *The Orient of the Boulevards: Exoticism, Empire, and Nineteenth- Century French Theater.* Philadelphia: University of Pennsylvania Press, 1998.

Parry, Benita. "Overlapping Territories and Intertwined Histories: Edward Said's Postcolonial Cosmopolitanism." In *Edward Said: A Critical Reader*, ed. Michael Sprinker, 19–47. Cambridge, MA: Blackwell Publishers, 1992.

Pathak, Zakia, Saswati Sengupta, and Sharmila Purkayastha. "The Prisonhouse of Orientalism." *Textual Practice* 5, no. 2 (1991): 195–218.

Paton, Cindy, and Benigno Sánchez-Eppler, eds. *Queer Diasporas.* Durham, NC: Duke University Press, 2000.

Payne, Michael, ed. *A Dictionary of Cultural and Critical Theory.* Malden, MA: Blackwell Publishing, 1997.

Peltre, Christine. *Orientalism in Art.* Trans. John Goodman. New York and London: Abbeville Press Publishers, 1998.

Peterfreund, Stuart. "Identity, Diaspora, and the Secular Voice in the Works of Isaac D'Israeli." In *The Jews and British Romanticism: Politics, Religion, Culture*, ed. Sheila A. Spector, 127–47. New York: Palgrave/Macmillan, 2005.

———. "Not for 'Antiquaries,' but for 'Philosophers': Isaac D'Israeli's Talmudic Critique and His Talmudical Way with Literature." In *British Romanticism and the Jews: History, Culture, Literature*, ed. A. Spector, 179–96. New York: Palgrave/Macmillan, 2002.

Poliak, Abraham N. "Alroy, David." *Encyclopaedia Judaica*, 2:750–51. Jerusalem: Keter, 1972.

Porter, Dennis. "Orientalism and Its Problems." In *Colonial Discourse and Postcolonial Theory: A Reader*, ed. Patrick Williams and Laura Chrisman, 150–61. New York: Columbia University Press, 1994.

Potkay, Adam. "Beckford's Heaven of Boys." In *Three Oriental Tales*, ed. Alan Richardson. Boston: Houghton Mifflin, 2002. Originally appeared in *Raritan.* (Summer 1993).

Powell, Timothy, ed. *Beyond the Binary: Reconstructing Cultural Identity in a Multicultural Context.* New Brunswick, NJ: Rutgers University Press, 1999.

Pratt, Mary Louise. *Imperial Eyes: Travel Writing and Transculturation.* London: Routledge, 1992.

Praz, Mario. *The Romantic Agony.* 2nd ed. London: Oxford University Press, 1970.

Qian, Zhaoming. *Orientalism and Modernism: The Legacy of China in Pound and Williams, 1913–1923.* Durham, NC: Duke University Press, 1995.

Ragussis, Michael. *Figures of Conversion: "The Jewish Question" and English National Identity.* Durham, NC: Duke University Press, 1995.

Rajan, Balachandra. "Feminizing the Feminine: Early Women Writers on India." In *Under Western Eyes: India from Milton to Macaulay*, 118–138. Durham, NC and London: Duke University Press, 1999.

Rajan, Tillutama, and Julia Wright, eds. *Romanticism, History, and the Possibilities of Genre.* New York: Cambridge University Press, 1998.

Reiman, Donald H., ed. *The Romantics Reviewed: Contemporary Reviews of British Romantic Writers.* New York: Garland Publishing, 1972.

Rev. of *Alroy*, by Benjamin Disraeli. *American Monthly Review* 4 (October 1833): 279–81. Rpt. Disraeli, Benjamin. *Alroy.* Ed. Sheila A. Spector. *Romantic Circles Electronic Editions.* Gen. eds. Neil Fraistat and Steven E. Jones. http://www.rc.umd.edu/editions/alroy.ns.

Rev. of *Alroy*, by Benjamin Disraeli. *The Court Journal* 5 (1833): 202–203, 279–81. Rpt. Disraeli, Benjamin. *Alroy*. Ed. Sheila A. Spector. *Romantic Circles Electronic Editions*. Gen. eds. Neil Fraistat and Steven E. Jones. http://www.rc.umd.edu/editions/alroy.ns.

Rev. of *Alroy*. *The London Literary Gazette: Journal of Belles Lettres, Arts, Sciences, &c.*, no. 842 (March 9, 1833): 146–48. 279–81. Rpt. Disraeli, Benjamin. *Alroy*. Ed. Sheila A. Spector. *Romantic Circles Electronic Editions*. Gen. eds. Neil Fraistat and Steven E. Jones. http://www.rc.umd.edu/editions/alroy.ns.

Rev. of *A Discourse on the Institution of a Society*, by William Jones. *Critical Review* 59 (1785): 19–21.

Rev. of *The Missionary: An Indian Tale*, by Sydney Owenson. *The Anti-Jacobin Review* 38 (1811): 377–85.

Rev. of *The Missionary: An Indian Tale*, by Sydney Owenson. *British Critic* 37 (1811): 651.

Rev. of *The Missionary: An Indian Tale*, by Sydney Owenson. *Critical Review* 23 (1811): 182–95.

Rev. of *Sacontalá*, translated by William Jones. *Analytical Review* 7 (1790): 361–73.

Rev. of *The Wild Irish Girl: A National Tale*. *Monthly Review* 57 (1808): 378–81.

Rev. of *Woman: Or, Ida of Athens*, by Sydney Owenson. *Quarterly Review* 1 (1809): 50–52.

Rice, Edward. *Captain Sir Richard Francis Burton*. New York: Barnes and Noble, 1990; rpt. 1999.

Richardson, Alan, ed. *Three Oriental Tales*. New Riverside Editions. Boston: Houghton Mifflin, 2002. Contains *History of Nourjahad, Vathek,* and *The Giaour*.

Roessell, David. *In Byron's Shadow*. New York: Oxford University Press, 2003.

Romer, Mrs. [Isabella Frances]. *A Pilgrimage to the Temples and Tombs of Egypt, Nubia, and Palestine, 1845–6.* 2 vols. London: Richard Bentley, 1846.

Roth, Cecil. *Benjamin Disraeli*. New York: Philosophical Library, 1952.

Roy, Arundhati. "The New American Century." *Nation*, February 9, 2004, 11–14.

Rycaut, Paul. *History of the Present State of the Ottoman Empire*. London: Joanne Brome, 1682.

Saglia, Diego. "William Beckford's 'Sparks of Orientalism' and the Material-Discursive Orient of British Romanticism." *Textual Practice* 16, no. 1 (2002): 75–92.

Sahni, Kalpana. *Crucifying the Orient: Russian Orientalism and the Colonization of Caucasus and Central Asia*. Bangkok, Thailand: White Orchid Press, 1997.

Said, Edward. "Afterword." *Orientalism*. New York: Random House, 1994 (1978).

———. *The Anti-Aesthetic: Essays on Postmodern Culture*. New York: New Press, 1983.

———. *Culture and Imperialism*. New York: Alfred A. Knopf, 1993.

———. "The Horizon of R. P. Blackmur." *Reflections on Exile*, 246–67.

———. "Humanism?" *MLA Newsletter* (Fall 1999).

———. "Opponents, Audiences, Constituencies, and Community." In *Reflections on Exile and Other Essays*, 112–47.

———. *Orientalism*. New York: Vintage Books, 1978.

———. "Orientalism Reconsidered." In *Reflections on Exile and Other Essays*, 198–215.

———. *Out of Place: A Memoir*. New York: Knopf, 1999.

———. *Reflections on Exile and Other Essays*. Cambridge, MA: Harvard University Press, 2000.

———. "Representing the Colonized." In *Reflections on Exile*, 293–316.

———. "An Unresolved Paradox." *MLA Newsletter* (Summer 1999).

Saint Claire, William. *That Greece Might Still Be Free*. London: Oxford University Press, 1972.

Sanders, Paula. "The Victorian Invention of Medieval Cairo: A Case Study of Medievalism and the Construction of the East." *Middle East Studies Association Bulletin 37*, no. 2 (2003): 179–98.

Sardar, Ziauddin. *Orientalism*. Buckingham: Open University Press, 1999.

Schlegel, Fredrich. *Über diese Sprache and Weisheit der Indier*. Heidelberg: Mohr & Zimmer, 1808, 44–59. Quoted in Said, *Orientalism,* 98.

Schmitt, Cannon. *Alien Nation: Nineteenth-Century Gothic Fictions and English Nationality*. Philadelphia: University of Pennsylvania Press, 1997.

Schneider, Jane. *Italy's "Southern Question": Orientalism in One Country*. New York: Berg Publishers, 1998.

Schopenhauer, Arthur. *The World as Will and Representation*. 2 vols. Trans. E. F. J. Payne. New York: Dover Publications, 1969.

Schor, Naomi. *Reading in Detail: Aesthetics and the Feminine*. New York: Methuen, 1987.

Schueller, Malini Johar. *U.S. Orientalisms: Race, Nation, and Gender in Literature, 1790–1890*. Ann Arbor: University of Michigan Press, 1986.

Schwab, Raymond. *The Oriental Renaissance: Europe's Rediscovery of India and the East 1680–1880*. Trans. Gene Patterson-Black and Victor Reinking. New York: Columbia University Press, 1984.

Secor, Anna. "Orientalism, Gender and Class in Lady Mary Wortley Montagu's Turkish Embassy Letters: To Persons of Distinction, Men of Letters & C." *Ecumene* 6, no. 4 (1999). *Academic Search Premier*. EBSCO. Plymouth State University, Lamson Library, January 17, 2004. http://www.epnet.com/.

Sedgewick, Eve Kosofsky. *Between Men: English Literature and Male Homosocial Desire*. New York: Columbia University Press, 1985.

Serghini, El Habibi Benrahhal. "William Beckford's Appropriation of the Oriental Context." In *Oriental Prospects: Western Literature and the Lure of the East*, ed. C. C. Barfoot and Theo D'haen, 43–64. Amsterdam, Netherlands: Rodopi, 1998.

Shakespeare, William. *Othello*. Ed. Barbara A. Mowat and Paul Werstine. New York: Washington Square Press, 1992.

Sharafuddin, Mohammed. *Islam and Romantic Orientalism: Literary Encounters with the Orient*. London: I. B. Tauris, 1994.

———. " 'Positive Orientalism: Islam in the Eyes of the West,' an Exploration of Positive Images of Islam in Western Literature." Discussion at Al-Hewar Center, November 28, 2001. http://www.alhewar.org/mohammed sharafuddin_positive_orientalism. htm.

Sharpe, Jenny. *Allegories of Empire: The Figure of the Woman in the Colonial Text*. London and Minneapolis: University of Minnesota Press, 1993.

Shaw, Ezel Kural. "The Double Veil: Travelers' Views of the Ottoman Empire, Sixteenth through Eighteenth Centuries." In *English and Continental Views of the Ottoman Empire, 1500–1800*, ed. Ezel Kural Shaw and C. J. Heywood, 1–29. Los Angeles: University of California, 1972.

Shelley, Mary. Note on *Hellas*. *Shelley: Poetical Works*, ed. Thomas Hutchinson, 480–82. London: Oxford University Press, 1970.

———. *The Last Man*. Ed. Brian Aldiss. London: Hogarth Press, 1985.

Shelley, Percy. *Hellas*. In *Shelley: Poetical Works*, ed. Thomas Hutchinson, 446–80. London: Oxford University Press, 1970.

———. *Letters*. Ed. Roger Ingpen. Vol. 10. London: Julian Edition, 1926.

———. *Letters*. Ed. Frederic Jones. 2 vols. Oxford: Clarendon Press, 1964.

———. *A Philosophical View of Reform: Shelley and His Circle*, ed. Donald H. Reiman, 6:961–1066. Cambridge, MA: Harvard University Press, 1973.

Simmons, Diane. "Narcissism and Sinophobia: The Case of Thomas De Quincey." *Journal of Psychoanalysis of Culture and Society* 7, no. 2 (2002): 179–89.

Simon, Reeva Spector. "Commerce, Concern, and Christianity: Britain and Middle-Eastern Jewry in the Mid-Nineteenth Century." In *The Jews and British Romanticism: Politics, Religion, Culture*, ed. Sheila A. Spector, 181–94. New York: Palgrave/Macmillan, 2005.

———, Philip Mattar, and Richard W. Bulliet, eds. *Encyclopedia of the Modern Middle East*. 4 vols. New York: Macmillan Reference USA, 1996.

Smith, Sydney. Rev. of *Indian Missions*. *Edinburgh Review* 12 (1808): 151–81.

Snader, Joseph. *Caught between Worlds: British Captivity Narratives in Fact and Fiction*. Lexington: University of Kentucky Press, 2000.

———. "The Oriental Captivity Narrative and Early English Fiction." *Eighteenth-Century Fiction* 9 (1997): 267–98.

Snodgrass, Judith. *Presenting Japanese Buddhism to the West: Orientalist, Occidentalism, and the Columbian Exposition*. Chapel Hill: University of North Carolina Press, 2003.

Southey, Robert. Preface to *The Curse of Kehama*. *The Poetical Works of Robert Southey*. 10 vols. London: Longman, 1838.

Spector, Sheila A. "*Alroy* as Disraeli's 'Ideal Ambition.'" In *British Romanticism and the Jews: History, Culture, Literature*, ed. Spector, 235–48. New York: Palgrave/Macmillan, 2002. Rpt. 279–81. Rpt. Disraeli, Benjamin. *Alroy*. Ed. Sheila A. Spector. *Romantic Circles Electronic Editions*. Gen. eds. Neil Fraistat and Steven E. Jones. http://www.rc.umd.edu/editions/alroy.ns.

Spivak, Gayatri Chakravorty. *Death of a Discipline*. New York: Columbia University Press, 2003.

———. "Thinking about Edward Said: Pages From a Memoir." In Bhabha and Mitchell, 519–25.

Stamy, Cynthia. *Marianne Moore and China: Orientalism and a Writing of America*. Oxford: Oxford University Press, 1999.

Starr, G. A. "Escape from Barbary: A Seventeenth-Century Genre." *Huntington Library Quarterly* 29 (1965): 35–48.

Suleri, Sara. *The Rhetoric of English India*. Chicago: University of Chicago Press, 1992.

Tallis, John. *Tallis's History and Description of the Crystal Palace, and the Exhibition of the World's Industry in 1851*. 3 vols. London: Tallis and Co., 1852.

Tavakoli-Targhi, Mohamad. *Refashioning Iran: Orientalism, Occidentalism, and Historiography*. New York: Palgrave MacMillan, 2001.

Teltscher, Kate. "The Lama and the Scotsman: George Bogle in Bhutan and Tibet, 1774–75." In *The Global Eighteenth Century*. Ed. Felicity A. Nussbaum. Baltimore: Johns Hopkins University Press, 2003.

Terjék, József. "Alexander Csoma de Körős: A Short Biography." *Tibetan-English Dictionary*. Budapest: Akadémiai Kiadó, 1984.

Thackeray, William Makepeace. *Notes of a Journey from Cornhill to Grand Cairo*. 1846. In *The Works of William Makepeace Thackeray*, 8:5–92. New York: Collier, n.d.

Thomas, Nicholas. *Entangled Objects: Exchange, Material Culture, and Colonialism in the*

Pacific. Cambridge, MA: Harvard University Press, 1991.

Thorn, Jennifer. Eighteenth-Century British Orientalism. Course home page. Accessed January 16, 2004. http://www.asecs.press.jhu.edu/thorn.html/.

Till, Nicholas. Cited on http://www.mozartproject.org/compositions/k_384_.html.

Tudela, Benjamin. *The Travels of Rabbi Benjamin, The Son of Jonas of Tudela, Through Europe, Asia and Africa, From Spain to China, from the Year of our Lord 1160 to 1173*. . . . In John Pinkerton, *A General Collection of the Most Interesting Voyages and Travels in All Parts of the World, Many of Which are Not First Translated into English*. London, 1811. 7:8–9. Rpt. Disraeli, Benjamin. *Alroy*. Ed. Sheila A. Spector. *Romantic Circles Electronic Editions*. Gen. eds. Neil Fraistat and Steven E. Jones. http://www.rc.umd.edu/editions/alroy.ns.

Turhan, Filiz. *The Other Empire: British Romantic Writings about the Ottoman Empire*. New York: Routledge, 2003.

Turner, Bryan S. *Orientalism, Postmodernism, & Globalism*. London: Routledge, 1994.

Turner, Captain Samuel. *An Account of an Embassy to the Court of the Teshoo Lama in Tibet containing a Narrative of a Journey through Bootan and Part of Tibet*. London: W. Bulmer, 1800.

Vincent, John. *Disraeli*. Oxford and New York: Oxford University Press, 1990. 279–81. Rpt. Disraeli, Benjamin. *Alroy*. Ed. Sheila A. Spector. *Romantic Circles Electronic Editions*. Gen. eds. Neil Fraistat and Steven E. Jones. http://www.rc.umd.edu/editions/alroy.ns.

Vitkus, Daniel J. "The Circulation of Bodies: Slavery, Maritime Commerce and English Captivity Narratives in the Early Modern Period." In *Colonial and Postcolonial Incarceration*, ed. Graeme Harper, 23–37. London: Continuum, 2001.

———. "Early Modern Orientalism: Representations of Islam in Sixteenth-and Seventeenth-Century Europe." In *Western Views of Islam in Medieval and Early Modern Europe: Perception of Other*, ed. David R. Blanks and Michael Frasetto, 207–30. New York: St. Martin's, 1999.

———. *Turning Turk: English Theater and the Multicultural Mediterranean, 1570–1630*. New York: Palgrave, 2003.

Voltaire, François Marie Arouet de. *Mahomet*. In *The Works of Voltaire: A Contemporary Version*, ed. John Morley, trans. William F. Fleming, 16: 5–87. London: E. R. DuMont, 1901.

———. *The Tragedy of Zara*. Trans. Aaron Hill. London: J. Watts, 1736.

Warburton, Eliot. *The Crescent and the Cross; or, Romance and Realities of Eastern Travel*. 1844. 17th ed. London: Hurst and Blackett, n.d.

Watkins, Daniel P. *Social Relations in Byron's Eastern Tales*. Cranbury: Associated University Press, 1987.

Watt, Ian. *The Rise of the Novel*. Berkeley: University of California Press, 1957.

Weintraub, Stanley. *Disraeli: A Biography*. New York: Truman Talley Books/Dutton, 1993.

Wharton, Edith. "Harems and Ceremonies." In *Edith Wharton Abroad*, ed. Sarah Bird Wright, 187–209. New York: St. Martin's, 1995.

Wheatcroft, Andrew. *The Ottomans: Dissolving Images*. 1993. London: Viking, 1993.

Wilkinson, [John] Gardner. *Handbook for Travellers in Egypt*. London: John Murray, 1847.

Wilson, W. Daniel. "Turks on the Eighteenth-Century Operatic Stage and European Political, Military, and Cultural History." *Eighteenth-Century Life* 2 (1985): 79–92.

Wollstonecraft, Mary. *Vindication of the Rights of Woman*. Ed. Carol Poston. New York: Norton, 1988.

Woolf, Virginia. *The Waves*. 1931. New York: Harcourt, 1959.

Wright, Julia M, ed. *The Missionary* by Sydney Wenson (Lady Morgan). Peterborough, ON: Broadview Press, 2002.

Yeazell, Ruth Bernard. *Harems of the Mind: Passages of Western Art and Literature*. New Haven, CT: Yale University Press, 2000.

——. "Public Baths and Private Harems: Lady Mary Wortley Montagu and the Origins of Ingres's *Bain Turc*." *Yale Journal of Criticism* 7, no. 1 (1994): 111–38.

Yĕgenŏglu, Meyda. *Colonial Fantasies: Towards a Feminist Reading of Orientalism*. Cambridge: Cambridge University Press, 1998.

Zein, M. Faruk. *Christianity, Islam, and Orientalism*. London: SAQI Books, 2003.

Ziter, Edward. *The Orient on the Victorian Stage*. London: Cambridge University Press, 2003.

Zonana, Joyce. "The Sultan and the Slave: Feminist Orientalism and the Structure of *Jane Eyre*." *Signs* 18 (1993): 592–617.

JEFFREY CASS is associate provost and professor of English at Texas A&M International University. His research interests include nineteenth-century women writers, Orientalism, Milton, and popular culture. He has published articles on Maria Edgeworth, Elizabeth Gaskell, and Charlotte Brontë for *ANQ*, *Papers on Language and Literature*, *La questione romantica*, and *Dickens Studies Annual*.

G. TODD DAVIS is assistant professor at Kentucky State University. He received his Ph.D. in English in 2003 from Miami University, Ohio, where he wrote a dissertation that explored representations of Lord Byron.

JEANNE DUBINO is an associate professor of English and head of the English Department at Southeastern Louisiana University. She has taught in Massachussets, Turkey, and most recently Kenya. She has published articles on Virginia Woolf's essays, popular films, postolonial literature, and British travel writing about Turkey and Kenya. Among her works-in-progress is an anthology of Kenyan colonial and settler writing tentatively titled *Land of Sunshine and Sundowners: Remembering Kenya*.

MICHAEL J. FRANKLIN teaches in the English Department of University of Wales, Swansea. Since editing *Sir William Jones: Selected Poetical and Prose Works* (1995) and writing the critical biography *Sir William Jones* (1995), he has been investigating colonial representations of India and their various interfaces with Romanticism. He has edited *Representing India: Indian Culture and Imperial Control* (2000) and *The European Discovery of India: Key Indological Sources of Romanticism* (2001), and has written a series of articles on prominent members of the Hastings circle that forms the current focus of his research. His latest publication is *Romantic Representations of British India* (London: Routledge, 2006).

EMILY A. HADDAD is associate professor of English at the University of South Dakota, and the author of *Orientalist Poetics: The Islamic Middle East in Nineteenth-Century British and French Poetry* (2002) and of essays on the travel writing of Mungo Park and Florence Nightingale.

DIANE LONG HOEVELER is professor of English and coordinator of Women's Studies at Marquette University, Milwaukee, Wisconsin. She is author of *Romantic Androgyny* (1990), *Gothic Feminism* (1998); coauthor of *Charlotte Brontë* (1997) and the *Historical Dictionary of Feminism* (1996; 2004). Edited or coedited works include *Comparative Romanticisms* (1998), *Women of Color* (2001), *Approaches to Teaching "Jane Eyre"* (1993), *Approaches to Teaching Gothic Fiction* (2003), *Romantic Drama* (*ERR*, 2003), *Romanticism: Comparative Discourses* (2006), and *Wuthering Heights* (2001) and *Women's Literary Creativity and the Female Body* (2007). She has published over forty-five articles on a variety of topics, including the gothic, melodrama, women writers, and romanticism and gender, and she is also past president of the International Conference on Romanticism (2001–2003).

MARK LUSSIER is an associate professor of English and director of the Ph.D. Literature Program at Arizona State University. His last book, *Romantic Dynamics* (1999), pursued shared assumptions between Romantic poetics and the new physics of relativity and quantum dynamics. The essay in this volume is drawn from his most recent book project on Romanticism and Buddhism.

ALAN RICHARDSON is professor of English at Boston College. His books include *British Romanticism and the Science of the Mind* (2001); *Literature, Education, and Romanticism: Reading as Social Practice, 1780–1832* (1994); and *A Mental Theater: Poetic Drama and Consciousness in the Romantic Age* (1988). Edited or coedited works include *Three Oriental Tales* (2001); *Early Black British Writing* (2004); and *Romanticism, Race, and Imperial Culture 1780–1834* (1996). He has also published over forty essays on Romantic-era literature and culture, particularly in relation to gender, childhood and education, colonialism, and early neuroscience. Major honors and awards include fellowships from the Andrew W. Mellon Foundation, the National Endowment for the Humanities, and the John Simon Guggenheim Foundation, and the American Conference on Romanticism Book Prize for 1994.

SHEILA A. SPECTOR is an independent scholar who has devoted her career to studying the intersection between British culture and Judaica. In addition to a two-volume study of Blake as a Kabbalist—*"Wonders Divine": The Development of Blake's Kabbalist Myth* and *"Glorious Incomprehensible": The Development of*

Blake's Kabbalistic Language (2001)—she compiled *British Romanticism and the Jews: History, Culture, Literature* (2002) and *The Jews and British Romanticism: Politics, Religion, Literature* (2005). Her edition of Benjamin Disraeli's *The Wondrous Tale of Alroy*, the subject of her contribution to this collection, was published online in the Romantic Circles Praxis Series (2005).

FILIZ TURHAN is assistant professor of English at Suffolk Community College in New York. Her book *The Other Empire: British Romantic Writings about the Ottoman Empire* appeared in 2003. Dr. Turhan is currently working on a book about the life writings of Muslim women worldwide.

EDWARD ZITER is associate professor in the Department of Drama at New York University and author of *The Orient on the Victorian Stage* (2003). He is Book Review editor for *Theatre Survey* and was previously Performance Reviews coeditor for *Theatre Journal*. He is currently at work on a study of contemporary Syrian theater.

INDEX

A Day in Turkey; or Russian Slaves: A Comedy (Cowley), 78

Abercorn, Marquis of, 163; Sydney Owenson's dramatic performances in Abercorns' drawing room, 163, 165

Abercorn, Marchioness (Lady Anne Jane Gore Hamilton), 163, 176n20

Abdel-Malek, Annouar, 25

Abdullah, Mirza, 8

Abduction from the Seraglio (Mozart), 54, 225; abduction from seraglio as motif, 228

Abrams, M. H., 41

An Account of an Embassy to the Court of the Teshoo Lama in Tibet (Turner), 91, 106n7

Adrianopolis, 3

The Adventures of Hajji Baba, of Ispahan (Morier), 42

The Adventures of Mr. and Mrs. Sandboys (Mayhew and Cruikshank), 232, 236, 243n10

Aeschylus, 185, 193; *The Persians*, 193–94

aesthetics, 32, 149–50; feminist, 155n14; Indian, 168; language of, 147–48

Africa, 1, 87n4, 184; North Africa, 47, 57, 59, 64

Afro-Orientalism, 38

Aida (Verdi), 35, 225

Aladdin, 35, 224; Aladdin performed on pantomime stage, 238

Alloula, Malek, 70, 143

Alp Arslan, 129–30, 133–34

Al-Ro'I, David, 125. See also Disraeli, Benjamin.

Althusser, Louis, 140; post-Althusserian, 106n5

Anti-Jacobin Review, 166, 177n27, 178n37

Apter, Emily, 12, 28, 32–33, 57, 229

Arabian Nights, 81, 83, 139, 144, 178n35, 217, 238–40. See also *Thousand and One Nights*

Arnold, William, 91; "The Light of Asia," 91

Asia, 1, 20, 38, 41, 92–93, 103, 134, 191, 206, 216, 221; Central Asia, 38, 92, 101, 103, 222; South Asia, 179n53

Asiatick Society of Bengal, 13, 97–100, 102–103, 172

Asiatick Researches, 167, 180n61

Athenaeum, 236–39

Aubin, Penelope, 12, 51–52, 54

Auerbach, Erich, 31–32, 35, 45n2

Austen, Jane, 30, 177n23, 177n28

Bagchee, Shyamal, 42

Bage, Robert, 12, 59, 66–68; *The Fair Syrian*

baksheesh, 13, 84. See also *bakshish*

bakshish, 75–76, 83–86, 89n22, 89n23, 89n24. See also *baksheesh*

Banks, Joseph, 43

Barbour, Richmond, 38, 49

Bar Kokhba, 128, 131,136n14

Barrel, John, 88n10, 186

Barrow, Isaac, 170

Battle of Lepanto, 49

Bawer, Bruce, 119

bazaars, 13, 75–78, 81, 85–86, 88n11

Beauliu, Jill, 40

Beckford, William, 14, 55, 107–120, 135, 182, 198, 200, 213, 216–17, 220, 246, 248, 251–52, 257–60; critics of, 14–15, 109–111, 115, 119; pederasty, 14, 109–111, 115, 118–119; presumed psychosexual guilt, 14–15, 110–112, 118–19; *Vathek*, 14, 19, 55, 107–120, 135n1, 198, 213, 216–17, 221
bedouin, 89n24, 224, 240
Beethoven, Ludwig v., 84
The Beggar's Opera (Gay), 164
beggars, 73, 84–85, 87
Behdad, Ali, 11, 27, 73
Belmont and Constanze (Bretzner), 54
Bell, John, 97
Bennett, Tony, 229, 242n6,
Bentham, Jeremy, 43
Bevan, Samuel, 75–76, 79, 83, 88n9
Bhabha, Homi, 2–3, 11–12, 14, 28, 31, 33, 42, 45n1, 107
Bickerstaff, Isaac, 50, 247
Bin Laden, Osama. *See* Laden, Osama bin
Boer, Inge E., 38, 150, 157n34
Bogle, George, 90, 95–97
Bohls, Elizabeth, 148–49, 155n9, 155n14, 156n22
Bohrer, Frederick, 40
Brantlinger, Patrick, 44, 86
Brennan, Timothy, 29, 37, 44
Bretzner, Christoph Friedrich, 54
Britain, 1, 50, 57, 60, 66, 99, 121–23, 125, 135, 143, 156, 167, 182–84, 190, 196–97, 211, 218, 221, 228, 230, 241–42
British empire, 1, 10, 40, 124, 183–84, 191, 196, 231
British imperialism, 10, 100, 122, 135n5. *See also* imperialism
British Orientalism, 3, 11, 41–42, 176. *See also* Orientalism
British Raj, 1
Brontë, Charlotte, 43, 69
Brook, Peter, 226
Buddhism, 13–14, 41, 90–94, 99–100, 103–106, 106n2, 106n3
Burnham, Michelle, 53
Burton, Richard, 3, 8–11, 75, 78–79, 81, 83–84, 88n11, 89n151; Muslim impersonation, 9–10

Buruma, Ian, 40
Bush, George W., 44, 134
Bute, Lady, 141
Byron, Lady, 209
Byron, George Gordon, Lord, 3, 5–7, 10–11, 18–20, 47, 55, 91, 109, 112, 123, 135n1, 159, 162, 164, 176n13, 177n22, 198–212, 213–33, 238; *Childe Harold's Pilgrimage*, 176n13, 198; *The Corsair*, vi, 6, 18, 198–211, 238, 254; *Don Juan*, 18, 48, 198, 207; *Eastern Tales*, 204, 208, 211, 215, 221, 263; *The Giaour*, 19–20, 55, 113–117, 182, 201, 203, 207, 213–22, 223n2; *Lara*, 18, 198–211; *Manfred*, 198; *Sardana-palus*, vi, 18–19, 112, 198–211; Leila (*The Giaour*), 216–18, 220–21; Robert Rushton (page), 205;

Cannadine, David, 41
Cannon, Garland, 91, 97–98, 178n35
capitalism, 84; capitalist, 32, 84
Carey, Daniel, 3
Carrier, James, 40
Carter, Mia, 26, 28
Cartwright, Captain George, 229
Cass, Jeffrey, 11–12, 14, 38, 43
Castellan, Antoine Laurent, 7
Castlereagh, Lord, 163–65, 177, 197n1
Cervantes Saavedra, Miguel de, 49
Clarissa (Richardson), 141
class, 5, 10, 40–41, 45–48, 60–61, 65–67, 69, 98, 104, 107–109, 111, 139–42, 145–46, 148–50, 152, 154, 156–57, 161; British middle class, 12, 54, 69, 157, 161
Christensen, Jerome, 206–7, 212n2
Clifford, James, 2, 11, 28, 31–32, 36, 39
Colebrooke, Henry, 171, 179n50
Coleridge, Samuel Taylor, 41
Colley, Linda, 59, 62
colonialism, 12, 27, 43, 74, 90–94, 100, 106n5, 108, 117, 159–61, 182, 208, 220; and Orientalism, 27, 43, 91; spiritual, 90–94, 100
Cooley, Emily, 143, 151, 156n15
Compendium of Eastern Elements in Byron's Oriental Tales (Oueijan),

203–204, 207
Corinne (Staël), 160
Courtenay, William, 14, 109, 120n2
Cowley, Hannah, 50
Cranford (Gaskell), 43
Crisp, James, 60–61, 63
Critical Review, 17, 165, 167, 173, 175
Croker, John Wilson, 163, 176n17, 177n29
Crompton, Louis, 206, 212n2, 219
Crouching Tiger, Hidden Dragon, 18, 200
Cruikshank, George, 228, 231–32, 236
Csoma, Alexander, 13–14, 90, 93–94, 97,
    100–104, 106n9
Curtius, Ernst Robert, 31, 35

Dacre, Charlotte, 42, 118
Dallmayr, Fred, 38
Dalrymple, William, 8, 223
Dante, 32
David, Deirdre, 43
Davis, G. Todd, 17–18, 198
Davis, Samuel, 96, 106
De Laceys, French, 69, 185
De Quincey, Thomas, 18, 91, 182–197,
    212n1; Confessions of an English
    Opium Eater, 18, 182–97
Death of a Discipline (Spivak), 45. See also
    Gayatri Spivak
Dennon, Joseph, 38
Derrida, Jacques, 25
Dimond, William, 237
D'Israeli, Isaac (Benjamin Disraeli's
    father), 123, 135n1, 136n7
discourse, 16–17, 25, 27–28, 31, 37–39,
    41–41, 45–47, 57, 71n6, 73, 87, 143,
    148–49, 154–56, 161, 169–70, 176–77,
    180, 183, 200, 206–207; colonial/colo-
    nialist, 57, 99, 108, 156; hegemonic,
    27, 36; Orientalist/Orientalized, 12, 37,
    45, 57, 66, 115, 119, 153, 156, 183, 221,
    239–40
Disraeli, Benjamin, 15, 43, 121–36, 245,
    247, 249, 257, 259, 261, Alroy, 15,
    121–36; Coningsby, 15, 122; Contarini
    Fleming, 123; Henrietta Temple, 123;
    Jabaster (character in Alroy), 127–33;
    The Rise of Iskander, 123, Sybil, 115,
    122; Tancred, 15, 122; Vindication of

the English Constitution, 123–24; The
    Young Duke, 123
Dobie, Madeline, 38, 58, 70n1, 157n31
Dracula (Stoker), 202
Drew, John, 92, 106n1, 169, 177n24
Dris, Muly, 63
Drury, Henry, 206
Drury Lane, 226, 242
Dubino, Jeanne, 16–17, 58
Dutton, Michael, 26–28

Eagleton, Terry, 109, 166, 177n30
Eblis, 14, 113, 115–16, 120n2
Edgeworth, Maria, 213, 265
Edwards, Amelia, 75, 77–78, 80–81, 83,
    86, 88n7, 88n11, 88n12
Edwards, Holly, 40
Egypt, 12–13, 72–77, 79–80, 82–87, 87n4,
    88n7, 88n9, 88n10, 88n12, 88n15,
    88n18, 88n20, 88n21, 88n22, 88n26,
    126, 186, 227–28, 242; Egyptian mar-
    kets, 13, 73–79, 81, 83, 85, 87
Eisler, Benita, 6, 109
Elfenbein, Andrew, 209, 212n2
Enfield, William, 128–29, 136n14
England, 15, 51–52, 55–56, 58–59, 61,
    66–67, 97, 104, 118, 122–24, 128, 147,
    151, 176, 187–88, 197, 205–206, 208,
    238, 241–42. See also British empire
ethnography, 5, 20, 150, 157, 229, 234,
    242, 247, 249–50, 254; ethnographic,
    16, 20, 230, 234, 236, 239–40; pseudo-
    ethnographic, 228
exoticism, 20, 41, 108, 112, 167, 237

Faerie Queene (Spenser), 15, 125, 129. See
    also Spenser, Edmund
Fairbanks, Douglas, 225
Fairholt, Frederick, 75, 78–79, 85, 88n11,
    89n14, 89n19
Falwell, Jerry, 19, 215
Fanon, Franz, 28, 229
female captivity narratives, 12, 53, 61,
    65–66
Ferguson, Moira, 43
Ferrer, José, 221
Ferris, Ina, 17, 166, 177n31
Fidelio (Beethoven), 54

Fitzpatrick, William, 163, 164, 168, 176n19, 176n20
Fleming, K. E., 38
Forster, E. M., 39, 45n3
Foucault, Michel, 25, 28, 31–32, 42–43, 70n1, 110
Francis, Philip, 91
Franguestan, 220–21
Franklin, Michael, 17, 42, 91, 98–99, 106n8, 178n33
Fulford, Tim, 42, 106n5, 106n7

Galland, Antoine, 139, 154, 238
Gascoine, Earnest, 242
Gaskell, Elizabeth, 43
Geertz, Clifford, 31
Gikandi, Simon, 43
Gill, R. B., 111–12
Girardort, Norman J., 43
Godwin, William, 68–69
Goldsmith, Oliver, 213
Gordon, Major General Charles, 226–27
Gothic, 19, 42, 111, 118, 158n42, 168, 174, 203, 213; gothic rescue opera, 54–55, 70n3
Gramsci, Antonio, 70n1
Great Exhibition, 20, 228–29, 231–32, 235–36, 239, 243n10
Greenfield, Cathy, 26
Greenhalgh, Paul, 231, 243n8
Grosrichard, Alain, 49
Grundy, Isobel, 3, 5, 154n2

Haddad, Emily, 13, 43, 72
Hajj (pilgrimage to Mecca), 8–9
Halsband, Robert, 141, 154n2
Hamilton, John, 163
Hamley, William, 75, 80–82, 89n20
Handbook for Travellers in Egypt (Wilkinson), 80
harem, 3, 5, 12, 39–40, 50–52, 54–55, 57–59, 62–63, 65–70, 114, 117–18, 139, 143–44, 148, 150, 152, 154–55, 157, 193, 218, 224–25, 228, 237–38, 241–42; Wollstonecraft's critique of, 68;
Harlow, Barbara, 26, 28
Harlow, Vincent T., 1

Harootunian, Harry, 12, 32
Haywood, Eliza, 52, 54, 66; *The Fair Captive,* 66; *The Fruitless Enquiry,* 52; *Idalia,* 52; *Philidore and Placentia,* 52
Heffernan, Teresa, 156n20, 158n44
hegemony, 25, 36, 69, 109, 124, 152, 157, 207
Herder, 167
Hill, Aaron, 56, 59, 66, 158n40
History of Nourjahad (Sheridan), 54, 213, 217. *See also* Sheridan, Frances
Hoeveler, Diane Long, 12, 70n3
Holcroft, Thomas, 68–69
homoeroticism, 19; and Beckford, 14, 111–12, 114–15, 117–19; and Byron, 202, 207–208, 220–21; and Montagu, 148–49
Hourani, Albert, 48
Hussein, Abdirahman, 34, 253
Hussein, Saddam, 220
Hyam, Ronald, 186–87

ideology, 5, 20, 29, 31, 65, 107, 109, 119
Illustrated London News, 228, 230, 233–35, 237–40
imperialism, 29, 32, 44, 91, 106n5, 172, 182, 197, 228; Euroimperialism (Pratt), 87n4
India, 1, 2, 7–8, 17, 60, 90–99, 102, 106n2, 134, 160, 162, 164–65, 167–69, 172, 174, 177n22, 179n45, 181n63, 184, 214, 222n1, 223n4, 239–40; East India Company, 24, 43, 95–96, 100–101, 164–65; Orientalized India, 43
Internet, 44, 174, 219
Isabella, queen of Spain, 1, 47
Italian in Algiers (Rossini), 54

Jack, Malcolm, 112, 253
Jane Eyre (Brontë), 43
Jauss, Hans Robert, 18, 199–201, 204, 207–208, 210–11; *Toward an Aesthetic of Reception,* 199
Jervas, Charles, 4, 148–49, 238
Jews/Judaism, 15, 48, 64, 121–23, 125, 128, 130–31, 134–36, 176
Jones, Owen, 241
Jones, William, 13, 47, 90–91, 94, 97, 105,

162, 167, 170, 177, 179–80
Karatani, Kojin, 12, 34–35
Kashmiri, 101, 169–71
Kelly, Gary, 41
Kelsall, Malcolm, 42, 176n13
Khartoum, 226–27; *Khartoum! Or, The Star of the Desert* (melodrama), 227
Kidwai, Abdur Raheem, 217, 254
Kietzman, Mary Jo, 141, 150, 153, 154, 156n17, 157n30, 157n35
Kill Bill (Vols. 1 and 2), 18, 200
Kipling, Rudyard, 43, 134
Kirkpatrick, James, 8
Kirshenblatt-Gimblet, Barbara, 229, 242n7
Kismet (Wright and Forrest), 229
Kitson, Peter J., 42, 91, 99, 100, 106n5, 106n8, 251
Kneller, Godfrey, 4
Kontje, Todd, 38
Koran, 56, 116, 146, 214
Korte, Barbara, 16, 87n4
Kushigian, Julia A., 38

Laden, Osama bin, 19, 215, 222
Lalla Rookh (Moore), 7
Landry, Donna, 147–48, 156n25
Lane, Christopher, 44
Lane, Edward, 73, 75, 79–80, 88n8, 89n16, 89n17
Lasansky, Medina D., 38
Latour, Bruno, 43
Lawrence, T. E., 36, 165, 221; *The Seven Pillars of Wisdom,* 36
LeCompte, Elizabeth, 226
Lean, David, 221
Leask, Nigel, 42, 87, 91, 99, 204, 208, 210, 212n1
Lee, Anthony, 40
Lettres Persanes (Montesquieu), 57
Lew, Joseph, 42
Lewis, Matthew, 118, 206
Lewis, Reina, 39–40, 57, 69
Liakura, 221
liberal(ism), 14–15, 35, 45n2, 66–69, 106–111, 119, 145, 156n21, 172, 183, 191, 215, 217
Lindh, John Walker, 219, 221

literary commodification, 59, 70, 202
Loftie, William, 75, 83
Longino, Michele, 38, 255
Loomba, Ania, 11, 27, 108–109
Lowe, Lisa, 16, 39, 47, 70, 145–47, 156n24, 156n25, 157n29
Lussier, Mark, 13–14, 28, 90

Macfie, A.L., 25–26, 28
Machiavelli, 210
Mack, Robert, 118
Mackenzie, John M., 40, 70n1
Mahabharata, 167, 226
Mahavayutpatti, 102
Mahfouz, Maguib, 33
Mahomet, 49, 71n7, 113; Mahometanism, 68
Mahomet, ou le Fanatisme (Voltaire), 56–57, 225
Majeed, Javed, 43
Makdisi, Saree, 42, 91, 99
Manning, Samuel, 75, 85, 87n3, 89n24, 89n26
Marchand, Leslie, 205, 248
Margalit, Avishai, 40, 247
market, 74–78, 80–82, 86–88, 228, 236, 242; market as trope, 87n5, 89n17
Martel, Charles, 48
marranos, 48
Marrouchi, Mustapha, 12, 33–34
Marsh, Elizabeth, 12, 54, 58–63, 65–67, 70, 70n5, 249, 256; *The Female Captive,* 12, 58–62, 66
Marsh, Milborn, 60
Martineau, Harriet, 79, 83–84, 86, 89n18, 89n25
Mayhew, Henry, 228, 231–32, 243n10
McClintock, Ann, 43
McDayter, Ghislaine, 201–203
McGann, Jerome J., 204, 208, 217, 221
McLaren, Brian, 38
Mecca, 8, 10, 129, 180n59
Mejnoun and Leila: A Persian Romance (D'Israeli), 135
Melman, Billie, 5, 42, 65, 70n1, 139, 141–43, 154n1, 155n10, 155n13, 158n43
melodrama, 22, 226–27, 242
Meyer, Eric, 42, 70, 120n2

Mill, James, 43

Mills, Sara, 11, 28, 36, 57

Milton, John, 116, 143–44, 163, 167, 169, 172, 179–80, 248, 253, 259, 265; *Comus,* 172; *Paradise Lost,* 171

Mitchell, Timothy, 73–77, 82, 85, 87n4, 88n8,

Mitchell, W. J. T., 35, 45

Mnouchkine, Ariane, 226

Modern Language Association convention (San Diego), 213–214

Montagu, Edward, 147

Montagu, Lady Mary Wortley, v, vii, 2–5, 11, 16–17, 39, 50, 58–59, 62, 69–70, 139–58; and anti-Catholicism, 58, 122, 153, 158n43

Montesquieu, 39, 49, 57

Monthly Review, 135n1, 161, 176n7

Moorcroft, William, 13, 100–101

Moriscos, 48, 64

Morning Chronicle, 165

Morton, Timothy, 42

Mozart, Wolfgang A., 54, 70n3, 225

Mufti, Aamir, 12, 32, 45n2

Musgrave, Sir William, vii, 59–61

Muslim, 3, 8–9, 11–12, 15, 44, 46, 48, 52, 54–56, 59, 63–68, 121, 126–27, 130, 132–33, 135, 136n10, 184, 214–15, 217, 219–22, 225; anti-Muslim, 19, 61, 214

Nala, Rajah, 174, 180

Napoleon, 12, 50, 122, 124, 184–85; invasion of Egypt by, 12

Nathan the Wise (Lessing), 225, 242n1

nation, 15, 25, 36, 41, 45n2, 52, 122, 161; nationalism, 45n2, 99, 122, 162; internationalism, 234

Natural Supernaturalism (Abrams), 41

Newton, Isaac, 28, 152, 170, 172

Nietzsche, Friedrich, 14, 100, 104–105

Nile, 72–73, 77, 80, 85, 89n19; "To the Nile" (P. B. Shelley), 73, 87n1

Niro, Brian, 28–29

Nochlin, Linda, 40

Notes on a Journey From Cornhill to Grand Cairo (Thackeray), 72, 86

Oberon (Weber), 54

Occident, 69, 167, 174, 180n58, 217; and Orient, 11, 27, 28, 35, 174; Occidentalism, 36, 40–41, 220

O'Connor, Erin, 43

O'Flaherty. Wendy Doniger, 173, 180n55

O'Toole, Peter, 221

Orient, 2, 7, 11–13, 20–21, 25, 27–30, 32, 37, 40, 46, 52, 58, 63, 65, 69, 74, 99, 104, 108, 115, 120n2, 140, 149–50, 152, 177n22, 200, 203, 206, 207, 217, 226, 228, 237

Orientalism, 2–3, 10–13, 15–47, 68, 71, 73, 90–91, 98–99, 104, 106, 108–110, 115, 118–21, 134–35, 139–40, 149–50, 152–54, 156–57, 157n27, 158n39, 158n42, 158n44, 164, 170, 172–73, 176n11, 176n13, 176n22, 178n35, 187, 196–97, 200, 204, 207, 213–14, 216–17, 222, 223n2, 224, 226, 238, 242, 243n13; and humanism, 12, 30–38, 45n2, 209; and students, 15–21, 101, 139–50, 152–54, 156n25, 157n35, 162, 171, 173–74, 182, 186, 190–92, 197–200, 203–11, 213–14, 217, 219, 224–29, 231, 235, 239, 242; and teaching, 15–16, 18–20, 140–41, 179n46, 208, 213–215, 217, 222, 224–25, 228

Orientalisms, 11, 17, 41–42, 158, 160, 178, 227

Orientalists, 69, 73, 152, 156n23, 165, 171, 225

Oriental Other, 9, 11, 18–20, 27, 34–36, 108–109, 208, 214–15

Ormsby, Sir Charles, 171–72, 179

Ottoman empire, 2–3, 6, 49–50, 59, 69, 134, 147, 183–84, 191–92, 197n1, 218, 224. *See also* Turkey

Oueijan, Naji B., 203–204, 207–208

Owenson, Sydney (Lady Morgan), 17–18, 159–82; "Glorvina" (Owenson *persona*), 163–64; *Ida of Athens,* 162–63, 166, 176n13, 177n28, 177n29, 254, 259; and Ireland, 160–65, 175n5; *The Missionary,* 17, 43, 159–60, 162–66, 168–69, 171, 173–75, 177–81; *The Wild Irish Girl: A National Tale,* 165

Palestine, 33, 122

Panchen Lama, 94–95, 97. *See also* Teshoo Lama
Pao, Angela, 57, 227
Parry, Benita, 37
Paton, Cindy, 14
Payne Michael, 25, 28
pedagogical, 16, 21, 173, 182, 217
Peltre, Christine, 40
Persian, 9, 63, 89n22, 126, 129, 170
Phillips, Thomas, 6
Polo, Marco, 92
Pope, Alexander, 3, 142
Porter, Dennis, 11, 28, 36–37, 70n1
postcolonial 26–27, 32, 35, 37–39, 42, 107–109, 120n2; postcolonial critics, 11, 29–30; postcolonialism, 17, 21, 26; postcolonial studies, 29–30, 44, 75; postcolonial theory, 14, 42, 107
Potkay, Adam, 110, 117–18
Pound, Ezra, 38
Powell, Timothy, 2, 258
Pratt, Mary Louise, 5, 16, 58, 87n4, 143–44, 153, 183, 219–20, 231
Puntsog, Sangye, 101–102

Qian, Zhaoming, 38

race, 8, 39, 41, 45, 95, 107–109, 133, 147, 156, 159, 161, 165, 168–69, 183, 219–20, 239
Radcliffe Ann, 118
Rajan, Balachandra, 171–72, 177n31, 179n50, 179n51, 179n52
Rajan Tilottama, 250
The Rambler (Johnson), 213
Regnard, Jean-François, 51
Reiman, Donald H., 204, 211
religion, 15, 18, 38, 42, 45n2, 45n3, 47, 57, 67, 124, 131, 146, 155n13, 156n20, 169–70, 172, 183, 225; Buddhism, 92–106; Catholic(ism), 17, 48, 56, 58, 69, 92–93, 122, 124, 158n43, 169, 225; Christian(ity), 12, 15, 17, 19, 32, 47–51, 53, 55–65, 67–69, 92–94, 105, 106n2, 116, 121–23, 126–30, 135n4, 136n16, 144, 146, 151, 170, 172, 174–75, 177, 181n63, 183–85, 194–95, 217–21, 225; Christendom, 19, 184,

214; Hindu(ism), 17, 47, 64, 91–92, 98, 162, 165, 167–73, 174–75, 176n16, 178n34, 178n36; Islam, 12–13, 19, 35, 44, 46–50, 52, 54–55, 58–59, 62–64, 66–69, 153, 214–15, 217, 236, 242
Reni, Guido, 237
Restoring the Jews to their Homeland (Adler), 135n5
Ricci, Matteo, 93, 103
Richardson, Alan, 19–20, 42, 70n4, 115
Richardson, Jonathan, 4
Ricoeur, Paul, 29
Rimsky-Korsakoff, Nikolai, 35
Roberts, Mary, 40
Robinson, Mary, 68
Romanticism, 13, 46, 71n5, 90, 99, 104, 159, 176n14, 178, 182, 197, 212n2, 213
Romer, Isabella, 75, 83, 85, 89n21
Rossini, Gioacchino Antonio, 54
Rubinstein, Ida, 225
Rubruck, William of, 92
Rycaut, Sir Paul, 158n40, 184
Said, Edward, 2, 11, 25–30, 33, 35, 45–46, 73, 99, 135, 139, 176n11, 200, 229, 237, 243n13; *After the Last Sky*, 34; critics of, 11, 25–27, 29–31, 33–34, 37, 39, 43–44, 45n1, 45n2, 45n3, 47, 70n1, 150, 152–153, 156n25; *Culture and Imperialism*, 41, 47; *Orientalism; The World, The Text, The Critic*, 34, 45n2; *Sacontalá*, 167, 169, 178–79 (*see also Sakuntala*)
Saglia, Diego, 42, 111
Sahni, Kalpana, 38, 259
Sakuntala, 173. See also *Sacontalá*
Salome (Strauss), 225
Salome (Wilde), 225
Sanchez-Eppler, Benigno, 14, 107–109
Sardar, Ziauddin, 26, 28, 70n1, 115, 222
Saunders, Robert, 96, 106n7
Schwab, Raymond, 217
Schéhérazade (Diaghilev), 233
Schneider, Jane, 38
Schopenhauer, Arthur, 14, 104–105
Schor, Naomi, 143
Schueller, Malini Johar, 30
Scott, Walter, 123, 160
Secor, Anna, 16, 141–42, 147, 149, 152–58

Sedgewick, Eve Kosofsky, 111
September 11 (9/11), 19–20, 214–15, 222
Serghini, El Habib Benrahhal, 119
sexuality, 14, 52, 107, 109, 119, 145, 183, 205
Shakespeare, William, 143, 157, 202, 206; *Antony and Cleopatra*, 206; *The Merchant of Venice*, 202; *Othello*, 185
Sharafuddin, Mohammed, 42, 110, 217, 219, 222
Sharpe, Jenny, 43
Shelley, Mary, 69, 185, 191, 218; *Frankenstein*, 69, 185; *The Last Man*, 218
Shelley, Percy Bysshe, 160, 165, 168, 175n4, 178n38, 182–197; *Hellas*, 18, 182–83, 185–86, 190–93, 195–96, 197n6; *A Philosophical View of Reform*, 191; *Prometheus Unbound*, 169; *Queen Mab*, 73, 192; *The Revolt of Islam*, 182, 192, 197n2, 197n4
Sheridan, Frances, D., 55, 165, 213
The Siege of Damascus (Hughes), 62, 66
Simmons, Diane, 186
Smith, Charlotte, 68
Smollett, Tobias, 51
Snader, Joseph, 52–52, 65
Southey, Robert, 7, 42, 91, 135n1, 168, 173–73, 178n36; *The Curse of Kehama*, 42, 135, 168, 173–74, 178
Sowden, Reverend Benjamin, 141
The Spectator (Addison and Steele), 213
Spector, Sheila, 15, 121
Spenser, Edmund, 15, 125–26, 130, 157n29
Staël, Germain de, 7, 160
Stamy, Cynthia, 38
Starr, G.A., 53
Stockdale, John Joseph, 165, 177n24
Stoker, Bram, 202
Stoler, Ann Laura, 229
Suleri, Sara, 47, 70n1, 220–21
The Sultan (Bickerstaff), 50
Sumurum (Freska), 225
Syria, 239

Tawhid, 94
Teltscher, Kate, 95–97, 100
Tepeleni (birthplace of Ali Pasha), 5

Teshoo Lama, 94–97. *See also* Panchen Lama
Thackeray, William, 72–73, 75, 77–78, 82, 86–87, 87n4
Thalaba the Destroyer (Southey), 42
theater, 30, 74, 78, 82, 85–86, 219, 225–26, 238, 241
Thermopylae, 216, 221
The Thief of Bagdad, 225
Thistlethwayte, Anne, 147
Thomas, Nicholas, 11
Thorn, Jennifer, 147
Thousand and One Nights, 81–82, 238–39. See also *Arabian Nights*
Three Oriental Tales (Richardson), 213, 223n2
Tibawi, A. L., 25
Tibetan-English Dictionary, 22, 97, 100, 103
Tibetan Grammar (Csoma), 14, 102–103
Todorov, Tzvetan, 100
translatio, 32–33
travel, 3, 16–17, 88n10, 185, 239; travel writing, 13, 36, 38, 42, 75, 87n4, 87n5, 91, 139–40, 154, 239; travel as trope, 2
Treaty of Karlowitz, 155
Turhan, Filiz, v., 18, 182, 193, 197n6
Turkey, 2, 58–59, 77, 142, 147, 151, 153, 156, 158n37, 183, 187–88, 192–94, 196, 205–206, 217–18; Turkish, 3–4, 15–16, 50, 54–55, 58–59, 69, 77, 121, 126–27, 136n13, 139–40, 142–47, 149–50, 154, 154n3, 156n18, 156n24, 157n30, 157n36, 158n38, 182–191, 193–96, 205, 215, 221
The Turkish Embassy Letters (Montagu), 16, 59, 139–58
Turner, Bryan S., 25, 35–36
Turner, Samuel, 91, 95–97, 106n6, 106n7

Up the Nile and Home Again (Fairholt), 122

Vanmour, Jean-Baptiste, 12
Védánta, 169–70
Victorientalism (critical concept), 43
Villette (Brontë), 69
Vitkus, Daniel J., 47, 49, 57, 70, 262

Voltaire, 49, 55–57, 69, 225; *Mahomet the Prophet; or, Fanaticism* (*Mahomet, ou le Fanatisme*), 56, 225; *Tragedy of Zara,* 54–55

Wagner, Richard, 104; *The Valkyrie,* 104; *The Victors,* 164
Warburton, Eliot, 75, 78, 81, 83, 88n11, 88n13, 89n19
Wardell, Robert, 235, 237
Watkins, Daniel P., 204, 208, 210–11
Watt, Ian, 141
Western, 11, 13–14, 16, 26–28, 32, 34–37, 41, 46, 49, 50, 54–55, 57, 64–65, 67–70, 98–99, 101, 104–105, 121, 139, 142, 145, 150, 152, 155n12, 156n20, 157n35, 166, 168, 176n11, 184, 186, 191, 194–95, 200, 215, 218–19, 236–37, 240, 242; non-Western, 27–28, 32, 34–35, 47
Wharton, Edith, 64, 69
Wilkinson, John Gardner, 80

Wilde, Oscar, 225
Williams, William Carlos 38
Williams, Peter, 26–27
Wilson, Robert, 226
Wollstonecraft, Mary, 12, 43, 54, 62, 67–69, 71n7, 167, 250, 263; *Vindication of the Rights of Woman,* 67–68; *The Wrongs of Woman, or, Maria,* 67
Woolf, Virginia, 143
Wordsworth, William, 41
Wright, Julia, 171, 177n31, 178n41, 179n45, 179n49

Xavier, Francis, 93, 103, 106n2

Yeazell, Ruth Bernard, 68, 143, 156n17, 157n28, 158n41
Yeğenoğlu, Meyda, 16, 39, 152

Zein, M. Faruk, 38
Zionism/Zionist, 122–23
Ziter, Edward, 20, 43, 224, 242, n2
Zofloya (Dacre), 42